MARITIME INDIA

Trade, Religion and Polity in the Indian Ocean

MARITIME INDIA

Trade, Religion and Polity in the Indian Ocean

Revised Edition

Pius Malekandathil

PRIMUS
BOOKS

PRIMUS BOOKS
An imprint of Ratna Sagar P. Ltd.
Virat Bhavan
Mukherjee Nagar Commercial Complex
Delhi 110 009

Offices at CHENNAI   KOLKATA   LUCKNOW
AGRA   BANGALORE   COIMBATORE   DEHRADUN   GUWAHATI
HYDERABAD   JAIPUR   KANPUR   KOCHI   MADURAI   MUMBAI   PATNA

First published 2010
Revised edition 2013, 2015

ISBN: 978-93-80607-83-2

Published by Primus Books

Laser typeset by Digigrafics
Gulmohar Park, New Delhi 110 049

Printed at Sanat Printers, Kundli, Haryana

Contents

Foreword

It is an honour for me to write a short foreword to introduce Pius Malekandathil's collection of essays. Some of these are already published, but often in relatively obscure journals. They will be made more accessible by being presented in book form. This collection has a strong thematic unity, for all of the essays deal with the role of people and goods and ideas coming via the sea, and their influence on India. As he says in the Introduction, 'it is a study of the impact that the circuits in the Indian Ocean exerted on the socio-economic and political processes of India.' The author uses sources in many languages, and shows familiarity with broader historiographical trends.

Many readers will know of Malekandathil's previous work. I would single out especially his book on Cochin (*Portuguese Cochin and the Maritime Trade of India, 1500-1663*, New Delhi, 2001), which is an exemplary study of a port city. It stands out amongst the burgeoning port city literature because it deals in great detail with the immediate interior of Cochin, rather than simply concentrating on the city itself and its export trade. The author drew on his own Kerala heritage to use indigenous sources, especially those in Malayalam.

Malekandathil uses sources from most of the major European languages, but Portuguese ones are most often found. Many of these chapters deal, at least in part, with the Portuguese presence in India. He represents a new and moderate trend in studies of the Portuguese in India. There used to be a pronounced dichotomy. Some wrote of the valiant Portuguese bringing civilization to India, and dominating the trade of the Indian Ocean. Others took a contrary view, claiming the Portuguese had very little impact on the broad sweep of Indian history, or condemning them for introducing a new and extreme form of violence into what had been a peaceful trading world. Malekandathil takes a much more nuanced and sophisticated view, one which neither glorifies nor denigrates the Portuguese.

Historians are increasingly trying to bring the ocean into their studies of India and other Indian Ocean countries. It used to be thought that the sea had little influence on the broad sweep of the history of India. All of its conquerors, until the British, came overland from the north-west. Hindus, we were told, were discouraged from travelling over the Black Water by caste pollution notions. For Muslims, power consisted of control over land and people, not over the sea. But we now know that the sea in fact contributed much more to the history of India than these accounts would allow. For example, Hindus did travel by sea, and settle in many Indian Ocean port cities. Muslim rulers encouraged bullion imports.

One of the greatest events in the whole history of India was the flood of bullion which came from the Americas from the mid-sixteenth century. Most of this came by sea, and more of it came under local auspices via the Red Sea than in European ships around the Cape of Good Hope. Nor was the influx by sea new in the sixteenth century. Najaf Haider has shown how this trade commenced some centuries before the arrival of the Europeans. The present collection reinforces these trends by showing that Indian rulers in fact were well aware of the potentialities of fostering and taxing trade in their realms. Chapter 2 shows a Deccan ruler encouraging sea trade, while in Chapter 3 another local ruler fosters the migration of trading groups to his area, in this case Christians. The same theme is to be found in Chapter 5.

Most of these essays are to do with early modern trade and commerce in south India. However, there are some other themes represented. Chapter 1 goes to an earlier period to discuss Sassanian trade with India. The conclusion is that it had an influence only on the coast. Chapter 3 apart from trade includes a fascinating study of St. Thomas Christians. This was a time before the arrival of intolerant Counter Reformation Catholicism. This is excellent social history, showing mutual accommodation, and synthesis, between these Christians and other religious communities in Kerala. Two other chapters provide interesting comparisons between the activities of the Portuguese, and first the Chinese, and second the Ottomans. It would be interesting to know whether the Portuguese learnt anything from the activities of their predecessors, the Chinese. It is claimed that the arrival of the Ottomans, a formidable force indeed, made the Portuguese become more militaristic, as seen in their erecting more forts and building more war ships. Chapter 8 concerns something very much on the scholarly agenda today, that is the flow of information. Malekandathil shows how Muslims, and the Portuguese, tried to get faster and more reliable communications between the Indian Ocean region and the Mediterranean, the objective being to gain economic and political advantages.

I hope these essays will be widely read and discussed. They represent the work of an historian who now is in mid career, with a substantial body of work to his credit. We can hope that he continues to publish work which expands our knowledge of the role of maritime matters in the broader history of India.

Sydney   MICHAEL N. PEARSON
Australia

Acknowledgements

The author and publisher are grateful to the following for permission to reproduce the material first published by them:

'The Sassanids and the Maritime Trade of India during the Early Medieval Period', paper read at the Indian History Congress held at Guru Dev Nanak University, Amritsar, 2002, published in *The Proceedings of the Indian History Congress,* 2003, pp. 156-73; 'Maritime Trade and Political Economy of Goa, 800-1500', published under the title 'The Impact of Indian Ocean Trade on the Economy and Politics of Early Medieval Goa (*c.* 8-15century)', in *Deccan Studies,* vol. II, no. 1, January-June 2004, pp. 3-22; 'Dynamics of Economy, Social Processes and the Pre-Portuguese Christians of India, 800-1500', a modified version of the article earlier published under the title 'Christians and the Cultural Shaping of India in the First Millennium AD', in *Journal of St. Thomas Christians,* vol. 17, no. 1, January-March 2006, pp. 4-22; 'From the Trails of the Chinese to the Dominance of the Portuguese: An Overview of the Patterns of their Naval Voyages and Maritime Policies in India', a revised version of the paper originally presented at the Hall of St. Albert Kirche, Heidelberg, 15 September 1998; 'Maritime Polity and a Mercantile State: An Analysis of the Political Dynamics of Kerala, 1500-1663', a paper presented at the National Seminar on Kerala History organized by Kerala Council of Historical Research, Trivandrum, 16-18 March 2006. It is a revised version of the paper published earlier under the title, 'Maritime Malabar and a Mercantile State: Polity and State Formation in Malabar under the Portuguese', in *Maritime Malabar and the Europeans: 1498-1962,* ed. K. S. Mathew, Gurgaon and London, 2003, pp. 197-228; 'The Ottoman Expansion and the Portuguese Response in the Indian Ocean, 1500-1560', published in *Metahistory, History Questioning History: Festschrift in Honour of Teotonio R de Souza,* ed. M. N. Pearson and Charles Borges, Lisboa, 2007, pp. 497-508; 'From Merchant Capitalists to Corsairs: The Muslim Merchants of Malabar and their Responses to Portuguese Maritime Trade Expansion (1498- 1600)', published in *Portuguese Studies Review,* vol. 12, no. I, Winter-Spring 2004-5, pp. 75-96; 'Information Networking between India and the Mediterranean in the Sixteenth and Seventeenth centuries', an earlier version of this paper was delivered at Nirmala College, Muvattupuzha, 28 September New Delhi 2003; 'Bengal and the Commercial Expansion of the Portuguese *Casados*, 1511-1632', in *Trade and Globalization, ed.* S. Jeyaseela Stephen, New Delhi, 2003, pp. 161-90; 'Mercantile Wealth and the Estado da India: Changing Pattern of Portuguese Trade with India, 1570-1663', a modified version of the paper earlier published under the title 'Merchant Capitalists and the Estado da India: Changing Pattern of Portuguese Trade with India, 1570-1663', *The Proceedings of the XI International Seminar on Indo-Portuguese History: Global Trends*, ed. Charles Borges, Fatima Gracias and Celsa Pinto, Panjim, Goa, 2005, pp. 345-60.

PIUS MALEKANDATHIL

Introduction

Maritime India is a collection of ten research articles written at different time points, but within the larger frame of defining and understanding the historical trajectories and trails of that part of India which was shaped by the circuits in the Indian Ocean. The commonality of all the essays in this volume is that they address the larger question as to whether it is the collectivity of water which encircles its territorial land limits, or certain values emerging from the circuits in the water space of the Indian Ocean that constitute the consciousness of Maritime India. The circulatory cycles of commodities, men and ideas through the diverse channels of the Indian Ocean form the major focal themes of analysis in this book as to find out these values and to understand the meanings of power and social processes evolving out of them on the coastal fringes of the subcontinent.

There has been all through history two Indias, viz., the inland, or terrestrial India, and Maritime India, yet each mutually supplementing and complementing the other. Maritime (deriving from the Latin word *mare* = sea) India is the sea-oriented segment and it represents the long stretch of littoral India, which stands remarkably unique and different from its land-locked counterpart in its social, economic and political processes.[1] During the early medieval and medieval periods, because of the frequent movement of commodities, people and ideas from abroad, Maritime India was exposed to changes, novelties and foreign elements of different nature and categories, which necessitated it to be relatively much more accommodative, liberal and tolerant in contrast to the Inland India which was increasingly turning out to be inward looking, conservative and socially rigid in the process of feudaliz-ation and authority-fragmentation. However this cannot be viewed as a watertight division as they were mutually supplementing and complimenting each other, and the dividing lines were often blurred and foggy, making a mixture of features appear at the intermediate realms. [2]

Obviously ecology and geography of the sea played a vital role in shaping the ethos and mentality of people living on its fringes during medieval times. The fury of the sea, as well as the oddities and adversities waiting for them behind fatal waves and winds, were so common that these people had to discipline their wills and shape their behaviour in ways very different from those of agrarian space or of urban space, where things used to happen considerably on the basis of certain rhythms and patterns. The ecology of the sea used to be such that people bordering its rim were perennially invited to shape certain behavioural patterns while fighting against the fury of the sea to tap its vast resources and sustain their livelihood.[3] In this process of tapping the resources of the sea, a typical professional culture linked with fishing, salt-panning or a sea-borne trade, a food culture with rich ingredients of sea species, a religious culture where the sea becomes the central component of devotional practices and rituals, a social networking, where bonds established by collective sea-faring evolved over years, were made to become the basic features of the coastal societies of India, as in the case of any other country. One may call it features of coastal societies rather than constituents of the consciousness of Maritime India, for identifying which one has to look beyond the coastal fringes into the areas and zones shaped by the values supplied by maritime space.

The consciousness of Maritime India was shaped, at least during early medieval and medieval India, not only by the ecology and the geography of the coast alone, but also by the type of circuits and the value-condensed activities that the residents of a given geographical space resorted to using the channels or resources of its sea waters. It is quite natural that sea-oriented perceptions became integral to a society, if its sustenance had become impossible without depending on any of the sea-related activities like fishing, salt-panning, sea-borne trade, shipping and navigation. The more dependent a region on sea space and its resources for its survival is, the more intense maritime consciousness its residents would maintain. If the economy of a region, particularly its activities of production and distribution are conditioned by sea-borne trade, the region would have a great amount of maritime consciousness, even if it is physically and geographically relatively distanced away from the coast. Hence it is not the mere physiology of the coast alone that creates this consciousness, but the value-based dependence on sea space. In such cases the 'sea' would get more into the economy and culture of these inland spaces, as the rupture lines are not purely geo-physical. In this connection it is worth recalling the attempts of M.N. Pearson to see how far inland the maritime frontiers could be extended. His perception is that the notion is functional and discusses under maritime theme 'those land events which affect the ocean'.[4]

It is to a great extent the intrinsic connectivities of a region with the circuits of maritime space that translate maritime consciousness to it, however big or small its geo-physical extent is. In that sense maritime consciousness is constituted out of a wide variety of activities like the economic linkages with the sea-borne trade, the political processes based on the gains from sea-borne commerce, the cultural and religious processes entering through the channels of seas, social formation based on maritime circulatory processes, etc.[5] In this book are included a few aspects of economy, culture, society and polity from different maritime regions of early medieval and medieval India and analyzed as to show how a distinctive consciousness of Maritime India evolved over time out of the circuits in the Indian Ocean.

Something very much intrinsic to the consciousness of Maritime India was that its entire coastline was viewed as having uneven economic significance. A certain segment of its coastline was considered to be economically highly valued and hence politically highly coveted, while some other segments had fluctuating values and the others with less value. The value of a coastal segment was determined by the type of economic activity carried out over there, which also used to decide the nature of its social processes as well. During the medieval and early modern period, Maritime India did not mean the mere long stretch of sandy space located on the fringes of sea-space; it meant value-condensed segments in uneven forms scattered along the coastline and extending up to inland space where the economic activities of production and exchange, besides social and political processes, were shaped by the circuits in the Indian Ocean.[6]

The type and nature of economic activities, particularly production and exchange activities, of Maritime India, but linked with oceanic circuits, demanded the emergence of different kinds of maritime nodal points and outlets as ports for different microeconomic regions. However these ports were not of even importance and significance as far as the economy of a region was concerned; instead there used to be a hierarchy and gradation among the ports operative in each region. In the hierarchization of ports, one port used to evolve as the central and pivotal exchange centre attracting the bulk of overseas trade, while other ports were made to depend on it by converting them into its feeding satellite units or as its minor distribution centres. The creation of a principal port with several feeding ports in its vicinity was developed as a part of the strategy of the political elite and rulers to get the wealth from maritime trade concentrated on the pivotal port of each principality politically controlled by its chieftain, however crude this wealth was in form, content and manifestation. This was also a mechanism to reduce chances for the inferior rulers to get access to wealth, obviously a strategy that was meant to keep them always subjugated. This went hand in hand with the attempts to augment the possibilities for greater exchange activities in the port of the paramount ruler for the purpose of getting more wealth, which in turn was meant to empower his state further.[7]

The Indian Ocean has been a theme of historical study for quite some time, thanks to a contingent of scholars who, following Braudelian study on the Mediterranean,[8] tried to find unity and cohesion in this maritime space, as well, due to its circulatory processes. The otherwise scattered regions are said to have been linked together through the channels of trade or other forms of circulation. However, the strategic location of India in the ocean gave it a political meaning of great significance, which gets reflected in the early works of historians like K.M. Panikkar, for whom independence of India was intimately linked with assertion of authority over the Indian Ocean.[9] It was through the prism of politics and power exercise that several other early scholars also loved to look at the history of the space of Indian Ocean.[10] However, later a wide variety of themes linked with commerce, culture, social processes, science and technology used for sailing, shipping and navigation became the major concerns of historians who studied this ocean-space. This shift in historiographical tradition made its way very strongly from 1985 onwards, though its beginnings can be traced back to the writings of Hourani and Tibbetts.[11] A large number of scholars started re-defining the meaning of the Indian Ocean for the economically and socially changing Indians since mid-1980s, particularly against the background of new perceptions that evolved with the changes in the socio-economic policies in India at the national level. Having got out of the colonial hangover and moorings, the scholars began to look increasingly at the history of larger linkages of India, highlighting the nuances and complexities of trans-national connectivities and cultural interactions realized through the maritime channels of the Indian Ocean. Consequently a large corpus of historical literature on the Indian Ocean appeared widening its scope of study. The leading figures of this historiographical tradition were Ashin Das Gupta, M.N. Pearson, Satish Chandra, Sinnappah Arasaratnam, Kenneth McPherson, B. Arunachalam, Om Prakash, K.S. Mathew, K.N. Chaudhuri, Lotika Varadarajan, Himanshu P. Ray, Lakshmi Subrahmaniam, Patricia Risso et al. Movement of commodities, people and ideas through the maritime space of the Indian Ocean formed their focal themes of analysis and their historical studies up to the mid-1990s, probably with the exception of Patricia Risso, were predominantly Indo-centric in nature.[12] Ship-building and navigation in the Indian Ocean formed other important themes of this period, to which the works of B. Arunachalam, K.S. Mathew and Lotika Varadarajan could be added as major contributions.[13]

The conceptualizations of globalization, particularly in late 1990s, had its impact on the historiography of the Indian Ocean Studies, and the academic perception of the globalization phenomena made historians move away from Indo-centric approaches to see the larger linkages and connectivities in this maritime space with multiple centres. M.N. Pearson, particularly in his writings after 2000, began to emphasize very strongly the poly-centric dimensions of the Indian Ocean and argued for equal weightage of treatment for the temporal processes in the space between Australia and East Africa.[14] Another major historiographical trend of this period was to look in depth into the history of the Indian Ocean and its nature before the entry of the Europeans, when developments used to revolve around multiple centres. Historians like Himanshu P. Ray used to focus on the seafaring traditions of South Asia highlighting linkages between India and South East Asia during the ancient period,[15] while Ranabir Chakravarti made attempts to examine the role which the mercantile networks used to play in providing unity to this maritime space before the entry of the Europeans.[16] However, Najaf Haider argues that it was the monetary system that was in circulation that used to give unity and cohesion to the Indian Ocean prior to the arrival of the Europeans.[17] Obviously their studies did help to diversify the scope and nature of Indian Ocean studies, taking them to wider horizons.

This book is not a study on the Indian Ocean per se; on the other hand it is a study of the impact that the circuits in the Indian Ocean exerted on the socio-economic and political processes of India. The geography treated here is not the entirety of India; but the Maritime India comprising those regions over which the circulation processes in the Indian Ocean exerted qualitative influence. The time span of the themes discussed in this book stretches from early medieval to early modern giving a picture of the long-term histories that went into the shaping of Maritime India. Temporal processes in the vast stretch of coastal geography from Bengal to Gujarat are analysed, highlighting episodal changes and regional differences. In fact the central purpose of this work is to see the processes and mechanisms by which the consciousness of Maritime India evolved over time. This was done principally by analysing the socio-economic and political processes of some important regions of India, which were intimately linked with the circuits of the Indian Ocean.

The book starts with the chapter, which in fact looks into the way how early medieval India responded to the maritime trading activities of the Sassanids. Though this was a piece initially presented in the Indian History Congress and later published in its proceedings, in this volume it has a definite point to argue. On the one hand it shows how certain geo-physical segments of Maritime India linked with commercially active Sassanids looked like when a major chunk of inland India was falling increasingly into a socio-economic process often characterized by feudalization. On the other hand it indicates how the incorporation of Indian ports into the Sassanid mercantile networks led to the evolution of 'oasis of trade' or 'islands of commerce' on the maritime fringes lying between the Indian Ocean and the agrarian inland regions. The highly urbanized Sassanid Persia, with a very large segment of consumer class, emitted economic forces needed for the conduct of trade through these 'islands of commerce' along the border regions in the Indian Ocean, when wheels of trade in Europe and in inland India declined considerably.[18] In fact the mercantile links of the Sassanids extended up to South-East Asia and China, where their cargo was called Possu (which initially was a Chinese version of the place name Persia) merchandise. In India Revatidvipa or Gopakapattanam on the Konkan, which the Chalukyas occupied for their trade with the Sassanid Persia, Shingly or Cranganore on the Malabar coast, and Mahabalipuram on the Coromandel, which the Pallavas developed as an important port for their trading contacts with South-East Asia[19] formed the 'larger oasis of commerce' in this process. The traces of these mercantile linkages are obtained in the form of Pahlavi-inscribed crosses from a stretch of coastal terrain starting from Goa and extending up to Mylapore. However the intensity of commerce seems to have been very much limited and the movement of commodities was restricted mainly to politically active societies with considerable number of political elite and power groups, whose consumer habits used to stimulate the markets. In between these scattered societies there were equally similar situations in which the markets were either dormant or dull against the background of increasing feudalization in Europe, and more or less similar socio-economic formations in the major part of inland India and what emerged was only scattered 'islands of commerce'.

The second chapter deals with the participation of Goa in the Indian Ocean trade and examines how the gains from its sea-borne trade were converted for political processes in the region. This was originally published as an article in *Deccan Studies*; however in this volume it is included with the argument that in the face of intensification of Indian Ocean trade by the ninth and tenth centuries many of the local rulers began the practice of appointing foreign merchants as governors of the major ports with a view to mobilizing and attracting overseas commerce, as it happened in Goa, where it was used as a mechanism to generate sufficient wealth to assert their power and authority in the region. The other side of the development was that the gains from maritime trade were increasingly banked upon by the chieftains of coastal principalities for setting up political institutions and quasi-state structures as to make their power ostensibly visible. The Rashtrakuta ruler Indra III, reigning over the inland part of Deccan, appointed an Arab Muslim by name Madhumati (Muhammad) as the governor of Sanjana-mandala in AD 926.[20] What happened in Goa was that the Kadamba ruler Jayakesi I in his desire to attract more overseas merchants and thus foreign wealth to his emerging kingdom appointed an Arab merchant by name Sadhan as the governor of his major port, Gopakappattinam, in AD 1053. He was in fact the grandson of Madhumad (Muhammed) the Tajika (Arab) who saved Jayakesi's predecessor Guhalladeva, when he was shipwrecked on his way to Somnath.

Later this practice was followed by many other principality chieftains of coastal India including the Zamorin, who appointed a Mappillah Muslim for handling the affairs of coastal trade and a *paradesi* (foreign) Muslim for managing the overseas commerce of Calicut.[21] By focusing on Goa, the study also shows how certain merchants and ship-owners involved in the circuits of the Indian Ocean, as in the case of Jamal-ud-din of Goa, appropriated power and political authority over the region by translating the mercantile wealth into political assets.

Chapter 3 shows how foreign merchant groups, particularly migrant Christians from Persia, with sizeable mercantile wealth and networks were utilized by rulers of coastal regions of India, the Cheras and their regional chieftains in particular, for promoting overseas trade and for ensuring regular flow of wealth for the process of strengthening their hands against the background of their recurring wars with the Pandyas and the Cholas. The Christian mercantile migrant leaders of Quilon and their church that are analysed in this chapter were empowered by the local ruler with several commercial privileges by mid-ninth century for the purpose of getting overseas trade concentrated in Quilon. In the decision to bestow mercantile privileges on the foreign Christian merchant leaders and to empower them, even the Brahminical elements joined hands with the ruler, and in doing so their intention was mainly to weaken and shatter the commerce of the Buddhists and the Jains of Kerala, with whom the Brahminical religion had already initiated an ideological war from the eighth century onwards. Incentives to foreign Christian merchants were believed to have been developed as a mechanism to formulate an alternative mercantile community in Kerala, which would eventually replace the commerce of the Jains and the Buddhists, and finally deprive them of enough resources needed for sustaining non-Brahminical ideologies. In this socio-economic process the Christians eventually assumed the status of Vaisyas and borrowed from the neighbouring cultural space several caste rules including untouchability, the wearing of sacred thread, tuft, observance of *pula* (pollution related to birth, death, etc.) and *sradha*. Meanwhile there were also attempts to Christianize the notion of sacred space and god-concepts in various eco-regions and to formulate a different category of saints for different eco-systems. The practice of veneration of the Blessed Virgin Mary and the construction of churches in her name was made to become prominent in low-lying, paddy-cultivating zones of Christian settlements, in the process of weaning believers away from fertility cults common to such eco-zones. Similarly the practice of venerating St. George, who was associated with killing a snake-like dragon, was projected as a Christian alternative to wean believers away from worshipping snakes in upland regions bordering forest areas. The Christians had developed, long before the arrival of the Europeans, their own unique identity in India on the basis of the responses and meanings they derived from the social space in which they were frequently invited to interact and differentiate.

The fourth chapter deals with the larger geographical scenario of Maritime India against the backdrop of Chinese maritime contacts and Portuguese expansion with a view to seeing whether the Portuguese derived policy lessons from the voyage circuits of Cheng Ho in their attempts to establish hegemony over the coastal terrains of India. Though the Chinese were constantly in contact with India through maritime channels, the seven repeated voyages of Cheng Ho made the Chinese presence much more perceptible in several of the coastal exchange centres. The initial locations like Cochin, Calicut, Bengal, ports of Coromandel, Mangalore, Bombay and ports of Gujarat, where the Portuguese wanted to concentrate in India were interestingly trade centres that were repeatedly visited by Cheng Ho in several of his voyages. The Portuguese while strengthening their hold over the erstwhile locations of Chinese contacts, developed a maritime policy in which the west coast of India was made to become the focal area of their official expansion. This was mainly to obstruct flow of commodities to eastern Mediterranean and to protect the trade monopoly of the crown, for which several control devices like *cartaz-armada* and fortresses were set up on the western seaboard. Portuguese expansion on the east coast of India was realized with the help of the Portuguese private traders and renegades, who used to flee away from the control of their power centres on the west coast. The Church institutions and personalities acted as connecting links for integrating the scattered settlements of private traders with the official stream on the west coast. Thus, the Portuguese presence in India had different layers, with the official layer on the west coast, and the mercantile layer predominantly on the east coast, the layer of the renegades and freebooters extended to different inland kingdoms and principalities, where they used to sell guns, artilleries and commodities from various Portuguese settlements, the layer of the Portuguese adventurers who resorted to agriculture under a donatorial system in the vast stretch of land space between Thana and Daman, and finally the layer of the Portuguese *padroado* marked by church people and institutions that were constantly engaged in the process of integrating and legitimizing the second and third categories of the Portuguese elements. Through a process of commodity circulation and networking, these various scattered layers were bound together giving additional weight to the form of domination that the Portuguese state established with the instruments and devices of power exercise in Maritime India.

A study of the polity in Maritime India would provide answers to the question as to how the value-contents of the trade circuits in the Indian

Ocean gave a different format and character to the power processes in the region. Chapter 5 has attempted to do this by analysing the political dynamics of maritime Kerala, where some inland rulers of agrarian space shifted their seat of power to maritime centres of exchange against the backdrop of intensified sea-borne commerce from mid-fourteenth century onwards. The chief of Nediyiruppu *swarupam* shifted his power centre from the agrarian pocket of Eranadu to Calicut and the chief of Perumpadappu *swarupam* shifted his headquarters from Vanneri to Cochin by mid-fourteenth century for the purpose of procuring through trade enough resources needed for setting up institutions and instruments of power exercise. Zamorin and his al-Karimi merchant allies realized well that the state building ventures of Calicut depended very much on sustaining the Calicut-Red Sea-Venice trade routes that actually brought the major chunk of wealth needed for their political assertion in the region. Cochin, being another maritime principality, tried to emerge out of the political shadow of Calicut by ably converting the wealth that came to it in the form of customs duty and monetary rewards from the Portuguese into actual substance of power. With the intensification of sea-borne trade following the Portuguese commercial expansion, the state structures based on the gains from maritime trade had acquired precedence over the inland states that derived wealth from the agrarian sector. However the success of big political institutions having quasi-state structures like Cochin or Calicut rested chiefly on their ability and manipulation skills to keep a cluster of satellite inland power centres around them, not only as mere supportive political units, but also as feeding economic units, from where the former wielded power and derived wealth for sustaining power.

The sixth chapter dwells upon the type of expansion that the Portuguese and the Ottomans made into the Indian Ocean almost simultaneously but from two different directions and examines their repercussions on Maritime India. The Ottomans moved towards this maritime space from the western land-space, while the Portuguese entered it through the navigational channels of the Cape route. The study shows how the expansion of the Ottomans into Cairo, Suez, Basra, and their moves towards the various coastal regions of India made the Portuguese resort to increasing militarization and fortification of their settlements on the western sea-board of Maritime India. The Ottoman occupation of Cairo in 1516, Suez in 1517, Basra in 1534 and their visit of Vizhinjam in Kerala in 1538 and Bengal in 1545, followed by their siege of Diu in 1538 and 1546 and joint naval operation with the Malabar Muslims against the Portuguese in south India in 1553, were militarily responded to by the Portuguese who fortified their possessions on the west coast of India, equipping them with highly sophisticated weapons and fighting devices in places like Quilon (1519), Chaul (1521), Bassein (1534),

Diu (1536) and Daman (1559). Coastal Gujarat, which provided a maritime outlet for the production centres of north India and where the Ottomans used to get support from the Muzzafarid dynasty, became the major focal point of their activities in India, besides coastal south India where they had Malabar Muslims as their allies.[22] Fearing larger threats from them, the Portuguese resorted to the policy of militarizing their settlements in Maritime India and these fortifications were later reinforced in the seventeenth century to confront the greater challenges from the English and the Dutch. When the Ottomans later stopped their assertive policies in the politics of the Indian Ocean by the 1590s, the Armenians who had earlier operated as part of the Ottoman fighting force, began to get increasingly dispersed into the length and breadth of the Indian Ocean and began to get politically and commercially engaged in the principalities and kingdoms of Muslim rulers like Aceh, or the Mughals or the Adil Shahis, obviously negotiating between them and the Ottoman world.

The seventh chapter treats the way the traditional the Muslim merchants of Kerala, who had substantial mercantile wealth with them, got estranged from the Portuguese and how they eventually got themselves transformed into the Portuguese category of 'corsairs' in their attempts to define their role in the Indian Ocean commerce against the monopoly claims of the Portuguese. The Marakkar traders who had been collaborators of the Portuguese in the early days of their commerce, got antagonized and estranged from them, when the latter with a view to favouring the emerging commerce of the Portuguese *casados*, started confiscating the cargo of Marakkars and drowning their vessels under the pretext of checking *cartazes*. In turn, the Marakkars under the leadership of Kunjali retaliated by developing a strategy of attacking the Portuguese vessels, whenever needed, in order to create a space required for dispatching cargo regularly to the ports of the Red Sea. The wealth that they thus accumulated out of their mercantile ventures was eventually transferred for buying guns and weaponry to confront the Portuguese, which ultimately went to the extent of establishing a state like political institution with headquarters at Pudupattanam and setting up diverse instruments and devices of power exercise, followed by assumption of several highly power-denoting titles by Kunjali. However, later the entire process boomeranged, and the Zamorin, who initially was the mentor of Kunjali, soon smelled foul play and suspected that the rudimentary political process happening under the leadership of the latter in the vicinity of Calicut would eventually turn out to be a threat of severe magnitude to his authority. Acting on this premise the Zamorin joined hands with the Portuguese to capture Kunjali, who was later executed at Goa in 1600, and shattered and erased all the power-symbolizing institutions as well as structures of the latter. With this a good many of the Muslim merchants, who had till then been diverting the major chunk of their mercantile wealth for buying guns as well as weaponry to thwart the expansion of the Portuguese and for setting up diverse instruments as well as devices of power exercise instead of investing it in productive ventures, turned out to be highly pauperized and began to move towards the inland part of Malabar, resorting ultimately to agricultural activities. Meanwhile, a relatively considerable number of them, who were till then bound together and united as a disciplined band by the leadership of Kunjali fell apart and scattered all over the Arabian Sea. With the execution of Kunjali they began to resort to maritime criminality and piratical activities of a different nature.

The eighth chapter looks at the nature of information-networking between Maritime India and the Mediterranean at a time when the Portuguese made attempts to control the process of information-dissemination between the two worlds for the purpose of protecting their monopoly. However, both the worlds did not remain as isolated as was believed, since the information about the market conditions of the Mediterranean and the developments in Maritime India was exchanged at Mecca and Jidda through the channels of *haj* pilgrims and feeders of the traditional caravan routes. Access to updated information about the Mediterranean market conditions helped the local Muslim merchants to quote much higher prices in the production centres of south India, often depriving the Portuguese of the possibility of purchasing cargo at their fixed rate. The communication channels from India through the Persian Gulf, Baghdad, Aleppo and the Lavant ran for a considerable period of time along with the commodities flowing to the Mediterranean and also with the movement of people between the two worlds. An organized venture for information networking between India and the Mediterranean world overland started by the mid-1580s, when Italian and German business houses that took up the Indo-European trade from the Portuguese crown, wanted to communicate frequently with their trade agents in different parts of coastal India. Ferdinand Cron, who as the trade agent in India of the German business houses of the Fuggers and the Welsers, used to gather trade directives and information from Augsburg through this overland communication system. Later, even when the German and the Italian commercial establishments dropped the Indian contract, the same communication system was kept operative by Ferdinand Cron, who used it for his private trade and gathered information, not only about the demand factors of European markets, but also about the nature and size of the Dutch fleet moving to the Indian Ocean. He secured the credibility and acceptability of the Portuguese by passing on to them updated information about the character and intentions of the Dutch fleet in the Indian Ocean, which enabled the Portuguese to make timely preparations to thwart the Dutch attacks. Later, against the backdrop of increasing blockades on the navigational lines of the Portuguese by the Dutch and the English, the Portuguese crown wanted to institutionalize this overland communication system between India and Europe with Cron as the key figure, and supported by several nodal personalities at different information hubs of Asia and Europe. When this system failed the Portuguese authorities used the services of the Augustinian and the Carmelite monks then working in different parts of Saffavid Persia and the Ottoman territories to transmit messages to Europe, at times employing their own runners.

The ninth chapter deals with how the Portuguese *casados*, who moved to Bengal initially as private traders, eventually set up chains of mercantile settlements in different parts of Bengal, where their social and mercantile capital were considerably utilized by some Portuguese adventurers and traders for setting up territorial power units in the region later. The Portuguese private traders who used to roam around Bengal in the early quarter of the sixteenth century soon realized that it was not a destination in itself, but a wider door to a larger market located in the power centre of Delhi, and an alternative door to the scattered markets of Ming China. With the incorporation of Bengal into the wider market systems of Delhi-adminis-tration realized through the wielding of power from the Mughals by Sher Shah, particularly by 1540s, and the consequent construction of Grand Trunk Road connecting Bengal with Delhi there was an increasing flow of spices from Kerala to Bengal on a large scale, which was followed by an equally increasing flow of Portuguese private traders from Cochin and Goa to the deltaic regions of Bengal and to the banks of the river system of Hughli, where they slowly established their settlements. Gradually a chain of Portuguese settlements appeared in the gulf of Bengal in places like Pipli on the Orissa coast, Hijili located at the mouth of Rupanarayan, Chittagong, Satgaon, Buttor (Betor–Howrah), Dacca (particularly at *Feringhi Bazar*), Sripur (near Sonargaon), Chandecan (on the banks of a branch of Hughli), Bakla (identified with Chandradwip pargana), Catrabo (Katrabuh), Loricul (28 miles south of Dacca), Dianga, Bhulua, etc. They absorbed different categories of Portuguese migrants including the entrepreneurs, private traders, freebooters and renegades from the west coast of India, and there they soon emerged as a powerful social group noted for their skills of entrepreneurship, expertise in warfare with guns as well as artillery and acumen in political manoeuvring. While a segment of them were engaged in taking spices from Kerala to Bengal in return for long pepper, silk and rice, the other segment was involved in the political processes of Arakan and the neighbouring principalities, making themselves inevitable for any of these local rulers for asserting their authority in the region. Later, the absorption of Bengal into the Mughal administrative frame by Akbar in the mid-1570s gave the Portuguese private traders chances to engage in commodity movements up to the markets of Agra and Delhi through different intermediaries. Many Portuguese private traders and adventurers like Sebastião Gonçalves Tibau, Manuel de Matos and Domingos Carvalho, who wielded considerable clout in the region, translated a significant portion of their wealth and trade surplus into setting up territorial power units in the region, at times challenging the neighbouring chieftains as well as rulers, and on several occasions banking upon the power centre of Goa to get their ill-gotten political positions legitimatized and justified.

The tenth chapter analyses the phase of intensification of private trade in the sixteenth century and highlights the ways and means by which the mercantile wealth of the leading private traders in the Portuguese pockets of Maritime India was transferred for the sustenance of the politico-commercial edifice of the *Estado da India* at a time when the flow of wealth from Europe was severely obstructed. Though there was a sizeable amount of private trade in India in the early part of the sixteenth century already puncturing the trade monopoly of the Portuguese crown, it became rampant from the mid-1570s onwards, when the crown stepped down from being a merchant monarch and the Indo-European trade was handed over to the Germans as well as the Italians and later the Portuguese business houses. In fact the burden of procuring the required volume of cargo for Europe fell primarily upon these private business houses, and consequently the Portuguese *casado* private traders in Maritime India began to increasingly engage in intra-Asian trade, often with the support of officials who allowed the controlling mechanisms like *armada* as well as the administrative machinery of the state to get transformed into mechanisms for protecting their 'empire' of private trade. In this process of intensified private trade of the *casados*, their wealth in Cochin and Goa was eventually banked upon by the state for resorting to a chain of construction processes, ultimately producing magnificent and elegant structures as well as edifices and architecturally inscribing into their urban spaces notions and meanings of hegemony. By the seventeenth century with the increasing blockades on the navigational lines of the Portuguese by the Dutch and the English, the *Estado* had to depend on the mercantile wealth of the private traders for its sustenance. While the *casados* of Cochin liberally lent money to the state for maintaining its spice trade, the Saraswat Brahmins, who had relatives across the Maratha border and in the Northern Province, emerged by the early decades of the seventeenth century as the leading bankers and tax-farmers in Goa. When a considerable chunk of Portuguese population fled from the city of Goa because of frequent epidemics and pestilences, the financially sick Portuguese state was compelled to bank upon the wealth of private traders like Ferdinand Cron and tax-farmers from the Saraswat Brahmin community to run its business uninterruptedly. The locally generated mercantile wealth was thus made to become the inevitable supportive pillar for sustaining the Portuguese activities in India, at a time when the Dutch and the English blockades used to prevent the Iberian capital from reaching India.

These ten chapters dealing with diverse themes, geo-physical spaces and temporal processes are collectively indicative of the way the formation of the consciousness of Maritime India can be looked at. It is the integral linkages of the economic structures of various regions with the resources and the circulatory processes in the Indian Ocean that stands as the foundational base for the consciousness of Maritime India. The socio-cultural and the political processes emerging out of such linkages, or out of forces emanating from such economic structures, used to define the character of 'maritime' as a distinct entity quite different from the 'terrestrial'. As the consciousness of Maritime India was shaped by the nature and amount of impact that circuits in the Indian Ocean exerted on the socio-economic and political processes of various regions, the intensity of this consciousness used to vary from place to place and from time to time, on the basis of their partaking in the developments of maritime space.

This work was made possible because of the constant encouragement and support that I received from several institutions and persons, to whom I owe a great amount of debt. It is a pleasure to thank the many archivists and librarians who always extended ready support in my search for manuscripts and old volumes. I should extend my particular thanks to the staff of Arquivo Historico Ultramarino-Lisbon, Bibliotheca Nacional de Lisboa, Algemeen Rijksarchief–The Hague, the library of South Asian Institute of Heidelberg University-Heidelberg, the library of European University Institute-Florence, Historical Archives of Goa, the Xavier Centre for Historical Research-Alto Porvorim, the libraries of Goa University, Jawaharlal Nehru University, New Delhi, Sree Sankaracharya University of Sanskrit-Kalady and St.Joseph's Pontifical College, Alwaye.

I owe many thanks to Bishop Mar George Punnakottil, who has been a great source of encouragement and support all through my academic career and it is a pleasure to remember that his blessings are always with me. Prof. Dietmar Rothermund, Prof. K.S. Mathew, Prof. Teotonio R.de Souza, Prof. M.N. Pearson, Prof. Luis Filipe Thomaz and Prof. Reinhardt Hildebrandt were always there to bank upon whenever I needed academic help. I thank very specially Prof. M.N. Pearson for launching this book into the maritime space with his scholarly foreword. I cannot forget the concern and care showered on me by my friends in Lisbon, Leiden, Florence and Heidelberg, particularly by Br. Joseph of Benediktiner Abtei of Stift Neuburg and Bernhard Kotzur and family of Heidelberg, during my sojourns and short stays in Europe. My colleagues at the Centre for Historical Studies, JNU, have always been supportive of my academic activities and I recall all of them with gratitude and fond memories. I benefited a lot from the academic interactions with my colleagues, particularly from Rajat Datta, Yogesh Sharma, Ranabir Chakravarti, Himanshu P. Ray, Najaf Haider and Arvind Sinha. Finally, my heartiest thanks are due to all my friends and well wishers, who always want to sit behind the curtains and strengthen me with their love and affection.

NOTES

1. This idea was repeatedly highlighted by scholars like M.N. Pearson, Sinnappah Arasaratnam and Ashin Das Gupta, but in different categories. One of the most interesting pieces that gives a lot of insight is the notion of 'littoral' given by M.N. Pearson. M.N. Pearson, 'Littoral Society: The Case for the Coast', *The Great Circle*, 9, 1987, pp. 1-12; see also Ashin Das Gupta, 'The Maritime city', in Indu Banga, ed., *Ports and their Hinterlands in India*, New Delhi, 1992, pp. 359-74; Sinnappah Arasaratnam, *Maritime India in the Seventeenth Century*, Delhi, 1994.

2. M.N. Pearson has gone deep into the issues of land-sea relationship and tried to explain the nature of borders where land takes over and sea disappears. See M.N. Pearson, *The Indian Ocean*, London, 2003, pp. 27-9. In one of his recent works he dwells deep upon the economic meanings of the linkages between coast and the interior. See M.N. Pearson, *Port Cities and Intruders: The Swahili Coast, India and Portugal in the Early Modern Era*, Baltimore, 1998, pp. 63-100.

3. As both the coastal residents and the seafarers had to face the fury of the rough sea, very often unpredictable havoc created by water and wind currents, easy spread of water-related diseases, frequent outbreak of epidemics, besides scurvy, shipwrecks and piratical attacks to which sailors often succumbed to, steeled will-power emanating from repeated crisis-management experiences would be the most precious individual wealth for them. The harsh physical and social environment that the Portuguese sailors had to face is elaborated upon by A.J.R. Russel Wood, 'Men Under Stress: The Social Environment of the Carreira da India, 1550-1750', in Luis de Albuquerque and Inacio Guerreiro (eds.), *Il Seminario Internacional de Historia Indo-Portuguesa-Actas*, Lisboa, 1985, pp. 28-35.

4. See M.N. Pearson, 'The Indian Ocean and the Portuguese in the Sixteenth Century', in Luis de Albuquerque and Inacio Guerreiro (eds.), *Il Seminario Internacional de Historia Indo-Portuguesa-Actas*, Lisboa, 1985, p. 111.

5. This dimension is succinctly highlighted by authors like Janet L. Abu-Lughod. See Janet L. Abu-Lughod, *Before European Hegemony: The World System AD 1250-1350*, Oxford, 1991, pp. 261-86.

6. This forms the centrality of my arguments for including certain themes and sub-themes of this book under 'maritime' category, which for many others may appear to be inland developments and 'non-maritime'.

7. Pius Malekandathil, 'Port-Hierarchy and the Coastal Politics', Paper presented in the National Seminar on *Coastal Histories*, organized by CHS, JNU, 13-14

February 2007, pp.1-4; see also Ashin Das Gupta, *Indian Merchants and the Decline of Surat*, Wiesbaden, 1979.

8. Ferdinand Braudel, *The Mediterranean and the Mediterranean World in the Age of Philip II*, 2 vols., translated by Sian Reynolds, London, 1978.

9. K.M. Panikkar, *India and the Indian Ocean: An Essay on the Influence of Sea Power on Indian History*, London, 1951.

10. For representatives of this category see G.A. Ballard, *Rulers of the Indian Ocean*, London, 1927; K.A. Sridharan, *Maritime History of India*, Delhi, 1965; R.K. Mookerji, *Indian Shipping: A History of the Sea-borne Trade and Maritime Activity of the Indians from the Earliest Times*, Calcutta, 1957.

11. George F. Hourani, *Arab Seafaring in the Indian Ocean in Ancient and Early Medieval Times*, Princeton, 1951; G.R. Tibbetts, *Arab Navigation in the Indian Ocean before the Coming of the Portuguese*, London, 1971.

12. Ashin Das Gupta and M.N. Pearson, *India and the Indian Ocean*, New Delhi, 1987; Satish Chandra, *The Indian Ocean Explorations in History, Commerce and Politics*, New Delhi, 1987; K.S. Mathew, *Studies in Maritime History*, Pondicherry, 1990; idem, *Mariners, Merchants and Oceans: Studies in Maritime History*, Delhi, 1995; Kenneth McPherson, *The Indian Ocean: A History of People and the Sea*, Delhi, 1993; Sinnappah Arasaratnam, *Maritime India in the Seventeenth Century*, Delhi, 1994; Om Prakash, *Precious Metals and Commerce: The Dutch East India Company in the Indian Ocean Trade*, Aldershot, 1994; K.N. Chaudhuri, *Asia before Europe: Economy and Civilization of the Indian Ocean from the Rise of Islam to 1750*, Cambridge, 1990; Sinnappah Arasaratnam, *Maritime India in the Seventeenth Century*, Delhi, 1994; Himanshu Prabha Ray and Jean Francois Salles, *Tradition and Archaeology: Early Maritime Contacts in the Indian Ocean*, New Delhi, 1996; Patricia Risso, *Merchants and Faith: Muslim Commerce and Culture in the Indian Ocean*, Boulder, 1995; Lakshmi Subramaniam used to publish a lot on maritime history and Indian Ocean studies. One of her recent works is Lakshmi Subramaniam, *Medieval Seafarers of India*, Delhi, 2005.

13. Lotika Varadarajan, *Sewn Boats of Lakshadweep*, Panaji, Goa, 1998;K.S. Mathew, ed., *Shipbuilding and Navigation in the Indian Ocean Region AD 1400-1800*, Delhi, 1997; B. Arunachalam has written extensively on indigenous techniques of navigation and haven-finding. Satish Chandra, B.Arunachalam and V. Suryanarayan, *The Indian Ocean and its Islands: Strategic, Scientific and Historical Perspectives*, New Delhi, 1993; idem, 'The Haven-Finding Art in Indian Navigational Tradition and Cartography', in Satish Chandra, *The Indian Ocean Explorations in History, Commerce and Politics*, New Delhi, 1987, pp. 191-221. See his recent works, as well. B. Arunachalam, *Essays in Maritime Studies*, 2 vols, Bombay, 1999-2002.

14. See the recent major works of M.N. Pearson, *The Indian Ocean*, London, 2003; M.N. Pearson, *Port Cities and Intruders: The Swahili Coast, India and Portugal in the Early Modern Era*, Baltimore, 1998.

15. Himanshu Prabha Ray, *The Archaeology of Seafaring in South Asia*, Cambridge, 2003.

16. Ranabir Chakravarti, *Trade in Early India*, New Delhi, 2001.

17. Najaf Haider, 'The Network of Monetary Exchange in the Indian Ocean Trade, 1200-1700', in Himanshu Prabha Ray and Edward A. Alpers (eds.), *Cross Currents and Community Networks: The History of the Indian Ocean World,* New Delhi, 2007.

18. Scholars argue that that urban economy including commercial activities decreased in three stages, with the first stage during the period between AD 300 and 600, followed by the second stage that spanned 600 and 1000 and the last stage between 1000 and 1200. The changing perspectives of Indian feudalism admit the possibilities of growth of trade once again from 1000/1100 AD. For literature on Indian feudalism see D.D. Kosambi, 'On the Development of Feudalism in India', in *ABORI*, xxvi, 1956, pp. 258-69; R.S. Sharma, *Indian Feudalism*, Delhi, 1980; B.N.S. Yadav, *Society and Culture in North India in the Twelfth Century*, Allahabad, 1973; D.N. Jha (ed.), *Feudal Social Formation in Early India*, Delhi, 1987; R.S. Sharma, *Urban Decay in India, 300-1000 AD*, Delhi, 1987.

19. For a general history of the Pallavas, see C. Minakshi, *Administration and Social Life under the Pallavas*, Madras, 1938. Later the port-area of Mahabalipuram is believed to have been submerged in the sea, probably following an earlier tsunami or a turbulent geo-physical development of such nature. Ranabir Chakravarti, *Trade in Early India*, Oxford, 2001, p. 76. The contact of Sassanid merchants with Cranganore is evident from the Pahlavi-inscribed cross of that place (besides the other ones of Kerala), which *Jornada* is referring to in the sixteenth century. Pius Malekandathil (ed.), *Jornada of Dom Alexis de Menezes: A Portuguese Account of the Sixteenth Century Malabar*, Kochi, 2003, p. 216. Sassanid contact with the Chalukyan port of Revatidvipa or Gopakapattanam is evident from the Pahlavi-inscribed cross obtained from Agassaim (in the vicinity of Gopakapattanam) and also from the painting in Cave I at Ajanta that represents an embassy from Sassanid Persia to the Chalukyan court of Pulikesin II.

20. Ranabir Chakravarti, 'Merchants of Konkan (*circa* AD 1000-1500)', in *The Indian Economic and Social History Review*, vol. XXIII, 2, 1986, p. 208; For more details on the trade of Konkan during this period see Ranabir Chakravarti, 'Coastal Trade and Voyages in Konkan: The Early Medieval Scenario', in *The Indian Economic and Social History Review*, vol. XXXV, no. 2, April-June 1998, pp. 97-123.

21. W.W. Rockhill, 'Notes on the Relations and Trade of China with Eastern Archipelago and the Coast of Indian Ocean during the Fourteenth Century', *T'oung Pao*, 2nd Series, vol. XVI, Part IV, October 1915, pp. 454-7.

22. A Turkish fleet, with the support of Muslim sailors from Malabar, attacked Pearl Fishery Coast and captured 17 boats in April 1553. It was Vithala Nayak of Madurai who mobilized Muslim support to attack Punnaikayal and to burn down their churches, besides taking about 52 Portuguese soldiers, including the captain and their priest, as prisoners. Josef Wicki, *Documenta Indica*, vol. III, Rome, 1950, pp. 252-3; 238-9; Henry Heras, *The Aravidu Dynasty of Vijayanagara*, Madras, 1927, pp.150-65.

CHAPTER ONE

The Sassanids and the Maritime Trade of India during the Early Medieval Period

The traders from Sassanid Persia formed an important mercantile community that frequented the important exchange centres of the western seaboard of India and established several trading settlements along its coast during the early medieval period. In fact the commercial expansion of the Sassanids coincided with the relative sluggish phase that appeared in Rome's international commerce by third century AD,[1] and that was profitably made use of by the newly emerging Sassanids to lay foundations for wider and long-standing networks of commercial operations with India from the ports of the Persian Gulf. The ports of Gujarat, Konkan, South Canara, Malabar, Coromandel and Sri Lanka provided the chief doors for these Sassanid traders to interact with the regional economies of South Asia.

Though several studies have appeared on the trading activities of the Romans and the Arabs with India, as well as on their impact on Indian society and economy, little research has been done so far on the Indo-Persian commercial contacts during the time of the Sassanids, and still less on their impact on Indian society and economy. In fact it was mainly through the pioneering researches of D. Whitehouse and A. Williamson[2] that the Sassanid's maritime trade with India got rather highlighted and became a matter of academic debate. The article of Gerd Gropp,[3] published in 1997, has thrown immense light on the merchant groups involved in this trade between the western littoral of India and the ports of the Persian Gulf. A succinct survey of the Indian trade centres where the Sassanid merchants concentrated their economic activities was done in my own recent researches.[4]

The central purpose of this chapter is to see the nature of the maritime trade carried out between India and Sassanid Persia and also to see the impact

*This was first published in *The Proceedings of the Indian History Congress,* Amritsar, 2003, pp. 156-73.

which it exerted on Indian society and economy. This is elaborated by highlighting the principal mercantile settlements of the Sassanid traders in India and also by focusing on the mechanism by which the merchant groups from Sassanid Persia stabilized their commercial operation with the help of the spice-producing Christians of Malabar distributed in the fertile riverbeds of central Kerala. The evolving picture throws light into the diversification of their economic activities, which is reflected in their very settlement pattern.

THE INITIAL PHASE

As early as the time of king Ardashir, who laid foundations of the Sassanid rule in Persia by overthrowing the Parthians in AD 224, the stage was set ready for trans-oceanic trade with India. He founded or re-founded several ports in the Persian Gulf including Rew Ardashir (Rishahr on the Bushire Peninsula), Astarabadh Ardashir (formerly Charax), Bahman Ardashir (Forat of Maisan), Wahasht Ardashir, Kujaran Ardashir (on the Iranian coast) and Batn Ardashir (on the Arabian coast). This infrastructural arrangement was made to boost Persia's maritime trading activities with India, for realizing which he also transplanted large numbers of the Azdi tribe of Oman to Fars and to the Kirman-Makran coast.[5] The trade between India and the Sassanid ports in the Persian Gulf continued with vibrancy later during the time of Shahpur II (310-79). Both persecution (of Christians in his empire)[6] and maritime trading activities of Shahpur II ushered in a phenomenon of increasing movement of people from the Persian Gulf regions to different places in Asia including Malabar. As a result of Malabar-Persian Gulf maritime contacts, the diverse mercantile communities seem to have preferred the marts of Kerala for migration, where they seem to have initially operated as collection agents. The earliest evidence of such migration to Kerala is traceable in the case of the seventy-two mercantile families who came from West Asia under the leadership of Thomas of Cana and settled down in *Cornelur* (Cranganore) about AD 345.[7] It seems that the kings of Malabar were very much eager to attract the foreign traders by granting them privileges and special honours, as these merchants brought considerable revenue to the exchequer. The native ruler conferred upon Thomas of Cana and the seventy-two families privileges a status on par with those of the nobility (which were later enjoyed by the upper caste Hindus), including the privilege to use palanquins, carpets on the ground, to use sandals, to ride on elephants, etc. Moreover, a particular portion of *Mahodayapuram* (Cranganore), which had forests, was given to these mercantile families for clearance and habitation.[8] It seems that these seventy-two families formed only one segment of the different waves of migration from West Asia, which had started from the fourth century AD onwards. In fact, participation in the long-distance maritime trade in the Indian Ocean made many Christians move over to the littoral of India to establish settlements.

The important maritime bases of operation for the Sassanids in the Persian Gulf were Siraf, Rew Ardashir and Kharg Island.[9] The extensive excavations conducted at Siraf brought into the limelight the remnants of a Sassanid fort, which was also used as a naval base during the time of Shahpur II.[10] Rew Ardashir was a city on the coast of Fars, founded by Ardashir I[11] and from the fifth century onwards it was the seat of the Nestorian metropolitan of Fars (Persis of Persia).[12] The archaeological excavations conducted by Ghirshman in Kharg Island, 55 km north-west of Bushire, unearthed the remnants of a Nestorian monastery with a potential capacity to accommodate about a hundred persons.[13] This monastery seems to have been the main training centre for the formation of the missionaries meant for India and other regions in the Indian Ocean region.[14]

It is Palladius (the fourth century writer) who gives the first reference to Sassanid vessels (moving obviously for trade) in the Indian Ocean.[15] The active participation of Christian traders from the Sassanid Empire in the maritime trade and navigation in Indian waters is testified by the Nestorian annals of this period. Some time before AD 415, as the eleventh century chronicle of Seert mentions, the Sassanid ruler Yazdigird I (399-421) sent the Nestorian Catholicos, a certain Ahai, to Fars to investigate the piracy of ships returning from India and Ceylon.[16] Now the question is, why was a Catholicos deputed for handling piracy? It was highly probable that the merchant groups involved in the maritime trade between India-Ceylon and the Persian Gulf were predominantly Christian, and in that way he would be in a better position to gather more direct and immediate information about the piratical attacks on them, which, besides, must have been a matter of concern for the church dignitary as well. It could have also been because of the support, which he, as a Catholicos, would be able to mobilize from the Christian merchant-settlers located on the rim of the Indian Ocean to contain the problem of sea-piracy.

The Christian merchants from Fars (Persis) or Seleucia-Ctesiphon were considered to be the chief carriers of the Persian commodities to the different marts of the Indian Ocean. B.E. Colles refers to the account of Abraham Kashkar, a sixth century monk, who made his voyage to India as a merchant. He also mentions that Bar Sahde made several journeys to India before entering a monastery following the attack of his ship by the pirates.[17]

The early commercial and spiritual expansion of the trading community of the Christians from the Sassanid Empire in India, South-East Asia and China is evident from the resounding title of the bishop, who attended the synod of AD 410. The title runs as follows: 'Metropolitan of the Islands, Seas and Interior, of Dabag, Chin and Macin.' Chin and Macin (Mahachina) were parts of China, whereas Dabag was an island, probably Java.[18] A Syriac document of this period refers to the entry and settlement of Nestorian Christians in parts of South-East Asia through maritime channels;[19] however the earliest reference to the Nestorian Christians, who entered China by land, was in AD 578.[20]

Eventually as a result of the Sassanid's monopolistic hold over the Indian Ocean trade, commodities failed to reach Constantinople. The three main channels of Euro-Asian trade, viz., the land route often known as the Silk Route and the maritime routes emanating from the Persian Gulf as well as the Red Sea, through which eastern commodities used to enter the Mediterranean world, were monopolistically controlled by the Sassanids. The Byzantine emperors Justin (518-27) and Justinian (527-65) wanted to break the Sassanid hold on Indian trade by seeking the support of Abyssinian (Ethiopian) Christians, who were asked to go to the markets of south India and Ceylon to fetch silk and spices.[21] Emperor Justin had a larger project in his mind, which included attempts to control at Bab-el-Mandeb the trade emanating from India by keeping a pro-Byzantine Ethiopian ruler in Yemen. But the Sassanid ruler Khusrau (531-78) foiled this attempt by routing the pro-Byzantine Ethiopians from Yemen and appointing his governor there, which besides giving control over the Red Sea also denied access to the Byzantines to penetrate into the east, including India.[22]

THE EXCHANGE CENTRES AND THE MERCANTILE
SETTLEMENTS OF THE SASSANID TRADERS IN INDIA

Cosmas Indicopleustes (AD 525) refers to the important trading centres in South Asia frequented by the Christian traders from Sassanid Persia. They were: Sindu (Indus), Orrhota (Saurashtra), Kalliana (Kalyan), Sibor (Sindabor or Chandrapura in Goa), the five marts of Malabar, namely Parti(?), Mangaruth (Mangalore), Salopatana(?), Nalopatana (Valapattanam?), Pudopatana (Puthupattanam), and the ports of Marallo (Marava or Marawar) as well as Khaber (Kaveripattanam). These ports operated in a larger orbit, within which the circulation of commodities from the Indian Ocean region to the Mediterranean world through the Persian Gulf was realized.

He also makes reference to the principal port of Taprobane (Sri Lanka), identified with Mahatitha, where commodity streams from China, South-East Asia, the Deccan and the Sind intersected. The Christians (probably from Persia and Malabar) played a significant role in the commercial activities of this port of Ceylon. He adds that in Sri Lanka there was a church of the Christians, who had settled there and a priest, who was appointed from Persia, and a deacon together with the arrangements for public worship. Many ships came to this island from India, Persia and Ethiopia. From Tzinista (China) and other places (reference is evidently to South-East Asia), silk, aloes, cloves, sandalwood and so forth were imported to Taprobane. These were further taken to the entrepots on this side (evidently India), to Persia, Homerite (South Yemen) and Adule (Zula in Ethiopia).[23]

The extension of the commercial activities of these Persian Christians into the Indian Ocean region was followed by the formation of several trading colonies by them on its rim, leading to migration of Christians from West Asia in considerable numbers. In fact these Christian settlements were located near the important trade centres, the collection centres or the halting places of long-distance trade, where temporary stay was necessitated by the monsoon factor. The traders from West Asia moving to South-East Asia had to halt at Malabar or some other place on the western coast of India, for a considerable period of time till they got favourable wind for their long-distance voyage through the Bay of Bengal, where the North-East monsoon obstructed navigation during the period between October and February.[24] In the Arabian Sea, similarly, the South-West monsoon hindered trans-oceanic voyages during the period between May and September. The Christian merchants, who used to halt till they got favourable a monsoon laid the foundation for some of the principal settlements like that of Ceylon, Quilon, Sindabor or Goa, Kalyan, etc., which swelled in size, with the inflow of people in the succeeding periods. Of these, as Cosmas Indicopleustes says, Male (Koulam Male or Quilon) and Kalliana (Kalyan), where the bishop from Persia was residing, had vibrant Christian communities.[25] In course of time many Christian traders from West Asia began to settle down on the fringes of the Indian Ocean, from where easy movement of commodities and people to destinations of their choice was possible. These settlements seem to have been linked mutually by the network of exchange systems, in which they actively took part and, interestingly, commerce was a major unifying factor for these diasporas.[26]

The presence of these mercantile-cum-migrating communities on the fringes of the Indian Ocean is attested to by the discovery of stone crosses with Pahlavi (archaic Persian) inscriptions in several places in south-west India and Sri Lanka. So far only nine crosses with Pahlavi inscriptions are found in the entire Indian Ocean region (and all over the world, as well): one in Anuradhapuram in Sri Lanka, which was associated with the commercially oriented Christian community migrated from Persia,[27] and six in India, viz., Mylapore, Kottayam (two crosses), Kothanalloor, Muttuchira, Kadamattam,

Alengad and Agassaim near Gopakapattanam (the old capital and principal port of pre-Portuguese Goa). Among the various Pahlavi-inscribed crosses found in India, the one in St. Thomas Church of Mylapore[28] seems to be the oldest, which is traced back to the sixth century and probably as old as Anuradhapuram cross. The Pahlavi cross of Mylapore was excavated by the Portuguese in 1547[29] and since then strenuous and continuous attempts were made to decipher the inscription of Mylapore cross, which in the latest translation of Gerd Gropp (1970) is *Unser Herr Messias erbarme sich über Gabriel, den Sohn des Chaharbokht, den Enkel des Durzad, der dies (Kreuz) anfertigte*.[30] It could be translated as 'Our Lord Messiah may show mercy on Gabriel, the son of Chaharbokht (literally meaning having four sons), the grandson of Durzad (literally meaning born in distant land), who made this (cross).' However, it should be specially mentioned that scholars have not yet reached at an agreement on deciphering the cross-inscription, which for want of vowel-usage and familiarity with the letter-carvings of the inscription, was read differently.[31]

The Pahlavi crosses of Kottayam, Muttuchira, Kadamattam and Alengad seem to have been copies made later. It is highly probable that the copies of the cross of Mylapore, which was an important centre of trade and settlement for the migrating Christians, were later made and sent to the old churches of Malabar located in the interior.[32] The recent discovery of a granite stone cross with Pahlavi inscription from Agassaim (Goa) on 27 April 2001, by Fr. Cosme Costa s.f.x., shows that the activities of the Pahlavi-speaking mercantile Christian community was not restricted to south India alone.[33] This cross seems to have been of the seventh century, a dating done on the evidence of the Pahlavi inscription on the stone made in the form of an arch, which evidently speaks of an origin before the Islamization of the Indian Ocean trade in the eighth century.[34] It seems that the Christian merchants from West Asia began to establish links all through the Konkan region in general, and Goa in particular, during the time of the Chalukyan king Pulikesin II (610-642) of the Deccan, who sent commercial envoys to the Sassanid court.[35] It is said that a painting in Cave I at Ajanta represents a return embassy from Persia to the Chalukyan court.[36]

What is significant to note here is that most of the commercial places including Taprobane (Anuradhapuram in Sri Lanka), Male (Koulam Male or Quilon) and Sibor (Goa) mentioned by Cosmas Indicopleustes as centres of trade for Persian Christians have yielded remnants of Christian settlements in the form of Pahlavi-crosses or copper plates. Probably the bishop of Kalyan, about whom mention is already made by Cosmas Indicopleustes in the sixth century, must have spiritually fed the Christian settlement of Goa in the seventh century and later. Sindabor (Chandrapur), or Goa, at that time was an important port in the Konkan with hectic trading activities with the ports of Gujarat and Malabar.[37] Against this general background, it seems that the initial mercantile group, which was associated with the crosses of Goa and other places on the rim of maritime India was the migrating commercial group from Persia, a fact which is clearly evident from the Pahlavi inscription on the cross. (However the work of all these crosses seems to have been executed in the respective places.) But later, with the development of commercial networks all over the Indian Ocean, which they seem to have realized with the help of the native St. Thomas Christians of Kerala and Mylapore, the composition of this mercantile group must have included many local Christians, as well. Even though the mercantile Christian settlements on the rim of Indian Ocean were predominantly West Asian in the initial phase, with the commencement of joint commercial operations with the help of the St. Thomas Christians of Kerala (tracing back their origin to apostle St. Thomas, who preached the gospel in India between AD 52 and AD 72), these settlements became mixed in the intermediate period and eventually, in the course of time, they seem to have become purely indigenous with a lot of elements from St. Thomas Christian community.[38] That must have been the reason why the Portuguese added, at a later phase, to the Pahlavi inscribed cross of Goa the following words: *A de S.(Sao) Tome ...* or 'that which belongs to St. Thomas'.[39]

The various Christian settlements on the south-west coast of India including those located on the rim of the Indian Ocean were spiritually fed by the metropolitan of Fars. Rew Ardashir on the coast of Fars (Persis), just at the border of Khuzistan, was the seat of the Metropolitan of Fars, from where he attended to the spiritual needs of Bahrain, Oman, Socotora and India. Eduard Schau in his research article of 1916 has pointed out that the Nestorian church of this period was not a monolithic entity as was generally understood; but had several streams and subdivisions.[40] While the seat of the patriarch was at Ctesiphon after AD 420, and the patriarch ordained all the bishops of Asia, there appeared certain developments in Rew Ardashir, which eventually led to its emergence as a parallel ecclesiastical centre, as distinct from Ctesiphon. From AD 554 to 790, the Metropolitan of Fars with his seat in Rew Ardashir (which was differently named as Reshar, Rishar or Rashar) separated his diocese from the patriarch of Ctesiphon and himself ordained the bishops for the six bishoprics of Fars (including Istahr, Ardashir-Khorre, Bishapur, etc.). The six towns of Bet Qatraye/Bahrain-Oman, Socotora and coastal south-west India were also spiritually fed by the Metropolitan of Fars.[41] The Catholicos Isho-Yab III (650-8) records that in his day the Metropolitan of Rew Ardashir was responsible not only for the dioceses of Fars alone, but also for 'India', a geographical concept in which he included the places between the maritime borders of the Sassanid kingdom to the country called QLH (Syriac QLH is equivalent to the Arabic place name Qal'ah/Kedah, an important entrepot in the Malaya peninsula), covering a distance of 1200 *parasangs* and extending up to the doors of South-East Asia.[42]

The separation of the church of Fars (Persis) with its satellite Christian settlements in south-west India from the Nestorian Patriarch of Ctesiphon became inevitable with the increasing differences that appeared among them on vital issues related to monasticism, ordination of the bishops and on use of language. The church of Mesopotamia (Ctesiphon) had the liturgical celebrations in Syriac, whereas the church of Fars (Persia) had its own Bible translation in the Pahlavi (archaic Persian) language in the fifth century. In fact, this Pahlavi translation of the Bible (which was used in contrast to the Syriac Psita Bible) was made by bishop Ma'na of Rew Ardashir in AD 420. A copy of this translation was excavated in 1966 in Turfan in China, where it seems to have reached through the Silk Route, and is now kept in Berlin.[43]

The available evidences attest to the fact that the Pahlavi language used in Fars was also extended to south-west India, where the missionaries from Fars catered to the spiritual needs of the native Christians. The fact that the 'stone-crosses' discovered in south-west India carry Pahlavi inscriptions[44] and the copper plates granted to Mar Sapor and Mar Prodh bear Pahlavi signatures (the names of the witnesses using Pahlavi script are distinctly Christian)[45] speaks of the dominant use of the Pahlavi language in the churches of Malabar and coastal western India. Gerd Gropp says that up to the eleventh century, the church of Fars used Pahlavi language and ordained bishops for Oman, Socotra and India. It was only after 1040/50, with the advent of the Seljuk dynasty in Iran, that the Metropolitan of Rew Ardashir was extinguished. From that time on, the bishops for the Gulf and India were ordained by the patriarch of Baghdad.[46] It seems highly probable that Syriac came to be used as a liturgical and ecclesiastical language in Malabar only after these developments in the eleventh century, when the church of Kerala got linked directly with the seat of the East Syrian church.

The nature of the Sassanid trade, as a result of which the earlier mentioned cultural and material remnants were later obtained in India at different time periods, needs to be explained against the background of increasing ruralization and peasantization in major parts of India. The trade of this period was not, however, extensive or widespread; instead the wheels of its commerce were moving rather interruptedly through the 'islands of commerce' and in a limited way. On the one hand, there was the increasing feudalization in Europe and more or less similar socio-economic formations in north India and on the other hand, there were frequent commercial and political conflicts between the Sassanids and the Byzantines, inevitably necessitating ruptures in the circuits. The available sources suggest that the coastal nodal centres of Gujarat, Konkan, as well as Kerala and the port of Mahabalipuram of the Pallavas were the significant 'islands of commerce' with which the Sassanid traders were often engaged. Its impact seems to have been felt more on the society than on economy as it helped to pump in a lot of Christians from Persia as traders and migrants.

EVOLVING NEXUS BETWEEN THE MIGRATING
CHRISTIAN TRADERS AND THE
INDIGENOUS CHRISTIAN AGRICULTURISTS

With the increasing external demand for spices and the migration of West Asian Christian mercantile groups to Malabar and other parts of south-west India for better commercial activities, there appeared a tendency among the indigenous St. Thomas Christians of Malabar to go into the interior part of Kerala and to bring more landspace under cultivation. The movement of the St. Thomas Christians to the expanding agricultural zone to produce spices with a view to meeting the external demands from the West, is testified by the erection of new churches and Christian settlements in the inland-agrarian pockets of central Kerala from the third century AD onwards.[47] In fact the agrarian settlements of the Christian community used to establish their identity by erecting in their settlements churches or prayer centres, which turned out to be the principal cohesive factor for them. The first of these settlements came up at Pallipuram during the third century, followed by centres at Ambazhakad, Aruvithara, Kuravilangadu and North Pudukkad in the fourth century. In the fifth century churches and prayer centres were erected at Angamali and Muttuchira. The sixth century saw the rise of settlement at Kaduthuruthy, Enammavu, Mylakombu, Udayamperur and Edappally. Later, in the ninth century, centres were built at Kayamkulam, Athirampuzha and Kottayam, and, in the tenth century church settlements were raised at Arakuzha and Nedisala.[48] These are the important churches and settlements in the interior of Kerala, formed as a result of the inland movement of the indigenous Christians.

Interestingly the region, in which these settlements are distributed, formed the best landspace for spice cultivation in central Kerala. This reiterates the fact that the movement of the St. Thomas Christians to these places was not accidental or casual, but a part of the move to participate in the expanding pepper cultivation, accelerated by the demand from the Mediterranean world and the Persian Gulf. Most of these places were located on the banks of rivers or the channels of backwaters, which ensured regular irrigation and easy transportation. There eventually developed a strong rapport between the agriculturists and the traders, between the spice producing group and the exchange oriented group, where commonality of religion seems to have cemented the bond. The spice producing native Christians of Malabar and the Christian traders from West Asia created an economic axis for the flow of commodities through the window of the Persian Gulf to the Mediterranean world. There was added logic for the St. Thomas Christians in their participation in the spice production, which invited more Christian traders from Persia and with them many priests and bishops too, who would, in turn, cater to their spiritual needs. In the absence of native bishops, dependence on Persian traders, who guided and took ecclesiastical dignitaries from Persia to India, was an exigency of the time.[49]

With the support of the spice producing indigenous Christians from the hinterland of Malabar, the commercially oriented migrating Christians from West Asia started focusing on the maritime rim of India expanding their commercial networks and settlements. Their overseas commercial operations were carried out especially under the banner of *Anjuvannam* and *Manigramam,* in which the Christian traders of Malabar were members.[50] In fact these Christian merchant guilds (including *Korran*[51]) engaged in overseas trade, played a considerable role in the pre-Portuguese world system that operated in the Indian Ocean encompassing the regions of the Persian Gulf, the Red Sea and the Levant. Their maritime commercial expansion was realized with the patronage of the indigenous rulers of Malabar, as is evidenced by the special privileges and rights which the ruler of Venadu granted to Mar Sapor as well as Prodh (AD 849)[52] and those that king Rajasimhan (AD 1028-43) conferred on the Christian traders like Chathan Vadukan and Iravi Chathan, who were members of the *Manigramam* merchant guild.[53]

The Christian mercantile settlements in several parts of maritime India, particularly the Konkan and Gujarat coasts, were quite active even in the fourteenth century, as is evidenced by Friar Jordan Catalani of Severac, who was made the bishop of Quilon in AD 1329. He refers to the existence of vibrant Christian settlements in Thana on the island of Saslsette, Sopara and Broach at the time of his visit.[54] The mercantile settlement of the Christians in Gopakapattanam (Goa), from where the Pahlavi-cross was recently unearthed, is alluded to by Ibn Batuta in the mid-fourteenth century.[55] Probably they must have dispersed to other places of Goa including Ela (Old Goa) in due course of time, a fact which is inferred from the discovery of a cross from the walls of a destroyed building in 1510, when Afonso Albuquerque invaded Ela (Old Goa).[56] All these are indicative of the Sassanid commercial links with maritime India that facilitated the expansion of Christian mercantile expansion, even though these settlements underwent a phase of radical transformation with Islamic commercial expansion from the eighth and ninth century onwards.

From the foregoing discussions the following conclusions may be drawn: thanks to the frequent commercial contacts between maritime India and Sassanid Persia, several mercantile settlements of the Pahlavi-speaking Christians appeared in important maritime trading centres of south-west India. It was mainly through the ports and maritime doors of Gujarat, Konkan, Canara, Malabar, Coromandel and Sri Lanka that this movement of commodities, followed by the process of settlement of the Persian trading communities on the coastal nodal points of India took place. While these Pahlavi speaking Christian merchants seem to have concentrated more on the important trading centres on the Indian littoral, the native St. Thomas Christians were penetrating more and more into the interior parts of Kerala for the extension of spice cultivation, a fact which is deduced from the relatively large number of churches built in the inland part of Malabar during this period. The efforts for the expansion of spice cultivation have nothing to do with religion: other communities also seem to have participated in agrarian expansion. But what is significant with the spice cultivating St. Thomas Christians is that they succeeded in establishing a rapport with the commercially oriented Persian Christians, a rapport between the producer and the trader that revolved around the axis of a common religion, which ultimately turned out to be mutually beneficial. It should be specially mentioned that the foundations laid by the Pahlavi-speaking merchants from Sassanid Persia formed the substratum upon which the Arabs and the later Abbassid traders erected the commercial superstructure from the eighth and ninth centuries onwards.

NOTES

1. The crisis in Indo-Roman trade, which appeared by the end of the reign of Marcus Aurelius, was reflected in the debasement of coins and stoppage of gold *aurei*. The Roman debasement of the golden *aurei* could be seen as the epilogue of the bad internal situation of the Roman empire, caused partly by the export of precious metals to India, to buy spices and other luxury items. In fact Pliny the younger in a letter to his penfriend, the emperor Trajan, informs us that Rome exported over a hundred million of golden *sesterces* to Asia annually. Pliny, *Natural History*, 12, p. 84; E.H. Warmington, *The Commerce between the Roman Empire and India*, Cambridge, 1928, p. 274. This critical phase in Indo-Roman commerce continued for a considerable period of time until the appearance of Constantine. With the abdication of Diocletian in AD 305, there was indescribable confusion and civil war till 324, when Constantine united the whole empire. Only then began the phase of the revival of Roman commerce with the East.

2. D. Whitehouse and A. Williamson, 'Sassanian Maritime Trade', in *Iran*, 11, 1973, pp. 29-32.
3. Gerd Gropp, 'Christian Maritime Trade of Sasanian Age in the Persian Gulf', in *Internationale Archaeologie*, 6, 1997, pp. 86-9.
4. Pius Malekandathil, 'St. Thomas Christians and the Indian Ocean: 52 AD to 1500 AD' in *St. Ephrem's Theological* (International) *Journal*, vol. 5, no. 2, October 2001. Pius Malekandathil, 'Discovery of a Pahlavi-Cross from Goa: A New Evidence for Pre-Portuguese Christian Settlements in Konkan', in *Christian Orient*, vol. 23, no. 3, September 2002, pp.132-46.
5. D. Whitehouse and A. Williamson, 'Sassanian Maritime Trade', pp. 29-32.
6. The political rivalry between Rome and Persia played a vital role in shaping the religious policy of the Sassanids. When the Christians were persecuted in Rome till the proclamation of the Edict of Milan in AD 313, there was complete freedom for the Christians of Sassanid Persia. The church of Persia had during this period developed an episcopal structure with the bishop of the capital city of Seleucia-Ctesiphon as the primate. However, with the acquisition of freedom of worship in the Roman Empire in AD 313, and with the transformation of Constantine into a Christian emperor, the Sassanids looked upon Christianity as the religion of the enemies, as a result of which Shahpur II (310-79) started a phase of religious persecution in the kingdom. For details see Pius Malekandathil, 'St. Thomas Christians: A Historical Analysis of their Origins and Development up to 9th century AD', in *St.Thomas Christians and Nambudiris, Jews and Sangam Literature: A Historical Appraisal*, ed. Bosco Puthur, Kochi, 2003, pp.1-48.
7. Diogo do Couto, *Da Asia, Decadas* XII, liv. 3, chap. 5, tome 8, Lisboa, 1788, pp. 283-5. Though the authors may differ on the date of his arrival, a rough analysis of possible demographic increase per century after deducting the possible mortality rate would show that AD 345 could have been the probable year of his arrival. The copper plate inscription as referred to by the Portuguese writers of the sixteenth century says that Thomas Cana came with seventy-two families and 400 people. Damião de Gois, *Chronica de El-Rei D.Manoel*, Parte I, cap. 98, Lisbon, 1749, p.133. Currently this community, both belonging to the Catholic diocese of Kottayam and the Jacobite diocese of Chingavanam, would come to two lakhs in number. One has to see the possible demographic increase per century and find out whether sixteen and a half centuries are required to make the community reach two lakhs from the initial 400. The high mortality rate of the medieval and early modern periods is to be taken into special account, which seems to have made the demographic growth index proceed slowly till the twentieth century. However, it should be admitted that a very conclusive and definite answer to this problem of date can be given only after a thorough demographic analysis by studying micro-regions and verifying the baptismal registers and death records kept in their churches.
8. Monteiro d'Aguiar, 'The Magna Carta of the St. Thomas Christians', in *Kerala Society Papers* (Series 4), ed. T.K. Joseph, vols. I and II, Thiruvananthapuram, 1997 (reprint), pp. 169-200; see particularly the translation Roz' Portuguese text given by H. Hosten, ibid., pp. 180-3.

9. D. Whitehouse and A. Williamson, 'Sassanian Maritime Trade', pp. 30-43.

10. Ibid., pp. 33-5.

11. Muhammad ibn Jarir Tabari, *Annales*, ed. M.J. de Goeje et al., Series I, Leiden, 1879-93, p. 820.

12. J. St. Martin, *Memoires historiques et geographiques sur l'Armenie* , vol. II, Paris, 1819, p. 372; J. Marquart, *Eransahr nach der Geographie des Ps. Moses Chorenaci*, Berlin, 1901, pp. 138 and 147. The Nestorians, who were particularly numerous in northern Mesopotamia, formed an important minority in the Sassanid Empire and from time to time Nestorians filled key positions in the administration.

13. R. Ghirshman, *The Island of Kharg*, Tehran, 1960, pl. 12fols.

14. D. Whitehouse and A. Williamson, 'Sassanian Maritime Trade', p. 43. They make this inference on the ground that traditionally the captains approaching Basra used to put in at Kharg to engage a pilot before entering the Shatt al-Arab and the island thus played a significant role in the maritime trade of the Gulf. The importance of this monastery is to be seen against the background of the missionary expansionist activities of the Nestorians and the ecclesiastical administration of the Indian church by the metropolitan of Rew Ardashir. For a detailed discussion on whether the St. Thomas Christians were Nestorians, see Luis Filipe F.R. Thomaz, 'Were the St.Thomas Christians looked upon as Heretics?', in *The Portuguese and the Socio-Cultural Changes in India: 1500-1800*, ed. K.S. Mathew, Teotonio R. de Souza and Pius Malekandathil, Fundação Oriente, 2001.

15. D. Whitehouse and A. Williamson, 'Sassanian Maritime Trade', pp. 29-47; D.M. Derrett, 'The History of Palladius of the races of India and Brahmans', *Classica et Mediaevalia*, 21, 1961, pp. 64-135; D.M. Derrett, 'The Theban Scholasticus and Malabar in c.355-60', *J.A.O.S*, 82, 1962, pp. 21-31.

16. Addai Scher, *La Chronique de Seert in Patrologia Orientalis*, V, pp. 324-6; B.E. Colles, 'Persian Merchants and Missionaries in Medieval Malaya', *Journal of the Malaysian Branch of the Royal Asiatic Society*, XLII/2, 1969, pp. 10-47.

17. B.E. Colles, 'Persian Merchants and Missionaries in Medieval Malaya', pp. 11-47; A. Mingana, 'The Early Spread of Christianity in India', *Bulletin of the John Rylands Library*, X, 1926, p. 455.

18. D. Whitehouse and A. Williamson, 'Sassanian Maritime Trade', p. 47. It should be here specially remembered that there was a tradition in the sixteenth century Kerala that St. Thomas himself had gone to preach in China, Mahachina and Java. For details see Antonio de Gouveia, *Jornada Ido Arcebispo*, Coimbra, 1606, pp. 44-46; see also Pius Malekandathil, *Jornada of D.Alexios Menezes: A Portuguese Account of the Sixteenth Century Malabar*, Kochi, 2003, pp. 8-9.

19. B.E. Colles, 'Persian Merchants and Missionaries in Medieval Malaya', p. 11.

20. P.Y. Saeki, *The Nestorian Documents and Relics in China*, 1951, p. 85. He refers to the Chinese record which speaks of the arrival of 'a great Nestorian family of Mar Sargis from the western lands' in 578. It was a forerunner of the official mission of 635, which is recorded in an inscription from Singan fu in Shensi. D. Whitehouse and A. Williamson, 'Sassanian Maritime Trade', p. 47.

21. Ibid., pp. 30-47; Muhammad ibn Jarir Tabari, *Annales*, p. 965; R. Pankhurst, *An Introduction to the Economic History of Ethiopia from early times to 1800*, London, 1961, pp. 33-7. The Ethiopians (the Aksumite kingdom) who embraced Christianity around AD 300 were considered as an integral part of the eastern Christian world. The St. Thomas Christians of Malabar and the Coptic (referring to Koptos, the old generic term for Egypt) Christians of Ethiopia had good commercial relations in the medieval period. These diversified channels of commerce led to the flow of Sassanid silver *dirham* and the Byzantine gold *nomisma* to the marts of Kerala.

22. D. Whitehouse and A. Williamson, 'Sassanian Maritime Trade', pp. 29-47; Husain ibn Muhammad al-Marghani Thaa'libi, *Histoire des Rois de Perse*, ed. and tran. H. Zotenberg, Paris, 1900, pp. 615-19; J.B. Bury, *History of the Later Roman Empire, AD 395-800*, vol. II, 1889, pp. 322-7; Muhammad ibn Jarir Tabari, *Annales*, p. 965.

23. Cosmas Indicopleustes, *La Topographie Chretienne*, tran. Wanda Wolska, Paris, 1962, pp. 3-5.

24. Pius Malekandathil, 'St. Thomas Christians and the Indian Ocean: 52 AD to 1500 AD', *Ephrem's Theological Journal*, vol. 5, no. 2, October 2001, p.189.

25. Cosmas Indicopleustes, *La Topographie Chretienne*, p. 5. Male could also be a place name. It is difficult to say whether it stands for Malyankara near Cranganore or for Kulam Male (Quilon). It could be either of these two. In Geniza papers we find reference to Malibarat, which could have been Kulam Male. S.D. Goiteen, *Letters of Medieval Jewish Traders*, Princeton, 1972, p. 64. For identification of Malibarat see Pius Malekandathil, *The Germans, the Portuguese and India*, Münster (Germany), 1999, p. 4.

26. Pius Malekandathil, 'Discovery of a Pahlavi-Cross from Goa', p. 140.

27. B.J. Perera, 'The Foreign Trade and Commerce of Ancient Ceylon', *Ceylon Historical Journal*, I, 1951, pp. 110-13.

28. C.P.T. Winckworth, 'A New Interpretation of the Pahlavi Cross-Inscription of Southern India', in *Kerala Society Papers*, ed. T.K. Joseph, vols. I and II, pp.159-64, 267-9.

29. N. Figueiredo, ed., St. Thomas, the Apostle in Mylapore, Three Documents, Madras, 1934, doc. III, p. 1. However, Gaspar Coreeia says that this cross was discovered in 1546. See Gaspar Correia, *Lendas da India*, vol. III, p. 421. See also Pius Malekandathil, ed., *Jornada of D.Alexis Menezes: A Portuguese Account of the Sixteenth Century Malabar*, pp. 244-6, 308-16.

30. Gerd Gropp, 'Die Pahlavi-Inschrift auf dem Thomaskreuz in Madras', *Archaeologische Mitteilungen aus Iran, Neue Folge* Band 3, 1970, pp. 267-71.

31. C.P.T. Winckworth has translated the inscription as: 'My Lord Christ, have mercy upon Afras son of Chaharbukht, The Syrian, who cut this.' For details see C.P.T. Winckworth, 'A New Interpretation of the Pahlavi Cross-Inscription of Southern India', in *Kerala Society Papers*, ed. T.K. Joseph, vols. I and II, pp. 161-4. Winckworth has later revised his reading and interpretation as follows: 'My Lord Christ, have mercy upon Afras, son of Chaharbukht, the Syrian, who

preserved this (cross).' For details see 'Revised Interpretation of the Pahlavi Cross Inscription of Southern India', in *Kerala Society Papers*, ed. T.K. Joseph, vols. I and II, pp. 267-9. The first attempt to decipher the inscription on the cross was in 1561, when the Portuguese invited a reputed Brahmin scholar, Pingali Suranna from the Vijayanagara kingdom to decipher the inscription. He said that the inscription contained no less than 36 hieroglyphics, each of which was equivalent to a sentence. His version was as follows: 'That at the time of the sagamo Law, Thomas, a man of God, was sent by the son of God (whose disciple he was) to these parts to bring the people of this nation to the knowledge of God; that he had built there a temple and done miracles; and that finally when he was praying on his knees before that cross he had been run through with a lance by a Brahmin and that the cross was tinged with the blood of the Saint in His everlasting memory.' A.C. Burnell, the first European to attempt a translation of the said inscription in 1873, says the following: 'In Punishment by the Cross the suffering of this who is the true Christ and God above and guide ever pure.' A.C. Burnell, 'Pahlavi Inscriptions in South India', *Indian Antiquary*, 3, November 1874, p. 313; Herman D' Souza, *In the Steps of St. Thomas*, Madras, 1983, pp. 60-2.

32. These crosses are considered to be copies of the Mylapore cross on the basis of the fact all these crosses carry the same Pahlavi inscription as that of Mylapore and the churches where these crosses are found were built at a later period after eighth/ninth centuries (except Muttuchira). See also Gerd Gropp, 'Die Pahlavi-Inschrift auf dem Thomaskreuz in Madras', p. 267.

33. For more details about the cross discovered from Goa see Pius Malekandathil, 'Discovery of a Pahlavi-Cross from Goa: A New Evidence for Pre-Portuguese Christian Settlement in Konkan', *Christian Orient,* vol. XXIII, no. 3, September 2002, pp. 132-46. This cross has Pahlavi inscription in the form of an arch and a Portuguese inscription at the base, which runs as follows: *A de S.(Sao) Tome (....) de Ilez (ilhas ?) 642(1642).* The Portuguese inscription which would mean 'that which belongs to the St.Thomas Christians of the islands (Tiswadi) 1642', must have been added later to identify this cross and show its difference from the rest of crosses, a step which was necessary in the seventeenth century amidst the heightened tension between the Portuguese and the indigenous Christians.

34. The Archaeological Survey of India, Goa Branch has confirmed the antiquity of the cross.

35. Muhammad ibn Jarir Tabari, *Annales*, p.1052.

36. G. Yazdani and L. Binyon, *Ajanta, The Colour and Monochrome Reproductions of the Ajanta Frescoes based on Photography*, I, London, 1930-55, pl. XXXVIII; D. Whitehouse and A. Williamson, 'Sassanian Maritime Trade', pp. 30-47.

37. For details see Ranabir Chakravarti, 'Coastal Trade and Voyages in Konkan: The Early Medieval Scenario', *The Indian Economic and Social History Review*, vol. XXXV, no. 2, April-June 1998, pp. 97-123; Ranabir Chakravarti, 'Merchants of Konkan', *The Indian Economic and Social History Review*, XXIII, 2, 1986,

pp. 212-16; Ranabir Chakravarti, 'Candrapura/Sindabur and Gopakapattana: Two Ports on the West Coast of India (AD 1000-1300)', *Proceedings of the Indian History Congress*, Aligarh, 2000, pp. 153-61.

38. Pius Malekandathil, 'Discovery of a Pahlavi-Cross from Goa', p. 136.

39. For details see Pius Malekandathil, 'Christianity came before the Portuguese to Goa', *Navahind Times* (Panorama), Panjim, 13 May 2001, p.1.

40. E. Schau, 'Vom Christentum in der Persis', *Sitzungsberichte Preußischen Akademie der Wissenschaften*, Berlin, 1916, pp. 958-80.

41. Ibid., p. 965; Gerd Gropp, 'Christian Maritime Trade of Sasanian Age in the Persian Gulf', p. 85.

42. O. Braun, *Corpus Scriptorum Christianorum Orientalium: Scriptores Syri*, Ii, p.252; B.E. Colles, 'Persian Merchants and Missionaries', pp. 20-1.

43. Gerd Gropp, 'Christian Maritime Trade of Sasanian Age in the Persian Gulf', p. 85; E. Schau, 'Vom Christentum in der Persis', pp.960ff; See also Richard N. Fyre, 'Bahrain under the Sasanians', in *Dilmun: New Studies in the Archaeology and Early History of Bahrain*, ed. Daniel Potts, Berlin, 1983, p. 169. The church of Ctesiphon opted for Syriac in order to make its medium distinct from Pahlavi, a language that was predominantly used by the Zoroastrians. However, the church of Fars with its satellite ecclesiastical units in the Indian Ocean seems to have made its separation from the Ctesiphon Patriarch evident by adhering to the use of Pahlavi language.

44. Gerd Gropp, 'Die Pahlavi-Inschrift auf dem Thomaskreuz in Madras', *Archaeologische Mitteilungen aus Iran, Neue Folge*, Band 3, 1970, pp. 267-71.

45. See the copy of the copper plates given in T.A. Gopinatha Rao, *Travancore Archaeological Series*, vol. II, Madras, 1916, pp. 66-6. For a study on the Pahlavi signatures of the Quilon copper plates see, C.P.T. Winckworth, 'Notes on the Pahlavi Signatures to the Quilon Copper Plates', in *Kerala Society Papers*, ed. T.K. Joseph, pp. 320-3.

46. Gerd Gropp, 'Christian Maritime Trade of Sasanian Age in the Persian Gulf', p. 86.

47. The active involvement of St. Thomas Christians in the spice-production was testified by Bishop John Marignoli (AD 1348), who visited Malabar on his way back from Cambulac (Beijing in China) and referred to the Christians of Quilon as 'rich people' and as 'owners of pepper plantations'. Henri Yule, ed., *Cathay and the Way Thither*, vol. III, Nendeln/Liechtenstein, 1967, pp. 216-18, 248-57. Later, in the Portuguese documents, St. Thomas Christians were described as the major cultivators of pepper in central Kerala. For example, see ANTT, *Cartas dos Vice-Reis da India*, doc. 95. See also E.R. Hambye, 'Medieval Christianity in India: The Eastern Church', in *Christianity in India*, ed. E.R. Hambye and H.C. Perumalil, Alleppey, 1972, p. 34; Samuel Matteer, *The Land of Charity: A Descriptive Account of Travancore and its People*, New Delhi, 1991, pp. 237-8. In a letter written in 1529 to the king of Portugal, it was said that all the pepper was in the hands of the St. Thomas Christians and that the majority of the pepper that went to Portugal was sold by them. Antonio da Silva Rego, ed., *Documentação*

para a Historia das Missões, vol. II, pp. 175-6. Even in the sixteenth and seventeenth centuries, the process of agrarian expansion was in great progress, as is evidenced by *Jornada's* reference to several Christian settlements then in the forests. For details see also Pius Malekandathil, 'Agrarian Production and Procurement Strategies in Malabar under the Portuguese, 1500-1663', in *The Portuguese in Coastal India in the 16th and the 17th Centuries*, ed. Yogesh Sharma and Jose Ferreira, New Delhi, 2008.

48. The details about the antiquity of these Christian settlements and their churches is based on W. Hermann, *Die Kirche der Thomaschristen:Ein beitrag zur Geschichte der Orientalischen Kirchen*, Hütersloh, 1877, pp. 673-769, and on Fr. Bernard, *Marthoma Christianikal (The History of the St. Thomas Christians)*, Pala, 1916, pp. 296-327. The year of founding of these churches is taken from the respective diocesan directories. It is further corroborated with the help of field study, in which the statues, the church-bells, stone inscriptions (including in *Vattezhuthu*), *Pallipattukal* (church songs), etc., are studied to verify the antiquity of these settlements. For church songs see P.J. Thomas, *Malayala Sahithyavum Christianikalum*, Kottayam, 1961, pp. 63-4.

49. Pius Malekandathil, 'St. Thomas Christians and the Indian Ocean', pp. 186-7, 202.

50. For details on these Christian merchant guilds see Meera Abraham, *Two Medieval Merchant Guilds of South India*, New Delhi, 1988. Only *Manigramam* and *Anjuvannam* had the right to impose customs in the town of Quilon. For details of the text of the Sthanu Ravi Varma copper plate, which indicates a close connection between the Christian community of Quilon and the *Manigramam* guild, see T.A. Gopinatha Rao, *Travancore Archaeological Series*, vol. II, Madras, 1916, pp. 66-86; T.K. Joseph, 'The Malabar Christian Copper-Plates', in *Kerala Society Papers*, vol. I, Thiruvananthapuram, 1997, pp. 201-4.

51. Later in 1503 Francisco de Albuquerque bought 4,000 bhars of well-dried pepper from the traders of the merchant guild Korran. See 'Reisebericht des Franciscus Dalbuquerque vom 27 December 1503', in *Tagebuch des Lucas Rem aus den Jahren 1494-1541: Ein Beitrag zur Handelsgeschichte der Stadt Augsburg*, ed. B. Greif, Augsburg, 1861, p. 146. Jean Aubin and Genevieve Bouchon identify Korran with a native Christian guild. For details see Jean Aubin, 'L'apprentissage del'Inde Cochin 1503-1504', in *Moyen Oriente et Ocean Indien*, 1988; Genevieve Bouchon, 'Calicut at the Turn of the Sixteenth Century', in *The Asian Seas 1500-1800: Local Societies, European Expansion and the Portuguese*, Revista da Cultura, vol. I, Ano V, 1991, p. 44; Pius Malekandathil, *Portuguese Cochin and the Maritime Trade of India, 1500-1663* (South Asian Study Series of Heidelberg University, Germany), Delhi, 2001, p. 152.

52. Elamkulam Kunjan Pillai, *Studies in Kerala History*, Kottayam, 1970, pp. 370-7.

53. A. Sreedhara Menon, *Kerala Charitram* (Malayalam), Kottayam, 1973, p.135. The grant made to these two Christian merchants was recorded in the form of a *vattezhuthu* inscription on a granite slab, 74 inches by 51 inches, lying at the foot of the open air cross in front of the Catholic church at Tazhekkad in Irinjalakuda.

54. For details see Jordanus, *Mirabilia Descripta*, London, 1863; George Moraes, *A History of Christianity in India from Early Times to St. Francis Xavier: AD 52-1552*, Bombay, 1964, pp. 89-102.

55. Ibn Batuta, *Travels in Asia and Africa, 1325-1354*, tran. H.A.R. Gibb, New Delhi, 1990, pp. 238-40; George M. Moraes, *History of Christianity in India*, Bombay, 1964, p. 154.

56. Francisco de Souza, *Oriente Conquistado a Jesu Christo pelos Padres da Companhia de Jesus da Provincia de Goa*, vol. I, Lisboa, 1710, pp. 14-15; See also ANTT, *Corpo Cronologico*, I, Maço 17, doc. 30. Letter of Fr. Domingos de Sousa sent to the king D. Manuel from Goa, dated 22-12-1514. Francisco de Souza in *Oriente Conquistado* says that this cross was found hidden away in a wall a few days after the occupation of Goa in 1510. It was from this cross that *Rua do Crucifixo* of Goa was said to have got its name. The newly discovered cross was then taken in procession to the church for veneration. Francisco de Souza, *Oriente Conquistado*, pp. 14-15.

CHAPTER TWO

Maritime Trade and Political Economy of Goa, 800-1500

Goa, whose sea-oriented traditions have been significantly unique in Indian history, had evolved into an important maritime trading centre on the west coast of India by the early part of the medieval period. In fact, its maritime traditions seem to have taken shape during the commercial expansion of the Satavahana traders following the acceleration of the Indo-Mediterranean trade of the Romans, which also led to the settlement of *yavana* merchants on Goa's coast.[1] During the time of the Chalukyan ruler Pulikesin II, the Goan port of Revatidvipa was an important door through which various commodity strands of the Deccan found movement to the Persian Gulf, a development that appeared as a follow-up of the exchange of embassies between the Sassanids and the Chalukyans and that coincided with the Sassanid attempts to make the trading activities of the Indian Ocean converge in their territory by controlling the trade routes through the Red Sea, the Persian Gulf and the 'Silk Route'.[2]

The trade networks and mercantile settlements of these Sassanid traders formed the substratum upon which the Arab traders later erected an Islamic commercial superstructure in the Indian Ocean. The Islamized merchants from Arabia and Persia started expanding their commercial activities initially to the regions where the Sassanid traders had their collection centres or settlements. One of the important regional economic units in India that benefited much out of the fruits of the West Asian commercial expansion was the Konkan in general, and Goa in particular. The local mercantile community while linking the networks of the regional economy with the long-distance trade route of the Arab traders made trade

*This was first published under the title 'The Impact of Indian Ocean Trade on the Economy and Politics of Early Medieval Goa (c. 8-15c),' *Deccan Studies*, vol. II, no. 1, January-June 2004, pp. 3-22.

surplus accumulate in their settlements and their maritime centres of exchange.

ARAB TRADERS AND GOAN POLITY UNDER THE SILAHARAS

The commercially oriented activities of the Arabs increased in the Konkan region with the accession of Rashtrakutas, who not only maintained good relations with the Arabs, but also appointed Arabs as governors over Sanjan, as is evidenced by the appointment of a Muhammad the Tajjik as the governor of Sanjana-mandala in AD 926.[3] From this privileged politico-economic position enjoyed under the Rashtrakutas, it seems that some Arab traders extended their influence and maritime contacts to Goa, which was then ruled by the Silaharas, who were initially vassals of the Rashtrakutas. There are scholars like Ranabir Chakravarti, who say that the Silaharas renounced their allegiance to the Rashtrakutas when the latter placed Arabs in the Konkan region and that the Silaharas developed hostile relations with the Arabs.[4]

However, in Goa, which was ruled by the Goan Silaharas or the South Konkan Silaharas,[5] the Arab traders and Muslim mercantile settlements seem to have appeared at least by the end of the tenth century AD, as one can infer from the Goa plates of Kadamba Jayakesi I dated AD 1059. In fact this epigraphic narration refers to an Arab Madhumad (Muhammed) trading in Gove or Gopakapattanam (located on the banks of river Zuari in Goa), who was a *nauvittakadhimana* or a ship-owning merchant and who rescued the Kadamba ruler Guhalladeva, when he was shipwrecked on his way to Somanath.[6] However, this evidence also suggests that even before the intervention of the Kadamabas in the affairs of Gopakapattanam, there were ship-owning Arab merchants, who seem to have settled down in the region during the last phase of the Goan Silaharas, making it a *Hanjamannanagara.*[7]

Gerald A. Pereira suggests that Sanaphulla, the founder of the Goan Silaharas, must have based his political headquarters at Gopakapattanam,[8] when he received the land tract lying between the Sahya mountain and the sea from the Rashtrakuta king Krishna I (AD 758-73) for the help he extended to the latter to subdue the Konkan.[9] From the time of his son Dhammayira (795-820) onwards, Balipatana became an important maritime trade centre of the Goan Silaharas, where Dhammayira erected a fortress.[10] The importance of Balipatana as an important maritime trading centre of the Goans is evident from the Kharepatan plates of Rattaraja dated AD 1008. This record speaks of vessels from Chandrapura (south Goa) frequently visiting Balipatana, where ships from Cemulya (Chaul) and *dvipantara* (overseas) also used to come for commerce.[11]

The Goan Silaharas also wanted to control the maritime trade emanating from Chandrapura. In order to realize this goal, Aiyaparaja (820-45), the son of Dhammayira, conquered Chandrapura and made its ruler a vassal to him. From this time on, the Goan Silaharas controlled the affairs of Chandrapura by supporting its ruler in times of emergency, particularly when there were attacks from outside, a situation which the Silaharas could manipulate for their advantage.[12] During this period Gopakapattanam, Chandrapura and Balipattana seem to have formed one regional economic unit whose commercial links were expanding with the emerging maritime trade networks of the Arabs.

Corresponding to the intensification of Arab trade with Goa, mentioning of the name of Chandrapura (Goa's main port) became frequent in Arab writings. Al Masudi who visited the west coast of India in the first half of the tenth century refers to Sindabur and identifies its location in the Sea of Lata (Sea of Gujarat or the Arabian Sea) and says that it is in the kingdom of Baghara (Balhara or Rashtrakutas). Along with Sindabur, Al Masudi refers also to Kanbaya (Cambay), Sandan (Sanjan), Tana (Thana), Subara (Sopara), Saimur (Chaul) and Manibar or Mulaybar (Malabar) as the important maritime centres on the west coast of India for the trade of the Arabs.[13] All these places, which were earlier centres of commerce for the Romans, and later for the Sassanids, and in that way mutually connected by economic activities of distribution and exchange, operated as different links for the expanding commercial zone of the Arabs.

Al Idrisi (AD 1162) gives a vivid account of the city and port of Sindabur, which could be reached by a journey of four days from Broach. He writes, ' Sindabur is situated on a great gulf where ships cast anchor. It is a commercial town and contains fine buildings and rich bazaars.'[14] He also highlights the coastal trade relations, which Sindabur had with Tana (Thana), and Baruj (Broach). Sindabur was an important trade centre for the Arabs even in the thirteenth century as is evident from the account of Abul Fida, who speaks of Sindabur's contacts with Manjruth (Mangalore).[15]

POLITICS AND TRADE CIRCUITS

The Kadambas of Goa rose to the occasion to exploit the expanding maritime contacts of the Arabs to build up a relatively independent state structure on the basis of the gains accruing from this trade. The Kadambas were the *Mahamandalesvaras* of Western Chalukyas and their increasing involvement in maritime activities should be seen as part of their mercantilist desire to augment wealth with a view to strengthening power. The initial step in this direction was to appoint an Arab governor to attract more foreign traders from Arabia. However, in the selection of the candidate, preference went to Sadhan, a descendant of Madhumad (Muhammed) the Tajika (Arab) who saved Guhalladeva,[16] when he was shipwrecked on his way to Somanath. The copper plate inscription of Jayakesi I states that Sadhan, the grandson of Muhammed the Tajika, was made the governor of Goa by Jayakesi I on Friday, on the third day of *Vaisaka* in 975 of the Saka era (AD 1053).[17]

The appointment of the Arab trader Sadhan as the governor of the port city of Gopakapattanam is to be seen against the background of the expanding Islamic commerce, followed by the establishment of Arab settlement along the fringes of the Indian Ocean starting from the mouth of the river Indus and extending up to Indonesia, with sizeable indigenous Muslim communities of Navayats in Karnataka, Mappillas in Malabar and Ilappais as well as Marakkars in Coromandel, all linked together by a common *shafi'ite* tradition.[18]

The Arab ship-owning merchant Muhammed seems to have played a key position in the maritime trading activities of Gopakapattanam, during the time of Guhalladeva I (*c.* 980-1005/7), when the Kadambas of Goa confined themselves to the port of Chandrapura for their maritime trade. The immense wealth which this Arab trader bestowed upon Guhalladeva I after having rescued the latter from shipwreck was an added reason to get acceptability and legitimacy for his trading activities in the Kadamba port of Chandrapura, as well as in Gopakapattanam, of which the latter was then under the Goan Silaharas. However, later, with the annexation of Gopakapattanam by Shastha-deva (1007/8), the son of Guhalladeva I, it became an important port for the Kadambas.[19] During the initial phase when the Kadambas were establishing their hold over the affairs of Gopakapattanam including its maritime trade, Sameil (Ismail) one of the sons of the above-mentioned Arab trader Muhammed,[20] seems to have played a decisive role. In the battles, which the Kadamba rulers waged against the North Silaharas, his contribution in the form of money and personnel seems to have been significant.

It must have been against this background of increasing support from the Arab traders that Sadhan, the son of Sameil (Ismail), was appointed as his governor by Jayakesi I. With a view to attracting more Arab traders to Gopakapattanam, Jayakesi I took a pro-Muslim policy and gave up a part of his right to collect customs to Sadhan for the maintenance of the *Mijiguiti* (mosque), which the latter set up in this port city. The ruler allowed Sadhan to collect fixed amounts from the vessels coming from different parts of the Indian Ocean region for the up-keep of this mosque.[21] It seems that this Mijiguiti also operated like one of the links in the chain of *khanqahs*, which were established all over the Indian Ocean region from Gazirun near the Persian Gulf up to Zaytun (Ts'wan-chow-fu) in China.[22] In fact, the continuous linkage between the Arab traders and the Kadambas helped to integrate the exchange centres of Goa with the expanding commercial networks of the Arabs in the Indian Ocean.

By this time Gopakapattanam emerged as a major maritime trade centre in India having commercial contacts with different regional economies of Asia, as is evident from the copper plates of Jayakesi I (AD 1053). The important regions with which this port had commercial contacts were *Malaya-desa* (Malaya Peninsula), *Duluka Desha* (Tulu country), Gokarna (regions near Kumta), Saurashtra (Saurashtra), Gurjara (Gujarat), Lata (Coastal Gujarat), Sthanak (Thana), Konkana (Konkan), Veimulya (Seimulya or Chaul), Chippalona (Chiplun), Sangameshwar (near Ratnagiri), Valappattan (Baliapattana or Kharetan), Pindayana (Panayem?), Shivapur (near Chandor). Merchants from Simhala (Sri Lanka), Zangavar (Zanzibar), Kalah (QL'H in the Malaya Peninsula, now it is called Kedah),[23] Pandya (the southern portion of Coromandel coast), Chouda (Chola teritory), Gauda (Bengal), Khyata (Kuwait), Puxta (Pithapuram), Sri Sthanak (Thana), and Chandrapura (Chandor) all of which had frequent interaction with Gopakapattanam.[24]

Following the hectic trading activities, coins of a wide variety were in use in Gopakapattanam. The principal coin in circulation was *gadyanacas*, which all traders coming from overseas and far off places had to use as the monetary medium for making payments to the mosque of Sadhan. They had to pay two coins of *gadyanacas* to the mosque for each voyage.[25] In fact *Bhairava-gadyanakas* were pure gold and their weight varied from 76 to 86 grains.[26] The second category of coin that was used in trade transactions in Gopakapattanam was *dracmas*. The vessels coming from the trading centres of Duluka-desa, Gokarna, Valapattan, Chippalona, Sangameshwar, Shivapur, Pindayana (which means traders involved in coastal trade) were required to pay in *dracmas* to the mosque of Sadhan, which is also suggestive of the fact that the chief monetary medium for the coastal trade in Konkan was *dracmas*.[27]

The prime position, which Jayakesi I gave to the Arab traders is evident from the importance he attached to the mosque of Sadhan, for which tax was collected from every conceivable form of transaction. This partial relinquishment of taxes for the sake of the mosque was to attract more traders from Arabia, which would bring more wealth to strengthen his emerging kingdom. Taxes were collected from vessels coming and going, from slaves, from the sale and purchase of commodities, all for the maintenance of the mosque.[28] His commercial and religious policies favouring Arab merchants did not go unrewarded; the Muslim merchants began to supply liberally their resources (including personnel, money and vessels) for the political expansion of the Kadambas.

The Arabs are said to have joined hands with the Kadambas (Jayakesi I) to attack the North Konkan Silaharas.[29] This naval battle between the Silaharas and the Kadambas of Goa is pictured in a panel in a cave near the Borivili railway station near Mumbai.[30] Jayakesi I maintained a strong navy, probably incorporating the services of Arab seamen, with the help of which he defeated the principal maritime powers of the period like the Pallavas, the Cholas and the Latas, as is referred to in his Panjim copper-plate.[31]

However, things changed with the death of Jayakesi I in 1080/81, and his successor Guhalladeva II was a weak ruler. Anantadeva of the North Konkan Silaharas, as his Kharepatan plates (AD 1084) say, 'drove out the violent and vile soldiers of Muna (probably referring to Muhammad Nabi) who devastated the Kunkana territory' and took the title Lankeswara,[32] which would mean he had some control over parts of Goa, then called Lanka. This is indicative of the reverses, which the Arab-Kadamba alliance had to face from the North Konkan Silaharas. It seems that after the taste of defeat from Antantadeva, Guhalladeva II dropped Muslim officials and appointed Kelima (Kelivarma) as his principal official, mentioned in his copper-plates.[33]

However, this reverse was a temporary phenomenon, and under the later Kadamba rulers of Goa the maritime trade of Gopakapattanam and Chandrapura continued to flourish. Traders from across the seas were frequenting these ports, also because of the junctional position that Goa enjoyed in the flow of different commodity streams. From the eighth century onwards, there was the long distance trade route emanating from al-Basrah or Muscat or Sohar in Oman in the Persian Gulf and terminating in Canton in South China, into which Goa was incorporated as a satellite economic unit.

Long distance movement of commodities through this sea trade route flourished thanks to the existence of large empires at both ends of the route: on the one hand, there was the Abbassid Caliphate (750-1258) in Persia, which kept its capital at the commercially strategic city of Baghdad, and on the other hand, the Tang dynasty (618-907) of China that gave unbroken peace in the south for two and a half centuries.[34] Koulam Male or Quilon in Malabar was an important halting centre in India for the Arab traders involved in this long distance trade, who used to break long distance voyages there for want of favourable monsoon and change of shipping.[35]

The ports of the Konkan in general, and Goa in particular, had hectic trade relations with Koulam Male or Quilon, as is testified by the Jewish letters of Cairo Genizza.[36] The Jewish traders, who expanded their commerce along with the Arabs, either from Abbassid Persia or Fatimid Egypt, were the principal commercial intermediaries involved in this trade.[37] However, the main channel through which they used to take commodities to the Mediterranean world was via Aden, al-Qus, Fustat/Cairo and Alexandria.[38] These Jewish traders bolstered their economic positions by well-established family bonds and matrimonial links. One among them was Mahruz b. Jacob, a ship-owning Jewish merchant (*nakhoda*), who carried out trading activities with the ports of Konkan, Malabar and Egypt.[39] In his letter of *c.* AD 1145, Mahruz b. Jacob refers to Kanbayat (Cambay), Broach, Tana, Mangalore, Malibarath (Kulam Mali), and Kayakannur (Lower Kannur) as the important centres of Jewish trade on the western seaboard.[40]

More or less during the same period (AD 1116-17) we find one Allan b. Hassun, another Jewish merchant, making commercial voyages from Aden to Sindabur (Chandrapura) to sell storax and coral, which he collected from Mediterranean ports.[41] After having carried out trading transactions in the port of Sindabur (Chandrapura) he proceeded to Munaybar (Malabar), where the important ports (according to him) were Fakanaur (Barakur) and Kawalam (Koulam Mali),[42] of which the latter was the more important port, also for the Abbassid traders. Corresponding to the hectic trading activities of the Jews with the ports of Goa, the name of Chintabor (Sindabur or Chandrapura of Goa) also entered the famous Catalan map prepared by the Majorcan Jew called Abraham Cresques in 1375 for the King Charles V of France.[43]

The proximity to maritime trade accelerated the total output of primary production, as well as secondary production, and also the process of division of labour, as is evidenced by the wide variety of taxes imposed by the Kadambas of Goa on different agencies involved in various economic operations. These varied from *totadaya* (taxes on income derived from garden land), *kuniya sunka* (tax levied on pond or tank which supplied water to the fields), *totada batti sunka* (levy on garden products, collected at custom houses), *bagila vag* (house tax), *chittani kayalu dasom* (1/10 of levy of tax collected from the skilled workers), *talasari* (transit duty collected on income of the villagers), *handaruvani* (tax collected on the spot of the pandal) and *biruvani* (tax for the maintenance of the travelling merchants).[44] All these suggest that the tax paying ability of the people was relatively high, which is further indicative of the existence of an activated economy in the region.

From the tax called *totadaya* one may infer that there must have had an intensified cultivation of garden crops like coconut, and from *kuniya sunka* one may infer the intensification of agricultural activities, particularly paddy cultivation. *Chittani kayalu dasom* is suggestive of the intensification of craftworks and secondary production, and *biruvani* is indicative of intensification of trade, probably peddling trade. We find several *settis* or merchants being mentioned in the inscriptions of the Kadambas of Goa, evidently referring to the social group to which these traders belonged. Pattanasetti, Kotisetti, Sasanisetti,[45] Kavanasetti,[46] etc. were some of the leading Hindu merchants who took part in the flourishing trade of this time. The following taxes like *baledere* (tax on bangle manufacture), *ganadere* (tax on oil mills), *maggadere* (loom tax levied on weaving), *taila sarige* (tax on oil manufacture) highlight a wide variety of secondary production activities.[47] In short, all these were nothing other than auxiliary economic activities meant to feed the maritime trade carried out in Gopakapattanam and Chandrapura.

VICISSITUDES AND NEW ACTORS

Though the trading activities of Gopakapattanam continued for another two centuries, the amount of profit accumulation for the Kadamba rulers from its trade seems to have been less following the defeat of Guhalladeva II from Anantadeva of North Konkan Silaharas in 1084. However, the later Kadamba rulers like Jayakesi II and Permadi-deva, who was also called the 'Lord of the western ocean',[48] seem to have taken special interest to facilitate the maritime trading activities of Gopakapattanam. The title 'Lord of the western ocean', which Permadi-deva assumed, was evidently indicative of the formidable naval power that he possessed.

The maritime trade emanating from Gopakapattanam and Chandrapura seems to have experienced a dwindling phase in the fourteenth and fifteenth centuries. Several factors were operating behind the scenes. At the international level, the fall of Abbassid Caliphate in 1258 following the attacks of the Mongols (which cut off for a considerable period of time the long distance trade links between the Persian Gulf ports and Chinese ports) adversely affected the commerce of several traditional ports of India.[49] This also seems to have had repercussions on the maritime trade of Goa, as the trade of Gopakapattanam and Chandrapura depended very much on their linkage with other ports of the Indian Ocean region, which were in fact feeding ports or satellite units for this international trading network.

At the regional level, the frequent attacks on Goa by several invaders like Malik Kafur (1310), Muhammad-bin-Tughlaq (1327)[50] and finally Jamal-ud-din of Honavar (1342-4) drained the economic vitality of Gopakapattanam. Even during this phase of crisis, the expansion of the Delhi Sultanate to the Deccan and the consequent politico-commercial developments in the region introduced significant transformation in the commercial sector of Goa, a development which seems to have taken place probably because of its commercially strategic location for the import of horses from West Asia.

One of the most visible aspects of this development was the relatively high amount of capital accumulation in Goa, particularly in the hands of sea traders and ship operators. Some of them were even able to convert the new resources from trade into political assets, as in the case of Jamal-ud-din, who was a son of a Goan shipbuilder, and who became the ruler of Honavar (in the 1340s), because of his ability to transfer the trade capital accumulated from the ports of Goa for political dominance. This Goan Muslim merchant used his family's trade wealth to hire an army of 6,000 and a fleet of over 50, with the help of which he established himself as the sultan of Honawar. Later he dispatched from Honawar his naval force, consisting of 52 fighting vessels, under the command of Ibn Batuta and occupied the port of Gopakapattanam. With the occupation of the principal port of Gopakapttanam, the control over the Goan economy passed into the hands of Jamal-ud-din. It is true that Jamal-ud-din attacked this port from Honavar on the request of the prince of Gopakapattanam, who promised to accept Islam and to marry Jamal-ud-din's daughter, if his father was ousted.[51] However, what appears to be significant here is: if Jamal-ud-din could accumulate so much wealth from Goan ports as to bring the affairs of Honawar and Goa totally under his control, then how much trade surplus must have been accumulated in Goa during this period with the increasing maritime trading activity in its ports.

It seems that the scene of the naval battle depicted in the *Viragal* (hero-stone), belonging to the time of king Biravarma and now kept in the Goa State Museum, is representing the naval battle waged between the forces of Gopakapattanam and Honavar. This *Viragal* was set up to commemorate the death (in the sea battle) of a *samanta* of Biravarma, who seems to have ruled Gopakapattanam during this period.[52]

The various *Viragals* depicting sea battles and fighting ships, which are now kept in Goa State Museum, are indicative of the advanced technology employed in Goa in this period for building vessels for fighting purposes. In one of the *Viragals*, a vessel with an axial rudder is depicted; it has seven rowers in it. The representation of a vessel in another *Viragal* has nine oar holes and a stern-post rudder, which was a technological improvement on the axial rudder.[53] These depictions highlight the existence of a strong naval tradition in Goa, which continued uninterruptedly from the time of Chalukyan ruler Kirtivarman I (580) till the mid-fourteenth century, when Goa was reverted temporarily as political appendage to larger territorial powers.

In fact, the attack from the forces of Honavar was a severe blow to the trading activities of Gopakapattanam. For the next one and a half centuries, Goa was made a political appendage of several ambitious territorial powers like the Vijayanagara, the Bahmanis and the Adil Shahi of Bijapur. What these landlocked political powers wanted was a gateway for their maritime exposure and Goa suited most aptly to their designs.

SHIFT OF ECONOMIC CENTRE FROM ZUARI-BASED GOPAKAPATTANAM
TO MANDOVI-BASED ELA

The port of Ela, which seems to have evolved as a satellite port during the later period of the Kadambas, began to take precedence over the port of Gopakapattanam after Muslim invasions.[54] The 'Kadamba road' connecting Ela on the banks of river Mandovi with Gopakapattanam, located on the the Zuari, was the chief land route for inter-port interactions. It seems that the Vijayanagara rulers, who captured Goa in 1369,[55] concentrated much on Ela and Diwar, as is evidenced by the Saptakoteshwar temple, which they re-built in Diwar. It was the Vijayanagara minister Vasanta Madhav (1379) who played the key role in the reconstruction of this temple.[56]

Along with Ela, Raibandar also emerged as a significant trading centre[57] by this time, a process which eventually led to the shifting of Goa's economic centre of gravity from the ports of the river Zuari to the ports of river Mandovi. The silting of the port of Gopakapattanam had invited its own doom. Moreover, the proximity to timber-yielding Ponda forests, which would ensure regular supply of timber for shipbuilding activities, the closeness of the new port to the core centre of the Vijayanagara Empire (which reduced the distance for the transportation of the horses through the land route) and the relative distance from the Islamized city of Gopakapattanam, must have been the other prominent reasons for the Vijayanagara rulers to opt for Ela as their principal port. Eventually the Vijayanagara coin called *pratap* or *pagoda*, which is described in Portuguese sources as *pardao d'ouro*, became the common monetary medium of the new port.[58] However, as is suggested by the Portuguese sources, by the 1440s Goa seems to have been ruled by its own chief or Nayak, relatively independent of Vijayanagara's direct control, probably with Ela as its capital.[59]

With these changes some traders from Gopakapattanam also seem to have shifted their activities to Ela, as is evidenced by the discovery of a cross from the demolished building of Old Goa in 1510, when Afonso Albuquerque conquered it.[60] This must have been the remnant of the mercantile Christian community that migrated to this port from Gopakapattanam, where they had concentrated earlier to take advantage of the new commercial situation in Ela. Similarly, some Arab traders also seem to have moved over to this port to take part in the import trade of horses from Arabia and the Persian Gulf and to supply them to the Vijayanagara rulers to meet their war needs. This is inferred from the discovery of several Arab remnants from different places on the banks of river Mandovi, including Betim. It seems that many others like Krishna Sinai and Timoja were also equally interested in the growing maritime trade of this new port by the end of the fifteenth century.[61]

However, the city of Ela, which eventually fell into the hands of the Bahmani rulers, had a great many Muslim traders as settlers. Their number increased with the arrival of 400 Muslims (*navayats*) from Onor (Honavar) and Baticala (Batkal) in 1479, following their persecution by the Vijayanagara rulers for having supplied horses from Arabia and Persia to the Bahmani Sultan.[62] Later, with the disintegration of Bahmani kingdom in 1498, Yusuf Adil Shah (the Constantinople-born governor of Bijapur), who established his political power over a considerable tract of territory centred around Bijapur, also brought Goa under his control. The port of Ela was the chief entry point through which the trading networks of the Bijapur kingdom found maritime exposure. With the increase in the import of horses from Hormuz to this port for distribution in the Vijayanagara kingdom, the city of Ela received a considerable amount of wealth as custom duties, which Adil Shah claimed as his share.

The Portuguese sources say that the city of Goa paid 1,00,000 *pardaos* per year to Yusuf Adil Shah from the duties on the merchandise brought to this port,[63] whereas the duties collected on the objects of maritime trade in Goa and the neighbouring districts came to about 400,000 *pardaos*.[64] A large share of this wealth came from the trade in horses. It is estimated that about 10,000 horses were imported annually to India and the price of each horse in 1292 was 200 *livres tournois* (according to Marco Polo, which Yule equates with 190 pounds).[65] On the eve of Portuguese conquest, one horse was worth 800 *pardaos* in Ela.[66] As the documents of the second half of the sixteenth century say, each ship from Hormuz was bringing to Goa about 80 to 125 horses, which the traders used to sell at a value varying from 300 to 1000 *ducats*.[67] For each horse an amount of 20 *pardaos* were to be paid as tax at Ela during the pre-Portuguese times, and 40 *ducats* in the second half of the sixteenth century, which also suggest that the flow of wealth from the custom house of Ela to the exchequer of the territorial rulers was immensely high. Against this background of intensified maritime trade contacts with the ports of the Persian Gulf, it is highly probable that Juwa-Sindabur of the Tuluva coast (which means southern part of the Konkan) mentioned in the famous navigational treatise of Ibn Majid of the fifteenth century must have been Ela-Goa.[68]

Thus, we find that the Goan economy experienced a very activated phase during the early medieval period following the intensification of maritime trading activities in its ports. Different social groups engaged in secondary production, and craft works started giving preference to production of commodities that were in high demand for maritime trade, as is seen during the Kadamba period. Even before the European expansion, Goan trade had assumed a trans-regional character, because of the incorporation of its ports into the wider networks of international trade, running from the Indian Ocean to the Mediterranean and carried out principally by the Arab and Jewish merchants. Some local rulers promoted the maritime trade of Goa even by appointing Arab traders as their governors with a view to attracting more foreign trade to their ports, if they found that such a policy would ensure steady flow of resources needed for political dominance. However, politics and policies varied from time to time and from ruler to ruler. The Kadamba rulers and the Adil Shahis of Bijapur made attempts to grab a sizeable share from the maritime trade of Goa for empowering their states, whereas the Vijayanagara rulers tried to control Goan ports principally to ensure regular import of horses for meeting their increasing war needs in the Deccan. Another significant development was that various merchant groups which were involved in Goa's maritime trade turned out to be significant resource-mobilizing groups on the western coast of India, among which Jamal-ud-din's ability and success in establishing political dominance out of the trade surplus accumulated from the Goan ports stands as an exceptional entrepreneurial development. The end-result of these developments is that the various sectors of the Goan economy began to take more sea oriented dimensions where the production in the primary and secondary sectors was done principally for the sake of maritime trade. It was into this economically well-activated and commercially stimulated space that the Portuguese came in 1510.

NOTES

1. The discovery of the statues of Buddha executed in Greek artistic style and obtained from Colvale (in Bardez) evidently suggests that some of the Greek intermediaries (*yavanas*), who got converted to Buddhism, must have settled down in Goa, for the purpose of procuring cargo for commerce with Rome. See Pius Malekandathil, 'Maritime Activities of Goa and the Indian Ocean: A Study of the Society and Economy up to 1500 AD', in *Globalization in Pre-Modern India*, ed. Nagendra Rao, Delhi, 2005, pp. 144-68.

2. D. Whitehouse and A. Williamson, 'Sassanian Maritime Trade', *Iran*, 11, 1973, pp. 29-32. For details see also Pius Malekandathil, 'Discovery of a Pahlavi-Cross from Goa: A New Evidence for Pre-Portuguese Christian Settlement in Konkan,' *Christan Oriente*, 2002, pp.140-2; Muhammad bin Jarir Tabari, *Annales*, ed. M.J.de Goeje et al., serie I, Leiden, 1879, p. 1052; T. Noeldeke, *Geschichte der Perser und Araber zur Zeit der Sassaniden*, Leiden, 1879; *Epigraphia Indica*, vol. VI, pp. 4-9;

K.A. Nilakanta Sastri, *A History of South India*, New Delhi, 1999, pp. 134, 288; G. Yazdani and L. Binyon, *Ajanta: The Colour and Monochrome Reproductions of the Ajanta Frescoes based on Photography*, I, London, 1930-55, pl. XXXVIII.

3. Ranabir Chakravarti, 'Merchants of Konkan (circa AD 1000-1500)', *The Indian Economic and Social History Review*, XXIII, 2, 1986, p. 208; for more details on the trade of the Konkan during this period see Ranabir Chakravarti, 'Coastal Trade and Voyages in Konkan: The Early Medieval Scenario', *The Indian Economic and Social History Review*, vol. XXXV, no. 2, April-June 1998, pp. 97-123; for information on the cordial relations between the Arabs and the Rashtrakutas (Balharas), see M.H. Nainar, *The Geographers' Knowlede of southern India*, Madras, 1942; for information on the appointment of Mahumati the Tajjika (Arab) as the governor of Sanjana-mandala by king Krishna II (AD 878-915), see Chinchani Copper Plate of Indra III (AD 926), *Epigraphia Indica*, 32, pp. 45-60.

4. Ranabir Chakravarti, 'Merchants of Konkan', p. 211.

5. The existence of a distinct Goan branch of Silaharas is made known by the Kharepatan Plates of Rattaraja (AD 1008), the last of the known rulers of this dynasty. See *Epigrphia Indica*, vol. III, p. 292. V.R. Mitragotri says that the north Goa formed part of the Southern Silaharas till about AD 1010. See V.R. Mitragotri, 'Memorial Monuments of Shilahara-Kadamba period from Goa', in *Goa: Cultural Trends,* ed. P.P. Shirodkar, Panaji, 1988, p. 65.

6. We have got two accounts for this historical incident. One is the account given in the copper-plate inscription of Jayakesi I (dated AD 1053) which was sent to Lisbon in 1727 with a corrupt Portuguese translation. The entire text of this inscription is given in, P. Pissurlencar 'Inscrições Pre-Portuguesas de Goa', *O Oriente Portugues*, no. 22, Panjim 1938, pp. 386-98; see also Archivo da Secretaria Geral do Governo, *Monções do Reino*, no. 93, fol.1392. The other account is seen in the Panjim copper-plate of Jayakesi I (AD 1059) found at Panjim by Henry Heras and now kept in the Heras Institute of Historical Research, Mumbai. The text of this inscription is given in George Moraes, *Kadamba Kula*, New Delhi 1990, pp. 394-400, see especially pp. 399-400 and in P. Pissurlencar, 'Inscrições Pre-Portuguesas de Goa', pp. 398-9. However, in both the accounts there is a difference in the proper names of the Arab trader who rescued Guhalladeva. In the Panjim copper plate of Jayakesi I (1059) Aliya was mentioned as the rescuer of Guhalladeva. See George Moraes, *Kadamba Kula*, New Delhi, 1992, pp. 399-400. However, in the inscription of Jayakesi I (1053) later sent to Lisbon, Madhumad (Muhammed) is mentioned as the person who rescued Guhalladeva. P. Pissurlencar, 'Inscrições Pre-Portuguesas de Goa', pp. 387; 390-1. Here I follow the inscription of 1053, as it seems to be more true and reliable because of the great amount of minute details furnished there regarding the grantee and the wide variety of taxes that Sadan (the grandson of the Arab trader who rescued Guhalladeva) was allowed to collect for maintaining the *Mijiquiti* (Mosque).

7. For details on *Hanjamannanagara*, see Nandakumar Kamat, 'Simha and Gajasimha Motif in Goa Kadamba's Temple Architecture and Numismatics', in *Goa: Cultural Trends* ed. P.P. Shirodkar, p. 51; Nandakumar Kamat, 'Gopakapattana

through the Ages' in *Goan Society Through the Ages*, ed. B.S. Shastry, New Delhi, 1987, pp. 251-69.

8. Gerald A. Pereira, *An Outline of the Pre-Portuguese History of Goa*, Vasco da Gama, 1973, p. 30.

9. A.S. Altekar, *The Silaharas of Western India, Indian Culture*, vol. II, Calcutta, 1936, p. 399.

10. *Eigraphia Indica*, vol. III, p. 294; scholars have identified Balipatana differently: Valaulikar has identified it with Bali near Canacona. Varde Valaulicar, *Goecaranchi Goebhaili*, p. 6. P. Pissurlencar identifies it with Valavli in Sawant Wadi. See P. Pissurlencar, 'As primitivas capitais de Goa', *O Oriente Portugues*, no. 1, Decembro 1931, p. 3. Ranabir Chakravarti has identified it with modern Kharepatan. Ranabir Chakravarti, 'Merchants of Konkan', p. 212. It seems that Baliapattana was used in the Dravidian languages to signify a larger port–town and in that sense the identification of Ranabir Chakravarti (i.e. Khrepatan), seems to be more acceptable.

11. V.V. Mirashi ed., *Corpus Inscriptionum Indicarum*, vol. VI, Delhi, 1977, pp. 183-93.

12. Altekar says that Aiyaparaja won a victory over the ruler of Chandrapura. A.S. Altekar, *The Silaharas of Western India, Indian Culture*, vol. II, p. 399. From this time onwards, the rulers of Chandrapura were made vassals to Goan Silahara rulers, who were supporting the former when there was attack from outside. A.S. Altekar, *The Silaharas of Western India, Indian Culture*, vol. II, pp. 399, 401; Gerald A. Pereira, *An Outline of the Pre-Portuguese History of Goa,* pp. 30-1.

13. H.M. Elliot and John Dowson, *History of India as Told by its own Historians: Muhammadan Period*, vol. I, Delhi, 1867, pp. 21-2.

14. H. Elliot and J. Dowson, *History of India as Told by its own Historians*, vol. I, p. 89.

15. S.M.H. Nainar, *The Arab Geographer's Knowledge of Southern India,* p. 75.

16. P. Pissurlencar, 'Inscrições Pre-Portuguesas de Goa', pp. 387, 391. Guhalladeva I (whom George Moraes mistakenly considers as Guhalladeva II) was the real founder of the Goa branch of the Kadambas. See *Epigraphia Indica*, vol. XXX, p. 73. In the copper plate of 1053, the father of Sadhan was referred to as Sri Sameil (Ismail), who was one of the sons of Muhammed. P. Pissurlencar, 'Inscrições Pre-Portuguesas de Goa', pp.387, 391. However in the Panjim copper plate of Jayakesi I (1059) the father of Sadhan was mentioned as Madhumad (Muhammed), who was the son of Aliya. Cf. George Moraes, *Kadamba Kula*, pp. 399-400.

17. P. Pissurlencar, 'Inscrições Pre-Portuguesas de Goa', p. 391.

18. Andre Wink, *Al-Hind:The Making of the Indo-Islamic World*, vol. I (*Early Medieval India and the Expansion of Islam 7th –11th Centuries*), New Delhi 1999, pp. 69-70, 72-86; Victor d'Souza, *Navayaths of Kanara*, Dharwar, 1955.

19. The annexation of Gopakapattanam by Shasthadeva is alluded in the Narendra inscription of Jayakesi II. Scholars are of the opinion that the island of Lanka

mentioned in this inscription was not Sri Lanka but was only a metaphorical usage made to denote the island of Goa. See George Moraes, *Kadamba Kula,* pp. 174-5; *Epigraphia Indica,* vol. XIII, p. 310.

20. P. Pissurlencar, 'Inscrições Pre-Portuguesas de Goa', p. 391.

21. Ibid., p. 392; V.T. Gune, 'Goa's Coastal and Overseas Trade from the Earliest Times till AD 1510.', in *Goa Through the Ages,* ed. Teotonio R. de Souza, New Delhi 1990, p. 128.

22. For details on *khanqahs,* see S.A.A. Rizvi, *The Wonder that was India,* vol. II, (1200-1700), New Delhi, 1987, pp. 222-3. With the expansion of the Islamic trading activity, a chain of *khanqahs* (hospices) was established along the rim of Indian Ocean in honour of the Iranian Sufi saint Shaykh Abu Ishaq Guziruni (d.1035), who was considered as a patron saint of seafarers. The Muslim seafarers, when confronted with storms or pirates, used to pledge a certain amount of money to Shaykh's *khanqahs* for overcoming the crisis. On the coast such money was taken to the *khanqahs* for offering hospitality to the guests.

23. In the Geniza papers we find mention of Jewish traders conducting trade in Kalah in 1226, which place is identified as Kedah by S.D. Goitein. See S.D. Goitein, *Letters of Medieval Jewish Traders,* Princeton, 1973, p. 228.

24. P. Pissurlencar, 'Inscrições Pre-Portuguesas de Goa', pp. 388-90, 392-3.

25. P. Pissurlencar, 'Inscrições Pre-Portuguesas de Goa', pp.388-90, 392-3; see also F.N. Xavier, *Memoria sobre as moedas cunhadas em Goa,* p. 92.

26. V.T. Gune, ed., *Gazetteer of the Union Territory of Goa, Daman and Diu,* p. 118.

27. P. Pissurlencar, 'Inscrições Pre-Portuguesas de Goa', pp. 388-90, 392-4. It is surprising to note that *dracmas* were in circulation at such a late period. It was the Indo-Greek rulers (also called the Bactrian Greeks), ruling from 175 to 155 BC who introduced *dracmas* and *tedracmas* for the first time. These coins were then issued in silver and copper. For details see Pius Malekandathil, 'Coins of India and their History', *Numismatic Media,* vol. I, no. 1, Palghat, May 1996, p. 23. We know for certain that the Roman coins like gold *aurei,* and silver *denarii* were in circulation in India during the time of Roman trade, the Sassanid silver *dirham,* as well as the Byzantine gold *nomisma* during the time of Sassanid trade, and the gold *dinar* as well as the silver *dirham* during the period of Arab trade. See Andre Wink, *Al-Hind,* p. 11. *Dracma,* mentioned in the copper-plate of Jayakesi I seems to have been an indigenous coin minted by the Kadambas and its circulation seems to have been limited to the Konkan and Karnataka regions where the Kadambas had control.

28. P. Pissurlencar, 'Inscrições Pre-Portuguesas de Goa', pp. 391-3.

29. V.V. Mirashi, ed., *Corpus Inscriptionum Indicarum,* vol. VI, no. 19, p. 116; Ranabir Chakravarti, 'Merchants of Konkan', p. 211; J.F. Fleet, *Dynasties of Kanarese Districts of the Bombay Presidency,* Bombay, 1882, p. 91.

30. B.K. Apte, *A History of Maratha Navy and Merchant Ships,* Bombay, 1973, pp. 43-7.

31. George Moraes, *Kadamba Kula,* pp. 394-400.

32. V.V. Mirashi, ed., *Corpus Inscriptionum Indicarum*, vol. VI, no. 19, pp. 115-20.

33. See *Epigraphia Indica*, vol. XXX, pp. 71-7. He also shifted his capital from Gopakapattanam to Palasige (Halsi). George Moraes, *The Kadamba Kula*, pp. 465-7.

34. George Fadlo Hourani, *Arab Seafaring in the Indian Ocean in Ancient and Early Medieval Times*, Princeton, 1951, pp. 61-2, 64, 70-4; Pius Malekandathil, *The Germans, the Portuguese and India*, Münster (Germany), 1999, p. 4.

35. George F. Hourani *Arab Seafaring in the Indian Ocean in Ancient and Early Medieval Times*, pp. 70-4.

36. These are the wide variety of papers obtained from the Geniza of Cairo. Geniza is a place where discarded writings on which the name of God was written and deposited in order to preserve them from desecration. Most of the papers of the Cairo Geniza were preserved in a room adjacent to the synagogue. See for details, S.D. Goitein, *Letters of Medieval Jewish Traders*, Princeton, 1973, p. 3; S.D. Goitein, *A Mediterranean Society*, 5 vol., Berkeley, 1967-98; S.D. Goitein, *Jews and Arabs: Their Contacts through the Ages*, New York, 1964.

37. Pius Malekandathil, 'The Jews of Cochin and the Portuguese (1498-1663)', The *Proceedings of the Indian History Congress*, Aligarh, 2002, pp. 240-1; see also Andre Wink, *Al-Hind: The Making of the Indo-Islamic World*, pp. 86-91.

38. S.D. Goitein, *Letters of Medieval Jewish Traders*, pp. 175-229.

39. Ibid., p. 62.

40. Ibid., pp. 63-4; for the identification of these place names see also Pius Malekandathil, *The Germans, the Portuguese and India*, pp. 3-4.

41. S.D. Goitein, 'Portrait of a Medieval India Trader: Three Letters from the Cairo Geniza', *Bulletin of the School of Oriental and African Studies*, XLVIII, 1987, p. 457.

42. S.D. Goitein, 'Portrait of a Medieval India Trader', pp. 459-60; Ranabir Chakravarti, 'Chandrapura/ Sindabur and Gopakapattana: Two Ports on the West Coast of India (AD 1000-1300)', *Proceedings of the Indian History Congress* (Diamond Jubilee, 60th session, Calicut, 1999), Aligarh 2000, pp. 156-7. In fact, Fakanur (or Baknor of Ibn Batuta), which is often identified as Barakur, is located not in Malabar but in South Canara.

43. For details see Pius Malekandathil, *The Germans, the Portuguese and India*, p. 15; The original Catalan Map of 1375 from the Library of King Charles V of France is now kept in the Mazarine Gallery of the Bibliotheque Nationale in Paris (Spanish MSS. No. 30). See also, Henri Cordier, *L'Extreme-Orient dans l'Atlas Catalan de Charles V, roi de France*, Paris, 1894.

44. K.G. Vasantamadhava, 'Gove-Karnataka Cultural Contacts from AD 1000-1600', in *Goa: Cultural Trends*, ed. P.P. Shirodkar, p. 23.

45. See the Dharwar Inscription of Jayakesi II, in George Moraes, *Kadamba Kula*, pp. 401-3.

46. See the Mangundi Inscription of Jayakesi III, in George Moraes, *Kadamba Kula*, p. 414.

47. For details see Smita P. Surebanker, 'Taxation System in Halasige-12000: A Study', *Proceedings of the Indian History Congress* (Millennium, 61st session,

Kolkata 2000-1), Kolkata 2001, p. 245. For details of other taxes imposed by the Kadambas of Goa see ibid., pp. 242-51.

48. J.F. Fleet, *Dynasties of Kanarese Districts*, p. 569.

49. For a detailed discussion on this, see Pius Malekandathil, *The Germans, the Portuguese and India*, p. 9; B.J. Schrieke, *Indonesian Sociological Studies*, vol. I, The Hague 1955, pp. 7ff.

50. Muhammad Kasim Firishta, *Tarikh-i Firishta*, trans. J. Briggs under the title *History of the Rise of the Mahmoden Power in India*, vol. I, Calcutta 1909, p. 413; Ibn Batuta also refers to a city already erected by the Muslims in Gopakapattanam (apart from the city of the infidels) when they first captured the island. See Ibn Batuta, *Travels in Asia and Africa, 1325-1354*, tran. H.A.R. Gibb, New Delhi, 1990, pp. 239-40. This Muslim city within Gopakapattanam seems to have taken origin following the conquest of Malik Kafur and Muhammad-bin-Tughlaq.

51. Ibn Batuta, *Travels in Asia and Africa, 1325-1354*, pp. 239-41; Burton Stein, *Vijayanagara*, Cambridge, 1994, p. 74.

52. P. Pissurlencar, 'Inscrições Pre-Portuguesas de Goa', p. 391; pp. 418-19; Geral A. Pereira, *An Outline of the Pre-Portuguese History of Goa*, p. 65.

53. Jean Deloche, 'Iconographic Evidence of Boat and Ship Structures in India (2nd Century BC – 15th Century AD),' in *Tradition and Archaeology: Early Maritime Contacts in the Indian Ocean*, ed. Himanshu P. Ray and Jean Francoise Salles, New Delhi, 1996, pp. 199-224.

54. However, the port of Gopakapattanam did not disappear from the commercial map of Goa, even in 1471, when general Khwaja Muhammed Gawan conquered Gopakapattanam, it was referred as 'the major port of the land and as the cause of envy for all islands and ports of India'. See Sherwani, *Khwaja-i-Jahan Gawan's Campaigns in the Maharashtra*, p. 274; João Manuel Pacheco de Figueiredo, 'Goa Pre-Portuguesa', in *Studia,* nos. 13 and 14 (Janeiro-Julho), 1964, pp. 134-5.

55. Vasant Madhav, the minister of the Vijayanagara ruler Bukka I, defeated the forces of Bahmani Sultan and occupied Goa in 1369. For details see, João de Barros, *Asia, Dos feitos que os Portuguezes fizeram no Descobrimento e conquista doa Mares do Oriente*, ed. Livraria Sam Carlos (facsimile of the edition of 1777-8), Lisboa, 1973, *Decada* II, Livro V, Capitulo V, p. 135; B.A. Saletore, *Social and Political Life in the Vijayanagara Empire,* vol. I, Madras, 1934, p. 258.

56. Henry Heras, 'Pre-Portuguese Remains in Portuguese India', *Journal of Bombay Historical Society*, IV, September 1932, 2, pp. 7-11, 40; João Manuel Pacheco de Figueiredo, 'Goa Pre-Portuguesa', *Studia,* no. 13 and 14 (Janeiro-Julho), 1964, pp. 154-5.

57. Pratima Kamat, *Farar Far: Local Resistance to Colonial Hegemony in Goa, 1510-1912*, Panaji 1999, p. 22; K.G. Vasanth Madhava, *Karnataka Third World*, Haleangadi, 2001, p. 21:V.T. Gune, ed., *Gazetteer of the Union Territory of Goa, Daman and Diu*, p. 131.

58. The value of commodities available in Ela on the eve of Portuguese conquest was recorded by them in the Vijayanagara currency called *pardaos*, which was a corrupt form of Sanskrit *pratap. Pratap* or *pagoda* was a gold coin and it was

called *pagoda* because of the representation of *Varaha* or the Boar avatar of Vishnu on it. For detail, see Pius Malekandathil, 'Merchants, Markets and Commodities: Some Aspects of Portuguese Commerce with Malabar', in *The Portuguese, Indian Ocean and European Bridgeheads: Festschrift in Honour of Prof. K.S. Mathew*, ed. Pius Malekandathil and Jamal Mohammed, Fundação Oriente 2001, p. 245. *Pratap* had almost half the value of the gold coin *gadyanaca*.

59. The Portuguese accounts say that 40 years before its conquest by Bahmani Sultans in AD 1472, Goa had already freed itself from the dominion of Vijayanagara. See Gaspar Correia, *Lendas da India*, vol. II, Lisboa, 1921, p. 55; Gray Birch, ed, *The Commentaries of the Great Afonso Dalboquerque*, II, New York, 1975, p. 114; João Manuel Pacheco de Figueiredo, 'Goa Pre-Portuguesa', pp. 220-1. V.T. Gune says that Goa must have been ruled by one of the chiefs or Nayaks of Vijayanagara, just like other adjacent territories outside of the Vijayanagara since AD 1445. V.T. Gune, ed., *Gazetteer of the Union Territory of Goa, Daman and Diu*, p. 130.

60. Francisco de Souza, *Oriente Conquistado a Jesu Christo pelos Padres da Companhia de Jesus da Provincia de Goa*, vol. I, Lisboa, 1710, pp. 14-15; see also ANTT, *Corpo Cronologico*, I, Maço 17, doc. 30. Letter of Fr. Domingos de Sousa sent to the king D. Manuel from Goa, dated 22-12-1514. Francisco de Souza in *Oriente Conquistado* says that this cross was found hidden away in a wall a few days after the occupation of Goa in 1510. It was from this cross that *Rua do Crucifixo* of Goa was said to have got its name. The newly discovered cross was then taken in procession to the church for veneration–Francisco de Souza, *Oriente Conquistado*, pp. 14-15; G.M. Moraes, *History of Christianity in India*, Bombay, 1964, p. 154.

61. Gaspar Correia, *Lendas da India*, tom. II, p. 62.

62. Francisco de Souza, *Oriente Conquistado*, vol. I, div. I, 17. p.13; João de Barros, *Asia, Dos feitos que os Portuguezes fizeram no Descobrimento e conquista doa Mares do Oriente*, ed. Livraria Sam Carlos, (facsimile of the edition of 1777-8), Lisboa, 1973, Decada II, Livro V, Capitulo I, p. 434; Gaspar Correia, *Lendas da India*, II, p. 55; João Manuel Pacheco de Figueiredo, 'Goa Pre-Portuguesa', pp. 220-1.

63. Barros, *Da Asia, Decada II*, Livro V, Capitulo II, p. 24.

64. Tome Pires, *The Suma Oriental of Tomé Pires: An Account of the East Sea to Japan written in Malacca and India in 1512-1515*, ed. and tran. Armando Cortesão, vol. I, New Delhi, 1990, p. 58.

65. H. Yule, *The Book of Ser Marco Polo the Ventian Concerning the Kingdoms and Marvels of the East*, vol. II, London, 1926, p. 333; João Manuel Pacheco de Figueiredo, 'Goa Pre-Portuguesa', *Studia*, nos. 13 and 14 (Janeiro-Julho), 1964, pp.136-7.

66. Tomé Pires, *The Suma Oriental of Tomé Pires*, p. 58. During the time of Tome Pires one *pardao* was equivalent to 335 *reis*. Ibid., p. 58.

67. For details see Pius Malekandathil, *Portuguese Cochin and the Maritime Trade of India, 1500-1663*, (South Asian Study Series of Heidelberg University, no. 39, Germany), New Delhi 2002, p. 216. See also Karl H. Dannenfeldt, ed., *Leonhard*

Rauwolf: Sixteenth Century Physician, Botanist and Traveller, Massachussetts, 1968, pp. 121-2; Richard Hakluyt, *The Principal Navigations, Voyages, Traffiques and Discoveries of the English Nation,* vol. V, Glasgow, 1905, pp. 285, 33-4.

68. See G.R. Tibbetts, *Arab Navigation in the Indian Ocean before the Coming of the Portuguese* (original title of the book of Ibn Majid is *Kitab al Fawa'id fi usul al-bahr wa'l-qawa'id*), London, 1971, pp. 450, 454.

CHAPTER THREE

Dynamics of Economy, Social Processes and the pre-Portuguese Christians of India, 800-1500

The socio-economic processes of maritime India began to undergo decisive changes by the ninth century, when its vast coastal terrains were considerably influenced by the economic forces emitted by the long distance trade between the ports of the Persian Gulf regions and of Canton in China. One of the most significant impacts of this trade route on Indian economy was that the long distance traders, who had to temporarily break their voyage on the Indian coast because of adverse monsoon winds on the other side of the ocean, became instrumental in identifying and developing port sites near the mouth of various rivers, through which commodities held in high demand in other parts of the world could be obtained. Consequently a long chain of ports of varying degrees of economic importance began to emerge on the east and west coasts of India, making many regional economies located closer to these ports start producing commodities needed by the foreign merchants.

On the one hand, the process of production oriented towards market began to get relatively intensified in some of these places, while on the other hand, there was a concomitant phenomenon of migration of mercantile communities to India to take maximum advantage out of the changed situation. The local rulers who noticed the advantages of using these economic changes for their political advantages began to extend support and patronage to foreign merchants and mercantile migrants reaching their ports, who were eventually transformed as their supportive base for the political dreams of expanding their territories. One of the most evident cases of this

*Modified version of the article published under the title 'Christians and the Cultural Shaping of India in the First Millennium AD', *Journal of St. Thomas Christians*, vol. 17, no. 1, January-March 2006, pp. 4-22.

nature could be traced back to the set of commercial privileges granted by the ruler of the Ay kingdom to the Christian migrant traders of Quilon like Mar Sapor and Mar Prodh from the erstwhile Sassanid Persia in the mid-ninth century. Though the purpose of the grant was to generate enough wealth so as to strengthen the hands of the ruler and to realize his political plans, this grant bolstered and legitimized the increasing evolution of Christians as a significant trading group in Kerala, out of the economic linkage established between the spice producing Christians in the hinterland, and the migrant Christians from Persia, but having far-flung mercantile networks in the Indian Ocean. In this development, these Christians acquired certain traits from the social and cultural processes taking place in their neighbourhood that in turn were to form their distinctive marks for the centuries to come.

CHRISTIAN MERCANTILE MIGRANTS OF QUILON AND THE SOCIO-ECONOMIC SIGNIFICANCE OF THE THARISAPALLY COPPER PLATE

Among the different groups of Christian migrants to India at different time periods, the merchant leaders Mar Sapor and Mar Prodh, who reached Kurakeni Kollam (Quilon) in AD 823,[1] proved to be highly decisive because of the long-standing economic impact they had exerted in the deep south. They had erected a church at Kurakeni Kollam, called Tharisapally, which besides being a place of prayer eventually became the centre of economic life of the port town of Quilon.[2] The migration of these two Christian merchant leaders to Quilon was to be seen against the historical background of the expansion of traders from Abbassid Persia and the extension of their commercial networks into the Indian Ocean. It started with the shifting of the headquarters from Damascus of the Umayyad Khalifs to Baghdad by the Abassids (750-870) in AD 762, with a view to having access to the Indian Ocean via Tigris, and to controlling its trade. Generally the long distance trade from Abbassid Persia used to emanate from Oman or Sohar in the Persian Gulf and terminate in Canton controlled by the rulers of T'ang dynasty (618-907) of China.[3] With the increasing expansion of the political domains and commercial networks of the Abbassids, the Christian merchants who used to conduct trade in the erstwhile Sassanid territories, particularly in the Fars and the Persian Gulf regions, had to move over to safer destinations, including Kerala, where they had previous contacts.[4] The intensified commercial activities from Abbassid Persia must have prompted Mar Sapor and Mar Prodh to move towards Kerala, which had earlier been an important commercial destination for the Christian merchants from Sassanid Persia.

When they reached Quilon, they carried along with them an extensive network of commerce that the Sassanid merchants had earlier developed over centuries and they made use of these mercantile connections for keeping the wheels of commerce moving around the Tharisapally of Kollam.[5]

Though these merchant leaders were said to have reached Quilon in 823, the different economic privileges to the Tharisappally were granted only in 849, almost 26 years after their arrival in the town. This suggests that Ayyanadikal Thiruvadikal (ruler of the Ay kingdom), the feudatory of the Chera ruler Sthanu Ravi Varma, conferred the various privileges upon this mercantile community and its church not at their very first sight, but having tested the worth and utility of the recipients, both the church and the immigrant Christian mercantile community, in the process of resource mobilization. In fact, the various privileges were a reward for the Christian mercantile community for the activation of maritime trade in Kollam and for ensuring the flow of sizeable share of trade surplus into the coffers of the rulers as *Kopathavaram* (share of the king Sthanu Ravi Varma) and *Pathipathavaram* (share of the local ruler—Ayyanadikal).[6]

These privileges were inscribed on copper plates, which are often known as Tharisapally copper plate for the simple reason that the church of Tharisa of Quilon was the beneficiary of the grants. The most important among these privileges included the right to keep *parakkol*[7], *panchakandy*[8] and *kappan*[9] (different types of weights and measures) of the city of Kollam under its safe custody,[10] which the Christians of Quilon enviously held till 1503, when these were finally taken away from them following the malpractices by some of its trading members.[11] That the church was made the custodian of weights and measures of the city shows that Tharisapally was not merely a centre of worship alone, but represented an economic institution or a corporate body of traders that was entrusted with the responsibility of ensuring standardization of the weights and measures of the city and of enhancing the integrity of trade.

Ayyanadikal Thiruvadikal made a gift of four Ezhava families,[12] four Vellala families,[13] one *thachan*[14] and one Vannan (mannan)[15] family to the Tharisapally and handed over to it the right to collect a wide variety of taxes from them, which Ayyanadikal used to levy earlier for himself like *thalakkanam, enikkanam* (professional taxes from toddy tappers and tree-climbers), *mania meypan kollum ira* (housing tax), *chantan mattu meni ponnu* (tax for using the title *chantan*—Channan or Shanar—evidently to show high social status), *polipponnum* (tax given on special occasions), *iravuchorum* (*balikaram* or tax collected to feed the Brahmins, refugees and destitutes) and *kudanazhiyum* (collection of a *nazhi*, a type of liquid measurement of toddy as tax from each pot tapped).[16] Moreover, the church was also given the right to collect eight *kasu* from each cart that used to take merchandise by land into the market of Quilon (*vayinam*) and four *kasu* from each boat that was used to carry cargo to the port (*vediyilum*).[17] Though these details would give the impression that the local ruler was giving up much of his income for the sake of the church, in actual fact it was a small loss for the sake of appropriating larger gains by extending an attractive atmosphere for overseas merchants in the port of Quilon. The entire development is to be understood as a move to strengthen and empower the Christian mercantile community and probably many others involved in long distance trade that in turn was expected to facilitate easy flow of wealth to Quilon for the purpose of empowering the hands of the ruler.

As Ayyandikal Thiruvadikal prescribed in the copper plate, the merchant guilds, viz., *Anjuvannam*, *Manigramam* and *Arunnoottuvar* were entrusted with the right to protect the church and its property, obviously because of their economic importance.[18] *Anjuvannam* and *Manigramam* were also asked to inquire into contentious matters and find solutions, if somebody was to encroach upon the privileges conferred upon the church.[19] The fact that *Anjuvannam*, which is generally considered as a Jewish merchant guild and *Manigramam* of Kollam which is generally considered as a Christian guild,[20] had by this time assumed power as *karalars* of the city[21] would indicate that the merchant guilds had already wielded considerable amount of authority and power, with the help of which they were able to implement the will of the ruler inscribed in the copper plate and protect the church from all types of probable violations in the future. The context against which the *Manigramam* merchant guild of Kerala was mentioned in the copper plate (as custodian of a Christian church) suggests that its ethnic composition must have entirely been different from that of Tamilnadu, where its members had been predominantly Hindus. In Kerala this guild seems to have by this time evolved into a powerful commercial institution operating among the Christian merchants for the long distance movement of commodities in the Indian Ocean, particularly between Kerala and the economic zones of the Persian Gulf, the Red Sea and the Levant.[22]

The various economic privileges and rights which the ruler of Venadu granted to Mar Sapor Iso indicate the desire of the local rulers to keep themselves linked with the powerful Christian merchant groups by keeping them in good humour and by legitimizing their claims and ventures. The alliance between the local ruler and mercantile community became necessary because of the increasing dependence of the local ruler on the foreign Christian traders for the purpose of mobilizing wealth for strengthening his political institutions. The local rulers knew very well that the commercial ventures and the market systems could then be kept active and operational on the coastal pockets only with the help of overseas merchants, and that too, by the Christian merchants, against the background of declining trade in inland Kerala following the intensified feudalization process that started with proliferation of land grants and consumption-oriented production activities.[23] Consequently the ruler of the Ay kingdom and his master Sthanu Ravi Varma began to increasingly bank upon overseas merchants for obtaining wealth in the form of customs duties so as to get their hands strengthened particularly at a time when they were to counter the political and commercial challenges of the Pandyas.[24]

By this time, in the midst of the Chera-Pandya conflicts in the deep south, the Pandyas had managed to capture Vizhinjam along with the ruler and his relatives as well as treasures. When Vizhinjam was lost to the Pandyas, the Cheras turned towards Quilon, which the latter developed as the provincial headquarters of their kingdom. It was against this background of political developments that they encouraged the foreign Christian merchants to settle down in Quilon by conferring concessions and privileges upon them and their worshipping place. The attempts for the intensification of the trade of Quilon were necessitated not only for developing a competitor for the Pandyan controlled port of Vizhinjam, but also for generating sufficient wealth for the political ventures of the Cheras in the south.[25]

These developments in the long run empowered the foreign Christian merchants, and gave the Christians of Kerala an economic identity of being traders, following which in the evolving process of social spacing they were given the status of Vaisyas. It seems that there was already an attempt to create a trading caste in Kerala out of the foreign mercantile Christians, with the mass migration of Brahmins by the eighth century and the consequent appropriation of their hegemonic position, and this was necessitated not only to fill in the vacuum created by the absence of Vaisyas, but also to weaken the commerce of the Buddhists and Jains, who were also their religious rivals. In this process the Christians were kept in the social ladder on a scale equivalent to that of the Vaisyas of the areas north of Vindhya and Satpura.[26] Some crude traces of this phenomenon could be found in the Tharisapally copper plate, where it is mentioned that the *koyiladhikarikal* Vijayaraghava Devan[27] (probably a Brahmin minister) also joined hands with Ayyanadikal Thiruvadi (along with Ilamkur Rama Thiruvadi and others) in taking the decision to grant economic privileges to Tharisapally and its members, obviously to strengthen the economic and social standing of the latter. The encouragement given to Christian traders by way of privileges is to be viewed against the larger attempts of the dominant Brahmins to strike at the roots of the Buddhists and the Jains, against whom the Brahmanical religion had already started a crusade from the sixth and seventh centuries onwards.[28] For them, empowering Christian traders was an alternative device to weaken the trade of the Buddhists and the Jains, as it was the surplus from their trade that helped to uphold the ideology of both the religions in hegemonic position and to raise serious challenges to Brahminism.

PROCESS OF URBANIZATION AND THE NETWORK OF *ANGADIS*

The founding of the town (*Nagaram*) of Kurakkeni Kollam (Quilon) was attributed to Mar Sapor Iso (*Innakaram kandu neeretta Maruvan Sapiriso*), as per the information gathered from the Tharisapally copper plate. Kurakkeni Kollam, which was known differently as Koulam Male in Jewish Genizza papers[29] and in Arabic sources[30] as well as Gu-lin (in the Song period)/Ju-lan (in the Yuan period) in Chinese documents,[31] does not appear in any source prior to AD 823, which also suggests that the formation of the town must have taken place only after the arrival of Sapor Iso. The Malayalam calendar, often known as Kollam Era, was started in AD 825 and was attributed to have begun to commemorate the founding of the town of Quilon by Mar Sapor. Probably, the rich astronomical traditions, which Mar Sapor and other Chrisian merchants brought from the erstwhile Sassanid Persia, must have been instrumental in developing this calendar in the inceptional stage.[32]

By the time Suleiman visited Quilon in 841, it was already a town, as he writes in his *Salsalat-al-Taverika*.[33] Mar Sapor Iso seems to have brought elements of Sassanid urban culture along with him and exteriorized them physically at Quilon. Eventually, with the intensification of trade between Abbassid Persia and Tang China,[34] there appeared a port hierarchy in Kerala with a chain of satellite feeding ports revolving around the principal port of Quilon, which in turn was made to become the main port of call for long distance traders moving between China and Persia. This process in turn caused immense wealth to get concentrated in the town of Quilon, which by later period the Cholas wanted to appropriate by capturing this port town. In the midst of intense conflicts between the Cheras and the Cholas, Raja Raja Chola (985-1014) took over Quilon and its satellite port Vizhinjam. However, at this juncture, it was a Jewish merchant leader by name Joseph Rabban of Muyirikode (Cranganore), who came to the rescue of the Chera ruler Bhaskara Ravi Varma (962-1020), to whom the former handed over his ships, men and materials for the purpose of conducting war with the Cholas.[35] Despite these political vicissitudes, the trading activities of Quilon, being intensified by different merchant groups with international linkages, accelerated the process of urbanization in this port town, as was later testified by Benjamin of Tudela (c. 1170).[36] Foreign Christians from West Asia, Jews[37] and the Chinese[38] formed the mercantile elite in the port town of Quilon, where each segment seems to have had its own separate settlements and quarters.

When the foreign Christians from West Asia were involved in the overseas trade of Quilon, the indigenous Christians engaged in spice production in the hinterland of Kerala began to take part also in the regional trade supplying cargo to the Christian overseas merchants on the coast. Along with it, eventually there appeared the culture of clustered living[39] and trading activities around their settlements, symbolized by *angadis*. Most of these *angadis* were located around the churches of Christians and formed the nuclei out of which vibrant urban centres later developed in central Kerala. The *angadis* developed as trading establishments with accommodation facilities for the Christian merchants, who conducted trade in the front of the edifice facing the street, while the interior was used for their lodging as in any normal house. The spice producers of St. Thomas Christians used to sell their cargo in these *angadis* located near their churches and commodity movement from hinterland to the port of Quilon meant networking of different *angadis* through the transportation means of bullock-carts on land routes, and boats through riverine channels. The economic identity of the Christians as traders was preserved and maintained in the inland Christian settlements with the help of *angadis*,[40] by which the enterprising local merchants linked the inland production centres with the mercantile networks of *Manigramam* and the wider channels of overseas commerce. Consequently, Christian traders linked with the *Manigramam* merchant guild spread to different parts of Kerala, in the process linking *angadi* trade of the region with the overseas commerce emanating from Quilon. Some of these traders were patronized by the inland local rulers, as is evidenced by the Thazhekkadu inscription (AD 1024) obtained from the premises of the Thazhekkadu church (near Irinjalakuda), which speaks of king Rajasimhan conferring privileges on the Christian traders like Chathan Vadukan and Iravi Chathan, who were members of the *Manigramam* merchant guild to establish *angadi*.[41]

By the end of fifteenth century the *angadis* of central Kerala were linked with the leading maritime centres of exchange like Cranganore, Cochin, Quilon and Kayamkulam, where the commercially oriented Christians began to concentrate in large numbers for trading purposes. In Cochin they were said to have been organized under a merchant guild called *Korran* (may be *Kuṟṟan* in Tamil), from which Francisco de Albuquerque bought 4,000 *bahars* of well-dried pepper in 1503.[42] The economic importance of the merchant group of St. Thomas Christians for Quilon is also evident from the fact that the leading members of this community were chosen as the commercial emissaries in 1502 by the queen of Quilon for the purpose of inviting Vasco da Gama from Cochin for conducting trade with her port.[43] The prominent Christian merchant in Quilon was Mathias,[44] and in Kayamkulam was Tarqe Tome (Tarakan Thomas),[45] from whom the Portuguese used to purchase pepper regularly since in 1503.

CHRISTIANS AS SPICE PRODUCERS AND FIGHTING FORCE IN CENTRAL KERALA

When commercially oriented Christians and descendants from foreign Christian merchants began to concentrate on the major junctional routes of trade and maritime centres of exchange, the traditional Christians who were often known as St. Thomas Christians and who used to trace back their origins to the apostolic work of St. Thomas,[46] still continued to be predominantly agriculturists and focused on spice production availing cargo for the commerce of the former. With the increasing demand from the revival of spice trade from the ninth century onwards, we find Christians specialized in spice production moving to the hinterland of Kerala in their attempts to extend spice cultivation. The increasing inland-movement of the St. Thomas Christians is evident from the establishment of churches in places like Kayamkulam (AD 824), Athirampuzha (853), Kottayam (ninth century), Nagapuzha (900), Manjapra (943), Mavelikara (943), Pazhuvil (960), Arakuzha (999), Nediasala (999), Kottekad (1000), Kadamattom (tenth century), Kanjur (1001), Kaduthuruthy Cheriapally (tenth century), Kunnamkulam (tenth century), Pala (1002), Muttam (1023), Cherpunkal (1096), Vadakara (eleventh century), Bharananganam (1100), Changanacherry (1117), Thripunithara (1175), Cheppadu (twelfth century), Chengannoor (twelfth century), Kudamaloor (twelfth century), Ernakulam (twelfth century), Kothanalloor (1220), Mulanthuruthy (1225), Kothamangalam Valiapally (1240), Karthikapally (thirteenth century), Kuruppumpady (thirteenth century), Alengad (1300), Muthalakodam (1312), Njarackal (1341), Koratty (1381), Poonjar (fourteenth century), Alleppey (1400), Kanjirappilly (1450), Kothamangalam Cheriapally (1455), Kudavechur (1463), etc.[47] All theses churches were established during the period between the ninth and the fifteenth centuries, along the fertile riverbeds of central Kerala as a development that took place following the expansion of spice cultivation.

The active involvement of St. Thomas Christians in the spice production was testified by Bishop John Marignoli (*c.* 1346), who visited Malabar on his way back from Cambulac (Beijing in China) and referred to the Christians of Quilon as 'rich people' and as 'owners of pepper plantations'.[48] The increasing role of St. Thomas Christians in the production of spices is also attested to by the Portuguese documents which say that 'all the pepper was in the hands of the St. Thomas Christians and that majority of the pepper that went to Portugal was sold by them'.[49] Their continued involvement in the expansion of spice cultivation by resorting to the clearance of forest areas is referred to in *Jornada*, which says that there were several Christian settlements then in the forests.[50]

Meanwhile, a considerable number of St. Thomas Christians began to be recruited as a fighting force for the local rulers, particularly with the disintegration of the Cheras and the consequent fragmentation of central authority in the twelfth century. Most of the Christian settlements had their own *kalaris* (schools for training in martial arts and fencing) run mostly by Christian *panikkars* and in places where there was no Christian *kalari* they had to join the *kalaris* run by Nairs.[51] Mention is also made in the *Jornada* that some Christian *panikkars* had eight to nine thousand disciples, both Christians and Nairs, getting trained as a fighting force for the local rulers.[52] One of the most famous Christian *panikkars* of this period was Vallikkada Panikkar who had his *kalari* at Peringuzha on the banks of river Muvattupuzha, one of whose descendants was Mar Ivanios, who later got reunited with the Catholic Church in 1930, laying the foundation for the Syro-Malankara Church in India.[53]

The rulers of Vadakkenkur and Cochin banked very much upon the Christian fighting force for their wars of defence and expansion. In 1546 the king of Vadakkenkur offered the Portuguese about 2,000 soldiers from the St. Thomas Christian community for the purpose of helping them to lift the Ottoman siege on Diu.[54] Later in 1600 the king of Cochin also offered St. Thomas Christian soldiers to the Portuguese for the project of conquering Ceylon, though the project did not materialize for other reasons.[55] The military tradition of the St. Thomas Christians was preserved by this community as something integral to it, and they even resorted to the usual practice of the fighting force to form *chaverpada* (suicidal squad) to protect their bishop Mar Joseph from being arrested by the Portuguese by the end of 1550s. About 2,000 Christian soldiers organized themselves into an *amoucos* or suicidal squad to prevent the Portuguese from arresting their bishop.[56]

The St. Thomas Christians used to attend church services carrying their swords, shields and lances, as Antonio de Gouvea mentions in *Jornada*.[57] Eventually weapon houses (*Ayudhapurakal*) were constructed in front of the churches for the purpose of keeping of swords, guns and lances during church services, and the remnants of these weapon stores are now visible in front of the churches of Ramapuram, Pala and Cherpunkal.[58] However, later, when all the smaller principalities of central Kerala were amalgamated into Travancorean state between 1742 and 1752 and with the creation of a standing army under Marthanda Varma, the importance of the Christians as a fighting force for the regional political players declined considerably. He put an end to the *kalari* system of martial training of the St. Thomas Christians and the Nairs, as it produced soldiers for local rulers causing threat to his centralized state.

SOCIAL SPACING

Out of these nuanced developments in the economy and polity, there emerged certain dynamic forces for rearranging the format of the society of Kerala which also defined the social functions of Christians. It was a time when Brahminical ideology and temple centred economic activities were reshaping the social life of the Keralites by constructing and reconstructing new castes out of various professional and artisan groups, particularly during the period from the ninth to the thirteenth centuries. All the intermediaries standing between the landowner (Brahmin) and the tiller (sudra or *pulaya*) were put into one or another caste in a way that would facilitate and ensure Brahminical hegemony.[59] In this process of social spacing the commercially oriented Christians were made to evolve as a trading caste, almost like the Vaisyas. Consequently the Christians were given a social function in the evolving world and in many places they were used for touching and purifying the oil and utensils to be used in the temples and palaces, but being 'polluted' by the touch of the artisans.[60] Concomitantly certain Christian families were specially invited, offering them land and were made to settle down near the temples and palaces for the purpose of touching and purifying the oil (*enna thottu kodukkan*) and for purifying the vessels being 'polluted' by the touch or use of lower caste people.[61] In the new developments following the establishment of Brahminical hegemony and dissemination of notions of 'pollution' that would help the Brahmins to maintain their dominant position with Nairs subordinate to them, the Christians were made to become an inevitable social ingredient in central Kerala, who were in turn made to evolve as a bridging social group between the polluting artisan groups and the dominant castes.

The other side of the picture was that the Christians started borrowing several social customs and practices (like the ceremonies related to birth, marriage and death)[62] of the dominant castes to present themselves as fitting well into the newly evolving socio-cultural order. The spice producing St. Thomas Christians as well as the descendants of the foreign Christian merchants, together seem to have imbibed a lot of elements from the neighbouring cultural space in this social process. One of the most important social practices that the indigenous Christians imbibed was the practice of untouchability. The Christians believed that by touching low castes they would remain polluted, which would deter them from interacting with the Nairs and Brahmins.[63] As this would ultimately affect their trading activities, the Christians were keen to observe untouchability rather meticulously in their dealings with artisan groups and lower castes. They also used to wear sacred thread (*puunuul*),[64] *kudumi* (tuft), but the only difference from that of the Brahmins was that the Christians used to insert a silver cross into their tuft (*kudumi*).[65] The practice of St. Thomas Christians wearing sacred thread was later quoted by Robert de Nobili for justifying his wearing of the sacred thread as a part of his missionary method of inculturation experimented in Madurai in the seventeenth century.[66] The Christians also keenly observed birth-related pollution as well as *pula* (perception of the family as being under pollution after the death of a member) and resorted to *pulakuli* (the feast usually held on tenth day after the funeral) and *sradham* (a feast held once a year after the funeral, when the souls were believed to come back).[67]

Though some scholars like Placid Podippara argue that these customs entered the social life of St. Thomas Christians because of their Brahminical origins, and that a considerable number of them were descendants of Brahmins converted by St. Thomas in the first century,[68] it seems that the Christians of Kerala imbibed these social and cultural practices only during the period between the ninth and thirteenth centuries, when caste practices and norms were being increasingly fabricated and disseminated under the hegemonic supervision of the Brahmins, who assigned different caste identities to the already existing artisans, social groups and communities. The wide variety of social customs and practices that the St. Thomas Christians imbibed from their cultural neighbourhood, along with the ritual practices that they borrowed from West Asia eventually came to be collectively called *Thomayude Margam* or the 'Law of Thomas', which they did not want to get changed at any cost.[69] The bitter and long-standing conflicts between the St. Thomas Christians and the Portuguese in the sixteenth and seventeenth centuries were actually on the question of changing these cultural practices from the former.[70] They used to follow the East Syrian Liturgy, which had originally taken shape in Seleucia-Ctesiphon and its ritual content varied immensely from the Latin liturgy introduced in India by the Portuguese in the sixteenth century.[71]

At a time when Brahmins and Brahminical institutions controlled the processes of social formation of low-lying wetland agricultural zones suitable only for paddy cultivation, the central upland parts of central Kerala, which was the heartland of pepper-cultivation and where the St. Thomas Christians principally got distributed as producers of spices, traders and fighting militia, experienced a different type of social formation. It was principally the wealth coming from spice-production and spice-trade that sustained the process of social formation in central upland Kerala, where the St. Thomas Christians had already set up about 78 churches before the arrival of the Portuguese[72] and interestingly this geographical space happened to remain for long as the peripheral zones of Brahminical intervention.

One would obviously be interested to know whether there were not any socio-economic conflicts between the two representing two eco-systems and how these Christians survived at a time when all the existing belief systems of Kerala like Buddhism and Jainism as well as the folk religious traditions were swallowed by the Brahminical socio-religious processes and were made to become a part of the religious and social system that projected superiority to the Brahmins. Though the available documents do not throw much light on this aspect, it is inferred that the caste status equivalent to the Vaisyas being fabricated by the Brahmins for the Christians at this point of time was already developed as a mechanism to accommodate such social and economic tensions between the two, as it kept Christians relatively inferior to the Brahmins, although stories of Christians being converted from Brahmins by St. Thomas used to circulate frequently among the St. Thomas Christians. However, they sustained their faith through a process of social formation revolving around spice-producing upland regions, which helped them to keep a reasonably respectful distance to the type of social formation happening around Brahmins and Brahminical temples in the wetland cultivational zones. It was probably the forces emitted by the wealth from their spice-production and exchanges that helped the St. Thomas Christians to carve out a distinctive space for themselves that prevented them from being swallowed by the Brahminical socio-religious processes and the immense political acceptability that this community gained over centuries before the local rulers as expert fighting force and wealth generators by way of their participation in spice-cultivation and trade gave them a vast range of immunity needed for preserving their faith.

CHURCH ARCHITECTURE AND POPULATION

The earliest historical record that speaks of the existence of an architectural structure of church among the Christians of Kerala was the Tharisapally copper plate given to Mar Prodh and Mar Sapor in AD 849 by Ayyanadikal Thiruvadikal,[73] which refers to the church of Tharisapally being constructed in Quilon by Mar Sapor (*Maruvan Saporiso*), during the time between 823 and 849.[74] Since the church of Tharisapally was constructed by Mar Sapor hailing from Persia, there is the high possibility that it must have been erected on the architectural theology of the Persian Church. However, *Jornada* mentions that by end of the sixteenth century almost all the churches of the St. Thomas Christians were constructed on the models of temples.[75] It is evidently known that the tradition of temple architecture got disseminated in Kerala during the period between the eighth and thirteenth centuries. It is highly probable that since the same carpenters and masons who built the temples were hired for constructing churches in Christian settlements, the Christian churches also seem to have got modelled on the temple architectural format, as *Jornada* testifies. However, the identifying mark for the Christian churches was the huge granite cross being erected in front of them.[76] Meanwhile, intense theological meaning was also inscribed into the church space, by structuring it in three levels and keeping the congregation on the lower space for participating in a liturgical celebration that runs progressively from intermediate space (*bema*) to apex space (*madbeha*), which was equated with the heavenly Jerusalem. The way the interior of the church space was structured and the spatial articulation of East Syrian architectural theology into it, made the Christian prayer house look different.[77]

All the churches of indigenous Christians, though they externally looked like temples, had a huge granite cross in front of them. The Cross of Quilon which Giovanni di Empoli saw in 1503[78] and the granite cross erected by Mar Thana (Jacob Abuna) and Mar Avu (Denha) in 1528 at Muttuchira[79] are only a few of this category, to which the crosses of Angamali and Arakuzha could also be added. These crosses used to have a decorative basement with space for pouring oil and lighting lamps exactly in the same way as temple lamps were lighted during those days. Devotees used to light the oil lamps of the crosses (*vilakkumadams*) during the night,[80] either to get their wishes fulfilled or to express their gratitude for favours already received. These *vilakkumadams* also evolved as fire-preserving mechanisms particularly in the rural belts, from where the low caste people with less resource potentials to make fire, or preserve fire daily, could take fire for meeting their needs. Till recently, the St. Thomas Christians, particularly in connection with annual church feasts, used to crawl on knees around this granite cross from the main entrance of the church either as a penitential service or as a part of the vow they had taken for the materialization of certain wishes.[81]

The Portuguese had noticed that at least about 78 churches were already in existence in different parts of Kerala prior to their arrival.[82] However, the distribution of this Christian community was not even: Quilon, Angamaly, Kaduthuruthy and Cranganore had the largest number of St. Thomas Christian population. Giovanni Empoli, who came to Quilon in 1503, estimates that there were more than 3,000 St. Thomas Christians in Quilon alone, where they were called *Nazareni*.[83] The same number of Christians (3,000) were in Quilon according to the estimate given by the

German artillerist, who accompanied Vasco da Gama in 1502/3.[84] Tome Pires who wrote *Suma Oriental* estimates that the total number of St. Thomas Christians of Kerala varied between 60,000 and 75,000.[85] In 1564[86] and in 1568[87] the total number of the St. Thomas Christians was estimated to be 1,00,000.

ECOSYSTEMS AND PATRON SAINTS

The Christian responses to the cultural challenges around them initiated a particular process in the distribution pattern of patron saints in the Christian settlements. The St. Thomas Christians used to venerate chiefly four saints, viz., St. Mary, St. George, Mar Prodh and Sapor and St. Thomas, till the Portuguese intervention by the end of the sixteenth century, and their churches were erected in the name of one of these saints. In the first place was the blessed Virgin Mary, who was the patron saint for the churches located particularly in the low-lying paddy cultivation zones like Kuravilangadu,[88] Arakuzha,[89] Nediasala, Nakapuzha, Manarcadu, Enammavu, etc.[90] These churches had St. Mary as their patron saint, who was considered as the best spiritual refuge and asylum during the times of natural calamities and adverse weather that affected the course of agricultural operations. This spiritual symbol helped to wean the Christian settlers away from the different types of fertility cults, and mother-goddess worship practices prevalent among the indigenous people of the low-lying paddy cultivating zones and to get them integrated with the Christian perception of fertility.[91]

A relatively significant number of Christian settlements like those of Diamper,[92] Kothanalloor, Parur,[93] etc., located either at the junctional points of trade routes, or in areas having a considerable number of trading members, had Mar Prodh and Mar Sapor as their patron saints, who were the prominent personalities linked with the Tharisapally and *Manigramam* merchant guild associated with the trade of Quilon. This practice of assuming patron saints from a trade-related background in places having commercial importance is suggestive of the fact that it operated as a mechanism that linked spiritual life with the economic order.[94] Later Dom Alexis de Menezes tried to change the patron saints of these churches and rename them as All Saints' churches; however believers resented the move refusing to accept the change of their patron saints.[95]

The Capadocean saint, St. George, who was associated with the killing of a dragon, was the next important saint venerated in the Christian settlements that appeared either in the newly cleared forest areas or on the way to the newly created spice producing pockets infested with snakes like the settlements of Edappally,[96] Aruvithara,[97] Muthalakodam,[98] etc. Christians, who moved to inland regions for clearing forest areas and for expansion of spice cultivation began to take St. George as their patron in their combat against the snakes in the newly cleared forest areas. In the process of fight against the physical threats from the snakes, the spiritual symbol of St. George helped to wean the Christians from the practice of worshipping serpents (as their culturally different neighbours continued to do) to the practice of venerating the killer of snakes (the very saint himself). Eventually it turned out to be a cultural symbol that bolstered the ability of man to confront and kill the snakes, if possible, rather than to fall at their mercy by feeding them, a mentally and emotionally empowering process required at a time when cultivation activities were extended to larger areas prone to snake attacks.[99]

The fourth category of saint was St. Thomas, whose name was often given to the churches that were linked by oral tradition with the apostolic preaching of St. Thomas in Kerala like Malayattoor, Mylakombu, etc.[100] Mud from these churches, or from the church of St. Thomas of Mylapore, where the mortal remains of St. Thomas were believed to have been kept, was sprinkled on the mother and the child as a part of the initiating ritual for admitting a mother and child after delivery.[101]

Thus, the different types of Christian settlements of the period up to AD 1500 developed equally different concepts of patron saints corresponding to the ecosystems in which they were located. Though apparently there was a uniform cultural homogeneity evolving among the Christians, the rhythm of celebrations and cultural pattern as well as spiritual details evolving around the concepts of each patron saint and the respective ecosystem, made each Christian settlement develop separately from the other, which converted them into cultural micro-regions.

FOOD CULTURE AND DRESS CULTURE

The synthesis between indigenous Christians and the immigrant Christians on the one hand, and between non-Christians and Christians on the other, led to a fusion of foreign and Indian food habits and dress habits. The wide variety of food items of the Nazarani Christians like *neyyappam, kallappam, avalose podi, avalose unda, achappam, ottada, uzhunnappam,* etc., form important constituent elements of India's food culture, and they seem to have evolved with the movement of Christians into low-lying rice producing zones,[102] where rice and black gram were used to make edibles similar to the ones they had in their homelands in West Asia. The use of rice flour, coconut milk or powder and the adding of toddy for fermentation for preparing toffees, gave a different taste to the confectionary tradition they developed in Kerala.

Several dress habits like the use of *chatta* with long sleeves, *mundu* with *jnori, neriyathu* (veil) extending from the head down to the feet of the ladies were apparently West Asian in origin. While the womenfolk of this community were made to confine themselves to the conservative West Asian dress culture of *chatta, mundu* and veil, the men followed a liberal dressing pattern, which evolved as a result of their adaptation to local habits. Women used to cover their entire body with a long veil, which stretched from head to feet. Unlike women, men used to wear *mundu* around their loin.[103] The St. Thomas Christians used to grow their hair and beard till the third quarter of the eighteenth century. The hair was tied together with a string or hair locks as to form a *kudumi*, into which they used to insert a small cross of gold or silver as a visible sign to distinguish themselves from the Nairs, who also had the same type of dress as that of the St.Thomas Christians.[104]

FORMAT OF ADMINISTRATION

The bishops coming from West Asia formed the spiritual heads of the Church, while the actual head of the community was *jathikkukarthaviyan* or the archdeacon.[105] The archdeacon wielded a great amount of power because of being the administrative head of this Christian community, engaged in trade, agriculture and military activities. The native rulers of Kerala never wanted to antagonize the archdeacon fearing alienation of the resourceful Christian community from them and when there were occasions of contestations of power like the one between the archdeacon and Archbishop Alexis de Menezes, all the local rulers stood behind the archdeacon, despite the invitation of immense amount of wrath from the archbishop.[106] The priests and the members of the community owed their loyalty principally to the archdeacon, who was the administrative head and key decision-taking figure in the community, rather than to the foreign bishop from Babylon, who was often not fluent enough in the local language. However, the archdeacon's decisions were conditioned mostly by the pulse and views of the representative bodies of the community including *palli yogams*, whose membership then was restricted only to aristocratic families and landed gentry. There was little scope for a matter, which was vetoed by *yogam*, to get implemented at any level of church activities. However, this arrangement infused into the church administrative system elements of democratic practice, making decisions to emerge from the grass roots levels. The local church as a body enjoyed the prerogative to judge such key matters including the admission of people to priesthood, administration of sacraments, etc. The relative uncertainty about the availability of bishops at different time periods, for catering to the spiritual needs of the Christians, and their equally temporary stay in Kerala with little knowledge of the language of the land, made the archdeacon emerge as the key figure in the general administrative system of the St. Thomas Christians and the *yogams* as powerful mechanisms at the grass roots level. As the feudal European notion of episcopacy as a benefice for a noble obtained from the ruler was absent in Kerala, temporality was detached from an episcopal post, which, as per Oriental tradition was meant to be an exclusively spiritual one. Thus, the type of church administration that evolved among this community turned out to be immensely different from the ecclesiological perceptions of Europe.[107]

The foregoing discussions show that the period between the ninth and sixteenth centuries witnessed the increasing merging of the Christians into the socio-cultural processes of the region, causing them to develop the identity of a trading caste for themselves, although a considerable number of them were also engaged in spice production and military jobs. The maritime trade that brought many Persian Christians to the shores of Kerala also emitted the required amount of energy and forces for the inland movement of the traditional St. Thomas Christians for the purpose of expanding spice cultivation to meet the external demands. The Chera rulers and their feudatories promoted maritime trade by conferring privileges on the foreign merchants, both Christians and Jews, in their attempts to generate wealth for the purpose of strengthening their hands and for countering the southern attacks initially from the Pandyas, and later from the Cholas. The foreign Christian merchants in their turn developed a network of trade linking the spice production centres of the hinterland with the principal seaport, in which process the inland settlements of the spice producing St. Thomas Christians were made to develop a quasi-market mechanism in the form of *angadis* around their churches. Through these circuits, there was a constant process of mixing of foreign Christians and the spice producing St. Thomas Christians, which besides ethnic mingling led to the indigenization of church architecture and regional adaptation of food and dress cultures.

The other part of the story was that the Brahmins, who constructed caste categories out of the existing professional groups and social classes during the period between the ninth and the thirteenth centuries in their attempt to establish hegemonic position for themselves in the society, wanted to promote Christians as a trading caste and this was a part of their strategy to weaken the commerce of their religious rivals, the Jains and the Buddhists. By creating a tradition in which Christians were attributed to have the 'ability' to touch and purify the polluted oil and utensils of temples and palaces of central Kerala, they were made to become the part of the caste-based social process in which they were to play the role of a social group bridging the gulf between the artisan castes and the dominant castes. The Christians in their turn kept themselves acceptable before the Brahmins and the Nairs by meticulously maintaining caste regulations of untouchability, and by adhering to all cultural practices of the dominant castes, like the wearing of sacred thread (*puunuul*), a tuft (*kudumi*), and the observance of pollution by birth and death. However, they lived their religion with a world-view shaped by the geophysical space in which they were distributed in different parts of Kerala, and correspondingly, they developed a certain type of religious geography in which different categories of patron saints were conceived and developed for the diverse ecosystems of their habitat. In this early process of adapting Christianity to the Indian situation, even the core of administration moved away from a foreign bishop to a local community leader, whose power and strength was augmented by the reinforcements provided by the representative bodies of the wealthy elite at different levels. Thus, though the Christians formed only a feeble strand within the cultural fabric of India during the period up to 1500, they operated as a leavening substratum in pockets of their interaction through the economic forces that they disseminated, and through the identity that they stamped, besides the ideology they upheld.

NOTES

1. The Syriac document *Anecdota Syriaca* states that three Syrian Missionaries (two of them probably Nestorian Persians Mar Sapor and Mar Peroz or Prodh) came to Kollam in AD 823 and got leave from the king Shakirabirbi to erect a church there. K.P. Padmanabha Menon, *History of Kerala*, vol. I, New Delhi, 1982, p. 273. See also M.G.S. Narayanan, *Cultural Symbiosis*, 1972, Calicut, pp. 31-2. The word 'Kurakkeni Kollam' was often used in Malayalam for Quilon so as to differentiate it from another early medieval port town known as Pandarayani Kollam, which actually corresponds to present day Koyilandy.
2. For details see Meera Abraham, *Two Medieval Merchant Guilds of South India*, New Delhi, 1988.
3. George Fadlo Hourani, *Arab Seafaring in the Indian Ocean in Ancient and Early Medieval Times*, Princeton, 1951, pp. 61-2, 64, 70-4; Pius Malekandathil, *The Germans, the Portuguese and India*, Münster, 1999, p. 4.
4. In fact the decisive battle in which the Arabs defeated the Sassanid power took place at Nihavand in AD 641. Though the emperor Yazdirgird III fled and continued resistance, a great part of Persia came under the Arabs with his death in AD 651. Andre Wink, *Al-Hind: The Making of the Indo-Islamic World*, vol. I *Early Medieval India and the Expansion of Islam 7th-11th Centuries*, New Delhi, 1999, p. 9. During the period after the Arab occupation, there started migration of people (including Christians and Zoroastrians) in considerable numbers, who opposed Islam, to different parts of the Indian Ocean region. These Zoroastrians

laid the foundation for the Parsi community in Konkan region. See also Pius Malekandathil, 'St.Thomas Christians and the Indian Ocean: 52 AD to 1500 AD', *Ephrem's Theological Journal*, vol. 5, no. 2, October 2001, pp. 193-4.

5. This fact is evident from the Tharisapally copper plate. For details see T. A Gopinatha Rao, *Travancore Archaeological Series*, vol. II, Madras, 1916, pp. 66-75.

6. See T. A. Gopinatha Rao, *Travancore Archaeological Series*, vol. II, p. 68.

7. *Parakkol* seems to have derived from *Bhara-kol* or the balance by which commodities and solid materials were weighed. The literal meaning must have been balance to weigh *Bharam* units. Each *bharam* corresponds to 20 *thulams* or 200 kg. Probably it must have been the crude form of *vellikol* that existed till recently as a weighing mechanism in Kerala.

8. This also seems to be a device for measuring solid articles of trade like *para*, which was in use till recently. Probably it must have been used for bulk measurements of rice and pepper. Commodity measured by one *panchakandy* must have been equivalent to five *kandis*, another type of weight prevalent in Kerala till recently. Or it could also refer to a type of weights generally spaced out into five (*panchakandy* as a device with *pancha-khandas* or five measuring segments).

9. *Kappan* seems to have been a device to measure liquid items. It must have been the crude form of a *thudam* device with a handle, with the help of which oil was measured till recently. The word *kappan* must have been derived from *thappu pathram*.

10. T. A. Gopinatha Rao, *Travancore Archaeological Seiries*, vol. II, p. 68.

11. Walter de Gray Birch, ed., *The Commentaries of the Great Afonso Dalboquerque: Second Viceroy of India*, New York, 1875, p. 15.

12. As mentioned in the first plate of Tharisapally copper plate. Four families of Ezhavas and eight *Ezhakkaiyyar*. T. A. Gopinatha Rao, *Travancore Archaeological Series*, vol. II, p. 67.

13. As mentioned in the second plate of Tharisapally copper plate. T. A. Gopinatha Rao, *Travancore Archaeological Series*, vol. II, p. 68.

14. Ibid., p. 67.

15. Ibid., p. 68.

16. Ibid., pp. 63-7.

17. Ibid., pp. 68-71.

18. Ibid., pp. 67, 71.

19. Ibid., pp. 68, 71.

20. M.G.S. Narayanan, *Perumals of Kerala*, Calicut, 1996, p. 155; For a discussion on the different types and cultural composition of Manigramam guild see Rajan Gurukkal, *The Kerala Temple and the Early Medieval Agrarian System*, Sukapuram, 1992, p. 92; Raghava Varier and Rajan Gurukkal, *Kerala Charithram*, Sukapuram, 1991, pp. 135-6.

21. Ibid., pp. 68, 71.

22. Pius Malekandathil, 'Christians and the Cultural Shaping of India in the First Millennium', in *Journal of St. Thomas Christians*, vol. 17, no.1, January-March 2006, p. 10.

23. The evolving process of feudalization in the low-lying rice cultivating space is analyzed by Rajan Gurukkal. See Rajan Gurukkal, *The Kerala Temple and the Early Medieval Agrarian System*, Sukapuram 1992.

24. A typical case of this nature for the later period is mentioned by M.G.S. Narayanan in the instance of privileges given to Joseph Rabban by Bhaskara Ravi Varma AD 974. See M.G.S.Narayanan, 'Further Studies on the Jewish Copper Plates of Cochin', *The Indian Historical Review*, vol. XXIX, p. 69.

25. M.G.S. Narayanan, *Cultural Symbiosis in Kerala*, Trivandrum 1972, pp. 31-3.

26. Pius Malekandathil, 'Christians and the Cultural Shaping of India in the First Millennium', p. 11.

27. T. A. Gopinatha Rao, *Travancore Archaeological Series*, vol. II, pp. 68, 71.

28. The intensity of this conflict between the evolving Hindu religion and heterodox sects like Buddhism and Jainism, is very much evident in the Bhakti literature of this period. See R. Champakalakshmi, 'From Devotion and Dissent to Dominance: The Bhakti of the Tamil Alvars and Nayanars' in *Tradition, Dissent and Ideology: Essays in Honour of Romila Thapar*, ed R. Champakalakshmi and S. Gopal, 2001, p. 143.

29. For details of Koulam Mali mentioned in the Genizza papers, see S.D. Goitein, *Letters of Medieval Jewish Traders*, Princeton, 1972, pp. 64.

30. The earliest Arab source is Suleiman's account of AD 841 entitled *Salsalat-al-Taverika*. For other Arab sources on Kollam, see George Fadlo Hourani, *Arab Seafaring in the Indian Ocean in Ancient and Early Medieval Times*, Princeton, 1951, pp. 70-4.

31. For details on Chinese references to Kollam, see Haraprasad Ray, 'Historical Contacts Between Quilon and China', in *The Portuguese, Indian Ocean and European Bridgeheads: Festschrift in Honour of Prof. K.S. Mathew*, ed. Pius Malekandathil and Jamal Mohammed, Tellicherry/Lisbon, 2001, pp. 386-8.

32. Pius Malekandathil, 'Christians and the Cultural Shaping of India in the First Millennium', p. 15.

33. Suleiman's account titled *Salsalat-al-Taverika* was written around 841.

34. George Fadlo Hourani, op. cit., pp. 61-74; Pius Malekandathil, *The Portuguese, the Germans and India*, p. 4.

35. In return he was conferred with seventy-two privileges and prerogatives of aristocracy in about AD 1000 by the Chera ruler. For details, see Elamkulam Kunjan Pillai, *Studies in Kerala History*, Kottayam, 1970; M.G.S. Narayanan, *Cultural Symbiosis in Kerala*, Trivandrum, 1972, p. 82; Pius Malekandathil, 'Winds of Change and Links of Continuities: A Study on the Merchant Groups of Kerala and the Channels of their Trade, 1000-1800', *Journal of Economic and Social History of the Orient*, vol. 50, no. 2, 2007, p. 263.

36. M.N. Adler, *The Itinerary of Benjamin of Tudela*, London, 1907, pp. 63-4.

37. For details on Jewish traders in Quilon, see S.D. Goitein, *Letters of Medieval Jewish Traders*, pp. 62-4; S.D. Goitein, 'Portrait of a Medieval India Trader: Three Letters from the Cairo Geniza', *Bulletin of the School of Oriental and African Studies*, XLVIII, 1987, pp. 457-460.

38. For details on Chinese contacts with Quilon, see W.W. Rockhill, 'Notes on the Relations and Trade of China with the Eastern Archipelago and the Coast of the

Indian Ocean during the Fifteenth Century', *T'oung Pao*, vol. XV, Leiden, 1914, pp. 437-8. Henry Yule and Henry Cordier, *Cathay and the Way Thither*, vol. III, Nendeln/Liechtenstein, 1967, pp. 63, 133-7, 141, 217.

39. C. Achyuta Menon, *The Cochin State Manual*, Ernakulam, 1911.

40. For a detailed discussion on these *angadis* as markets, see Pius Malekandathil, *Portuguese Cochin and the Maritime Trade of India*, pp. 50-80; for details on the churches having *angadis*, see Pius Malekandathil, ed., *Jornada of Dom Alexis de Menezes: A Portuguese Account of the Sixteenth Century Malabar*, Kochi, 2003 (henceforth referred to as Antonio de Gouvea, *Jornada of Dom Alexis de Menezes*), pp. 126-462.

41. A. Sreedhara Menon, *Kerala Charitram* (Malayalam), Kottayam 1973, p. 135. The grant made to these two Christian merchants was recorded in the form of a *vattezhuthu* inscription on a granite slab, 74 inches by 51 inches, lying at the foot of the open air cross in front of the Catholic church at Thazhekkadu near Irinjalakuda.

42. Reisebericht des Franciscus Dalbuquerque vom 27 December 1503, in B. Greiff, *Tagebuch des Lucas Rem aus den Jahren 1494-1541: Ein Beitrag zur Handelsgeschichte der Stadt Augsburg*, Augsburg, 1861, p. 146. Genevieve Bouchon and Jean Aubin identify *Korran* with a native Christian guild. See Jean Aubin, 'L'apprentissage de l'Inde. Cochin 1503-1504', *Moyen Orient et Ocean Indien*, 1988; Genevieve Bouchon, 'Calicut at the Turn of the Sixteenth Century', *The Asian Seas 1500-1800: Local Societies, European Expansions and the Portuguese*, Revista da Cultura, vol. I, 1991, p. 44.

43. Nationalbibliothek in Wien, Nr. 6948; Christine von Rohr, *Neue Quellen zur zweiten Indienfahrt Vasco da Gamas*, Leipzig, 1939, p. 51.

44. Raymundo Antonio Bulhão Pato, ed., *Cartas de Affonso de Albuquerque seguidas de documentos que as elucidam*, tom. II, Lisboa 1884, pp. 30, 258-9, 268.

45. Ibid., tom. VI, pp. 114, 398-9.

46. For details on the origin of Indian Christians, see Mathias. Mundadan, *Sixteenth Century Traditions of St. Thomas Christians*, Bangalore, 1970, pp. 38-67; Joseph C. Panjikaran, 'Christianity in Malabar with Special Reference to the St.Thomas Christians of the Syro-Malabar Rite', *Orientalia*, vol. VI, 1926, pp. 103-5; Jonas Thaliath, *The Synod of Diamper*, Rome, 1958; Fr. Bernard, *The History of the St. Thomas Christians*, Pala, 1916; Placid J. Podippara, *The Thomas Christians*, Bombay, 1970.

47. The dating of these Christian settlements and the founding of their churches is done on the basis of information from W. Hermann, *Die Kirche der Thomaschristen: Ein Beitrag zur Geschichte der Orientalischen Kirchen*, Hütersloh, 1877, pp. 673-769; Fr. Bernard, *The History of the St. Thomas Christians*, pp. 296-327. The year of founding of these churches is taken from the respective diocesan directories, which is further cross-checked with the help of field-study, in which the statues, the church-bells, stone inscriptions, church-songs (*pallipattu*), etc., are used to verify their chronology. See also P.J. Thomas,

Malayala Sahithyavum Kristhianikalum, Kottayam, 1961, pp. 63-4; Pius Malekandathil, 'St. Thomas Christians and the Indian Ocean', pp. 186, 194-5, 198-9.

48. Henry Yule, ed., *Cathay and the Way Thither*, vol. III, Nendeln/Liechtenstein, 1967, pp. 216-18, 248-57.

49. Antonio da Silva Rego, ed., *Documentação para a Historia das Missões*, vol. II, pp. 175-6. For example, see ANTT, *Cartas dos Vice-Reis da India*, doc. 95. See also E.R. Hambye, 'Medieval Christianity in India: The Eastern Church', in *Christianity in India*, ed. E.R. Hambye and H.C. Perumalil, Alleppey, 1972, p. 34; Samuel Matteer, *The Land of Charity: A Descriptive Account of Travancore and its People*, New Delhi, 1991, pp. 237-8.

50. Antonio de Gouvea, *Jornada do Arcebispo*, Coimbra, 1606. See particularly pp. 132-3, 192-269.

51. Antonio de Gouvea, *Jornada of Dom Alexis de Menezes*, pp. 116-18, 252-3.

52. Ibid., p.117.

53. O.M. Varghese Olickal, *Vazhakulam: Oru Charithra Veekshanam*, Muvattupuzha 1985, pp. 15-16.

54. Arquivo Nacional da Torre do Tombo, *Cartas de Dio a D.João de Castro*, fol. 93, Letter of Damião Vaz to Dom Alvares de Castro, dated 6-8-1547; Georg Schurhammer, *Die Zeitgenössischen Quellen zur Geschichte Portugiesisch-Asiens und seiner Nachbarländer zur Zeit des hl. Franz Xavier (1538-1552)*, Rome, 1962, no. 3224, p. 212.

55. See Historical Archives of Goa, *Livro das Monções*, no. 8 (1601-2), fol. 106. For details on the military expertise of these Christians, see Antonio de Gouvea, *Jornada of Dom Alexis de Menezes*, pp. 252-3.

56. Josef Wick, ed., *Documenta Indica*, vol. III, Rome, 1960, p. 801.

57. Antonio de Gouvea, *Jornada of Dom Alexis de Menezes*, pp. 116-18, 129-35, 165-8.

58. Pius Malekandathil, 'Kothamangalam Roopathayude Charitra Paschatalavum Kraisthava Koottayamakalude Verukalum', in *Anpinte Anpathandu, Kothamangalam Roopathayude Charitram, 1957-2007*, ed. Pius Malekandathil, Kothamangalam 2008, p. 38.

59. This coincided with the attempts of the Brahmins to create as much distance as possible between the actual tiller (*pulaya*) and the owner (Brahmin) by constructing different types of intermediaries in the social ladder. In the process of gradation, the *naduvazhi* chief was kept at the top, followed by *uralar* (land owners and temple trustees), *karalar* (tenants and intermediary landholders), *kudiyar* (settled tenant cultivator) as well as *adiyar* (bonded service classes) on the lowest strata. For details, see M.G.S. Narayanan and Kesavan Veluthat, 'The Traditional Land system in Kerala: The Problem of Change and Perspective', *Logan Centenary Seminar on Land Reforms in Kerala*, Kozhikode 1981; M.G.S. Narayanan, 'Social and Economic Conditions during the Kulasekhara Empire (800 AD to 1124 AD)', unpublished Ph.D. thesis, University of Kerala, 1972.

60. The common saying was '*Paulose thottal athu sudhamayidum*'. It will get purified if it is touched by a Christian (Paulose). See P.G. Rajendran, *Kshetra Vijnanakosam*, Kottayam, 2000.

61. BNL, *Reservados Cod*, no. 536. *Noticias do reino do Malabar anteriores a chegada dos Portugueses e ate ao sec. XVIII. Geografia, Clima, Etnais, Linguas, Costumes, Politica, Religões, confronte entre Carmelitas, e Jesuitas e a Cristandade de São Tome*, fol. 6.

62. For details of these borrowed customs that existed till the Diamper synod of 1599, see Scaria Szacharia, *The Acts and Decrees of the Synod of Diamper*, Edamattom 1994.

63. Antonio de Gouvea, *Jornada*, p. 258.

64. Leslie Brown, *The Indian Christians of St. Thomas*, p. 177.

65. Antonio de Gouvea, *Jornada of Dom Alexis de Menezes*, p. 251.

66. Ines G. Zupanov, *Disputed Mission*, New Delhi, 2001, pp. 58, 93-8; D. Ferroli, *The Jesuits in Malabar*, Bangalore, 1939, vol. I, pp. 300-60.

67. Antonio de Gouvea, *Jornada of Dom Alexis de Menezes*, pp. 251, 257; Leslie Brown, *The Indian Christians of St. Thomas*, Cambridge, 1982, pp. 205-6.

68. Placid Podipara, *The Thomas Christians*, Bombay, 1970.

69. Antonio de Gouvea, *Jornada of Dom Alexis de Menezes*, pp. 57, 124, 212 -14.

70. Ibid., pp. 212-14.

71. Eugene Tisserant, *Eastern Christianity in India*, tran. E.R. Hambye, Calcutta, 1957; Placid Podipara, *The Thomas Christians*, Bombay, 1970.

72. For details see the geographical location of the churches of the St. Thomas Christians visited by Archbishop Dom Alexis de Menezes in 1599. See also the map of Kerala showing the itinerary of the Archbishop. Antonio de Gouvea, Pius Malekandathil (ed.), *Jornada of Dom Alexis de Menezes*, Appendix. Some of the churches of this Christian community were located also in low-lying paddy-cultivating zones, however their number was insignificant when compared with the large number of churches seen in upland terrains of central Kerala.

73. For details see T.A. Gopinatha Rao, *Travancore Archaeological Series*, vol. II, Madras 1916, pp. 66-75.

74. Ibid.

75. Antonio de Gouvea, *Jornada of Dom Alexis de Menezes*, pp. 29, 244.

76. Ibid., pp. 244-5.

77. Pius Malekandathil, 'Common Heritage of the St. Thomas Christians', *Journal of St. Thomas Christians*, vol. 19, no. 3, July- September, 2008, pp. 11-12.

78. Giovanni di Empoli, 'Viaggio fatto nell'India per Gionni da Empoli fattore su la nave del serenissimo re di Portugallo per conto de marchioni di Lisbona', in *Delle Navigationi et Viaggi nel qual si contiente la descrittione dell'Africa, et del Paese del Prete Joanni, con varii Viaggi, dal Mar Rosso a Calicut, et in fin all'isole Molucche, dove nascono le Spetieri, et la Navigatione attorno il Mondo*, ed. G.B. Ramusio, Venice, 1550, fol. 57.

79. *Kerala Society Papers*, vol. I, Trivandrum, 1928, pp. 253ff.

80. Antonio Gouvea, *Jornada of Dom Alexis de Menezes*, p. 194.

81. Pius Malekandathil, 'Common Heritage of the St. Thomas Christians', p. 9.

82. Antonio de Gouvea, *Jornada of Dom Alexis de Menezes*, pp. 120-497.

83. Giovanni di Empoli, 'Viaggio fatto nell' India per Gionni da Empoli fattore su la nave del serenissimo re di Portugallo per conto de marchioni di Lisbona', in *Delle Navigationi et Viaggi nel qual si contiente la descrittione dell'Africa, et del Paese del Prete Joanni, con varii Viaggi, dal Mar Rosso a Calicut, et in fin all'isole Molucche, dove nascono le Spetieri, et la Navigatione attorno il Mondo*, ed. G.B. Ramusio, Venice, 1550, fol. 57; Pius Malekandathil, 'The Portuguese and the St. Thomas Christians: 1500-1570', in *The Portuguese and the Socio-Cultural Changes in India, 1500-1800*, ed. K.S. Mathew, Teotonio R de Souza and Pius Malekandathil, Fundação Oriente, Lisboa, 2001, p. 128.

84. See the report of the German artillerists given in Gernot Giertz, *Vasco da Gama, die Entdeckung des Seewegs nach Indien: ein Augenzeugenbericht 1497-1499*, Tübingen, 1980, p.188. For the detailed report of the same see Horst G.W. Nüsser, *Frühe Deutsche Entdecker: Asien in Berichten unbekannter deutscher Augenzeugen (1502-6)*, München, 1980, pp. 126-40.

85. Tome Pires, *A Suma Oriental de Tome Pires e o Livro de Francisco Rodrigues*, ed. Armando Cortesão, Coimbra, 1978, p.180. In this connection the recent research works of the Portuguese scholars like João Teles e Cunha, João Paulo Oliveira e Costa and Luis Filipe F.R. Thomaz deserve special mention because of their objective painstaking research. See João Teles e Cunha 'De Diamper a Mattancherry: Caminhos e Encruzilhadas da Igreja Malabar e Catolica na India: Os Primeiros Tempos (1599-1624)', *Anais de Historia de Alem-Mar,* vol. V, 2004, pp. 283-368; João Paulo Oliveira e Costa, 'Os Portugueses e a Cristandade Siro-Malabar (1498-1530), *Studia*, 52, Lisboa, 1994; Luis Filipe F.R. Thomaz, 'Were Saint Thomas Christians Looked upon as Heretics?', in *The Portuguese and the Socio-Cultural Changes in India, 1500-1800*, ed. K.S. Mathew, Teotonio R. de Souza and Pius Malekandathil, Fundação Oriente, Lisboa, 2001, pp. 27-92.

86. Josef Wicki, ed., *Documenta Indica*, vol. VI, Roma, 1948, p. 180.

87. Ibid., vol. VII, p. 475.

88. Antonio de Gouvea, *Jornada of Dom Alexis de Menezes*, p. 50, no. 65; p. 436, no. 89.

89. Ibid., p. 432, no. 83.

90. Paulinus of St. Bartholomew, *India Orientalis Christiana*, Roma, 1794, p. 267; Antonio de Gouvea, *Jornada of Dom Alexis de Menezes*, p. 50, no. 65; 432, no. 83; 436, no. 89; 443, no. 104.

91. Pius Malekandathil, 'Christians and the Cultural Shaping of India in the First Millennium', pp. 14-15.

92. Antonio de Gouvea, *Jornada of Dom Alexis de Menezes*, pp. 302-3, no. 1.

93. Ibid., p. 449, no. 108.

94. Pius Malekandathil, 'Christians and the Cultural Shaping of India in the First Millennium', p. 14.

95. Antonio Gouvea, *Jornada of Dom Alexis de Menezes*, p. 302. Later these churches were given the names of St. Protasius and St. Gervasius, whose names sound phonetically similar to those of Mar Prodh and Sapor.

96. Antonio Gouvea, *Jornada of Dom Alexis de Menezes*, p. 425, no. 75.

97. Ibid., p. 441.

98. Ibid., p. 433, no. 86.

99. Pius Malekandathil, 'Christians and the Cultural Shaping of India in the First Millennium', p. 14.

100. Paulinus of St. Bartholomew, *India Orientalis Christiana*, p. 267.

101. Antonio de Gouvea, *Jornada of Dom Alexis de Menezes*, p. 244.

102. Pius Malekandathil, 'Christians and the Cultural Shaping of India in the First Millennium', p. 13.

103. For details on the dress culture of the Christians till the Diamper Synod, see Antonio de Gouvea, *Jornada of Dom Alexis de Menezes*, pp. 249-59.

104. Ibid., p. 251.

105. Jacob Kollaparambil, *The Archdeacon of All India*, Kottayam, 1972.

106. Antonio Gouvea, *Jornada of Dom Alexis de Menezes*, pp.162, 164-5, 176, 190, 200-4, 220-1.

107. Pius Malekandathil, 'Common Heritage of the St. Thomas Christians', pp. 13-14.

CHAPTER FOUR

From the Trails of the Chinese to the Dominance of the Portuguese: An Overview of the Patterns of their Naval Voyages and the Maritime Policies in India

The first state-sponsored naval voyages and explorative ventures in the Indian Ocean seem to have been initiated by the sailors from Ming China, which took place almost one century prior to the entry of the Portuguese into the scene. In fact, Indian ports had been the exchange venues for the Chinese right from time immemorial and were integrated as intermediate economic units for the tributary trade system of the Mongols. Indian rulers, particularly the Cholas, used to maintain a very special commercial linkage with China, for cementing which the former repeatedly sent embassies to the Sung court. However, the voyage circuits of Cheng Ho from Ming China stands as something different from the commercial trips of earlier *junks*, not only because of their state-sponsoring, but also because of the size of the vessels and the man-power employed for the purpose, the places visited and the time-span involved in the exploration. The trails of the early Chinese travellers must have been used by Cheng Ho to reach up to coastal western India; however his travells to East Africa definitely necessitated skills of exploration. The Portuguese, on the other hand, explored the sea-route from Lisbon up to East Africa, from where they banked upon indigenous sailors and traders for procuring sufficient information to reach India and, later, other locations in the Indian Ocean. Though both were explorers, the Chinese explored the Indian Ocean from east to west, whereas the Portuguese explored it from west to east with the backing of the state for the expeditions. On the other hand the Chinese disappeared from the scene when Cheng Ho

*Revised version of the paper originally presented at ther Hall of St. Albert Kirche, Heidelberg, Germany, 15 September 1998.

stopped his voyages, while the Portuguese managed to establish hegemony over the waters of India for more than a century. Attempts for comparing the voyage patterns of the Chinese under Cheng Ho and the Portuguese were already made by scholars like Roderich Ptak.[1] This chapter basically looks into the features and patterns of the Chinese maritime contacts with India at different time points and tries to analyse the naval voyages of Cheng Ho and the Portuguese, for the purpose of seeing whether the Portuguese drew lessons of experience from the voyages of Cheng Ho for developing a policy that would facilitate their domination over the fringes of maritime India.

EARLY MARITIME CONTACTS BETWEEN INDIA AND CHINA

The waters of the Indian Ocean formed an important medium for the Chinese at different time points to enter India.[2] Fa-Hsien's account of his return journey from India to China by sea during AD 411-13 is a good example of the sea voyages between the two regions. He boarded a Chinese vessel from Tamralipti on the Bengal coast and proceeded to Sri Lanka, from where he went on to China.[3] Though Hiuen Tsang (602-64) resorted to the 'Silk Route' to reach India and travel back to China,[4] I-Tsing (635-713) took the sea route to reach India via Srivijaya and Kedah. The same sea route was taken by him to reach back to T'ang China after 25 years of his travel.[5] This was a time when long distance trade circuits between Abbassid Persia (750-1258) and T'ang China (618-907) had incorporated several ports and regional economies of maritime India into their orbits. The long distance commodity movements from al-Basrah or Muscat or Sohar in Oman in the Persian Gulf and terminating in Canton in China had several halting centres or feeding units including Koulam Mali (Quilon) along the coastal fringes of India.[6]

Against the backdrop of these contacts, the Indian Ocean was subdivided into several interlocking circuits, each being controlled by a set of political and economic actors who resorted to different methods and devices to translate trade profits into political assets. Though the initial phase of the long distance trade started in the eighth century, the developments began to take the form of an all-pervasive economically stimulating phenomenon only by tenth century, activating the processes of production and exchange in larger zones of the Indian Ocean. In fact, the very shifting of capital from Damascus to Baghdad was motivated by the desire of the Abbassids to appropriate a sizeable chunk of profit accruing from the trade in the Indian Ocean. The various maritime zones in the Indian Ocean like the Arabian Sea, the Bay of Bengal and the South China Seas had different circuits of trade, which were necessitated by the inevitable breaks in the long distance travel between Abbassid Persia and T'ang China: the first break was at Koulam Mali, or Quilon, where a trader from Abbassid Persia reached after a travel of 30 days, while the second break was at Kedah in the Malay Peninsula after another 30 days. It took another 30 days for the Persian traders to terminate their journey at Canton.[7] Meanwhile, the trade circuits of the Abbassid merchants in the Arabian Sea were further strengthened by parallel lines of circuits developed by the Jewish traders linked with Fatimid Cairo.[8] Consequently, by the tenth and eleventh centuries, economies throughout Asia expanded considerably and new political powers such as the Kadambas on the Konkan,[9] the Cholas in southern India, the Khmers in Angkor, the Burmese at Pagan, the Ly in Vietnam and the Sung on the Chinese mainland emerged out of the resources generated from these maritime circuits.[10]

The Cholas formed one of the important political houses that tried to take maximum economic benefits out of the Chinese trade in India. The core area of maritime trade in the Coromandel coast eventually got shifted from Mahabalipuram to Nagapattinam with the accession of the Cholas to power.[11] Because of the nature of segmentary state only a small portion of the agrarian resources is said to have reached the central coffers of the Cholas, and, hence, the latter began to increasingly bank upon overseas trade for gathering enough resources needed for their political activities.[12] They had to bank upon the Tamil merchants for wealth generation, which prompted them to facilitate expansion of their maritime trade with South-East Asia and China. Eventually by the eleventh century, the Tamil traders got increasingly organized into different commercial corporations, evidently with the support of the Chola state.[13] The Cholas realized that more wealth could be generated by accelerating commercial activities with China, for realizing which they sent embassies to the Sung court in 1015, 1033 and 1079.[14] In fact the first embassy of 1015 is said to have taken the longest time span (1,150 days) for travel to China. Quoting Chinese records Tansen Sen traces the route of the Chola embassy of 1015, which started its journey from Na-wu-tan-shan (Nagapattinam?) and passed through So-li his-lan (Ceylon), Chan-bin (Jambi in Sumatra?), I-mo-lo-li (the Irrawady River in Burma?), Ku-lo (in Java?), Chia-pa (Langkwai islands), Kou-pu-lao (Cham?), Chou-pao-lung (Salat Sembilan River in Singapore?), San-fo-Ch'i (Srivijaya), Man-shan (Muntok in the Banda islands?), Tien-chu-shan (Pulo Aor in the Malayan peninsula), Pin-t'ou-lang-shan (Panduranga in southern Vietnam), Yang shan (Pulo Gambir in south-eastern Vietnam), Chiu-hsing shan (near Honk Kong or Macao) and finally it reached Canton after a journey of 1,150 days.[15] He further argues that while the later embassies took shorter routes to reach

China, the first envoys travelled in Arab mercantile ships, which made circulatory trips in the South-East Asian region for commercial purposes increasing the time span of the embassy to reach Canton.[16]

Later, the attempts to protect the commercial interests of the Tamil merchants in China inevitably dragged the Cholas into the politics of the archipelago. Probably it was on the question of controlling maritime trade with China that the Cholas entered into conflicts with the rulers of Srivijaya and finally the clash of economic interests prompted them to make raids against Srivijayan ports in 1025. Quoting Chu fan che, written by Chau-Ju-kua in the beginning of the thirteenth century, Tansen Sen says that the Srivijayans used to prevent ships from foreign countries from passing through the straits of Malacca, if they did not stop first at their ports. They used to attack and drown the vessels that resisted their moves. Against this background he views that the attacks on the Tamil ships going to China resisting Srivijayan demands must have been the reason for the trade war between the Cholas and the Srivijayans.[17]

Later, when the tributary-trade system was initiated under the Yuans (Mongol rulers-1279-1368), most of the leading ports of thirteenth century India were absorbed into the system. The Muslim traders and the indigenous Christian merchants of Quilon (mentioned in Yuan sources as Ju-lan)[18] were referred to as having sent a commercial mission to the court of Kublai Khan. Wu-tsa-erh-sa-li-ma (Ishob Mar Salom?), the chief of the Yeh-li-k'owen (whom Rockhill identifies with the Christians of Quilon) in 1282 sent a messenger with gifts to the Mongol emperor, 'a gorget set with different kinds of jewels and also flacons of drugs'.[19] This was reciprocated by an official Mongol mission dispatched to Quilon in 1283 carrying with it a golden badge for Wa-ni, the king of Koulam Mali, on whom the Chinese emperor conferred the title of Fu-ma or imperial son-in-law.[20] These details evidently indicate the nature of tributary trade carried out between India and China in the thirteenth and fourteenth centuries.

With the intensification of Chinese trade with the Indian Ocean, in 1293 private trade of the Chinese abroad in gold, silver and copper cash, ironware, male and females slaves, silk thread, satins, gold brocades, provisions, military equipments was strictly forbidden. This was followed by prohibition of gold and silver export from China in 1296 and by strict restriction and regulation on Chinese trade with Ma'bar, Kulam (Koulam Mali or Quilon) and Fandarina (Pantalayani Kollam near Koyilandy) to the small sum of 50,000 *ting* worth of paper money.[21] These details are indicative of the pressure that the Chinese authorities were compelled to exert on private trade with India due to the increasing outflow of wealth from China to India for fetching expensive spices and other commodities. In fact, when

Cheng Ho started his naval voyages into the Indian Ocean in 1405, he did not start from zero, but had built upon the rich tradition of sea voyages, shaped by the frequent movement of people and commodities between China and India over a long span of time.

PATTERN OF CHENG HO'S VOYAGES

Cheng Ho, who headed the seven naval voyages to Indian Ocean from Ming China, was originally known as Mǎ Sānbǎo (1371-1433). It is the Ming emperor Yongle who is said to have given him the name Cheng Ho in 1404, in recognition of his services. The span of the state-sponsored naval voyages under Cheng Ho commissioned by the Ming emperor Yongle was 28 years, covering different maritime zones and ecosystems. Different arguments were given for the series of voyages of Cheng Ho into Indian Ocean, ranging from the search for the lost brother of the emperor to the need for legitimizing Yongle's emperorship by diplomatic linkages against the background of usurpation of the throne from his nephew Jianwen.

Obviously the naval expedition under Cheng Ho was to carry some elements of Chinese power into the Indian Ocean, which can be inferred from the large size of the vessels and the number of men used for the expedition. In fact, his navy consisted of 27,800 men and a fleet of 62 treasure ships supported by approximately 190 smaller ships.[22] It is obvious that diplomatic embassies do not need such a large number of vessels, sailors as well as manpower. It could have been for creating an impressive picture of the Chinese among the various political personalities and traders of the Indian Ocean and to induce them to come to China to submit tribute and to conduct supplementary trade.[23] Evidently one may not be able to delink elements of power from the entire exercise of Cheng Ho's chain of voyages.

Cheng Ho's was not the only naval expedition sent by the emperor Yongle. Rockhill says that in 1403 Ma Pin was sent on a similar mission to Java, Aceh, Calicut, Quilon and other places. Hou Hsien who travelled initially between Tibet as well as Nepal (1403-13), and later to eastern India in a ship in 1415, was another famous traveller of this time.[24] But it was Cheng Ho who undertook a long chain of voyages and that too for a very long span of time (twenty-eight years) touching the remotest trade centres of those days like Mogadishu and Melinde in Africa.[25]

If we analyse the places that Cheng Ho visited during his seven expeditions, it becomes clear that almost all of them were commercially the most strategic centres in the different economic zones of the Indian Ocean referred to in the original sources as 'western seas'.[26] According to Rockhill, the period of the first voyage of Cheng Ho was from 1405 till 1407, while that of second was from 1408 till 1411. The third was between 1412 and 1415 and the fourth was between 1417 and 1419. He views the fifth expedition in 1421 to be of a short time duration of less than a year. Cheng Ho started his sixth voyage in 1424 and returned in 1425, while the seventh expedition was in 1430.[27] The major places that he frequently visited in his chain of voyages were Annam, Java, Kamboja, Timor, Palembang, Siam, the Nicobar Islands, the Singapore Strait, Malacca, Brunei, Acheh, Aru, Calicut, Cochin, Kayamkulam, Quilon, Coromandel, Kayal (Kayalpattinam), Jurfatan, Lambri, Cambay, Ceylon, Pahang, Kelantan, Hormuz, Brawa, the Maldives, Bengal, Juba, Mogadishu, Aden, Zeila, Djofar, Mecca, Sunda, etc.[28] Out of these various commercially important centres of the Indian Ocean, Bengal (Peng-ka-la), Orissa (Wu-tieh), Cail or Kayal (Kayalpattinam), Calicut (Ku-li-fo), Cochin (Ko-Chih), Kayamkulam (Hsiao Ko-lan), Quilon (Ta-Kolan), Hili or Mount Eli (Hsia-Li), Mangalore (Hsu-wen-na), Honavar (Hua-lo), Bacanore (Peng-kia-lo), Bombay (Fang-pai) and Cambay (K'an-pa-i) were the most frequently visited ports in India, as per the information given by Ma Huan and Fei Hsin.[29]

Cheng Ho was almost as tall as Vasco da Gama as far as his voyage expertise and navigational skills were concerned; however, he was definitely taller than the latter as far as the number and time span of the voyages were concerned. Nevertheless, Cheng Ho's expeditions died out with him without leaving behind any link of continuity, as the later Ming rulers were reluctant to pursue costly naval expeditions into the Indian Ocean, whereas the Portuguese crown allowed the voyage traditions of Vasco da Gama to continue through their able sailors and naval commanders.

Through the repeated voyage circuits of Cheng Ho there clearly emerged a notion of five different maritime zones in the Indian Ocean, with the first comprising the South China Seas and the South-East Asian regions. In most of his voyages Cheng Ho used to visit Malacca, giving the impression that this port, which had already been a prominent trade centre by 1400,[30] was the actual maritime door for the South-East Asian region. The second circuit of Cheng Ho was in the Bay of Bengal, where the junks used to frequent the ports of Bengal, Orissa and Coromandel.[31] The third maritime zone was the west coast of India, where the pepper ports of Kerala like Calicut, Cochin and Quilon formed the core area of his circuits, which at times used to extend up to Mangalore, Bombay and Cambay. Hormuz of the Persian Gulf and the Arbian ports of Aden and Mecca formed pivotal exchange centres that he visited in the maritime zone of coastal Arabia and Persia. The fifth zone was East Africa, where his voyages concentrated mostly on Mogadishu and Melinde.[32] Interestingly, the Portuguese later focussed on these major exchange centres of the Indian Ocean that were once repeatedly visited by Cheng Ho and established their fortresses and other control mechanisms for the purpose of maintaining their trade monopoly in a big way in this maritime space.

PATTERNS OF PORTUGUESE EXPANSION IN INDIA

Portuguese expansion in the East in general, and in India in particular, was realized at three different levels: On the one hand, there was the official expansion sponsored by the Portuguese crown and limited principally to the coastal regions between Gujarat in the north and Quilon in the south. The official expansion was carried out by the officials, instruments and devices of the state in areas lying on the west coast of India. On the other hand, there was the expansion realized in the space lying to the east of Cape Comorin (Coromandel, Bengal and the South-East Asian regions) by the Portuguese private traders and renegades in the process of extending their individual commercial and entrepreneurial activities to a free space reasonably away from the power centres on the west coast of India. As the east coast of India was relatively free from Portuguese state control and official interference, any enterprising Portuguese individuals on reaching Goa or Cochin moved over to Coromandel, Bengal and to South-East Asia for establishing their private initiatives. The third level of Portuguese expansion was carried out through the medium of ecclesiastical institutions and personnel, particularly through the missionaries and evangelizing devices of *Padroado*, which also acted as links connecting the privately expanded Portuguese settlements with the official segment.[33]

The west coast of India was the major area of concern for the Portuguese king because of its being the sources of spices and other commodities dear in Europe, and its closeness to the Red Sea-Venice routes, through which spices and other cargo were diverted to Europe undermining the monopoly claims of the Portuguese. This made the Portuguese focus on the west coast of India with several devices and mechanisms for controlling the movement of commodities in the Arabian Sea. A network of fortresses, reinforced by a regular patrolling fleet, was introduced to prevent the diversion of spices and other commodities reserved for the crown under the category of royal monopoly, from the diverse production centres of Asia to the eastern Mediterranean through the ports of the Red Sea and the Persian Gulf. Interestingly, the earliest Portuguese fortresses in India were erected in places where Cheng Ho had made repeated voyages in the fifteenth century. The first Portuguese fortress was erected at Cochin in 1503,[34] which was later modified in 1505, when it was made the seat of *Estado da India*.[35] The next fortresses (Kilwa in East Africa, Cannanore and Anjediva) were also constructed in places either visited by Cheng Ho or in their vicinities. In 1507 the fortress of Sofala was erected and in the following year the construction work on St. Angelo fort of Cannanore was completed.[36]

In 1510 when Afonso Albuquerque took charge as the governor of *Estado da India*, the sea-oriented policy of his predecessor Francisco da Almeida was abandoned for a land-oriented imperial policy. An imperialist expansionist policy was henceforth initiated to keep under Portuguese control various commercially and strategically important centres and resourceful places of the Indian Ocean, that could ably be utilized for the building up of the Lusitanian commercial empire. Meanwhile, the Portuguese had also understood the value of developing Malacca as the door for South-East Asia, Hormuz as the maritime portico for the Persian Gulf regions, and Aden as the chief portal for the Red Sea regions and tried to capture them for controlling the trade of these regions. In fact, these three trade centres were the major destinations of Cheng Ho in his chain of voyages; but the Portuguese wanted to give new political meanings to these economically strategic centres by erecting fortresses over there. Malacca was captured in 1511 and a fortress was erected by Afonso de Albuquerque.[37] In 1515, Hormuz in the Persian Gulf was captured and a Portuguese fortress was constructed there.[38] In the new scheme of developments Goa, captured in 1510[39], was made to be the focal point of Portuguese circuits, where the seat of *Estado da India* was finally shifted in 1530.[40] However, the attempts of Albuquerque to capture Aden failed. The Portuguese tried to compensate the failure in capturing Aden by extending regular patrolling up to the mouth of the Red Sea.

The next fortresses erected by the Portuguese were in the pepper ports of Quilon (1519),[41] and Cranganore (1536),[42] mainly for the purpose of preventing spices from falling into the hands of Muslim traders. This was followed by the erection of fortresses at the Konkan port of Bassein (1534),[43] the Gujarat port of Diu (1536)[44] and Daman (1559).[45] Their desire to control the maritime trade of the erstwhile Vijayanagara ports of Karnataka led to the erection of fortresses at Mangalore (1568),[46] Barçelor (1568)[47] and Honawar (1569).[48]

The controlling efficiency of these fortresses was further enhanced by regular coastal patrolling along the western seaboard. There were basically three maritime zones which were regularly checked and controlled by the patrolling fleet (armada). The southern armada was meant to patrol the western coastline from Cape Comorin up to Cochin, while another patrolling fleet patrolled the western coast from Cochin up to Goa and the third one from Goa up to Cambay and for a considerable period of time up to the mouth of the Red Sea.[49] Only those vessels having the licenses (*cartaz*) from

Portuguese authorities could ply in the Arabian Sea. In the *cartaz*, the place of origin of the cargo, the destination of the vessel, the types of cargo contained in the vessel, etc., were to be indicated, as to ensure that the ship was not involved in commercial activities with places that would undermine the royal monopoly of the Portuguese. In fact the patrolling fleet was necessitated to see whether the ships moving in the maritime space had actually got *cartazes*[50] and to check clandestine trade. However, the system of licences or *cartazes* meant much more than the denial of opportunities for Asian trade; it was principally designed as a device to regulate the intra-Asian trade as to suit the larger commercial interests of the Portuguese crown. The Muslim merchants of Cochin and Cannanore, who were the principal suppliers of spices for the Indo-European trade of the Portuguese were given *cartazes* even to send vessels and commodities to Red Sea ports, despite the amount of challenges it raised to the royal monopoly on the spice trade.[51]

While the west coast of India experienced the weight of Portuguese power in the process of expansion, the east coast of India was kept as a liberal space for the commerce of the Portuguese private traders. In order to keep it as a commercial space the Portuguese authorities refrained from introducing control devices like fortress and patrolling fleet on the Coromandel coast. Consequently, a considerable number of Portuguese people, who were married to Muslim women, began to move over to the various ports of the Coromandel coast, particularly after 1510, making use of the mercantile networks of their Muslim relatives. They lived in different parts of Coromandel without being disturbed by the institutions and machineries of the Portuguese state and by 1520 their number rose to 300, causing a long chain of Portuguese enclaves with deserters and traders to evolve along the south-eastern coast of India. Punnaikayal and Vedalai on the Pearl Fishery coast, Nagapattinam on the mouth of Kaveri, Devanapattinam near Pondicherry, Pulicat and Mylapore near Madras were the principal settlements for these Portuguese private traders and settlers. Though the Portuguese officials tried to bring them back to the west coast of India for the purpose of getting them subjugated to stately and ecclesiastical authorities, the freedom loving Portuguese private traders and renegades refused to go back.[52] Eventually using Coromandel as a springboard, these private traders expanded to different parts of coastal eastern India and South-East Asia.

In the long run, the Portuguese state tried to appropriate these settlements and integrate them into the larger *Estado* edifice through the services of ecclesiastical institutions and personnel extended to the east coast of India. Initially they were brought under Vicar Generals sent by the Funchal diocese and later under the dioceses of Goa (1534), and finally of Cochin (1558).[53] Various Religious Orders like the Franciscans, the Augustinians, the Jesuits and the Dominicans were encouraged to establish churches and religious institutions in these settlements so that the freedom-loving traders and renegades might be 'disciplined' and made to be 'spiritually fit' so as to operate within the frames of *Estado da India*. In 1606, a diocese was erected at Mylapore mainly to cater to the spiritual needs of the Portuguese *casados* of the Coromandel coast,[54] being loosely integrated with the power centre at Goa.

However, the number of Portuguese renegades and private traders preferring to stay in different places distanced themselves from the control of the ecclesiastical and civil authorities of the Portuguese went on increasing. Some of them used to sell advanced European weapons, techniques and military expertise to the native rulers and made capital for their private commercial ventures. Against the background of frequent wars in south and in Deccan, the rulers vied with one another to lure the Portuguese renegades to procure advance military technology and weaponry from them. It was Zamorin, who realized the intensity of damages that could be brought to human beings and property with guns and artilleries that lured the Europeans first. He won over two Milanese artillerists of the Portuguese army for the purpose of manufacturing artillery and guns for Calicut in 1503.[55] Later we find several Portuguese *casados* going into the interior parts of Kerala to sell guns and artilleries to inland rulers of spice growing territories. From them the king of Vadakkenkur had bought eight *berços* and two *falcões* in 1546, while the ruler of Diamper purchased 25 *falcões* and that of Cranganore 17 *falcões*. These Portuguese traders helped the ruler of Thekkenkur to fabricate artilleries as well as cannons in his kingdom and he thus possessed about 15 *falcões* by this time.[56]

Several Portuguese renegades were found in the lands of Bijapur, Golconda, Vijayanagara , Gujarat, Bengal and the Marathas either selling guns and armaments or serving as fighting militia. As early as 1521, Portuguese renegades were found to be operating in Bengal as soldiers.[57] Interestingly, some of the Portuguese renegades and adventurers like Sebastião Gonçalves Tibau, Manuel de Matos and Domingos Carvalho, who appropriated a lot of wealth and clout in the region, later established state like political institutions in the Bay of Bengal. In Gujarat about 50 Portuguese gunners and artillerists were used by Bahadur Shah to fight against the Mughal forces under Humayun in the mid-1530s. While a good many of these Portuguese forces were offered by the Portuguese governor in return for the ceding of Bassein to them,[58] at least a few of them seem to have been Portuguese renegades. Some of the Portuguese renegades living in the land of Adil Shahis (Bijapur) and Qutb Shahis (Golconda) later embraced Islam and settled down there.[59] The Portuguese captain of Bassein reports in 1659 that one Ruy Leitao Viegas along with 340 Portuguese had joined the naval fleet of the Marathas in their military operations, and that he finally managed to persuade Viegas from joining the Maratha alliance.[60] Many Portuguese deserters and soldiers were seen plundering the city of Surat along with the Marathas in 1664, evidently suggesting the linkage of Shivaji with Portuguese renegades and deserters in the earlier phase.[61]

In the process of Portuguese expansion, there thus appeared different enclaves in different parts of India with sizeable Portuguese presence having different levels of authority exercise. While the west coast of India experienced the intensity and the heavy weight of power exercise, with the core centre being Goa, the east coast of India enjoyed a liberal air needed for mercantile expansion. Later, the Portuguese authorities appropriated the mercantile achievements on the east coast of India through the *Padroado* devices and ecclesiastical institutions and integrated them to the *Estado* structure. Another important mechanism resorted to by the Portuguese crown was conferring of urban privileges and concessions on these settlements of east coastal India, which ultimately helped to keep their urban dwellers attached to the *Estado da India* frames for carrying out the larger agenda of the crown. The Portuguese renegades conducting trade and arms supply outside the Portuguese areas of control formed an important link in the commodity movements of the *casados* in Asia. However, the meaning of Portuguese hegemony in maritime India was inscribed not merely by the few scattered settlements on the west coast of India, but by the assortment of activities being carried out on different levels by the various categories of Portuguese settlers in India, who had sizeable mercantile capital by way of private trade, and social and political capital by way of political and military linkages. This added to the most advanced technology of gun and artilleries, together with the huge sized vessels coming from Portugal, augmented the weight of their dominance on the Indian waters.

FROM MERCANTILISM TO LAND ADVENTURISM

Initially the Portuguese had only mercantile motives and they used to occupy only tiny pockets for settlements adjacent to the major maritime trade centres of India. Eventually they developed a desire for appropriating a considerable chunk of landed territories, first in Goa, and later on the northern Konkan in areas lying between Chaul and Daman, often known as the Northern Province. With the occupation of Bardeza and Salcete in Goa in 1543,[62] the Portuguese claimed considerable agrarian space to bank upon for feeding their population in the power centre. Simultaneously, the Portuguese authorities encouraged Portuguese individuals to settle down in the long stretch of land lying between Chaul and Daman and to resort to agriculture.

Though Portuguese settlers were in Chaul from 1521 onwards, when the governor Diogo Lopes de Sequeira built a fortress there,[63] and in Bassein since 1534,[64] the process towards land adventurism in this area commenced only after the victory of the Portuguese in lifting the siege the Ottoman Turks laid on the city of Diu in 1546. The Portuguese viceroy Dom João de Castro liberally granted land to many Portuguese individuals including the settlers of Cochin and Goa, who risked their lives during the siege and who had supported the *Estado* with men and material.[65] In fact, he had taken about 1,500 men from these urban centres to Diu on 20 September 1546 to confront the Ottomans, and on gaining victory, these participants were rewarded either with commercial voyages or with landed property.[66] Land in the Northern Province was rented out to the Portuguese individuals as a form of incentive for the services rendered and some of them were given on lease entire villages and islands, where they could resort to agricultural activities. With this the donatorial-captaincy (*foreiro*) system of colonization (which the Portuguese had resorted to Brazil in the 1530s) was introduced for the first time in India in their Northern Province. The Portuguese holders of *foreiro* were in fact given land on a quit-rent basis which was the paying of rent at one go, and the tenure could stretch to a couple of years and could be renewed. Technically, this land could not be sold or leased since it was under the possession of the crown, and it could not be divided among the sons of the landlord.[67] The tenure of the land given under the *foreiro* system varied from place to place and usually it went up to 30 years. However later, for want of reliable land records, the landholders used to get it transferred to their successors.[68]

The donees were to live in the city, maintaining a household, and must have a horse (sometimes two) and guns, procured by the returns from the land.[69] Under the donatorial system the Portuguese authorities wanted to ensure that (a) sufficient Portuguese civil population in their cities like Bassein and Daman in the Northern Province; (b) security and defence of the Portuguese possessions against the background of frequent attacks from the Marathas, the Siddhis and the Adil Shahis; and (c) sufficient income to the *Estado* in the form of rents. During the period between 1576 and 1596 a number of fiefs were allotted to Portuguese people in the Northern Province, who later resorted to sub-infeudation. A large portion of the island of Bombay was the property of the family of Garcia de Orta.[70]

With the dwindling of Portuguese trade in the seventeenth century, and with the frequent blockades on the navigational lines of the Portuguese by the Dutch and the English, there was a shift of policy among the Portuguese from mercantilism to land adventurism. There was a great flow of Portuguese population to the Northern Province in the seventeenth century, when most of the Portuguese possessions were in financial trouble. Thanks to the increasing flow of people, several settlements with perceptible Portuguese presence appeared in Karanja, Bombay, Bandra, Trindade, Pare, Thana, Palle, Nirmal, Agashi, Mahim, Tarapur, Dhanu, Salsette, Solgao, Hedad, Kaman, Anjer, Panchnad, Kairna, Shahbaj and Bassein; however, the greatest among them was Bassein, which was also the capital of the Northern Province.[71]

When trade became difficult, landed property in Northern Province became a major source of revenue for the Portuguese crown, with about 1,61,274 *xerafins* from Bassein alone in the year 1682.[72] Though a considerable amount of their wealth was appropriated by the Portuguese state in the form of rents, the Portuguese landholders by residing in the cities of Bassein or Daman or Chaul pumped a significant share of their agrarian surplus from their holdings in Northern Province into their urban habitat, where it was used for architecturally articulating the image of their status and the power that they wielded. Most of their settlements were developed as highly visually impressive urban centres. Around the 1630s there were about 400 Portuguese *casados* in Bassein with several *fidalgos* (nobles) as well as 300 rich indigenous Christians each having attendants of three or four black slaves and several local serfs, as per the account of Antonio Boccaro.[73] With immense wealth flowing from the agrarian space of the Northern Province, many used to take the title of noble (Dom) and emulated aristocratic practices, probably for compensating the loss of social status that they suffered under dwindling trade and for creating a new social meaning for themselves. Manuel Godinho later writes in the middle of the seventeenth century that 'there were in Bassein so many people of both sexes entitled to be addressed as "Dom" that the city itself came to be called "Dom Baçaim".'[74]

Though the Chinese and the Portuguese reached India from two different directions, they also exerted two different types of impact on India. The Chinese were basically traders and their expeditions were principally for making the Indians participate in their tributary trade and probably to create a favourable atmosphere for their commerce on Indian shores. The Portuguese too came initially as traders, but the long distance from their homeland compelled them to have a territory based activity and preferential treatment in Indian markets, which they were compelled to secure with the help of weapons of war. Eventually their desire to establish royal monopoly over the Indian Ocean trade led to violence and war. They had to resort to several control mechanisms like the erection of a chain of fortresses at commercially strategic centres, reinforced by the *cartaz*-system and the armada patrolling the coasts.

In this process, interestingly, the key commercial centres frequented by Cheng Ho were the major locations where the Portuguese established their strongholds. In other words the Portuguese developed devices and mechanisms needed for their power exercise and domination following the trails of the Chinese sailor Cheng Ho. The fact that João de Barros, Gaspar Correia, Fernão Lopes de Castanheda and Garcia de Orta[75] referred considerably to the Chinese voyages of the fifteenth century, suggests that the information about the places visited by Cheng Ho must have played a vital role in shaping the Portuguese policies and attitudes towards the various locations, regions and commercial centres of maritime India. Very seldom did the Portuguese deviate from the trails traversed by Cheng Ho, while setting up their commercial and military establishments in India. This fact gives the impression that Cheng Ho's voyages of the fifteenth century provided an informational base for the Portuguese to build up their commercial empire with its nodal points stretched to the centres frequented earlier by Cheng Ho.

However, the Portuguese managed to establish considerable dominance in the Indian Ocean for a relatively long span of time, unlike the Chinese. This was mainly because of the pattern of expansion that they resorted to in India. The official expansion that was carried out initially on the west coast of India had all the tools and devices of power exercise for establishing their dominance in the Arabian Sea. However, these devices eventually became bereft of actual substance of power, due to the corruption of the officials, maladministration and for want of timely updating of technology and lack of funds. At such junctures, the mercantile settlements, on both the coasts, pumped in resources to sustain the imperial edifice of the *Estado* in times of crisis. The role played by the *Padroado* institutions and personnel in incorporating the diverse mercantile settlements of the Portuguese with the *Etado* fabric cannot be underestimated. The renegades who used to go into interior places located farther away from the Portuguese power centres on the west coast, though appearing to be anti-Portuguese in their attitude, were in fact links for the trade of the *casados* who connected the official domain with the unofficial realms. When the mercantile wealth diminished in the seventeenth century, it was the agrarian surplus from the Northern Province that sustained the power image of the Portuguese for a considerable period of time. Though the actual content of Portuguese power varied from place to place and from eco-zone to eco-zone, they managed to give outwardly the impression that they were the masters of Indian waters, who the Indians feared till the arrival of the Dutch, as well as the English, in the second half of the seventeenth century, and by the Marathas in the eighteenth century.

NOTES

1. Roderich Ptak, *China, the Portuguese and the Nanyang: Oceans and Routes, Regions and Trades (c. 1000-1600)*, Ashgate 2004; idem, 'China and Portugal at Sea: The Early Ming Trading system and the Estado da India Compared', *The Asian Seas 1500-1800: Local Societies, European Expansion and the Portuguese, Revista de Cultura*, vol. I, ano V, 1991; see also Roderich Ptak, 'Ming Maritime Trade to Southeast Asia, 1368-1567: Visions of a "System"', in *From the Mediterranean to the China Sea: Miscellaneous Notes*, ed. Claude Guillot, Denys Lombard and Roderich Ptak, vol. 7, Wiesbaden, 1998, pp. 157-91.

2. For details on the trade routes between India and China, see Haraprasad Ray, *Trade and Trade Routes between India and China, c.140 BC–AD 1500*, Kolkata, 2003.

3. H. Giles, *The Travels of Fa-Hsien*, Cambridge, 1923, pp. 65-83; James Legge, *A Record of Buddhistic Kingdoms: Being an Account by the Chinese Monk Fa-Hien of his Travels in India and Ceylon (AD 399-414) in search of the Buddhist Books of Discipline*, New York, 1965, chap. XL.

4. Sally Hovey Wriggins, *Xuanzang: A Buddhist Pilgrim on the Silk Road*, Westview Press, 1996.

5. I-Tsing, *A Record of the Buddhist Religion: As Practised in India and the Malay Archipelago (AD 671-695)*, tran. J. Takakusu, New Delhi, 2005.

6. George F. Hourani, *Arab Seafaring in the Indian Ocean in Ancient and Early Medieval Times*, Princeton, 1951, pp. 70-4.

7. Ibid., pp. 60-80.

8. See for details, S.D. Goitein, *Letters of Medieval Jewish Traders*, Princeton, 1973; S.D. Goitein, *A Mediterranean Society*, 5 vols, Berkeley, 1967-98; S.D. Goitein, *Jews and Arabs: Their Contacts through the Ages*, New York, 1964.

9. Pius Malekandathil, 'The Impact of Indian Ocean Trade on the Economy and Politics of Early Medieval Goa (c.8-15c.)', *Deccan Studies*, vol. II, no. 1, January-June 2004, pp. 17-22.

10. Janet L. Abu-Lughod, *Before European Hegemony: The World System AD 1250-1350*, Oxford, 1991, p. 268.

11. K.A. Nilakanta Sastri, *The Cholas*, Madras, 1955, pp. 603-10; K.R. Kenneth Hall, *Trade and Statecraft in the Age of the Cholas*, Delhi, 1980.

12. George W. Spencer, *The Politics of Expansion—The Cola Conquests of Sri Lanka and Srivijaya*, Madras, 1983.

13. Burton Stein, 'South India' in *The Cambridge Economic History of India*, ed. Tapan Raychaudhuri and Irfan Habib, vol. I, Cambridge, 1982, pp. 14-42.

14. K.A. Nilakanta Sastri, *The Cholas*, p. 219.

15. Tansen Sen, 'Maritime Contacts between China and the Chola Kingdom (AD 850-1279)', in *Mariners, Merchants and Oceans: Studies in Maritime History*, ed. K.S. Mathew, New Delhi, 1995, pp. 27-8.

16. Ibid., pp. 28-9.

17. Tansen Sen, 'Maritime Contacts between China and the Cola Kingdom', pp. 35-6; for another perspective see George W. Spencer, *The Politics of*

Expansion—The Cola Conquests of Sri Lanka and Srivijay; K.A. Nilakanta Sastri, *The Cholas* , pp. 183, 199-200, 211-18, 252-3.

18. See Haraprasad Ray, 'Historical Contacts between Quilon and China', in *The Portuguese, Indian Ocean and the European Bridgeheads: Festschrift in Honour of Prof. K.S. Mathew*, ed. Pius Malekandathil and Jamal Mohammed, Lisbon, 2001, pp. 386-8.

19. W.W. Rockhill, 'Notes on the Relations and Trade of China with the Eastern Archipelago and the Coast of Indian Ocean during the Fourteenth Century', *T'oung Pao*, vol. XVI, 1915', pp. 437-8. Rockhill suggests that Yeh-li-kowen could be the Nestorian Christians. See ibid., p. 437; the attempt to identify Wu-tsa-erh-sa-lima is made by the author.

20. Ibid., pp. 437-8.

21. Rockhill, 'Notes on the Relations and Trade of China with the Eastern Archipelago and the Coast', pp. 425-6.

22. L. Edward Dreyer, *Zheng He: China and the Oceans in the Early Ming, 1405–1433 (Library of World Biography Series)*, London, Longman, 2006, pp. 122-4; K.N. Chaudhuri, *Trade and Civilization in the Indian Ocean: An Economic History from the Rise of Islam to 1750*, New Delhi, 1985, p. 60.

23. See Roderich Ptak, 'China and Portugal at Sea: The Early Ming Trading system and the Estado da India Compared', *The Asian Seas 1500-1800*, pp. 23-4.

24. W.W. Rockhill, 'Notes on the Relations and Trade of China with the Eastern Archipelago and the Coast of the Indian Ocean during the Fourteenth Century', part II, *T'oung Pao*, 2nd series, vol. 16, no.1, March, 1915, p. 84.

25. Ibid., p. 83.

26. Ibid., p. 80.

27. Ibid., p. 81. There are others who view that the first voyage of Cheng Ho was during the period between 1405 and 1407, when he visited the major countries of the South-East Asian archipelago, like Champa, Java, Palembang, Malacca, Sumatra, Lambri (Sumatra), Ceylon in South Asia and the Indian ports of Quilon, Cochin as well as Calicut. According to them the second voyage was between 1407 and 1409, when he visited Champa, Java, Siam, Cochin and Ceylon. They maintain that the third voyage was during the period between 1409 and 1411, when he visited Champa, Java, Malacca, Sumatra, Ceylon, Quilon, Cochin, Calicut, Siam, Lambri and Kayal. During his fourth voyage (1413-15), a large number of countries were visited by him like Champa, Java, Palembang, Malacca, Sumatra, Bengal, Ceylon, Cochin, Calicut, Kayal, Pahang, Kelantan, Aru, Lambri, Hormuz, Maldives, Mogadishu, Melinde, Aden, Muscat and Dhufar (Arabia). In the fifth voyage (1416-19) Champa, Pahang, Java, Malacca, Sumatra, Lambri, Ceylon, Cochin, Calicut, Hormuz, Maldives, Mogadishu, Brawa, Malindi and Aden were his major destinations. Cheng Ho's vessels of the sixth voyage (1421-2) visited mostly the ports of the Persian Gulf like Hormuz, and of the Arabian peninsula as well as east Africa. In the last voyage (1430-3), the major destinations were Champa, Java, Palembang, Malacca, Sumatra, Ceylon, Calicut, Hormuz, etc.

28. W.W. Rockhill, 'Notes on the Relations and Trade of China with the Eastern Archipelago and the Coast of the Indian Ocean during the Fourteenth Century', part II, *T'oung Pao*, 2nd series, vol. 16, no. 1, March 1915, pp. 75, 82.

29. See Ma Huan, Ying Yai Sheng lan 12-'Kochih' as translated by W.W. Rockhill, 'Notes on the Relations and Trade of China with Eastern Archipelago and the Coast of Indian Ocean during the Fourteenth Century', *T'oung Pao*, 2nd series, vol. XVI, part IV, October 1915, pp. 435-67; Fei Hsin, *Hsin Ch'a Sheng lan 30*, 'Kochih', in as translated by W.W. Rockhill, 'Notes on the Relations and Trade of China with Eastern Archipelago and the Coast of Indian Ocean during the Fourteenth Century', *T'oung Pao*, vol. XVI, 1915, p. 452.

30. M.R. Tarafdar, 'Trade and Society in Early Medieval Bengal', *The Indian Historical Review*, vol. IV, no. 2, 1978, pp. 274-86; B. Schrieke, *Indonesian Sociological Studies*, part I, The Hague, pp. 9-15; M.A.P. Meilink-Roelofsz, *Asian Trade and European Influence in the Indonesian Archipelago Between 1500 and about 1630*, The Hague, 1962, pp. 15, 18-21.

31. For a study on Cheng Ho's activities in the Bay of Bengal see Haraprasad Ray, *Trade and Diplomacy in India-China Relations: A Study of Bengal in the Fifteenth Century*, New Delhi, 1993.

32. W.W. Rockhill, 'Notes on the Relations and Trade of China with the Eastern Archipelago and the Coast of the Indian Ocean during the Fourteenth Century', part II, *T'oung Pao*, 2nd series, vol. 16, no. 1, March 1915, p. 81.

33. For a detailed discussion on the pattern of Portuguese expansion in the East, see Luis Filipe Thomaz, *De Ceuta a Timor*, Liboa, 1994.

34. Gaspar Correia, *Lendas da India*, tom. I, cap. IV, Lisboa, 1921, pp. 393-5.

35. ANTT, Gavetas, 14, Maço 3, doc.14; Gaspar Correia, *Lendas da India*, tom. I, cap. XV, pp. 625-33; cap. XVI, pp. 633-7.

36. Gaspar Correia, *Lendas da India*, tom. I, pp. 583, 728, 784; Sanjay Subrahmaniam, *The Portuguese Empire in Asia 1500-1700: A Political and Economic History*, London, 1993, p. 72; Fernão Lopes Castanheda, *Historia do Descobrimento e Conquista da India pelos Portugueses*, liv. I, Coimbra, 1924, pp. 226-8. Later Anjediva was abandoned in 1507 and Kilwa in 1512.

37. João de Barros, *Asia. Dos feitos que os Portugueses fizeram no Descobrimento e Conquista dos Mares e Terras do Oriente*, decada II, part ii, Lisboa, 1973, pp. 40 ff.

38. Duarte Barbosa, *The Book of Duarte Barbosa: An Account of the Countries Bordering on the Indian Ocean and their Inhabitants*, tran. Mansel Longworth Dames, vol. I, Nendeln, 1967, p. 59.

39. R.A. de Bulhão Pato ed., *Cartas de Affonso de Albuquerque seguidas de documentos que as elucidam*, tom. I, Lisboa, 1884, pp. 21 ff; Diogo do Couto, *Da Asia dos feitos que os Portuguezes fizeram na Conquista e Descobrimento das Terras e Mares do Oriente*, decada IV, liv. X, cap. iv, Lisboa, 1973, p. 426.

40. Vitorino Magalhães Godinho, *Os Descobrimentos e a Economia Mundial*, vol. III, Lisboa, 1982, p. 34.

41. Gaspar Correia, *Lendas da India*, tom. II, p. 577.

42. Antonio Silva Rego, *Documentação para a Historia das Missões do Padroado Português do Oriente*, vol. I, Liboa, 1949, pp. 352-4.

43. S.S. Pissurlencar, *Regimento das Fortalezas da India*, Bastora/Goa, 1951, p. 302; Gaspar Correia, *Lendas da India*, tom. II, p. 689.

44. Luis Filipe Thomaz, *A questão da pimento em meados do seculo XVI. Um debate politico do governo de D.João de Castro*, Lisboa, 1998, p. 79.

45. Artur Teodoro de Matos, ed., *O Tombo de Damão 1592*, Lisboa, 2001, p. 295.

46. S.S. Pissurlencar, *Regimento das Fortalezas da India*, p. 494.

47. Antonio Bocarro, *Livro das Plantas de todas as fortalezas, cidades e povoações do Estado da India Oriental*, vol. II, transcrição de Isabel, Lisboa, 1868, p. 313.

48. Diogo do Couto, *Da Asia dos feitos que os Portuguezes fizeram na Conquista e Descobrimento das Terras e Mares do Oriente*, decada VIII, cap. xxxii, pp. 275-81.

49. M.N. Pearson, *Merchants and Rulers in Gujarat, the Response to the Portuguese in the Sixteenth Century*, London, 1976, pp. 44-5; João de Barros, decada I, part I, p. 181.

50. Though the *cartaz* system was introduced from 1502 onwards, the traders who collaborated with the Portuguese initially were conceded greater amount of freedom in the movement of commodities within Asia, as a mechanism to ensure their cooperation. However, only after 1509 against the background of the prevailing imperial designs chalked out by Afonso Albuquerque that the coastal patrolling and rigorous checking of *cartaz* seem to have become frequent. Consequently, all the native ships had to take *cartazes* which contained such details as the name of the vessel and of the captain, the nature of the cargo, its origin and destination as well as the name of the authority issuing the *cartaz*. For details, see Pius Malekandathil, *Portuguese Cochin and the Maritime Trade of India*, pp. 125-6; 220-1; Luis Filipe Thomaz, 'Portuguese Control on the Arabian Sea and the Bay of Begal: A Comparative Study,' *Commerce and Culture in the Bay of Bengal*, ed., Om Prakash and Denys Lombard, Delhi, 1999.

51. Letter of Francisco de Souza to the king, Cannanore dated 14 January 1535, in *As Gavetas da Torre do Tombo*, vol. X, Lisboa, 1974, pp. 606-9.

52. For details on the early Portuguese mercantile settlements on the Coromandel coast, see S. Jeyaseela Stephen, *Portuguese in the Tamil Coast: Historical Explorations· in Commerce and Culture, 1507-1749*, Pondicherry, 1998; S. Jeyaseela Stephen, *The Coromandel Coast and its Hinterland: Economy, Society and Political System, 1500-1600*, New Delhi, 1997; Sanjay Subrahmanyam, *Improvising Empire: Portuguese Trade and Settlement in the Bay of Bengal, 1500-1700*, Delhi 1990.

53. For details on the erection of the diocese of Goa and Cochin, see Casimiro Christovão de Nazareth, *Mitras Lusitanas no Oriente: Catalogo dos Prelados da Igreja Metropolitana e Primacial de Goa e das Dioceses Suffraganeas*, Lisboa, 1894, pp. 15-22; 40-1; for details of the papal bull, see BNL, Fundo Geral, cod. no. 737, *Erecção da Villa em Cidade (de Cochim), Creação do bispado a pedido de D. Sebastião 1557*, fol. 273.

54. It was erected chiefly for the lands of the Nayak, Tanjore, Nagapattinam, Masulipattainam, Bengal and Tennasserim. Casimiro Christovão de Nazareth,

Mitras Lusitanas no Oriente: Catalogo dos Prelados da Igreja Metropolitana e Primacial de Goa e das Dioceses Suffraganeas, p. 95.

55. For details on these Milanese renegade artillerists, see George Percy Badger, ed., *The Travels of Ludovico di Varthema in Egypt, Syria, Arabia Deserta and Arabia Felix in Persia, India and Ethiopia: AD 1503 to 1518*, New York, 1863, p. 260; O.K. Nambiar, *The Kunjalis: Admirals of Calicut*, London, 1963, pp. 49-51.

56. Elaine Sanceau, *Colecção de São Lourenço*, vol. II, p. 309.

57. Genevieve Bouchon and Luis Filippe Thomaz, eds., *Voyage dans les deltas du Gange et de L'Irraouaddy, 1521*, Paris, 1988, p. 51.

58. Bibliotheca Nacional de Lisboa, *Fundo Geral*, 299, fol. 1-41v; Georg Schurhammer, *Die Zeitgenössischen Quellen zur Geschichte Portugiesisch-Asiens und seiner Nachbarländer zur Zeit des Hl.Franz Xaver (1538-1552)*, Rome, 1962, pp. 16, 17; Teresa Albuquerque, *Bassein: The Portuguese Interlude*, Mumbai, 2004, p. 14.

59. See Joseph Thekkedath, *History of Christianity in India*, vol. II, Bangalore, 1988, pp. 299, 419. In Bijapur there were thousands of Portuguese renegades who fled from Goa at different time points. Ibid., p. 419.

60. G.V. Scammell, 'European Exiles, Renegades and Outlaws and the Maritime Economy of Asia, *c.*1500-1750', in *Mariners, Merchants and Oceans: Studies in Maritime History*, ed. K.S. Mathew, New Delhi, 1995, p. 128.

61. Afzal Ahmad, *Portuguese Diplomatic Relations with South-West Indian States in the Seventeenth Century (1600-1663)*, Ph.D. thesis submitted to the Department of Portuguese and Brazilian Studies, King's College, University of London, 2005, p.117; Pandurang S.S. Pissurlencar, *Portugues e Marathas*, in Boletim de Vasco da Gama, 1926-7, no.1, pp. 48-98; no.2, pp. 66-92.

62. In 1543 the Governor Martim Affonso obtained from the Adil Shah the perpetual donation of Salcete and Bardez to the Portuguese crown.

63. Gaspar Correia, *Lendas da India*, tom. II, pp. 659-61.

64. S.S. Pissurlencar, *Regimento das Fortalezas da India*, Bastora/Goa, 1951, p. 302; Gaspar Correia, *Lendas da India*, tom. II, p. 689.

65. For details, see Antonio Baião, *Historia Quinhentista (inedita) do Segundo cerco de Dio*, Coimbra, 1927.

66. See Bibliotheca do Palacio da Ajuda, *Livro das Merces que fez D.João de Castro*, 51-8-46; Antonio Baião, *Historia Quinhentista (inedita) do Segundo cerco de Dio*, p. 298.

67. R.J. Barendse, *The Arabian Seas: The Indian Ocean World of the Seventeenth Century*, New Delhi, 2002, p. 55. See also Teotonio R. de Souza, 'North-South in the Estado da India', *Mare Liberum*, numero 9, Julho 1995, pp. 454-5.

68. R.J. Barendse, *The Arabian Seas*, pp. 355-6.

69. Livia Baptista de Souza Ferrão, 'Tenants, Rents and Revenues from Daman in the late 16th Century', *Mare Liberum*, no. 9, Julho 1995, pp. 140-1.

70. R.J. Barendse, *The Arabian Seas*, p. 329.

71. Joseph Thekkedath, *History of Christianity in India*, vol. II, pp. 366-88.

72. R.J. Barendse, *The Arabian Seas*, p. 322.

73. Antonio Boccaro, *Livro das Plantas de todas as fortalezas, cidades e povoações do Estado da India Oriental*, vol. II, transcrição de Isabel, Lisboa, 1992.

74. John Correia-Afonso, ed., *Intrepid Itinerant: Manuel Godinho and His Journey from India to Portugal in 1663*, Bombay, 1990, pp. 30-1.

75. João de Barros, *Asia. Dos feitos que os Portugueses fizeram no Descobrimento eConquista dos Mares e Terras do Oriente*, decadas I-IV, Lisboa, 1973; Fernão Lopes Castanheda, *Historia do Descobrimento e Conquista da India pelos Portugueses*, 4 vols., Coimbra, 1924-33; Gaspar Correia, *Lendas da India*, 4 vols. in 8 parts, Coimbra, 1921-5; Garcia da Orta, *Coloquios dos simples e drogas da India*, 2 vols., Lisboa, 1977.

 CHAPTER FIVE

Maritime Polity and a Mercantile State: An Analysis of the Political Dynamics of Kerala, 1500-1663

The process of state formation and the nature of power structure in different parts of Kerala underwent a considerably significant change following the intervention of the Europeans and familiarization with their ideas as well as with their tools of power exercise. The Europeans entered Kerala at a time when its principal maritime exchange centres like Cannanore, Calicut, Cochin and Quilon were involved in the process of emerging as the new power centres by making gains from their vibrant maritime trade. Among them, Calicut was taking a decisive turn almost towards the direction of a pan-Kerala dimension with the increasing political and expansionist moves of the Zamorin. However, the intervention of the Europeans arrested the state-formation moves of the Zamorin, who had to be satisfied with the territories north of Cochin, a development which kept the Kerala polity in a fragmented state for a considerable period of time.

Following the multiple facets of these developments, different types of power structures appeared in Kerala, each varying from the other depending upon the eco-systems in which the locus of power was fixed, and on the ability of the rulers to accumulate surplus for strengthening their hands. The geophysical space, comprising principally the maritime centres of exchange of the littoral, with or without its spice producing hinterland, exhibited a certain type of state formation, while the predominantly low-lying paddy

*This essay was presented at the National Seminar on *Kerala History* organized by Kerala Council of Historical Research, Trivandrum, 16-18 March 2006. It is a revised version of the paper published under the title 'Maritime Malabar and a Mercantile State: Polity and State Formation in Malabar under the Portuguese', in *Maritime Malabar and the Europeans: 1498-1962,* ed. K.S. Mathew, Gurgaon, 2003, pp. 197-228.

cultivating regions exhibited another type of formation as far as their power structures were concerned. The forest zone, from where hill produce were collected in plenty, both for domestic as well as international trade, remained either as a separate entity having its own unique political formation or as a part of the political configuration of the central upland regions, depending upon their economic utility for the rulers of the latter. With the advent of the Europeans, the political units exercising control and power over maritime centres of exchange began to take precedence over the political units controlling low lying paddy cultivation zones, eventually making the 'maritime states'[1] much more powerful than the 'inland states'.

State formation of medieval Kerala had been a theme of great interest among academicians since the 1970s and several scholars like M.G.S. Narayanan,[2] Kesavan Veluthat[3] and K.N. Ganesh[4] had already discussed in detail the nature and different aspects of state formation in medieval Kerala. The various aspects of the secondary and tertiary stages of state formation in Kerala were examined by M.R. Raghava Varier,[5] by analysing the Svarupam organization of the medieval period. Wielding of power and formation of state structures in Kerala on mercantilist lines following the Portuguese intervention has already been highlighted in one of our earlier papers.[6] However, little work has been done to bring out the various aspects of state formation and political activity that appeared in Kerala as a response to the early European expansion in the Indian Ocean regions. The central purpose of this chapter is to see the dynamics behind the process of state formation, as well as political activities experienced in Kerala after the arrival of the early Europeans, and to see how far the European challenges necessitated a reshaping of the existing power structures. This is made clear by focussing on two aspects: on the one hand, by analysing the processes and mechanisms by which the power centres were shifted from one zone to another effecting a shift in the core area of political activity, and also by analysing the diverse devices and tools used for making power visible in these respective zones. On the other hand, by examining the channels and devices by which the individual units of local power got linked with the networks of world systems, making the political activity of Kerala intrinsically connected with global developments.

HISTORICAL SETTING: EVOLUTION OF A
POLITICAL EDIFICE OUT OF RUINS

Following the collapse of the Kulasekharas of Mahodayapuram, there appeared a wide variety of political structures and power exercising units in various parts of Kerala, with different organizational forms and nomenclatures like *svarūpams*, *nātuvāḷis*, *dēsavāḷis*, *kaimals*, *karthas*, etc., all indicating the fragmenting nature of central authority.[7] Most of them had an agrarian base, deriving resources predominantly from the low-lying paddy cultivating regions. The strength of these diverse political units and their superiority/ inferiority relationship depended greatly upon their ability in mobilizing wealth from paddy fields, the *cērikkal* land in particular, as well as from *parambu* upland areas of food and cash crops.[8] However, with the revitalization of trade principally by the Muslim merchants (who, by the thirteenth century, had already become an important commercial group capable of operating independently of Christian and Jewish guilds)[9] in the thirteenth and fourteenth centuries, the maritime exchange centres in Kerala began to get activated, leading to intensification of exchange related activities in several nodal centres of the coastal belt. Consequently, by the middle of the fourteenth century, a new phenomenon characterized by the shifting of the headquarters of rulers from inland agrarian regions to maritime centres of exchange started appearing in Kerala in the attempt to carve out independent states with the gains accruing from trade. The most important among them was the transfer of the royal residence of the Nediyirappu Svarupam from the inland pocket of Nediyirappu in Ernad (Malappuram District) to the maritime trade centre of Calicut, which the Zamorin captured from the ruler of Polanadu, evidently with an eye to earn profit from trade.[10] In fact, the emergence of Calicut as the principal port strengthened by a chain of satellite ports is traceable to the developments that took place in international trade routes following the collapse of Baghdad. With the Mongol attack on the Baghdad Caliphate (1258), the international trade emanating from the Persian Gulf and terminating in China got blocked, as a result of which the flow of commodities to Quilon located on this trade route declined, inflicting a severe blow on the state formation ventures of the Venadu rulers. However, the Mamluks of Egypt, who defeated the Mongols at Ain Jalut in 1260, used this crisis phase as an opportunity to develop another international trade route keeping Cairo as the basis, whose focal areas of relations were the northern ports of Kerala, including Calicut, which so far had been in twilight. This attempt of the Mamluk rulers of Egypt carried out with the help of Al-Karimi traders of Cairo stimulated the Calicut-oriented commercial operations from the ports of the Red Sea. The entrepreneurial groups of the Arab/Al-Karimi traders of Cairo gradually settled down in the city for the furtherance of their trade, which in turn favoured the rise of Calicut as a prominent exchange centre in the Indian Ocean region. Coinciding with these developments and particularly with a view to getting a share from its maritime trade and getting it transferred for his state building ventures, the Zamorin shifted his headquarters from the inland agrarian space to the evolving trade centre of Calicut.[11]

After having secured a permanent base for the exercise of power at a place that ensured regular flow of wealth from trade, the Zamorin consolidated his political and commercial position in Kerala with the help of Arab/Al-Karimi merchants. He realized that the fragmented polity of Kerala represented by petty kingdoms and chiefdoms, which in fact was the debris of the Kulasekahara's political edifice, was the greatest divisive force against which he had to fight for realizing the target of a strong state structure. With the help of the Muslim mercantile groups, the Zamorin started extending his power southwards and conquered the neighbouring principalities of Nilambur, Manjeri, Malapuram and Kottakkal. Subsequently, the Zamorin succeeded in wresting away state rights and powers from these local chieftains and amalgamated them for the process of making a territorial state centred around Calicut, besides making them units of the hinterland for the procurement of spices. These territorial amalgamations were strengthened by a cultural process linked with Mamankam, which turned out to be a state building mechanism with Zamorin's occupation of Tirunavai (located on the banks of Bharatapuzha) from the Valluvanad ruler. The acquisition of the privilege of presiding over the Mamankam or Pan-Kerala festival (which was held once in every 12 years) ensured the Zamorin of a relative pan-Kerala identity, besides conferring on him the legitimacy and official sanction required for the expansion of his state.[12]

Meanwhile another local chief also started moving from an inland agrarian space to the maritime exchange centre of Cochin, which emerged in 1341 following the great flood in Periyar.[13] It was none other than the chief of the Perumpadappu Svarupam, who was moving from Vanneri down to the south to escape from the attacks of the Zamorin. First, he moved over to Mahodayapuram, from where he proceeded further to Cochin around 1405.[14] The pattern of his movement clearly suggests that his shifting of capital from Vanneri to the maritime trade centres (at first to Mahodayapuram, and later to Cochin) was necessitated not only by the conquests of the Zamorin alone, but also by his deeper desire to appropriate profit from maritime trade for the purpose of building up a strong state structure that could counter the expansionist moves of the Zamorin.[15] Cochin's hectic commercial contacts including those with the Ming China (paved by Cheng Ho's repeated voyages)[16] and the Arab world[17] offered the resources needed for such a political move of the Perumpadappu Svarupam.

By the end of the fifteenth century there was a development evolving in Cannanore to carve out a petty maritime state structure under the Mamale as separate and distinct from Kolathunad, though its political fruition came only in the sixteenth century.[18] Meanwhile, in the south, the ruler of Quilon, whose state power also depended on the returns from its port maintained a petty kingdom, whose smallness was greatly compensated by its rich spice producing hinterland.[19] In the first case, with the intensification of commerce, the leader of Cannanore Muslims began to accumulate more and more power and appropriate administrative rights, which initiated the process of his transition from mercantile stature to quasi-kingly stature.[20] However, in Quilon the mercantile group of St. Thomas Christians, who though they were greatly weakened by the shift of bulk trade to Calicut, continued to collaborate with the native ruler as allies in state formation.[21]

In fact, on the eve of the Portuguese arrival there were twofold developments, as far as the polity of Kerala was concerned: on the one hand, there was the development towards the formation of 'the maritime state units' with resource bases located in maritime centres of exchange, but empowered by a sizeable spice producing hinterland. These 'maritime state units' were by now increasingly taking precedence over their land-locked counterparts in the inland part of Malabar. On the other hand, among these different power units on the maritime belt, Calicut was slowly emerging as a relatively full-fledged state entity,[22] appropriating and accumulating power and authority from the neighbouring principalities by weapons of war and tools of culture.

INITIAL FLUIDITY OF THE PORTUGUESE STATE
AND THE RESPONSE OF KERALA POLITY

The first Portuguese vessels visited the ports of Kerala for the purpose of trade only;[23] but they carried with them the strong machineries of a mercantile state that had evolved since the battle of Aljubarrota (1385), in which the divisive forces of old nobility and their Castilian allies were exterminated with the help of a rising middle class engaged in trade.[24] In the political structure, which the Portuguese developed, the state itself functioned as a trader.[25] During the first seven years the Portuguese artilleries and guns that opened the gates of Indian markets for their commerce, were only exterior manifestations of a fluid and imperceptible state that appeared in Kerala as an appendage of the Lisbon administration. In fact, initially, the Zamorin and his Muslim allies were fighting against this fluid structure, whose strength and weakness were beyond their perception and calculation. The site for the Portuguese factory, which they obtained from the king of Cochin in 1500,[26] was the base for their initial economic operations and a feeble nucleus for their emerging power in India. During the first seven years, even this fluid political structure of the Portuguese was visible only at the time of the arrival of annual Portuguese fleet that entered Indian waters principally for trade. However, its visibility assumed a definite and concrete form with the helping hand extended in times of emergency by the king of Cochin, between whom and the Portuguese there emerged reciprocal ties of protection and mutual support.[27] From Cochin, the roots of the expanding Lusitanian state were eventually penetrating into the soil of Quilon and Cannanore,[28] whose local rulers hoped that trade with the Portuguese would empower them for economic and political assertion. In fact, however, they ended in becoming secondary politico-economic feeding units for the emerging power structure of the Portuguese, which the Zamorin now looked at with caution and concern.

Realizing the importance and decisive role of guns and artilleries in mercantile wars, the Zamorin sought the help of Milanese renegades to manufacture them for his schemes of war against the expanding state of the Portuguese.[29] In fact, Calicut was the only full-fledged state in the Indian Ocean region at that time that really could apply the brakes and control the penetrating movements of the Portuguese into the region. Calicut's resistance though started regionally in 1500[30] was strengthened in 1502/3 and 1504;[31] however, it took a global dimension in 1509, when the Zamorin's forces joined hands with the Mamluks, the Turks and the Venetians off Diu with a determination to oust the Portuguese from the Asian waters.[32] The forces that came together to fight against the Portuguese in the latter tussle were the principal beneficiaries of the old trade route (Calicut-Aden-Cairo-Alexandria-Venice), which sustained the old world system comprising the Indian Ocean and the eastern Mediterranean.[33] Though outwardly this tussle gave the impression of political conflicts between the Portuguese and the beneficiaries of caravan route trade, in effect it turned out to be a politicized manifestation of the conflict between the old world system and the new world system, in which the commercially oriented power centres of three continents merged in vain to nip the bud of the emerging Portuguese power structure, which represented the new world system. The effect of this conflict was reflected in differing degrees in the economy, society, religion and politics of Kerala.

LOCALIZATION OF POWER AND THE
CONFLICTING FRAMES OF STATE

The structure and form of the Portuguese state (*Estado da India*) that was slowly emerging in India in the beginning of the sixteenth century was almost like that of a political archipelago with connections hidden beneath the surface. The first step towards this was to give permanence to the power so far moving about in fluid form, by setting up fortified headquarters at Cochin with a permanent residing viceroy in 1505. The attempts to localize power were reinforced by erecting armed fortresses in Cannanore, Anjedive and Kilwa.[34] In fact, only by 1510, with the land-oriented expansion of Afonso de Albuquerque, was the extent of the fluid power of the Portuguese solidified into a perceptible territorial entity. Occupation of Goa (1510), Malacca (1511) and Hormuz (1515)[35] defined the territorial limits of the power units that emerged in the form of an archipelago. Frequent shipping and movement of forces of state between these territorial units and the mother country, made this political archipelago take shape within the frames of the emerging world system that appeared following new geographical discoveries. Economic penetrations ensured the circulatory process required for the feeding of this network.

However, the greatest problem that appeared in the process of extending the mercantile state of Portuguese India[36] was that of insufficient population supportive of the state. Afonso de Albuquerque tried to solve this problem by making Portuguese citizens marry Indian women, which would ensure a generation supportive of Portuguese dominance.[37] He was even ready to give permission to the soldiers, the vital apparatus of a state, to forego their profession and get married for achieving a longer goal of ensuring demographic strength. For their sustenance he allotted petty trade, and permitted them to set up shops and manufacturing units including shoe making, baking and tailoring.[38] The viceroys and governors following Albuquerque were in favour of empowering these married Portuguese citizens and for carving out a free space in the eastern part of the Indian Ocean for their commerce.[39] While the corpus of the state of Portuguese India was located principally on the western coast of India, its sponging fingers were extended to the Bay of Bengal and South-East Asia by these *casado* traders, with whose help the Portuguese authorities tried to procure merchandise for Lisbon from the eastern space of the Indian Ocean. By the 1520s the Portuguese *casado* traders emerged as capable of ousting the Muslim mercantile intermediaries from the Indian Ocean trade and eventually turned out to be suppliers of cargo from various Asian marts for Lisbon-bound vessels.[40] Meanwhile, the crown wanted to bring the most profitable strand of Indo-European trade under state control by monopolizing the spice trade and the movement of commodities via the Cape route.[41]

However, the use of Portuguese forces, which was represented by the armed vessels and fortresses, was targeted mainly against the agencies and collaborators of the Zamorin, including the Al-Karimi/*paradesi* Muslim merchants, whose commerce with the Red Sea Mediterranean ports enabled accumulation of wealth and power in Calicut. The strength and power of

Calicut were pruned, and its *paradesi* Muslims including the al-Karimi merchants were made to quit the city[42] by enthroning a pro-Portuguese ruler in Calicut after having poisoned the reigning Zamorin in 1513. The consequent signing of a peace treaty, converted the mighty power of Calicut, at least temporarily, into a feeding satellite political unit for the Portuguese state.[43] Correspondingly, Calicut's economic forces were also held in check and control by lowering the market price of spices at Calicut and keeping it steady and fixed, so as to make it to be on par with that of Cochin and Cannanore.[44] Eventually, with the establishment of fortresses in Cannanore (1508),[45] Quilon (1519),[46] and Cranganore (1536),[47] it seemed as if the entire maritime zone of Malabar was passing on into Lusitanian control, making the territorial units of the Portuguese colonial archipelago appear sizeably significant.

By the middle of the 1520s, the processes involved in state formation took a decisive turn thanks to the changing politico-economic milieu. On the one hand, the increasing pressure on the Marakkar merchants from the Portuguese authorities of the post-Albuquerquian period, who frequently attacked and confiscated Marakkar vessels under the pretext of checking *cartazes*, made many of them incapable of mobilizing enough resources for their commercial ventures and out of this situation the Portuguese *casados* carved out a space for their expanding trade in the Indian Ocean. On the other hand, these estranged Marakkar traders including Kunjali Marakkar shifted their residence and base of operation from Cochin to Calicut by 1524, where their navigational expertise and mercantile resources were promptly utilized by Zamorin for his battles to attack the Lusitanian hegemony from 1525 onwards.[48]

In fact, the relationship between the Zamorin and the Portuguese had already got strained, and in 1525 Calicut reverted to independent political stature cutting relations with the Portuguese.[49] During the interval of twelve years (1513-25), when Calicut remained as a political appendage of the Portuguese state, the entire mechanisms that were earlier operating here for the building up of a unified territorial state came to a standstill. However, with the cessation of ties with the Portuguese, the Zamorin began to give keen attention to the means and ways of exerting his power. He extended instruments of power to the maritime zone by dispatching a regular fleet under Kunjali Marakkar for patrolling the coast, which involved the dual operations of exercise of power and creation of space for conducting trade with the destinations of their choice, the links of which often terminated in the Red Sea and Mediterranean ports.[50] Portuguese pockets of tension in Kerala were identified, and the Zamorin's forces always joined hands with the anti-Portuguese groups, which earned for Calicut the privileged position of being the only parallel state structure existing then in Kerala that could stand on a par with the Portuguese. He eventually expanded the apparatus of state to a wide space of maritime and territorial zones. It was the Marakkar fleet that was engaged in extending the Zamorin's spheres of influence on the western coast as well as on the Pearl Fishery coast till their defeat in Vedalai and Negombo in 1538-9.[51] However, keeping their base in Dharmapattanam, Kunjali Marakkar and his men operated as the dominance-establishing units for the Zamorin in the Indian Ocean. On the land front, the solidified power of Calicut state was easily exteriorized. In fact, the conflicts between Edappilly and Cochin over the island of Cochin (1530s),[52] between Cranganore and Cochin over the temple money of Cranganore (1540-60)[53] as well as that of the Vadakkenkur kingdom and Cochin over the control of Vaduthala and its temple money (1548-52),[54] in which the Portuguese invariably stood for the ruler of Cochin, turned out to be virtual struggles between two states: Calicut and the Portuguese. Other principalities and political units were relatively subverted to the position of feeding political entities to them. However, the king of Cochin was increasingly proclaiming his authority as *Koviladhikarikal* (custodian of temples)[55] to use the temples under his jurisdiction for the formation of state ventures, as in the cases of Cranganore and Vaduthala, where attempts were made to enter into the temples and thus into the jurisdictional boundaries of Cranganore and Vadakkenkur, respectively. It was his intent to augment resources for the expansion of his state. Following this conflict Vadakkenkur, temporarily, and Cranganore permanently, changed sides and began to shape their political activities in conformity with the designs of Calicut.[56]

The ruler of Cochin, whose sudden growth and prosperity was traceable to the commercial activities of the Portuguese, was in no way a silent partner to the mercantile designs of the Lusitanians. Annual *copa* and the golden crown[57] given to the ruler of Cochin, were the frequent silencing tools employed by the Portuguese to win his cooperation. However, the politico-economic developments in his territory, caused mainly by the acceleration of trade with the entry of the Portuguese, were moving towards the direction of forming a quasi-state in Cochin. With the hectic private trading activities of the Portuguese *casado* traders, especially favoured by the Portuguese authorities in the post-Albuquerquian period, large wealth had accumulated in the Portuguese city of Cochin. The king of Cochin wanted to draw a share from the proceeds by way of customs duty as early as 1520s. In 1529 he wrote a letter to the king of Portugal, John III making his claim on the port dues collected from the private traders (a claim raised on the fact that the port of Cochin was situated in his kingdom) saying that it would lessen the burden of his expenditure.[58] The governor Lopo Vaz de Sampayo, who was completely against the sharing of customs duties with the native ruler and who knew very well that concession of such a right would mean ceding of a part of the stately powers, reacted to it by interning the king of Cochin in his own palace.[59] However, in 1530 King John III of Portugal renounced all rights to collect customs duties at Cochin and gave over this right to the native ruler,[60] which later received viceregal confirmations in 1543, 1550 and 1561.[61] With the acquisition of customs right, the ruler of Perumpadappu Svarupam got access to the wealth required for strengthening the instruments of state. Initially, the rate of customs duty collected at Cochin by the native ruler was 6 per cent, which was equivalent to that of Goa and other Portuguese customs houses. Later, in order to attract more trade to Cochin, the king of Cochin reduced the rate to 3.5 per cent for the Portuguese *casado* traders. However, all the non-Portuguese private traders, who had wares destined for Cochin, had to go first to Goa and pay 6 per cent duties there, and only then were allowed to visit Cochin. In fact the native traders involved in Asian trade overcame this situation by entering into side-deals with the *casados* of Cochin, who used to bring the goods of local traders through the customs-house of the Perumpadappu ruler claiming ownership.[62] Nevertheless the lower customs rate charged by the Cochin raja was an attraction not only for the Portuguese *casado* traders, but also for the indigenous merchants, who operated as links in the private trade of the Portuguese, the end-result of which was the emergence of a powerful lobbying group involved in the creation of a parallel commercial network sidelining the *Estado da India* set up. The Portuguese often resorted to increase the customs share partially as a mechanism to please the native ruler on occasions of tensions with him, as for example, in the case when tensions boomed up in the late 1540s on plundering the wealth of Palluruthy temple,[63] etc.

However, in 1583 steps were taken to make the customs rate of Cochin port equivalent to that of Portuguese trade centres (i.e. 6 per cent), which in turn would reduce the evasion of private trade to Cochin and in that way also the amount accruing in the exchequer of the Perumadappu king. Moreover, this agreement also stipulated that all private traders should pay compulsory exit-tax to the Portuguese Treasury.[64] Kesava Rama Varma, the king of Cochin, who wanted to keep a rather lower customs rate (which would invite more traders and in that way more money) than a higher rate and fewer traders, was not at all happy with this arrangement. Nonetheless this deal provoked great popular protest—the most significant pre-modern bourgeoisie uprising in Kerala—in which 15,000 armed men (10,000 people of the land and 5,000 Portuguese) marched into the church of St. John in Cochin to defend their commercial liberties. The agitated crowd including the

Portuguese *casado* traders, who were said to have had the backing of the king, Kesava Rama Varma, even attacked the Portuguese captain in his fort.[65] In the agreement, which was made in 1585, clauses were included to satisfy the demands of the native king and his commercial associates, the Portuguese *casado* traders, by fixing their share at 3.5 per cent.[66]

The annual income for the king of Cochin from the customs, as evidenced from a document of 1605, was 60,000 *pardaos*,[67] which increased to 80,000 *pardaos* in 1612.[68] However, the customs right being handed over to the king of Cochin by the Portuguese was in fact empowering the hands of this local ruler and weakening the integration process targeted in the mercantile state structure of the Lusitanians. The increasing gains from trade made the Perumpadappu king more assertive from the 1520s onwards, which eventually transformed Cochin from the position of a politico-economic feeding unit of the Portuguese state into that of a partner power unit with individual designs. In the seventeenth century, with accumulating immense wealth by way of customs duty from private trade, the king of Cochin emerged as a powerful factor in the Malabar polity often asserting his claims and postulating his interests in the forefront. His move towards greater assertion and independent stature could be seen in his selection of anti-Portuguese Jews like David Levi and Samuel Castiel as councillors.[69] His policy decisions of this period were greatly influenced by these Jewish councillors, under whose instigation he even tried to establish commercial ties with the Dutch in 1618[70] and the ruler of Aceh in 1627[71] to make the political will of Cochin prevail over the extracting tendencies of the Portuguese state. Frequent conflicts between the subjects of the native ruler and the Portuguese broke out against this background of Cochin king's empowerment. As early as 1615 he even started demanding an amount of 14,000 *pardaos* as his share for the cargo taken from other marts to Goa by the residents of the Portuguese city of Cochin,[72] a claim postulated to show that the Portuguese settlement was a part of his territory and its settlers were his subjects. However, the king of Cochin did not want to throw away the yoke of Portuguese power and influence from his territory, as he knew very well that his ability to accumulate stately powers was drawn from the political support and commercial activities of the Portuguese.

Meanwhile, the developments in Kolathunad leading towards the formation of a quasi-state in Cannanore also began at this juncture of intensification of commerce. The initial steps towards the carving out of a nucleus of power in Cannanore were taken by the Muslim merchants of Kolathunad, where the local ruler had already given a great amount of administrative rights and political power to the Muslim *regedor*, Mamale and his successors Poca Amame and Pocaralle. By keeping the Maldives as an integral part of the economic operations of Cannanore, these *regedors* could easily generate wealth from the Cannanore–Maldives–Red Sea trade for setting up infrastructure and diverse apparatus of state in course of time.[73] However, the evolution of the Muslim *regedor* from a merchant to the head of a state became complete by 1545, when Ali Raja (on the assassination of his uncle Pocaralle by Belchior de Souza) came to power and thereby laid the foundation of the Muslim dynasty of the Ali Rajas of Cannanore.[74]

At about the same period, the economy of Travancore, which was till then lying in the twilight zone, started getting stimulated with the increasing commercial activities of the Portuguese private traders within its territory. The Portuguese private traders who used to take commodities to South-East Asia for trade used to stop at the southern nodal points of Travancore, in the sixteenth and seventeenth centuries, both for collection of goods from the markets of Travancore for their further trade, as well as for the sale of copper and other commodities brought from Portugal, and horses imported from Arabia. Thus, a large number of Portuguese traders started concentrating their trade in Travancore, among whom Dom João de Cruz who used to take horses from Cochin for their sale in Travancore in 1536-7 was the prominent one.[75] Their stay in the southern ports, though initially for temporary periods, eventually became longer with their penetration into the markets of Travancore. This in turn activated the economy of Travancore, particularly its trading activities. With the stimulation of commerce, the Travancorean ruler started focusing on its exchange centres and made attempts to control the trade of the region by erecting a fortress in Quilon by the end of the sixteenth century.[76]

Though the Portuguese political will and power had an overwhelming predominance over coastal Malabar, the indigenous rulers controlling the maritime states began to assert themselves emphatically by mobilizing wealth from the maritime exchange centres under their custody, which they in turn transferred for their ventures of state formation and power exercise. In fact, the entire process was linked with two world systems: on the one hand, there was the state of Calicut and the quasi-state of Cannanore that operated within the orbit of the traditional world system, which encompassed the Indian Ocean region and the Red Sea–Mediterranean region.[77] While Calicut operated as a major political entity wielding a considerable amount of power and tools of control in this world system, Cannanore was rather a politico-economic feeding unit for the commercial networks and power structures linked with the traditional world system. On the other hand, there was Cochin that operated as one of the principal state units of the new world system,[78] which emerged following the geographical discoveries integrating the Indian Ocean world economy with the Atlantic world economy. The linkage with this new world system helped the king of Cochin to generate wealth required for setting up various tools and institutions of state. Thus, the principal territorial power units and stately entities, which evolved on the maritime zone of Malabar, represented the two macro-world systems, though their expressions varied on the basis of the evolving global political character.

POLITICAL LINKAGES BETWEEN THE MARITIME POWER UNITS AND
THEIR SATELLITE POWER CENTRES

With the relative empowerment of states or quasi-states linked with maritime centres of exchange in the sixteenth and seventeenth centuries following the accumulation of wealth from trade, on the one hand, the different political units that developed in low-lying paddy cultivating space or in the central upland regions of Kerala by this time (represented by the nomenclatures *nātuvāḷis, dēsavāḷis, kaimals, karthas,* etc.), began to increasingly shape their politico-economic developments around one of the former, depending upon the port that provided an outlet for the movement of their commodities. On the other hand, the rulers controlling the maritime trade chalked out diverse strategies to make the rulers of inland territories including those of spice producing regions increasingly dependent upon them. Since these maritime exchange centres acted as doors for the entry of food materials, luxury goods and bullion into their provinces from other parts of India as well as overseas markets, besides providing an outlet for the flow of spices and other commodities produced in the inland regions, the intensity of the dependence of the inland rulers on the former was augmented. Though in the fifteenth century several attempts were made by the Zamorin to conquer and to keep resourceful territories, particularly the spice producing hinterland under his custody, in the sixteenth and seventeenth centuries the chances of annexations and territorial conquests were minimized by the prevailing presence of the Portuguese and their stately control devices. Hence, the Zamorin and other political magnates had to resort to several alternative strategies, principal among them being the practice to manipulate succession issues of the ruling houses of the spice producing hinterlands in their favour.[79] The Travancorean ruler used the developments in the ruling houses at Gundara (Kundara), Batimena (Venmani) and Marta (Karinagappilli) in 1599 to spread his spheres of influence to the port of Quilon, with whose help he also attempted to control the maritime trade of southern Kerala.[80]

In the sixteenth and seventeenth centuries several petty principalities started resorting to the strategy of adoption, instead of conquests, to increase their size and power, by which the adopting ruling family incorporated the territories of the adopted families as its integral part. Adoption eventually turned out to be a device that kept small principalities revolving around the states that took shape in the maritime belt, ensuring their empowerment. In most of the adoption cases, members from the ruling house controlling the spice production centres were often preferred. Thus, when the Vadakkenkur did not have a male member to succeed, the heir was adopted around 1598 from the Kizhumalainadu, who was also its ruler with his base at Karikodu near Thodupuzha.[81] With this the political entity of Kizhumalainadu ceased to exist; however, its vast cultivation space got attached to Vadakkenkur effecting integration with Cochin as its hinterland, and also as a satellite power centre supportive of the kingdom of Cochin. In 1603, the ruler of Thodupuzha was the chief supplier of spices to the Portuguese in Cochin.[82] In 1658, the Perumpadappu Svarupam adopted princes from the Vettathu royal family of Tanur[83] as a strategy of extending its areas of influence up to the doors of Calicut, which also comprised a significant agrarian space. In fact, the strategy of adoption was also used as a device to change the existing equation of power, by appropriating more political linkages and ability for more resource mobilization, which augmented not only the strength of the adopting family but also the number of satellite power centres revolving around it. In the event of such adoption what the adopting ruling family received was not merely one or two princes but they also obtained access to extensive political linkages that the adopted royal family developed for years adding to their resources.[84]

The Portuguese saw to it that their supportive chieftains and principalities got sufficiently strengthened. This was done by a system of affiliations, whereby the supportive rulers of inland territories were invited to be brothers in arms with the king of Portugal. Consequently, attempts were made to keep Porcad (Purakadu or Chembakasseri), Gundara (Kundara), Batimena (Venmani) and Marta (Karinagappilli) together under them by developing the political device of a brotherhood in arms. This was a device to contain the adoption strategy developed by the indigenous rulers to strengthen themselves. However, the power of the Portuguese state was ostensibly made evident in the Malabar polity, in the form of the armada, guns and artilleries, battalions of soldiers, armed fortresses, transportation conveyance, control systems, intriguing diplomats and military functionaries, ecclesiastical office-holders, etc. These agencies of state were in active operation to make the various principalities of Malabar subservient to the politico-economic designs of the Lusitanians. Very often feuds in the royal families gave the Portuguese opportunities to intervene in the native kingdoms and principalities. As family relations and ties cut across territorial limits, such a policy of intervention for mercantilist gains, though they offered temporary rewards for the Portuguese, very often invited long-standing conflicts for them, as in the case of Cranganore (1540-60).[85]

Meanwhile, as early as 1533 onwards, the Portuguese tried to incorporate the supportive rulers like the kings of Cochin, Thekkenkur, Vadakkenkur, Alengadu, Diamper, Parur, Porcad (Purakkadu) and the Karta of Alwaye within their political structure by conferring annuities on them. The king of Cochin was given an annual *copa* amounting to 640 *cruzados* and a golden crown, the reception of which, as the oath-formula clearly indicates, necessitated him to acknowledge his vassalage to the Portuguese crown.[86] The rulers of Vadakkenkur, Thekkenkur, Alengadu, Parur, Diamper as well as Porcad were given 72,000 *reais* each, and the Karta of Alwaye an amount of 42,000 *reais* per annum in return for their help in supplying spices to the Portuguese factory at Cochin.[87] By 1605, the king of Thodupuzha also began to receive 72,000 *reais*.[88] In fact this system of annual monetary rewards ensured easy and regular penetration into the spice hinterland by the Portuguese and served the purpose of integrating the far-flung production centres with the Portuguese factory located at Cochin. Moreover, this system of providing monetary rewards was much cheaper than any military expedition for achieving this target, and more long standing and cohesive than political occupation of these territories. Above all these monetary rewards carried with them the extent of the Portuguese power into the interior regions.

Politically, the Portuguese practice of giving annuities made the local chiefdoms and principalities controlling spice producing central upland regions to be appendages of the Portuguese state, and through its mediation they were made to be the satellite power centres revolving around Cochin. Though for all practical purposes they remained to be separate political units, they collectively formed the hinterland for the port of Cochin and their economic operations were rather uniformly carried out according to the designs of the Portuguese, which factor linked them integrally with the kingdom of Cochin.[89] All these inland chieftaincies, which also had access to the surplus from the paddy cultivating low-lying regions, continued to support the kingdom of Cochin in all its wars against Calicut, as long as they received annuities from the Portuguese. In other words the Portuguese system of monetary rewards given to the inland rulers acted as a device not only to keep them away from the Zamorin's sphere of influence but also to operate as appendages of Cochin state, which added the weight to its power at the height of its position in the political ranking. Even after the stopping of the practice of giving annuities to them in the 1620s, with the increasing economic crisis being experienced by the Portuguese then, the bond between them was so well-cemented by usage and the passage of time that their political rapport still continued. Though Porcad went out of the union by this time,[90] others still continued as feeding satellite power centres and economic units till their dismemberment by Marthanda Varma in the mid-eighteenth century.[91]

Corresponding to these developments, the inland rulers also resorted to several strategies for mobilizing resources for instituting the tools of power exercise and also for strengthening their political structures. Some of them like the Vadakkenkur king set up customs houses on the banks of Urupule (Muvattupuzha River)[92] and at Bardela (Vaduthala)[93] for collecting their share of the profit from the traders using water channels for movement of commodities to the Portuguese factory. While some other rulers, both from the maritime zone as well as from the inland belt, started appointing ministers from communities having linkages with either agrarian operation or trade, which in turn facilitated the process of mobilization of wealth for the purpose of setting up instruments of power. Thus, the Zamorin had a minister from the *paradesi* Muslim segment to look after the overseas trade of Calicut and a native Muslim minister to take care of its domestic and coastal trade. The ruler of Kayamkulam had a Muslim as his chief minister in the 1590s,[94] who was chiefly instrumental in promoting and activating its trade. The principality of Poonjar comprising a major portion of the present day High Ranges that supplied the Portuguese a wide variety of hill produce like cardamom, sandalwood, lac, timber, ginger and pepper, had one of its ministers from the St. Thomas Christian community,[95] which was then involved in the process of spice production and dealership of hill produce. The king of Cochin appointed Jewish ministers in his council in 1620s,[96] which is indicative of the desire of the ruler to expand his trading activities using Jewish connections and to get access to larger mercantile resources. Following the increasing flow of wealth by way of trade, the inland rulers started appropriating several European weapons and tools of power exercise. They acquired a great number of artilleries and a large volume of gun-powder with the help of Portuguese private traders. Thus, the king of Vadakkenkur had strengthened his military position with eight *berços* and two *falcões* in 1546, while the artillery of Diamper included 25 *falcões* and that of Cranganore 17 *falcões*. The ruler of Thekkenkur made use of the service of the European experts to fabricate artilleries and cannons in his kingdom, as a result of which 15 *falcões* came under his possession.[97] The appointment of a German soldier as the private secretary of the king of Cochin in 1548[98] is indicative of the desire of the ruler to utilize his service for the purpose of instituting several instruments of power and also for mobilizing the forces on European models.

The Portuguese state in Malabar in the seventeenth century with all its political, military and ecclesiastical edifices and structures appeared to be a huge tree but with a hollow trunk, with increasing depopulation in Cochin (almost one-third shifted residence to other parts of the Indian Ocean region) and increasing loss of vessels and cargo following the attacks of the Dutch and the English.[99] With mounting economic pressure the Portuguese state turned towards the bourgeoisie group of Portuguese private traders of Cochin for survival. The Portuguese *casado* traders, who amassed huge wealth during the hectic phase of private trade following the liberalization of the Indo-European trade of the crown in 1570, started lending wealth liberally to the *Estado da India* for its diverse politico-economic activities. In 1606, the amount borrowed from them was 93,744 *xerafins* at 10 per cent interest rate,[100] which increased to 1,21,971 *xerafins* in 1610. In 1611, the amount raised by the state as loan from the private Portuguese traders like Manuel da Fonseca, Isabel Ferreira, Francisco Barbosa, etc., rose to 71,200 *xerafins*.[101] By the middle of the second decade of the seventeenth century, the loan from the private traders to the sick state rose to 60,000 *cruzados*, which was never paid back.[102] The Portuguese state had already gone to sick bed by the third decade of the seventeenth century, and the *casado* traders realized that they would not be able to nurse the sick state for a long time with their hard earned money, which made most of enterprising *casado* traders move over to different areas (like Nagapattanam, Mylapore, Bengal, Pegu and Ceylon),[103] which were by then outside the direct control of the Portuguese state.

Thus, we find that the ventures for state formation and political manipulation during this period depended very much on the ability and success in using the mechanisms which the 'maritime states' developed for keeping a cluster of satellite inland power centres around them, not only as mere supportive political units but also as feeding economic units, from where the former wielded power and derived wealth for sustaining power. Because of the intensification of sea-borne trade following the European commercial expansion, the state structures based on the gains from maritime trade had acquired precedence over the inland states that derived wealth from the agrarian sector. The gains from the long distance maritime trade, which terminated either in Mediterranean ports or in Atlantic ports, ensured the accumulation of wealth and consequently power in the states having the ability to do so. Unlike Travancore in the later period, which generated agrarian surplus for sustained process of state-building and power maintenance, the state of Calicut and the quasi-states of Cochin and Cannanore depended only on the trade surplus generated by their linkages with the two world systems: Calicut and Cannanore were linked with the trade networks of a world system that terminated at the ports of the Red Sea or the Mediterranean, whereas Cochin was incorporated into the commercial axis of the new world system that had its core centre in the Atlantic. The newly evolving world system could not integrate entire Malabar, as a considerable part of it was still in the orbit of the old world system, the transformation from which to the new, however, did really take place only later during the time of the Dutch and the English. However, the Portuguese expansion of commerce followed by various apparatuses and instruments of a mercantile state to Malabar enabled them to set up a global politico-commercial archipelago, in which a considerable chunk of Malabar became constituent units. However, they could not integrate them permanently and continuously into their orbit, as the process of intensification of commerce, triggered off with the geographical discoveries, equally empowered the native principalities, chiefdoms and regional powers, which were moving fast towards the process of state-formation. In fact, the state, which evolved during this period, whether operating in the globalized system or in the localized system, was shaped on mercantile lines empowering states by the wealth obtained from trade. In the localized level, the mercantile interests of the Portuguese were cutting across those of native rulers including Calicut, which gave opposing pull to the state formation tendencies in Malabar. The introduction of a Portuguese mercantile state facilitated the appearance of a state formation process and political phenomena in Kerala, pulled by the dynamics of trade and its related economic activities, in which the native rulers realized that concentration of wealth was equivalent to concentration of power.

NOTES

1. The concept of the maritime state, which may at first appear to be an ambiguous notion, here refers to a state that sustains itself by banking upon diverse maritime activities, the principal among which being maritime trade. Unlike inland states, it is the resources procured by way of maritime trade that enable the maritime state to set up different instruments and apparatuses of power. These maritime states are different from aqua states, which have got only nominal land space, but extensive water space as its territory. The maritime states may have considerable land space in the hinterland, but their core area would be maritime centres of exchange from where they derive the major share of resources for sustaining their stately activities. The subjects of maritime states may resort to maritime trade as their principal economic activity, or its related areas or a wide variety of maritime activities including ship-building, navigation, naval enterprise and so on. The different tools and instruments of power exercise in a maritime state would be shaped greatly by the needs raised by their multiple sea-oriented activities.

2. M.G.S. Narayanan, *Perumals of Kerala*, Calicut, 1996; his recent study, where he views the Chera state as a 'visible and bold Brahmin oligarchy thinly disguised as

a monarchy', is also worth mentioning. M.G.S. Narayanan, 'The State in the Era of the Cēramān Perumāls of Kerala', in *State and Society in Pre-Modern South India*, ed. R. Champakalakshmi, Kesavan Veluthat and T.R. Venugopalan, Thrissur, 2002, pp. 111-19.

3. Kesavan Veluthat, *Political Structure of Early Medieval South India*, Delhi, 1993.

4. K.N. Ganesh, 'Structure of Political Authority in Medieval Kerala', in *Perspectives on Kerala History: the Second Millennium*, ed. P.J. Cherian, Trivandrum, 2000.

5. M.R. Raghava Varier, 'State as *Svarūpam*: An Introductory Essay', in *State and Society in Pre-Modern South India*, pp. 120-30.

6. Pius Malekandathil, 'Maritime Malabar and a Mercantile State: Polity and State Formation in Malabar under the Portuguese', in *Maritime Malabar and the Europeans*, London 2001.

7. Cf. M.G.S. Narayanan, *Foundations of South Indian Society and Culture*, Delhi, 1984, p. 22.

8. For details see M.R. Raghava Varier, 'State as *Svarūpam*: An Introductory Essay', in *State and Society in Pre-Modern South India*, ed. R. Champakalakshmi, Kesavan Veluthat and T.R. Venugopalan, Thrissur, 2002, p. 124.

9. Pius Malekandathil, 'St. Thomas Christians and the Indian Ocean: AD 52 to AD 1500', *Ephrem's Theological Journal* (International Journal), vol. 5, no. 2, 2001, pp. 190-200; Andre Wink, *Al-Hind: The Making of Indo-Islamic World*, vol. I, New Delhi, 1999, p. 71.

10. For details regarding the shifting of the royal residence of the Nediyirappu Svarupam, see K.V. Krishna Ayyar, *The Zamorins of Calicut*, Calicut, 1938, pp. 1-2. By the middle of the fourteenth century or by the time Ibn Batuta visited Calicut (1343), it had become the most important port of Kerala. Ibn Batuta, *Die Reise des Arabers Ibn Batuta durch Indien und China*, ed. Hans von Mzik, Hamburg, 1911, p. 302. Hermann Gundert, ed., *Keralolpathiyum Mattum*, Kottayam 1992, pp. 190-200.

11. Ashin Das Gupta, *Malabar in Asian Trade: 1740-1800*, Cambridge, 1967, pp. 5, 19; B.J. Schrieke, *Indonesian Sociological Studies*, vol. 1, The Hague, 1955, pp. 7 ff; Pius Malekandathil, *The Germans, the Portuguese and India*, Münster, 1999, p. 9; For details about the Al-Karimi merchants in India, see Eliyahu Ashtor, 'The Venetian Supremacy in Levantine Trade: Monopoly of Pre-colonialism', *Journal of European Economic History*, vol. III, Rome, 1974, p. 27; Walter J. Fischel, 'The Spice Trade in Mamluk Egypt', *Journal of the Economic and Social History of the Orient*, vol. I, 1958, p. 165; Pius Malekandathil, 'From Merchant Capitalists to Corsairs: The Role of Muslim Merchants in Portuguese Maritime Trade of the Portuguese' *Portuguese Studies Review* (Canada), 12(1), 2004, pp. 77-80.

12. William Logan, *Malabar Manual*, vol. I, New Delhi, 1989, p. 278; A. Sreedhara Menon, *A Survey of Kerala History*, Kottayam, 1970, pp. 178-9; Pius Malekandathil, *Portuguese Cochin and the Maritime Trade of India:1500-1663* (South Asian Study Series of Heidelberg University, Germany), Delhi, 2001, pp. 50-1. In fact, the project of conquering Tirunavai was proposed and supported by the Calicut Koya. For details, see K.V. Krishna Ayyar, *The Zamorins of Calicut*, Calicut, 1938, pp. 91-2.

13. W.W. Hunter, *The Imperial Gazetteer of India*, vol. IV, London, 1885, p. 11; K. Rama Varma Raja, 'The Cochin Harbour and the Puthu Vaippu Era', *The Bulletin of the Rama Varma Research Institute*, no. 2, Cochin, 1933, pp. 49-51.

14. A. Sreedhara Menon, *A Survey of Kerala History*, Kottayam, 1967, pp. 173-4; Ramesan Thampuran, *Gosri Rajavamsavali: Geneology of Cochin Royal Family*, Cochin, 1989, p. 6; C. Achyuta Menon, *The Cochin State Manual*, Ernakulam, 1911, p. 2; Pius Malekandathil, *Portuguese Cochin and the Maritime Trade of India*, pp. 30-2.

15. By the end of the fifteenth century, the Zamorin had already deprived the chief of the Perumpadappu Svarupam of many stately rights including the right to strike coins and to roof his palace with tiles, which right he wanted to regain. Cf. Duarte Barbosa, *The Book of Duarte Barbosa: An Account of the Countries Bordering on the Indian Ocean and their Inhabitants*, tran. Mansel Longworth Dames, vol. II, Nendeln, 1967, p. 95.

16. For details about Cheng Ho's voyages, see W.W. Rockhill, 'Notes on the Relations and Trade of China with the Eastern Archipelago and the Coast of the Indian Ocean during the Fourteenth Century', in *T'oung Pao*, vol. XVI, Leiden, 1915, pp. 45-452.

17. The place name Saudi in Cochin is indicative of Arab contacts with this port. Some local historians view that this place located the south end of Fort Cochin got its name from Saudi Arabia. K.L. Bernard, *History of Fort Cochin*, Cochin, 1991, p. 2.

18. For details, see Genevieve Bouchon, *Regent of the Sea: Cannanore's Response to Portuguese Expansion, 1507-1528*, tran. Louise Shackley, Delhi, 1988, pp. 23-5, 44-5, 151-64; Pius Malekandathil, 'The Maritime Trade of Cannanore and the Global Commercial Revolution in the 16th and the 17th Centuries', in *Cannanore in the Maritime History of India*, ed. M.O. Koshy, Kannur, 2002, pp. 46, 48-9.

19. Earlier the rulers of Desinganad (Quilon) had been very powerful. Vira Ravi Varma Sangrama Dhira of Desinganad defeated the Pandyas and the Cholas between 1299 and 1312 and was crowned at Kanchi. K.M. Panikkar, *A History of Kerala, 1498-1801*, Annamalainagar, 1960, p. 7.

20. Genevieve Bouchon, *Regent of the Sea*, pp. 151-75; Pius Malekandathil, 'From Merchant Capitalists to Corsairs', pp. 89-90.

21. The weakening of this mercantile group is evident from the fact that the privilege of keeping the seal and standard weight under the custody of the St. Thomas Christians, a privilege which they enviously enjoyed as members of the mercantile guild right from ninth century onwards, was taken away by this time. For details, see Walter de Gray Birch, ed., *The Commentaries of the Great Afonso Dalboquerque, Second Viceroy of India*, New York, 1875, p. 15. However, the increasing dependence of the ruler on this mercantile community is evident from the fact that the ruler (queen) had chosen merchants from St. Thomas Christian community for the delegation sent to Cochin in 1502 to invite Vasco da Gama to Quilon. Nationalbibliothek in Wien, Nr. 6948; Christine von Rohr, *Neue Quellen zur zweiten Indienfahrt Vasco da Gamas*, Leipzig, 1939, p. 51; Pius Malekandathil, 'St.Thomas Christians and the Indian Ocean', p. 200.

22. It was the diverse state apparatuses that Calicut developed during this period that enabled it to counter the forces of the Portuguese from 1498 onwards, and confront them along with the international forces in 1509.

23. The seat of the Portuguese Government in India was first established only in 1505 with the arrival of Francisco de Almeida. Till then the Lusitanian vessels were making annual visits to the shores of Malabar principally for trade. For details of the early commercial contacts of the Portuguese, see Pius Malekandathil, *Portuguese Cochin and the Maritime Trade of India*, pp. 37-40, 166-7.

24. Cf. Carl A. Hanson, *Economy and Society in Baroque Portugal, 1668-1703*, London, 1981, p. 110. The chief aim of mercantilism was to strengthen the state authority itself and to use economic forces for the furtherance of the interests of the state. Cf. Eli F. Heckscher, *Mercantilism*, tran. Mendel Shapiro, vol. I, New York, 1962, pp. 22, 24, 33-4. Portugal had by this time developed a political philosophy to realize this target. For details, see Pius Malekandathil, 'Maritime Malabar and a Mercantile State', pp. 201-2.

25. The Portuguese commerce with the new discoveries was, in fact, the commerce of the king, carried in his ships, guarded by his army and navy and paid for by his revenue. P.E. Pieris and M.A.H. Fitzler, *Ceylon and Portugal*, part I, Leipzig, 1927, p. 335. In fact, there was hardly any demand for European goods in Asia but there was an increasing demand for Asian goods in Europe, a phenomenon which magnified the dimensions of trade for the Portuguese. For details, see Dietmar Rothermund, *Asian Trade and European Expansion in the Age of Mercantilism*, Delhi, 1981, pp. 11-17.

26. F.C. Danvers, *The Portuguese in India: Being a History of the Rise and Decline of their Empire*, vol. I, New Delhi, 1988, p. 72; William Brooks Greenlee, ed., *The Voyage of Pedro Alvares Cabral to Brazil and India from Contemporary Documents and Narratives*, London, 1938, p. 143.

27. The king of Cochin initially gave accommodation to the Portuguese in his own palace in times of crisis, besides granting them a site for their factory and settlement. He liberally gave them loans for the purchase of spices and used to stand as surety, when the Portuguese experienced shortage of capital. The Portuguese on their turn were always there to defend the king of Cochin in his battles against the Zamorin of Calicut. For details of these reciprocal ties and mutual support, see K.S. Mathew and Afzal Ahmad, *Emergence of Cochin in the Pre-Industrial Era: A Study of Portuguese Cochin*, Pondicherry, 1990, pp. iii-x; K.M. Panikkar, *A History of Kerala*, p. 213; Pius Malekandathil, *Portuguese Cochin and the Maritime Trade of India*, pp. 37-40, 150-1.

28. The Portuguese established commercial contacts with Cannanore in 1501 and with Quilon in 1503. However, the evident instruments of the Portuguese state reached Cannanore with the erection of St. Angelo fortress (1508) and Quilon with their fortress at St. Thomas completed in 1519. For details, see Gaspar Correia, *Lendas da India*, tom. I, Lisboa, 1921, pp. 583, 728; tom. II, pp. 577; Antonio da Silva Rego, *Documentação para a Historia das Missões do Padroado Portugues do Oriente*, vol. I, Lisboa, 1948, p. 403.

29. For more details about these two Milanese *bombardeiros,* see George Percy Badger, ed., *The Travels of Ludovico di Varthema in Egypt, Syria, Arabia Desrta and Arabia Felix in Persia, India and Ethiopia: AD 1503 to 1508,* New York, 1863, p. 260; O.K. Nambiar, *The Kunjalis: Admirals of Calicut,* London, 1963, pp. 49-51.

30. The Zamorin's anger towards the Portuguese was aroused in 1500 by the brutality, which Pedro Alvares Cabral committed in Calicut and his consequent bombardment of the city. For details see William Brooks Greenlee, op. cit., pp. 147-8.

31. The war of 1502 was fought against the king of Cochin on the departure of Vasco da Gama in 1503 demanding the surrender of Portuguese factors to the Zamorin. The 1504 war was, in fact, a continuation of this belligerent atmosphere. After the departure of the Afonso Albuquerque and his cousin Francisco, who reinstated the king of Cochin on the throne, the Zamorin attacked Cochin, which was, in turn, foiled by the timely action of Duarte Pacheco. For details, see C. Achyuta Menon, op. cit., pp. 65-9; K.M. Panikkar, *A History of Kerala,* p. 54.

32. K.S. Mathew, 'The first Mercantile Battle in the Indian Ocean: The Afro-Asian front against the Portuguese, 1508-1509', A Paper presented in the *II Seminario Internacional da Historia Indo-Portuguesa,* Actas, Lisboa, 1985, pp.179-82.

33. For details on the world system that existed before the European hegemony, see Janet L. Abu-Lughod, *Before European Hegemony: The World System AD 1250-1350,* New York, 1989.

34. Sanjay Subrahmanyam, *The Portuguese Empire in Asia 1500-1700: A Political and Economic History,* London, 1993, p. 72; Jaime Cortesão, *Os Descobrimentos Portugueses,* vol. VI, Lisboa, 1978, pp. 141-2.

35. Raymundo Antonio de Bulhão Pato, *Cartas de Affonso de Albuquerque seguidas de documentos que as elucidam,* tom. I, Lisboa, 1884, pp. 21 ff; João de Barros, *Asia. Dos feitos que os Portuguezes fizeram no Descobrimento e conquista dos Mares do Oriente,* Lisboa, 1771, decada, II, part II, pp. 40 ff, 181, decada III, part II, pp. 451-2; Joaquim Verissimo Serrão, *Commentarios de Afonso de Albuquerque,* tom. I, Lisboa, 1973, p. 140; Duarte Barbosa, *The Book of Duarte Barbosa: An Account of the Countries Bordering on the Indian Ocean and their Inhabitants,* tran. Mansel Longworth Dames, vol. I, Nedeln, 1967, p. 59.

36. For details on the evolution of the Portuguese state within mercantilist conceptual frame, see Pius Malekandathil, 'Maritime Malabar and a Mercantile State'. For details of the mercantilist thinkers of Portugal, see Carl A. Hanson, *Economy and Society in Baroque Portugal, 1668-1703,* London, 1981, pp. 112-40. Antonio Sergio, *Antologia dos Economistas Portugueses (Seculo XVII),* Lisboa, 1974, pp. 68-74; Duarte Gomes Solis, Manuel Severim de Faria, Duarte Ribeiro de Macedo, Alexandre Gusmão and D.Luis da Cunha were the most important mercantilist thinkers of Portugal. For details, see Moses Bensabat Amzalak, *Do Estudo da Evolução das Doutrinas Economicas em Portugal,* Lisboa, 1928, p. 25; for the mercantilist views of Duarte Gomes Solis, see Duarte Gomes Solis, *Discursos sobre los Commercios de las Indias,* ed. Moses Bensabat Amzalak, Lisboa,

1943; Duarte Gomes Solis, *Alegacion en Favor de la Compañia de la India Oriental y Comercios ultramarines que de Nueuo se Instituyo en el Reyno de Portugal*, ed. Moses Bensabat Amzalak, Lisboa, 1955. The mercantilist ideas of Duarte Ribeiro de Macedo, who had been a Portuguese ambassador during the years of Colbert's tenure (1661-83), had a great impact on Portugal. He wanted to expand and diversify the agrarian capitalism already existing in Brazil, by starting cultivation of oriental plants like cinnamon (which was introduced in Brazil even before the fall of Ceylon into the hands of the Dutch), other spices and cotton. If they were produced on a large scale in Brazil (particularly Maranhão region), then they could be made available in European markets at prices lower than the rates of the Dutch. His plan was to transfer Asian plants to Brazil, in the same way as orange trees were brought to Portugal from China by way of Goa in 1635. Duarte Ribeiro de Macedo, *Observações sobre a transplantação dos fructos da India ao Brazil*, 1675; Duarte Ribeiro de Macedo, *Obras Ineditas*, Lisboa, 1817, pp. 102-10, 118.

37. Cf. K.M. Panikkar, *Malabar and the Portuguese, 1500-1663*, Bombay, 1929, p. 84.

38. Cf. Ibid. Antonio da Silva Rego, *Documentação para a Historia das Missões do Padroado Portugues do Oriente*, vol. I, Lisboa, 1948, doc. 44, p. 118.

39. Sanjay Subrahmanyam, *The Portuguese Empire in Asia*, 1500-1700, p. 97.

40. Cf. Pius Malekandathil, 'The Portuguese *Casados* and the Intra-Asian Trade, 1500-1663', *Proceedings of Indian History Congress*, Millenium 61st Session, Kolkata 2000-1, part I, Kolkata, 2001, pp. 385-96.

41. J.H. da Cunha Rivara, *Archivo Portuguez Oriental*, fasciculo 5, part I, New Delhi, 1992, pp. 10, 46-8.

42. These Al-Karimi merchants fled en masse to the ports of Gujarat, Vijayanagara, Hormuz and the Red Sea. For details, see Raymundo Antonio de Bulhão Pato, *Cartas de Affonso de Albuquerque*, tom. I, p. 126; Genevieve Bouchon, 'Calicut at the Turn of the Sixteenth Century', *The Asian Seas 1500-1800: Local Societies, European Expansions and the Portuguese, Revista de Cultura*, vol. I, Ano V, 1991, p. 46.

43. ANTT, *Chancelaria de Manuel I*, liv. II, fol. 83, '*Capitulos de pazes entre Afonso de Albuquerque e o Samorin de Calicut*', Lisboa, 26de Fevreiro de 1515.

44. Cf. Duarte Barbosa, *The Book of Duarte Barbosa*, vol. II, pp. 226ff; Pius Malekandathil, 'Merchants, Markets and Commodities: Some Aspects of Portuguese Commerce with Malabar', in *The Portuguese, Indian Ocean and European Bridgeheads: Festschrift in Honour of Prof. K.S. Mathew*, ed. Pius Malekandathil and Jamal Mohammed, Fundação Oriente, Lisboa, 2001, p. 247.

45. Gaspar Correia, *Lendas da India*, tom. I, pp. 583, 728.

46. Ibid., tom. II, Lisboa, 1921, p. 577.

47. Padduronga S.S. Pissurlencar, *Regimentos das Fortalezas da India*, Bastora/Goa, 1951, p. 227.

48. Pius Malekandathil, 'The Portuguese *Casados* and the Intra-Asian Trade, 1500-1663', pp. 387-8.

49. Cf. Faria y Souza, *Asia Portuguesa: The History of the Discovery and Conquest of India by the Portuguese*, tran. John Stevens, vol. I, London, 1695, p. 284.

50. Pius Malekandathil, 'From Merchant Capitalists to Corsairs', p. 16.

51. For the developments in Vedalai and Negombo, see Georg Schurhammer, 'die Geschichte Ceylons, 1539-1552', in Georg Schurhammer and E.A. Voretzsch, *Ceylon zur Zeit des Königs Bhuvaneka Bahu und Franz Xavers, 1539-1552*, vol. I, Leipzig, 1928, pp. 1-78; Gaspar Correia, Lendas da India, tom. III, pp. 818-37; tom. IV, pp. 77-84; Jorge Manuel Costa da Silva Flores, *Os Portugueses e o Mar de Ceilão, 1498-1543: Trato, Diplomacia e Guerra*, Mestrado Dissertation submitted to the Faculdade de Ciencias Sociais e Humanas da Universidade Nova de Lisboa, 1991, pp. 211-15.

52. In fact, the perennial conflict between Edappilly and Cochin centred around the island of Cochin, which was presented by the king of Edappilly as a gift in the fifteenth century to the ruling king of Perumpadappu Svarupam, who happened to be his son. But later when Cochin developed into a flourishing port and attained economic importance, the successors of the Edappilly king wanted to regain it from the Perumpadappu Svarupam. In this constant rivalry, the Zamorins used to champion the cause of Edappilly rulers, who in turn happily provided a base for the military operations of the Zamorin against Cochin. Very often the Zamorins used to come down to Edappilly for performing their coronation ceremony in the traditional manner. The attempts of the new Zamorin to get his coronation ceremony performed at Edappilly intensified tension in the 1530s. For details, see Francisco d'Andrade, *Chronica do muyto alto e muyto Poderoso Rey destes Reynos de Portugal, Dom Joao III*, parte III, Coimbra MDCCLXXXXVI, pp. 97-105, 114, 167; K.P. Padmanabha Menon, *History of Kerala*, vol. II, Ernakulam, 1929, pp. 69-71; K.M. Panikkar, *A History of Kerala, 1498-1801*, Annamalainagar, 1960, p. 24.

53. ANTT, *Gavetas*, 20-1-45; Elaine Sanceau, *Colecção de São Lourenço*, vol. III, Lisboa, 1978, pp. 9-17; Diogo do Couto, *Da Asia. Dos feitos que os Portuguezes fizeram na Conquista e Descobrimentos das Terras e Mares do Oriente*, decada VII, parte II, liv. 8, cap.14 and liv. 9 cap. 10.

54. ANTT, Corpo Cronologico, II, Maço 242, doc. 44; ANTT, Gavetas, 15-20-8; Elaine Sanceau, *Colecção de São Lourenço*, vol. III, p. 15; Faria y Souza, op. cit., tom. II, p. 159.

55. In fact, the full official designation of the king of Cochin was *Perumpadappu Gangadhara Vira Kerala Trikkovil Adhikarikal*. For details, see C. Achyuta Menon, op. cit., p. 39.

56. Elaine Sanceau, *Colecção de São Lourenço*, vol. III, Lisboa, 1978, pp. 9, 15; Diogo do Couto, *Da Asia*, parte II, liv. 8, cap.14 and liv. 9 cap.10.

57. The amount annually given to king of Cochin as *copa* was 640 *cruzados*. For details, see Simão Botelho, 'Tombo do Estado da India (1554)', in *Subsidios para a Historia da India Portugueza*, ed. by R.J. de Lima Felner, Lisboa, 1868, p. 25; Paduronga S.S. Pissurlencar, *Regimentos das Fortalezas da India*, Bastora/Goa, 1951, pp. 217-19; Vitorino Magalhães Godinho, *Les Finances de l'etat Portugais des Indes Orientales (1517-1635): Materiaux pour une Etude Structuralle et*

Conjoncturelle, Paris, 1982, p. 306. Account of Francisco da Costa, in Antonio da Silva Rego, ed. *Documentação Ultramarina Portuguesa*, vol. III, Lisboa, 1963, p. 310. The golden crown offered by the Portuguese in 1505 was used for the coronation ceremony of the kings of Cochin all through this period.

58. ANTT, *Corpo Cronologico*, I, Maço 52, doc. 23.

59. Cf. K.M. Panikkar, *Malabar and the Portuguese*, pp. 111-13.

60. K.S. Mathew and Afzal Ahmad, eds., *Emergence of Cochin in the Pre-Industrial Era: A Study of Portuguese Cochin*, Pondicherry, 1990, doc. 53, pp. 73-6; Sanjay Subrahmanyam, 'Cochin in Decline, 1600-1650. Myth and Manipulation in the Estado da India', in *Portuguese Asia: Aspects in History and Economic History (Sixteenth and Seventeenth Centuries)*, ed. Roderich Ptak, Stuttgart, 1987, p. 67.

61. K.S. Mathew and Afzal Ahmad, ed., *Emergence of Cochin in the Pre-Industrial Era*, doc. 53, pp. 73-84.

62. M.N. Pearson, *Coastal Western India*, p. 55; Sanjay Subrahmanyam, *The Political Economy of Commerce: Southern India, 1500-1650*, New York, 1990, pp. 218-19.

63. Vitorino Magalhães Godinho, *Os Descobrimentos e a Economia Mundial*, Lisboa, 1984, vol. III, pp. 22-3; Francisco d'Andrade, *Chronica do muyto alto e muyto Poderoso Rey*, parte III, pp. 233-4.

64. Diogo do Couto, *Da Asia*, decada X, part I, liv. IV, cap. XIII, pp. 472-80.

65. Ibid., M.N. Pearson, *Coastal Western India: Studies from the Portuguese Records*, New Delhi, 1981, pp. 55-6.

66. K.S. Mathew and Afzal Ahmad, eds., *Emergence of Cochin*, doc. 53, pp. 77-83.

67. Francisco da Costa, in Antonio da Silva Rego, ed., *Documentação Ultramarina Portuguesa*, p. 315.

68. BNL, Cod.11410, fol.116v, *Orçamento de 1612* Cochin.

69. Pius Malekandathil, 'The Jews of Cochin and the Portuguese (1500-1663)', in *The Proceedings of the Indian History Congress*, Aligarh, 2002, pp. 240-7.

70. T.I. Poonen, *A Survey of the Rise of the Dutch Power in Malabar (1603-1678)*, Trichinapoly, 1949, p. 52.

71. ANTT, *Livros das Monções*, no. 24, fols. 69v-70; no. 27, fol. 156; ANTT, *Documentos Remettidos da India*, liv. 24, fols. 69v-70.

72. AHU, *Caixas da India*, Caixa 3, doc. 31, dated 25-1-1615; doc. 34, dated 29-1-1615.

73. Cf. Genevieve Bouchon, *Regent of the Sea*, pp. 151-75; Pius Malekandathil, 'The Maritime Trade of Cannanore', p. 49.

74. Diogo do Couto, decada V, parte II, pp. 431-7; Gaspar Correia, *Lendas da India*, tom. I, pp. 425ff; Genevieve Bouchon, *Regent of the Sea*, p. 172.

75. The king of Travancore needed a lot of horses for meeting the increasing war needs, particularly for his battles against the king of Cape Comorin. The Portuguese horse trader, Dom João de Cruz, promised to supply horses regularly to him on the condition that he would allow his subjects to embrace Christianity. On this condition horses were regularly supplied by the Portuguese from Hormuz and about 80,000 Travancoreans became Christians. ANTT, *Corpo Cronologico*, I, Maço 60, doc.44; Pius Malekandathil, 'Merchants, Markets and

Commodities: Some Aspects of Portuguese Commerce with Malabar', in *The Portuguese, Indian Ocean and European Bridgeheads: Festschrift in Honour of Prof. K.S. Mathew*, ed. Pius Malekandathil and Jamal Mohammed, Fundação Oriente, Lisboa, 2001, p. 254.

76. The attempts to erect the fortress of Quilon started in 1599. For details, see Pius Malekandathil, ed., *Jornada of Dom Alexis de Menezes: A Portuguese Account of the Sixteenth Century Malabar*, Kochi, 2003, pp. 146-53, 375-85, 402-3.

77. This traditional world system can be tentatively equated with the East-West Axis of K.N. Chaudhuri, comprising Malacca, Calicut, Cambay, Aden, Cairo, Alexandria and Venice. For details on East-West Axis see K.N. Chaudhuri, *Asia before Europe: Economy and Civilization of the Indian Ocean from the Rise of Islam to 1750*, New York, 1990, p. 343.

78. For details on this World System, see Immanuel Wallerstein, *The Modern World System II: Mercantilism and the Consolidation of the European World Economy, 1600-1750*, New York, 1980, pp. 273 ff.

79. Corresponding with this attempt, the Zamorin conveniently used Edappilly as a pliable political entity for his designs and interventions in the south. For details, see Francisco d'Andrade, *Chronica do muyto alto e muyto Poderoso Rey destes Reynos de Portugal, Dom Joao III,* parte III, pp. 97-105, 114, 167; K.P. Padmanabha Menon, *History of Kerala*, vol. II, pp. 69-71; K.M. Panikkar, *A History of Kerala*, p. 24.

80. Pius Malekandathil, *Jornada of Dom Alexis de Menezes*, pp. 340, 398.

81. As early as 1599 the king of Thodupuzha was mentioned as the legalized son and heir of the Vadakkenkur kingdom. For details, see Pius Malekandathil, *Jornada of Dom Alexis de Menezes*, pp.176-9.

82. Account of Francisco da Costa, in Antonio da Silva Rego, ed., *Documentação Ultramarina Portuguesa*, vol. III, Lisboa, 1963, pp. 310, 312.

83. C. Achyuta Menon, op. cit., p. 88; K.M. Panikkar, *Malabar and the Portuguese*, p. 156.

84. In the sixteenth and seventeenth century many of the adopting royal families swallowed the territories of the adopted families, which also served as an integrating and consolidating mechanism.

85. Cf. Supra nos. 51 and 52. Though it was a war between Cochin and Cranganore, the Portuguese were eventually dragged into the conflict. It was in fact the Portuguese interference in the family feuds of Perumpadappu Swarupam that brought in their own collapse in 1663.

86. Cf. Damião de Gois, *Cronica do Felicissimo Rei D.Manuel*, parte II, Coimbra, 1953, pp. 26-30; for details about the oath of fealty to the king of Portugal taken by the rulers of Cochin at the time of coronation, see Antonio Silva Rego, ed., *Documentação Ultramarina Portugueza*, vol. III, Lisboa, 1963, pp. 359-60.

87. Paduronga S.S. Pissurlencar, *Regimentos das Fortalezas da India,* Bastora/Goa, 1951, p. 217-19; For details, see Simão Botelho, 'Tombo do Estado da India (1554)', in *Subsidios para a Historia da India Portugueza*, ed. R.J. de Lima Felner, Lisboa, 1868, p. 25; Paduronga S.S. Pissurlencar, *Regimentos das Fortalezas da*

India, pp. 217-19; Vitorino Magalhães Godinho, *Les Finances de l'etat Portugais des Indes Orientales (1517-1635): Materiaux pour une Etude Structuralle et Conjoncturelle,* p. 306. Account of Francisco da Costa, in Antonio da Silva Rego, ed., *Documentação Ultramarina Portuguesa,* vol. III, p. 310.

88. Francisco da Costa, in Antonio da Silva Rego, ed., *Documentação Ultramarina Portuguesa,* p. 310.

89. Pius Malekandathil, 'The Portuguese and the Ghat-Route Trade: 1500-1663', in *Pondicherry University Journal of Social Sciences and Humanities (PUSH),* Pondicherry, vol. I, no. 1&2, pp. 144-45.

90. The king of Porcad started entertaining the Dutch from 1642 onwards. For details, see M. Antoinette P. Roelofz, *Die Vestiging der Nederlander ter Kuste Malabar,* 's-Gravenhage, 1943, p. 106.

91. With the conquest of Vadakkenkur, Thekkenkur, Alengadu, etc., by Marthanda Varma, their spice hinterlands were cut off from Cochin and also their political ties. Attempts were taken to link them with Travancore by developing around 1763 the port of Alleppey to which commodities were made to flow.

92. Diogo Gonçalves, *Historia do Malavar,* ed. Joseph Wicki, Münster, 1955, pp. 87-8.

93. Ibid., p. 88.

94. Pius Malekandathil, *Jornada of Dom Alexis de Menezes,* p. 373.

95. Ibid., p. 332.

96. Cf. nos. 68, 69, 70.

97. Elaine Sanceu, *Colecção de São Lourenço,* vol. II, p. 309.

98. His name was Marcos Roiz Dalemanha. Ibid., p. 9. For details, see Pius Malekandathil, *The Germans, the Portuguese and India,* Münster, 1999, p. 40.

99. Pius Malekandathil, *Portuguese Cochin and the Maritime Trade of India,* pp. 208-9, 217, 255-6.

100. AHU, *Caixas da India,* Caixa 1, doc. 101, Devassa feito ao vedor da Fazenda, dated 25-2-1611.

101. AHU, *Caixas da India,* Caixa 2, doc. 89, fols. 1-4, 11, 15, dated 27-1-1613, details about the money borrowed from the Portuguese *casados.*

102. AHU, *Caixas da India,* Caixa 3, doc. 174, dated 2-1-1616.

103. AHU, *Caixas da India,* Caixa 2, doc. 107. The letter of the city council of Cochin sent to Philip III of Spain (also referred to as Philip II of Portugal) giving an account of the economic condition of Cochin, dated 21-12-1613.

CHAPTER SIX

The Ottoman Expansion and the Portuguese Response in the Indian Ocean, 1500-1560

The Ottomans, who had already expanded into the maritime space of the Mediterranean in the fifteenth century, attempted to control the traditional trade routes connecting Asia with Europe by occupying the key strategic trade centres lying on the maritime rim of the Indian Ocean. The Portuguese efforts to monopolize the eastern trade by making the commodities flow to Europe through the Cape route had started at the cost of the Ottomans and reduced the flow of wealth to the treasury of the Ottomans. This process in turn invited the latter to come out from the role of being the controller of inland caravan trade to be the key factors deciding the course of commodity movements through maritime channels. Though the Ottomans did not make any substantial impact on India by controlling sizeable chunk of its land through their frequent attempts to enter into the maritime space of Indian Ocean and particularly into the diverse maritime exchange centres of India as well as their unbroken commercial linkages with the Marakkar traders of Kerala, they created multifaceted challenges to the Portuguese, who, while responding to them, developed a set of politico-military arrangements including the devices of fortresses and patrolling, which eventually had greater impact on the politico-economic history of India. The central purpose of this chapter is to see the processes and mechanisms by which the Ottomans expanded into the Indian Ocean for the purpose of controlling its trade and also the ways as well as the means by which the Portuguese managed to contain the Ottoman expansion and retain their predominant position in conducting the Indian trade. This is done chiefly by locating the Ottomans in the context of Portuguese commercial expansion in the Indian waters.

*This chapter was first published in M.N. Pearson and Charles Borges (ed.), *Metahistory, History Questioning History: Festschrift in Honour of Teotonio R de Souza*, Lisboa 2007, pp. 497-508.

This chapter will provide a glimpse into the parallel stream developments of the sixteenth century in this maritime space.

HISTORICAL SETTING

The Ottoman desire to control the trade routes between Europe and eastern world as well as the strategic centres located in this trade route got ignited with the capture of Constantinople in 1453 by Mohammed II.[1] The developments following this decisive incident indicate that the Ottoman interest was not confined to the mere control of eastern trade routes alone, but extended to the farthest possibilities of tapping wealth from the very sources of trade in India and establishing spheres of influence at different levels. We find many adventurers and entrepreners moving over to India from Constantinople during the period following the Ottoman occupation of that city. The most evident case is that of the Constantinople-born Yusuf Adil Shah, who later became the governor of the Bahmanis over a vast land space in Konkan including Bijapur and Goa. In fact, the hands of Yusuf Adil Shah were strengthened by the Navayat Muslims, who had come as a group of 400 from Onor (Honawar) and Baticala (Batkal) in 1479, following their persecution by the Vijayanagara rulers for having supplied horses from Arabia and Persia to the Bahmani Sultan.[2] Later, with the disintegration of the Bahmani kingdom in 1498, Yusuf Adil Shah established his political power over a considerable tract of territory centred around Bijapur and brought Goa under his control. The port of Ela (Goa) was the chief entry point through which the trading networks of the Constantinople-born ruler of Bijapur found maritime exposure. With the increase in the import of horses from Hormuz to this port for distribution in the Vijayanagara kingdom, the city of Ela accumulated a considerable amount of wealth as custom duties, about 100,000 *pardaos* per year, which Adil Shah claimed as his share.[3] However, the duties that he collected on the objects of maritime trade in Goa and the neighbouring districts figured tentatively about 400,000 *pardaos* per year.[4] These developments suggest that the advent of the Ottoman adventurers like Yusuf Adil Shah in India took place against the background of their desire to bag trade surplus for carving out strong state structures at commercially strategic sites. Meanwhile, the Ottoman adventurers and traders also seem to have been in frequent contacts with the political and economic activities of Gujarat over a protracted period of time, which made the Ottomans concentrate on its ports as the most vulnerable targets in India.[5]

On the other side, the capture of Constantinople by the Ottomans and the re routing of oriental trade according to their larger politico-economic designs started affecting severely the fate of the commercial centres of the Bratislava-Hapsburgs, which had till then been thriving on eastern trade. Correspondingly, the Ottoman intervention began to be increasingly reflected in the price index of oriental wares in Europe, as well. During the period between 1450 and 1495 (especially after the fall of Constantinople) the prices rose steadily in the trade centres of Europe.[6] However, the Ottomans supplied spices at cheaper prices to the Venetians, which kept the price of pepper in Venice between 42 ducats and 49 ducats during the period between 1495 and 1497, a period when its price fluctuated between 66 and 75 ducats in Mamluk Cairo. In 1498, when the price of pepper in Cairo varied between 61 and 81 ducats, it was kept between 56 and 57 ducats in Venice.[7] This shows that even when the Mamluks imposed a high price on the spices in Cairo since the declaration of royal monopoly on its trade in Egypt in 1428, the Ottomans managed to make available pepper and other spices at a cheaper price to the Venetians.[8] This is to be seen against the background of the deeper economic ties that the Venetians and the Ottomans developed over decades on the trade traffic of oriental wares, the gains from which were ably translated by the Ottomans for their frequent wars of expansion into Europe. Moreover, the Venetian traders and Italian markets were needed for the Ottomans to break the backbone of the trade of Eastern Europe and the Bratislava-Hapsburgs as a part of their larger political strategy to weaken and bring Eastern Europe under their subjugation.

However, commodity flow through the Ottoman territories dwindled following the discovery of a sea-route to India and the consequent diversion of the spice trade to the Atlantic port of Lisbon via the Cape route. In 1501, Pedro Alvarez Cabral procured a cargo of 104,920 kg. of pepper, 20,984 kg. of ginger and 31,476 kg. of cinnamon for transshipment to Lisbon,[9] which rose to 1,154,120 kg. of pepper and 23,607 kg. of ginger in 1505.[10] The commodities taken to Lisbon were further distributed in Europe through the royal factory at Antwerp since 1501.[11] The principal loser in this reorientation of the spice trade of the Indian Ocean space was the Ottomans, who had captured Constantinople earlier for the purpose of controlling oriental trade. The increasing pepper shortage experienced in the Ottoman territories and in its supporting Italian markets following the entry of the Portuguese in Indian trade centres is evident from the high price (100 ducats per quintal) quoted for pepper in 1500 in Venice.[12]

Later with the land oriented expansion of Afonso de Albuquerque and with the occupation of Goa (1510), Malacca (1511) and Hormuz (1515),[13] Portuguese control over the trade in Asian waters carried out with the help of their *cartaz*-armada-fortress systems became considerably decisive and the flow of commodities through caravan routes started dwindling. During the early decades of the sixteenth century, Malacca, Aden and Hormuz were viewed as the principal entrance points of the Indian Ocean, through which commodities were distributed all over Eurasia. The Portuguese believed that all trade between Europe and the Indies could be forced to go round the Cape of Good Hope by blocking its traditional outlets, viz., the straits of Malacca, the Persian Gulf and the Red Sea.[14] However, Ottomans were quick to grasp the deeper nuances of these developments. On the one hand, it meant slackening of trade in the Ottoman markets, which also meant dwindling of resources. On the other hand, the Ottomans smelt a severe political danger in their neighbourhood. Till 1515, the Europeans appeared to be an enemy of the Turks only in the western front. But in that year with the occupation of Hormuz (lying in the eastern part of the Turkish Empire) by the Lusitanians, the Ottomans found themselves being virtually encircled by the Europeans, which in fact sent political messages of caution to the Ottomans. The evolving economic pressure and the political threats emerging from the encircling European expansion made the Ottomans turn their attention increasingly to the politics of the Indian Ocean regions and interfere in them to their advantage.

THE EASTWARD EXPANSION OF THE
OTTOMANS AND THE INDIAN OCEAN TRADE

It was during the time of Selim I (1512-20) that the Indian Ocean was, for the first time, looked upon as an area of great political and economic significance for the Ottomans. He took decisive steps to control the various trade centres located on the rim of the Indian Ocean by undertaking a chain of conquests starting with the occupation of Chaldiran in 1514 from the Safavid ruler Shah Ismail. The attack of Mamluk forces at Marj Dabiq in 1516 enabled the Ottomans to become masters of the eastern trade passing through Aleppo and Damascus. With the capturing of Cairo from the Mamluks in 1517, almost all the transit centres of the caravan trade connecting the Indian Ocean with the Mediterranean passed into the hands of the Turks. Meanwhile, Selim I also established a naval base at Suez with a view to availing timely naval and military assistance for the purpose of controlling the international trade routes from the east but terminating in the western rim of the Indian Ocean.[15]

By this time the Marakkar[16] traders of Cannanore and Cochin, who were originally from Kayalpattanam, Kilakarai and Kunimedu but engaged in the coastal trade between Coromandel and Malabar,[17] had already started frequenting the ports of the Ottomans in the Red Sea for the purpose of trade.[18] The emergence of the Marakkars as a principal merchant group conducting trade with the Red Sea ports was made possible with the mass exodus of the Al-Karimi traders from Calicut in 1513 following the entry of the Portuguese in that city after having signed a peace treaty with the new Zamorin.[19] With the flight of the Al-Karimis from Calicut to the safer ports of Gujarat, Vijayanagara, Hormuz and the Red Sea fearing vengeance from the Portuguese, the Marakkar traders of Cochin and Cannanore carved out a commercial niche of their own and started sending spices to the ports of the Red Sea, particularly after the Ottoman expansion into the western doors of the Indian Ocean following the occupation of Cairo and Suez from the hands of the Mamluks. The flow of commodities between the spice ports of Kerala and the Ottoman territories grew considerably with the increasing help extended to the Marakkar traders by the private trading lobby among the Portuguese officials.[20] However, this rapport did not continue for long, as the Portuguese officials themselves began to attack and confiscate the vessels of the Marakkar traders supporting the Ottoman trade centres under the pretext of checking *cartazes*.[21] Kuti Ali, one of these Marakkar traders, is said to have become a corsair later when the Portuguese governor, who previously joined hands with him to send pepper to the Red Sea ports, himself confiscated the whole as contraband and appropriated the vessel.[22] However, the available evidence suggests that the linkage with the Marakkars of Kerala continued to ensure the Ottoman ports of the Red Sea area with sizeable cargo for the purpose of trade, and for meeting the consumer demands of its far-flung territories even during the last years of Selim.

The Marakkar traders of Cannanore had by this time started diverting commodities to the Ottoman trade centres of the Red Sea region by using the Maldives as the base of their operation.[23] The grand design of the Ottoman ruler Selim I to create a pan-Islamic network uniting the Muslim East also strengthened the commercial moves of the Muslim traders of Cannanore and Cochin, who in turn linked the production centres of the spices in India with the trading world of the Ottomans that extended up to Europe.[24] The Portuguese responded to this move by erecting as many fortresses as possible near the spice ports of Kerala so that the flow of spices through the Ottoman territory might be prevented. The immediate response of the Portuguese to these developments was the erection of a fortress in Quilon in 1519, as its spice was increasingly falling into the hands of the Muslim traders.[25] Meanwhile, search was also made for locating suitable sites for the erection of fortresses along the west coast of India with a view to making them as military devices to counter the possible expansion of the Ottomans into Indian waters in the years to come. Concomitantly many Ottoman adventurers moved towards the kingdom of Muzaffarid Gujarat, where some were absorbed into royal service giving them the rank of nobility. One of such nobles of the Muzaffarids was Malik Ayaz, a Russian Christian, who was captured and sold in the slave market of Constantinople by the Ottomans. He was bought by a merchant of Constantinople and taken along with his cargo to Gujarat, where he was presented as a gift to the sultan.[26] Seeing his skills in archery, Sultan Muhammad Begada of Gujarat deployed him for waging many of his wars since 1484.[27] Later he was freed from the status of a slave and made the governor of Junagadh (Sorath) and Diu.[28] In that capacity he organized a big fighting force, consisting of one lakh horses, one hundred elephants, a number of cannons, cannoneers, musketeers and archers,[29] and very often Turks formed an important segment of his fighting force.[30]

He developed Diu as a major trading centre of Gujarat, extending its commercial linkages with the ports of Red Sea and Persian Gulf and the wealth coming from Diu augmented the power of and clout of Malik Ayaz.[31] He mobilized the forces of Zamorin, Mamluk Egypt and the Venetians and incorporated the service of Turkish fighters in 1508 to fight against the Portuguese and oust them from the Indian Ocean, as the trade of the former had already been hammered by the commerce and coercive activities of the Portuguese in the western Indian Ocean.[32] Though the Portuguese finally came out victorious in the encounter, Malik Ayaz was allowed to rule as governor of Diu till almost 1521, when he fell out of the good books of the sultan.

THE OTTOMAN CHALLENGES AND THE PORTUGUESE *ESTADO DA INDIA*

The developments in the maritime space of the Indian Ocean captivated the attention of Suleiman the Magnificent (1520-66), even when issues and developments in Europe turned out to be his primary concerns. Selim's earlier attempts to link the various trade centres of the Indian Ocean with the Ottoman ports in the Red Sea with the help of different merchant groups had already found fruits by this time. The Marakkar traders of Kerala turned out to be a significant mercantile group that cooperated with the Ottomans in carrying out a greater share of Indian trade. Being dissatisfied with the Portuguese behaviour towards them and seeing the prospects of trading with the Ottomans, the leading Muslim merchants of Cochin including Kunjali Marakkar, his brother Ahmad Marakkar, their uncle Muhammadali Marakkar and their dependents shifted their base of operations from Cochin to Calicut by 1524.[33] Meanwhile, the Zamorin who expelled the Portuguese from Calicut in 1525 started making use of this opportunity to reorganize the trade of Calicut with the navigational expertise of the Kunjalis. Things really worked in the way the Zamorin and the Marakkars had planned. Commodity movements from Calicut to the ports of Ottoman Turks in the Red Sea had already become relatively frequent, particularly during the period between 1526 and 1527.[34]

Meanwhile, in the midst of the adverse situation created by the control mechanisms of the Portuguese, the Muslim traders of Cannanore managed to continue their business by developing a trade route outside the Portuguese control system that was finally interlinked with the Ottoman commercial network. From Cannanore they used to divert commodities first to the Maldives and then get it linked with the commodities coming from South-East Asia through the straits of Karaidu and Haddumati to Ottoman trade centres in the Red Sea and the Persian Gulf.[35] The surplus deriving from this trade and the benefits accumulated by way of controlling the island groups of the Maldives, were very effectively used for their state building ventures in Cannanore, which in turn prompted the Muslim merchants of Cannanore to maintain this network of trade running outside the Portuguese control system.[36]

In fact the commonality of religion made them join hands in diverting commodities to the network of Ottoman commerce. The revival of Venice trade from the 1540s onwards was made possible,[37] to a great extent, because of the joint and collective commercial activities of the Marakkar Muslim traders of Kerala and the Ottomans, from two different operational points. Meanwhile, Cranganore was identified as an important spice exchange centre,[38] whose commodities the Portuguese wanted to procure by instituting a fortress over there in 1536. The Portuguese found that a great portion of pepper from Cranganore was diverted to the Red Sea ports. The erection of the fortress at Cranganore is to be seen against the background of recurring Muslim attacks on the maritime trade centres of central and southern Kerala, which came as a result of the peripheral impact of the Ottoman's expansion into the Indian Ocean.[39] Meanwhile Khwaja Safar, the merchant governor of Gujarat and another leading noble of the Muzaffarid Gujarat had mobilized a fighting force of about 600 Turks for the purpose of realizing his political and commercial ventures that he had chalked out in India. Khwaja Safar was originally an Albanian Catholic, who later on his way to conduct trade in the Strait of Mecca with three ships was captured by Rax Sulaiman, the general of Mamluk Egypt.[40] Later he was appointed as the treasurer of the sultan, for holding which he was asked to embrace Islam. Taking the name of Khwaja Safar, he used to conduct trade with Indian ports including Gujarat and also participated with a vessel in the war against the Portuguese fought by the joint forces of the Mamluks, the Venetians, the Ottomans, Zamorin and the Muzaffarids off Diu in 1508.[41] Later he murdered Rax Sulaiman and moved to Gujarat with his harem, wealth of 300,000 cruzados, besides lot of jewellery, and a fighting force of 600 Turkish soldiers as well as a few pieces of artillery.[42] By 1537 he was one of the leading merchants of Diu[43] and it was because of his long-term links with the Ottomans that the Turkish forces were repeatedly invited to Gujarat to fight against the Portuguese in 1538 and 1546.[44] By 1538 he was appointed as the governor of Surat,[45] from which capacity he extended his commerce to the chief ports of the Ottomans in the Red Sea and the Persian Gulf. Under his governorship Surat was made to evolve as the principal trading centre of Gujarat competing with Diu, which the Portuguese occupied in 1536, while those of Surat were connected with the Ottoman world.

Khwaja Safar, the merchant governor of Surat,[46] who had been maintaining commercial linkages with many of the Ottoman ports, invited the Ottoman viceroy Khadim Sulaiman Pasha from Suez to come to Gujarat and fight against the Portuguese in 1538 for the purpose of capturing Diu.[47] In 1537, Khwaja Safar met Muhmmad Shah the new sultan and explained to him the need to attack the Portuguese settlement of Diu and promised him that the Turks would help the sultan in this attempt.[48] Meanwhile Khwaja Safar sent an invitation to Khadim Sulaiman Pasha for getting the Turkish force and mobilized a military force of 3,000 horses and infantry of 4,000.[49]

Concomitantly another invitation to Sulaiman Pasha for dispatching Ottoman forces to Pearl Fishery Coast to fight against the Portuguese went from Pate Marakkar. Being terribly upset by the mass conversion of Paravas depriving the Marakkars of the chances of controlling pearl trade any further, the Marakkars under the leadership of Kunjali Marakkar, Pate Marakkar and Ibrahim Ali Marakkar mobilized a large force consisting of 2,000 fighting people and 50 large vessels to attack and plunder the newly formed Christian villages of the Paravas and captured their boats.[50] At this juncture the Marakkars, who used to conduct trade with the Ottoman ports of Red sea from 1517 onwards also sought the help of the Turkish forces in 1538, who were making preparations for moving to Gujarati coast to capture Diu.[51] The sources evidently indicate that the Ottomans promptly responded to the request of their commercial partners, the Marakkars, as well, and in 1538 an Ottoman fleet reached the Kerala port of Vizhinjam and probably also Pearl Fishery Coast, against the background of clashes between the Marakkars and the newly converted Parava Christians.[52] The arrival of Ottoman fleet in Vizhinjam and Pearl Fishery Coast at a time when Kunjali and his Marakkar allies were increasingly chased and about to be defeated by the Portuguese at Vedalai and Negombo,[53] is indicative of the larger dimensions of the relationship that evolved by this time between the Ottomans and the Marakkar traders of Kerala.[54]

The Ottoman attack on Indian soil was done with lot of preparations. Vessels needed for the capturing of Diu were already being built at Suez as early as 1537, probably immediately after receiving invitation from Khwaja

Safar. Venetian sailors were recruited for manning their ships engaged in the expansionist battles of the Indian Ocean. First they moved to Aden, which they captured in 1538 and then they moved to Diu laying siege to it.[55] However, the Ottomans did not gain anything out of this venture, as the Portuguese viceroy promptly thwarted their moves and Khwaja Safar withdrew support to the Ottomans.[56]

The presence of the Turks in the vicinity alerted the Portuguese to a chain of defensive actions, including the erection of new fortresses and the strengthening of the existing ones. The Portuguese started tightening their grip on the west coast of India. A chain of new fortresses was instituted along the Konkan and Gujarat coasts, so that the Ottomans in collaboration with the Muslim rulers of these coastal regions of India might not make an alternative network to divert spices to the trading centres of the Ottomans in the Persian Gulf and the Red Sea. Accordingly, fortresses in Bassein (1534), Diu (1536)[57] and Daman (1559),[58] were erected to protect the Lusitanian commercial interests in the northern provinces.

Meanwhile with the capturing of Baghdad from the Saffavids in 1534 and later with the establishment of a naval base at Basra by the Ottomans in 1538,[59] the Persian Gulf turned out to be an Ottoman economic unit for all practical purposes. We find a lot of spices from the ports of Kerala moving to the markets of the Ottoman Turks and the Saffavid Persia through Basra from 1540 onwards. From Basra they were further carried to Tripoly of Syria by two routes: one through the desert route that terminated at Damascus, and the other passed by Baghdad. The merchants travelled in caravans up to the city of Aleppo, from where they were further taken to Tripoly of Syria.[60] The trade through the ports of the Persian Gulf continued to be active even later, as Leonhard Rauwolfd gives us an eyewitness account, with as many as twenty-five ships loaded with spices and drugs from India (evidently from Kerala) moving to Baghdad via Hormuz and Basra.[61]

In the changed situation, Suleiman I the Magnificent had made a suggestion to the Portuguese King John III through a letter dated 28 May 1544 that he was ready to buy 20,000 kg. of pepper and other drugs from the Portuguese, which the latter might hand over to the Ottoman governor in Aden.[62] This request might have been made to ensure regular supply of spices in the Mediterranean so as to sustain the Venetian trade revived by the 1540s. However this dream was not realized. This made the Ottomans make a much longer and time-consuming voyage from the Red Sea to Bengal, to procure spices coming from the ports of Kerala, for taking back to their homeland. In 1545 several Ottoman traders went to Bengal, Pegu, and Tenasserim to take pepper coming from the Kerala ports to the Ottoman ports of the Red Sea.[63]

It seems that these were the preparatory moves of Suleiman the Magnificent before taking direct involvement in the affairs of India.

The Ottomans vessels entered Indian waters to attack Diu for the second time in 1546. This time too the initiative for inviting the Ottomans was taken by Khwaja Safar, the merchant governor of Surat, who had by this time emerged as a leading merchant conducting business with the Ottoman ports of Red Sea. We find his vessels frequently going with cargo to Suez and Jiddah controlled by the Ottomans from early 1540s[64] and bringing back boxes of bullions in the form of gold *ashrafis*.[65] Though in the earlier days he used to take *cartaz* from the Portuguese to dispatch vessels to Ottoman ports, later with the increase in his wealth from the customs duty of Surat and also from his trade with Ottoman ports he got all the more empowered and wanted to do away with the Portuguese, who had by this time started extracting customs at Diu from the vessels going to West Asia. Consequently Khwaja Safar sent his envoys to Constantinople requesting Ottoman help to oust the Portuguese.[66]

On getting the invitation from Khwaja Safar, galleys were constructed in the Ottoman dockyard at Basra with timber brought down the Euphrates from the Mar'ash region of the southern Taurus Mountains.[67] A large fleet dispatched by Suleiman started laying siege on and attacking the Portuguese fort of Diu in 1546.[68] The Ottoman siege on Diu with the help of Gujarati soldiers supplied by Khwaja Safar continued for several weeks.

Against this background of the ubiquitous presence of the Ottomans in the visible vicinity of Portuguese possessions, the crown and its officials of the *Estado* started increasingly banking upon Cochin and Goa for mobilizing resources for the purpose of defending the *Estado* from the Ottoman attacks. Attempts were made to mobilize large material and human resources from these cities, when the Ottomans laid siege on Diu in 1546. D. João de Castro took about 1,500 men from Goa and Cochin to Diu on 20 September 1546.[69] While a good many of them like Antonio Leme,[70] Manoel de Sousa de Sepulveda,[71] Francisco da Silva,[72] Sebastião Luis, *alcaide-mor* of Cochin,[73] Antonio Correa, the very factor of Cochin,[74] etc., were mobilized from Cochin, a considerably great number was gathered from Goa, as well, like Lucas Veiga,[75] Dom Leitão,[76] Simão da Rocha,[77] Sebastião Lopez Lobato,[78] Francisco Navaes Pereira,[79] Vasco Rebello,[80] Pedro de Liao,[81] etc. The lifting of the siege on Diu was effected thanks to the help, both in the form of wealth and men, extended by Cochin and Goa.[82] Meanwhile, the Portuguese governor D. João de Castro rewarded the city-dwellers of Goa and Cochin who had fought in the war of 1546 to defend Diu by granting commercial voyages, in most cases, to Bengal or Malacca or Hormuz.[83]

Though in the Luso-Turkish encounter, the Portuguese ably kept the Ottomans out of Indian soil, the Ottomans attacked and temporarily occupied Muscat in 1552 with the help of a strong squadron consisting of 25 galleys, 4 galleons and a big ship with 850 troops under the command of Piri Reis.[84] The principal objectives of the Ottomans were to capture Hormuz and Bahrain islands, whose possession was deemed to be necessary to oust the Portuguese and to control the Indian Ocean trade. Though they could not achieve this target, Piri Reis and Seydi 'Ali Reis conquered the coasts of Yemen and Aden as well as Arabia and cleared the coastal belt up to Basra for the purpose of conducting easy trade with India.[85]

However, the Ottomans did not altogether leave the water space of India. In 1553 the Ottomans with the support of Marakkar Muslims of Malabar attacked the Pearl Fishery Coast in south India. Their target were the Portuguese, who started controlling the pearl-fishing of its coast. The Marakkar-Ottoman attack on the Portuguese churches and settlements had the tacit approval of Vittula Nayak of Madurai who actually wanted to control the pearlfishing. The chruches of Punnaikayal were burnt down and 52 Portuguese soldiers along with their captain and priests were taken as prisoners.[86] A major strand of Indo-Ottoman trade was through the port of Surat, whose trade happened to be predominantly controlled by Ottoman-related merchants or governors. In fact, it was the relative upper hand of the Turks in commercial matters of Surat since the time of Khwaja Safar that made it to evolve as major maritime door for conducting trade with the Ottoman commercial world, even after Akbar's occupation of Surat in 1574. In the beginning of 1580s the captain of the port of Surat, Qilij Khan Andijani, originally a Turk, started sending ships to the Ottoman ports of Red Sea without the Portuguese *cartaz* or licence, which led to a chain of conflicts between the Portuguese and the Mughals during the period between 1581 and 1585.[87]

As early as 1573 Akbar had made agreement with the Portuguese, adhering to which the latter started issuing every year free *cartaz* to a Mughal imperial ship going for *Haj* pilgrimage from Surat and granted exemption of customs duty on the cargo that it brought back.[88] We know that Akbar later appointed an officer called *Mir Haj* for organizing *Haj* pilgrimage, who took the first group of Mughal pilgrims consisting of Akbar'a aunt Gulbadan Begam, the empress Salima Sultan Begam and a few high-born women in 1576 from Surat to Jiddah in the ship *Ilahi*.[89] Eventually when the pilgrim vessels returning from Ottoman port of Jiddah took large bulk of cargo from Arabia, the farmers of revenue at Diu started capturing these vessels demanding customs duty. In August 1577, about five vessels returning from Jiddah but loaded with different types of cargo and the imperial ship with gold and silver worth the value of

600,000 *cruzados* were captured by the revenue-farmers at Diu, which created intense tension between Akbar and the Portuguese.[90] The Mughal governor of Gujarat had to plead before the Portuguese Viceroy to return the vessels to Akbar. Though finally things were sorted out and the vessel of Akbar was given back, it created a lot of tension and heat, which got aggravated with the spread of rumour that the Portuguese would henceforth impede the movement of ships from Surat to Jiddah. On hearing about it Akbar got disturbed and asked Quli Khan, one of the most powerful Mughal administrators of Gujarat to go to the seashore and do the needful for facilitating the *Haj* pilgrims to make their onward voyage to Jiddah.[91] By this time *Haj*, as we have argued elsewhere in this book, besides being a religious exercise of pilgrimage, was the largest moving market in the medieval and early modern times and was also the important economic channel for obtaining precious cargo including bullions from Jiddah, Mocha and other markets of Red Sea.

The Mughal nobles and royal ladies also used to dispatch ships regularly with indigo and textiles to Mocha and other Ottoman ports and bring back bullions. One of such vessels was Rahimi, which was sent to the Ottoman port of Mocha with a Portuguese *cartaz* by Maryam-uz-Zamani, mother of emperor Jahangir. However, the Portuguese captured the vessel along with the cargo, and 700 passengers, which angered Jahangir making him take such serious measures as temporarily stopping the traffic through Surat, an effort to capture the neighbouring Portuguese settlement of Daman, the closing of the Jesuit church in Agra, etc.[92] However, this conflict was only transient and the Mughal trade with the Ottoman ports of continued in the succeeding decades of the seventeenth century rather in high velocity.

It is interesting to note that in the fleet of Ottoman Turks, a large number of Armenians were employed as a fighting force. They entered the Indian Ocean in considerable numbers during the period 1520 and 1552, laying siege on Diu, and expanding the Ottoman authority to the western domains of this maritime space. However, when the Portuguese lifted the siege on Diu in 1546 and when the Ottoman navy in the Indian Ocean was later disbanded, the Armenian fighting men instead of going back to their original homeland got dispersed in the waters of Asia, entering into the service of different Muslim rulers like that of Aceh as mercenaries and mediating between them and the Ottomans on strategic matters including commerce.[93] Though the Armenians initially operated under the political and economic umbrella of the Ottomans, eventually they emerged as leading merchants and bankers in the Muslim states and principalities of Asia. They used to conduct their business through a network of Armenian diaspora spread out mostly in the Indian Ocean, but very much integrated with its core centre at New Julfa.[94] It is worth noting that though the Ottomans failed to sustain their mercantile interest in the Indian Ocean for a long period of time, their Armenian agents outlived them in matters of Indian Ocean commerce, probably imbibing the spirit from their masters. However, there is no doubt that their acceptability before the Muslim rulers of the Indian Ocean region was initially ensured mainly because of their onetime closeness to the Ottoman Turks.

Thus, the historical developments of the first half of the sixteenth century manifest a chain of actions and processes in Asian waters, in which the Portuguese expansion along the west coast of India is sequentially followed by the Ottoman expansion into the western rim of the Indian Ocean, evidently suggesting a causal linkage between the two. An analysis of the historical developments of the period is indicative of the fact that it was the Portuguese expansion into the major trade centres of coastal western India and into the Persian Gulf (Hormuz), as well as the regular patrolling of the mouth of the Red Sea that made the Ottomans turn towards the core areas of the caravan trade located in Egypt as well as West Asia and establish hegemony over there. The Marakkar traders of Kerala, who developed an alternative trading network outside the orbit of the Portuguese control systems, were the principal feeders from India for the trade of the Ottoman ports in the Red Sea and the Persian Gulf. The economic ties between the Ottomans and the Marakkars seem to have been well maintained and protected by the military devices and naval machineries of the Ottomans, as is suggested by the appearance of the Ottoman fleet in Vizhinjam in Kerala (1538), when the Marakkar traders were chased and frequently attacked by the Portuguese because of their linkage with Kunjali Marakkar. Though the frequent attempts of the Ottomans to enter the soil of India were repelled ably by the Portuguese, the amount of influence that they exerted on the shaping of the military structures of *Estado da India* was enormous. Against the background of the Ottoman expansion into the western fringes of the Indian Ocean, the Portuguese erected strong fortresses at key strategic centres of trade along the west coast of India, besides strengthening and reinforcing the existing ones. The very structuring and proliferation of these Portuguese fortresses were greatly necessitated by the different types of challenges raised by the diverse streams of Ottoman expansion into the Indian Ocean from 1517 onwards.

Though both the Portuguese and the Ottomans moved to the maritime space of Indian Ocean almost simultaneously (the gap was only of nineteen years, as the Ottomans reached Suez in 1517), the Portuguese managed to appropriate a major portion of it, as their primary concern was India and their secondary concerns were confined to other Indian Ocean regions. However, the prime concern of the Ottomans continued to be Europe and the Mediterranean regions even during this period. It is true that the Indian

Ocean regions captivated the attention of the Ottomans as economically important areas, from where they tried to mobilize resources for their empire building ventures; however, these regions happened to remain all through as supplementary feeding zones for the Ottomans. The Portuguese tried to obstruct the free flow of commodities to the Ottoman ports by erecting fortresses at strategic centres and junctional points of riverine and land routes, which they also developed as power-exercising devices. Though the degree of exercise of power varied and, in some places, the fortresses eventually turned out to be mere stone structures devoid of actual power of control as in the case of Cannanore, the chain of Portuguese fortresses erected along coastal western India did a lot to prevent the Ottomans from completely integrating the economic activities of India into their designs, which they were cherishing from the middle of the fifteenth century onwards.

NOTES

1. Pius Malekandathil, *The Germans, the Portuguese and India*, Münster, 1999, p. 10; Halil Inalcik, *The Ottoman Empire, The Classical Age, 1300-1600*, London 1973.

2. Francisco de Souza, *Oriente Conquistado a Jesu Christo pelos Padres da Companhia de Jesus da Provincia de Goa*, vol. I, div. I, 17. Lisboa 1710, p. 13; João de Barros, *Asia, Dos feitos que os Portuguezes fizeram no Descobrimento e conquista doa Mares do Oriente*, ed. Livraria Sam Carlos, (facsimile of the 1777-8 edition), Lisboa 1973, decada II, livro V, capitulo I, p. 434; Gaspar Correia, *Lendas da India*, II, Lisboa, 1925, p. 55; João Manuel Pacheco de Figueiredo, 'Goa Pre-Portuguesa', *Studia*, nos. 13 and 14, Janeiro-Julho 1964, pp. 220-1.

3. Barros, *Da Asia*, decada II, livro V, capitulo II, p. 24.

4. Tome Pires, *The Suma Oriental of Tomé Pires: An Account of the East Sea to Japan written in Malacca and India in 1512-1515*, ed. and tran. Armando Cortesão, vol. I, New Delhi, 1990, p. 58.

5. This is evident from the fact that the repeated attacks of the Ottomans on India in the sixteenth century were directed towards Diu.

6. Donald F. Lach, *Asia in the Making of Europe*, vol. I, *The Century of Discovery*, I, Chicago, 1965, p. 143.

7. Vitorino Magalhães Godinho, *Le repli venetien et egyptien et la route du Cap, 1496-1533, Eventail de l'histoire vivante, homage a Lucien Febvre*, vol. II, Paris, 1953, pp. 289, 294; Vitorino Magalhães Godinho, *L'Economie de L'empire portugais aux XVe et XVIe siecles*, Paris 1969, pp. 720-1, 725.

8. Pius Malekandathil, *The Germans, the Portuguese and India*, pp. 21-2.

9. 'The Anonymous Narrative' in *The Voyage of Pedro Alvarez Cabral to Brazil and India*, ed. William Brooks Greenlee, London, 1938, p. 86; Luis de Albuquerque, ed., *Cronica do Descobrimento e conquista da India pelos Portugueses: codice*

anonimo Museu Britanico, Egerton 20901, Coimbra, 1974, p. 25; Marino Sanuto, *I Diarii di Marino Sanuto: 1496-1533,* ed. G. Berchet, R. Fulin, N. Barrozi, F. Steffani and M. Allegri, vol. IV, Venice, 1879, cols. 66-7; Rinaldo Fulin, *Diarii e diaristi Veneziani,* Venice, 1881, pp. 157-64; Wilhelm von Heyd, *Histoire du commerce du Levant au Moyen Age,* vol. II, Leipzig, 1886, p. 512.

10. Marino Sanuto, *I Diarii di Marino Sanuto,* tom. IV, p. 544; tom. XVII, p. 191; tom. XXVII, p. 641; Pius Malekandathil, *Portuguese Cochin and the Maritime Trade of India, 1500-1663,* South Asian Study Series of Heidelberg University, Germany, No.39, New Delhi, 2001, pp. 166-67; Vitorino Magalhães Godinho, *Os Descobrimentos e a Economia Mundial,* vol. III, Lisboa, 1984, p. 73; K.S. Mathew, *Portuguese Trade with India in the Sixteenth Century,* New Delhi, 1983, pp. 114-29.

11. Vitorino Magalhães Godinho, *Os Descobrimentos e a Economia Mundial,* vol. III, Liboa, 1981, p. 184; Hermann van der Wee, 'Structural Changes in European Long-Distance Trade, and Particularly in the Re-export Trade from South to North, 1350-1750' in *The Rise of Merchant Empires, Long Distance Trade in the Early Modern World: 1350-1750,* ed. James D. Tracy, Cambridge, 1990, p. 28.

12. Vitorino Magalhães Godinho, *L'Economie de L'empire portugais aux XVe etXVIe siecles,* pp. 720-5.

13. Raymundo Antonio de Bulhão Pato, *Cartas de Affonso de Albuquerque seguidas de documentos que as elucidam,* tom. I, Lisboa, 1884, pp. 21ff; João de Barros, *Asia. Dos feitos que os Portuguezes fizeram no Descobrimento e conquista dos Mares do Oriente,* Lisboa, 1771, decada II, part II, pp. 40ff, 181; decada III, part II, pp. 451-2; Joaquim Verissimo Serrão, *Commentarios de Afonso de Albuquerque,* tom. I, Lisboa, 1973, p. 140; Duarte Barbosa, *The Book of Duarte Barbosa: An Account of the Countries Bordering on the Indian Ocean and their Inhabitants,* tran. Mansel Longworth Dames, vol. I, Nedeln, 1967, p. 59.

14. However, the attempts to control the gateway of the Red Sea by conquering Aden did not succeed.

15. Halil Inalcik, *The Ottoman Empire, The Classical Age, 1300-1600,* London, 1973; Halil Inalcik and Donald Quartaet eds., *A Social and Economic History of the Ottoman Empire;* D.S.Richards, ed., *Islam and the Trade of Asia,* Oxford, 1970.

16. Etymologically the word 'Marakkar' means captain or owner of a ship and is derived from the Tamil word 'Marakalam' meaning ship. For details, see O.K. Nambiar, *The Kunjalis: Admirals of Calicut,* London, 1963, p. 76.

17. Jayaseela Stephen, *The Coromandel Coast and Its Hinterland: Economy, Society and Political System (AD 1500-1600),* New Delhi 1997, pp. 137-139.

18. Pius Malekandathil, 'Making Power Visible: Portuguese Commercial and Military Strategies in the Indian Ocean with special Reference to Cannanore, 1500-1550', in *Winds of Spices,* ed. K.S. Mathew, Tellicherry 2006, pp. 3-9.

19. ANTT, *Chancelaria de Manuel I,* liv. II, fol. 83 'Capitulos de pazes entre Afonso de Albuquerque e o Samorin de Calicut', Lisboa, 26 de Fevreiro de 1515; Genevieve Bouchon, 'Calicut at the Turn of the Sixteenth Century', in *The*

Asian Seas 1500-1800: Local Societies, European Expansion and the Portuguese, Revista de Cultura, vol. I, ano V (1991), 46; Raymundo Antonio de Bulhão Pato, ed., *Cartas de Affonso de Albuquerque seguidas de documentos que as elucidam,* tom. I, Lisboa 1884, p.126.

20. Pius Malekandathil, 'From Merchant Capitalists to Corsairs: The Role of Muslim Merchants in Portuguese Maritime Trade of the Portuguese' in *Portuguese Studies Review,* 2004, 12(1), pp. 84-85.

21. Zaynuddin Shaykh, *Tuhfat-ul-Mujahidin,* tran. S.Muhammad Hussain Nainar, Madras, 1942, pp. 89-91; R.S. Whiteway, *The Rise of Portuguese Power in India,* New Delhi, 1989, p. 196.

22. R.S. Whiteway, op. cit., p. 196. Another important Muslim trader of Cochin to become a corsair, when the Portuguese captured the two ships sent by him to Cambay, was Pate Marakkar, who had been a great friend and collaborator of the Portuguese in the early days of their establishment. On the confiscation of his vessels, he went to Calicut and joined his nephew, Kunjali Marakkar as a corsair. *As Gavetas da Torre do Tombo,* vol. X, Lisboa, 1975, p. 577; Genevieve Bouchon, 'Les Musulmans du Kerala à L'Epoque de la Découverte Portugaise', *Mare Luso-Indicum,* II, Paris, 1973, pp. 52-3; See also Diogo Couto, *Da Asia dos feitos que os Portuguezes fizeram na conquista e descobrimento das terras e mares do Oriente,* decada V, parte 2, Lisboa, 1973, p. 4.

23. Genevieve Bouchon, *Regent of the Sea: Cannanore's Response to Portuguese Expansion, 1507-1528,* tran. Louise Shackley, Delhi, 1988, pp. 23-5, 44-5, 119, 142, 151-64; Pius Malekandathil, 'The Maritime Trade of Cannanore and the Global Commercial Revolution in the 16th and the 17th Centuries', in *Cannanore in the Maritime History of India,* ed. M.O. Koshy, Kannur, 2002, pp. 46-50.

24. It was in 1516 that the Mamluk Sultan Kansuh al-Gauri was completely defeated and killed by Selim near Aleppo. By the end of January 1517, Cairo was in Selim's hands and thereby he became the guardian and master of the holy places of Medina and Mecca, and also the controller of trade in the Red Sea. M.S. Anderson, *The Origin of the Modern European State System, 1494-1618,* London, 1998, p. 234; Jean Louis Bacque-Grammont et Anne Kroell ed., *Mamlouks, Ottomans et Portugais en mer Rouge. L'affaire de Djedda en 1517,* Supplement aux *Annales Islamologiques,* Le Caire, 1988.

25. Gaspar Correia, *Lendas da India,* tom. II, Lisboa, 1921, p. 577.

26. Tome Pires, *The Suma Oriental of Tomé Pires: An Account of the East, from the Red Sea to Japan written in Malacca and India in 1512-1515,* Nendeln, 1967, p. 34; João de Barros, *Asia. Dos feitos que os Portugueses fizeram no Descobrimento e Conquista dos Mares e Terras do Oriente,* Lisboa, 1973, tomo II, part I, pp. 210-14.

27. Mahomed Kisim Ferishta, *History of the Rise of the Mahomedan Power in India, A Persian History,* tr. John Briggs, vol. IV, New Delhi, 1981, pp. 39-41.

28. João de Barros, *Asia. Dos feitos que os Portugueses fizeram no Descobrimento,* tomo II, part I, pp. 212-14; Gaspar Correa, *Lendas da India,* tomo I, Coimbra, 1922, pp. 746-7.

29. This was the size of the fighting force that he mobilized for the wars against Abdullah Muhammad al-Malikki al-Asafi al Ulughkhani Hajji Ad, *Zafar ul Walih bi Muzaffar wa Alihi*, tr. M.F. Lokhandwala, vol. I, Baroda, 1970, pp. 102-3.

30. The Turks were included in the battle against the Portuguese in 1508. Damião de Gois, *Chronica do Felicissimo Rei D.Emmnauel de glorioso memoria*, Coimbra, 1933, part II, p. 132; Gaspar Correa, *Lendas da India*, tomo I, pp. 927-8.

31. K.S. Mathew, *Portuguese and the Sultanate of Gujarat (1500-1573)*, Delhi, 1986, pp. 24-40.

32. Ibid., pp. 30-1; Mahomed Kisim Ferishta, *History of the Rise of the Mahomedan Power*, vol. IV, p. 45; João de Barros, *Asia. Dos feitos que os Portugueses fizeram no Descobrimento*, tomo II, part I, pp. 173-218; Gaspar Correa, *Lendas da India*, tomo I, pp. 741-71.

33. Faria y Souza, *Asia Portuguesa: The History of the Discovery and Conquest of India by the Portuguese*, tran. John Stevens, vol. I, London, 1695, p. 284; Shaykh Zaynuddin, op. cit., 66; A.P. Ibrahim Kunju, *Studies in Medieval Kerala*, Trivandrum, 1975, p. 60.

34. Gaspar Correia, *Lendas da India*, tom. III, parte I, pp. 274-5.

35. Genevieve Bouchon, *Regent of the Sea*, pp. 118-19, 161; for details on the flow of commodities from the Cannanore to the ports of the Red Sea controlled by the Ottomans, see Pius Malekandathil, 'The Maritime Trade of Cannanore', pp. 47-53.

36. Pius Malekandathil, 'The Maritime Trade of Cannanore and the Global Commercial Revolution', pp. 45-54.

37. For revival of Venice trade, see Frederic C. Lane, 'The Mediterranean Spice Trade: Further Evidence of its Revival in the Sixteenth Century', in *Crisis and Change in the Venetian Economy in the 16th and 17th Centuries*, ed. Brian Pullan, London 1968, pp. 47-58.

38. Silva Rego, *Documentação para a Historia das Missões do Padroado Português do Oriente*, vol. I, Lisboa, 1949, pp. 352-4.

39. George Schurhammer, *The Malabar Church and Rome during the Early Portuguese Period and Before*, Trichinapoly, 1934, pp. 11-13; Pius Malekandathil, 'The Portuguese and the St. Thomas Christians: 1500-1570', in *The Portuguese and the Socio-Cultural Changes in India, 1500-1800*, ed. K.S. Mathew, Teotonio R. de Souza and Pius Malekandathil, Fundação Oriente, Lisbon/ MESHAR, Tellicherry, 2001, p. 133.

40. João de Barros, *Asia. Dos feitos que os Portugueses fizeram no Descobrimento*, tomo III, part I, p. 33; Jacinto Freire de Andrade, *Vida de Dom João de Castro*, Lisboa, 1968, pp. 79-80.

41. Jacinto Freire de Andrade, *Vida de Dom João de Castro*, pp. 80-2; Diogo do Couto, *Da Asia dos feitos que os Portuguezes fizeram na Conquista e Descobrimento das Terras e Mares do Oriente*, Decada IV, Lisboa, 1973, p. 211.

42. Jacinto Freire de Andrade, *Vida de Dom João de Castro*, p. 82; Fernão Lopes Castanheda, *Historia do Descobrimento e Conquista da India pelos Portugueses*, liv. viii, Coimbra, 1924, p. 248.

43. K.S. Mathew, 'Khwaja Saffar, the Merchant Governor of Surat and the Indo-Portuguese Trade in the Early Sixteenth Century', in *Vice-Almirante A. Teixeira da Mota: In Memoriam*, vol. I, Lisboa, 1987, p. 323.

44. Ibid., pp. 324-8.

45. Gaspar Correa, *Lendas da India*, tomo IV, pp. 143, 159; Diogo do Couto, *Da Asia dos feitos que os Portuguezes fizeram na Conquista e Descobrimento das Terras*, Decada V, part i, pp. 205-6.

46. Diogo do Couto, *Da Asia dos feitos que os Portuguezes fizeram na Conquista e Descobrimento das Terras*, tomo V, liv. i, pp. 205-6: Gaspar Correa, *Lendas da India*, tomo IV, pp. 143, 159.

47. Dejanirah Couto, 'Les Ottomans et I'Inde Portugaise', *Vasco da Gama et I'Inde*, vol. I, Calouste Gulbenkian Foundation, Paris, 1999, pp. 185–8; Salih Özbaran, *The Ottoman Response to European Expansion—Studies on Ottoman-Portuguese Relations in the Indian Ocean and Ottoman Administration in the Arab Lands during the Sixteenth Century*, Analecta Isisiana XIII, Istanbul, 1994, pp. 99-109.

48. Diogo do Couto, *Da Asia dos feitos que os Portuguezes fizeram na Conquista e Descobrimento das Terras*, tomo V, part I, pp. 202-5; João de Barros, *Asia. Dos feitos que os Portugueses fizeram no Descobrimento*, tomo IV, part ii, pp. 399ff; 616-17.

49. Ibid., p. 446; João de Barros, *Asia. Dos feitos que os Portugueses fizeram no Descobrimento*, tomo IV, part ii, pp. 616-22.

50. Georg Schurhammer, *Orientalia*, Lisboa, 1963, p. 248.

51. Ibid.

52. Gaspar Correa, *Lendas da India*, tom. III, p. 882.

53. João de Barros, *Asia. Dos feitos que os Portugueses fizeram no Descobrimento e Conquista dos Mares e Terras do Oriente*, Decada IV, liv. 8, Lisboa, 1973, pp. 12-14; Diogo Couto, *Da Asia dos feitos que os Portuguezes fizeram na Conquista e Descobrimento das Terras e Mares do Oriente*, Decada V, Lisboa, 1973, liv. 2, pp. 4–6, 8.

54. Pius Malekandathil, 'Winds of Change and Links of Continuities: A Study on the Merchant Groups of Kerala and the Channels of their Trade, 1000-1800', *Journal of Economic and Social History of the Orient*, vol. 50, no. 2, 2007, pp. 271-2.

55. M.S. Anderson, *The Origin of the Modern European State System, 1494-1618*, London, 1998, p. 227. For details on the practice of the Ottomans to employ European experts and technology for naval expeditions see A.C. Hess, 'The Evolution of the Ottoman Sea-borne Empire in the Age of the Oceanic Discoveries, 1455-1525', *American Historical Review*, vol. LXXV, 1969-70, p. 1901; Palmira Brummet, *Ottoman Sea Power and Levantine Diplomacy in the Age of Discovery*, New York, 1994, p. 93; B. Lewis, *Cultures in Conflict: Christians, Muslims and Jews in the Age of Discovery*, New York, 1995, p. 22; Giancarlo Casale, *The Ottoman Age of Exploration*, Oxford, 2010.

56. João de Barros, *Asia. Dos feitos que os Portugueses fizeram no Descobrimento*, tomo IV, part ii, p. 710.

57. Luis Filipe Thomaz, *A questão da pimento em meados do seculo XVI. Um debate politico do governo de D.João de Castro*, Lisboa, 1998, p. 79.

58. Artur Teodoro de Matos, ed., *O Tombo de Damão 1592*, Lisboa, 2001, p. 295.

59. Salih Özbaran, 'The Ottoman Turks and the Portuguese in the Persian Gulf, 1534-1581', *Journal of Asian History*, VI, 1, 1972, pp. 52-4. In 1538, the name of the Ottoman Sultan was stamped on the coinage and included in the *khutba* at Basra. In 1546 Basra was formally integrated into the empire.

60. Nycolão Gomçallves, *Livro que trata das cousas da India e do Japão*, ed. Adelino da Almeida Calado, Coimbra, 1957, p. 74.

61. Karl H. Dannenfeldt, *Leonhard Rauwolf: Sixteenth Century Physician, Botanist and Traveller*, Massachussetts, 1968, p. 121.

62. The letter of the Sultan to the Portuguese crown in ANTT, *Corpo Chronologico*, I, Maço 74, doc.108.

63. See the remarks of João Fernandes Galego about the flow of pepper to the various destinations in the Indian Ocean. ANTT, *Cartas dos Vice-Reisda India*, no. 75; Pius Malekandathil, 'Bengal and the Commercial Expansion of the Portuguese Casados, 1511-1632', in *Trade and Globalization: Europeans, Americans and Indians in the Bay of Bengal (1511-1819)*, New Delhi, 2003, p. 172.

64. Gaspar Correa, *Lendas da India*, tomo IV, p. 237.

65. Abdullah Muhammad al-Malikki al-Asafi al Ulughkhani Hajji Ad, *Zafar ul Walih bi Muzaffar wa Alihi*, pp. 231-2. It refers to the loss of a box full of gold *ashrafis* brought for Khwaja Safar.

66. Jacinto Freire de Andrade, *Vida de Dom João de Castro*, p. 88; Fernão Lopes Castanheda, *Historia do Descobrimento e Conquista da India pelos Portugueses*, liv. viii, p. 504.

67. Salih Özbaran, 'The Ottoman Turks and the Portuguese in the Persian Gulf, 1534-1581', p. 56.

68. João Paulo Oliveira e Costa, 'O Imperio Portuguese m meados do seculo XVI', in *Anais de Historia de Alem–Mar: Homenagem a Luis Filipe Thomaz*, ed. Artur Teodoro de Matos, p. 101.

69. Antonio Baião, *Historia Quinhentista (inedita) do Segundo cerco de Dio*, Coimbra 1927, p. 298.

70. Antonio Leme was given the permission to get a ship built in Malabar and to send commodities to any of the ports in Bengal as reward for fighting for the state at Diu. Antonio Baião, *Historia Quinhentista (inedita) do Segundo cerco de Dio*, Coimbra, 1927, p. 298.

71. On 21 February 1547, Manoel de Sousa de Sepulveda was permitted to send a ship to Bengal, for having served in Diu and for having spent a lot of money feeding the fighting forces. Ibid., p. 312.

72. The *casado* trader of Cochin, Francisco da Silva was given a grant of voyage on 23 November 1547 as reward for his role in the defence of Diu, by which he could send every year one ship each to Bengal, Arakan and Moluccas. Bibliotheca do Palacio da Ajuda, *Livro das Merces que fez D. João de Castro*, 51-8-46, fol. 193v.

73. ANTT, *Chancellaria de D.João III,* Doações 69, fol. 98v.

74. Antonio Baião, *Historia Quinhentista,* pp. 306, 309-10.

75. Lucas Veiga was given the voyage-concession to Bengal for his participation in the defence of Diu. Antonio Baião, *Historia Quinhentista,* p. 327.

76. Dom Leitão was permitted to send a ship to Maldives along with Jeronimo Butaqua as reward for his role in the defence of Diu. Ibid., p. 327.

77. Simão da Rocha was granted permission to send a vessel to Malacca as reward for his role in the defence of Diu. Ibid., p. 327.

78. Sebastião Lopez Lobato was made the *alcaide mor* of Goa. Ibid., p. 328.

79. Francisco Navaes Pereira was rewarded with a commercial voyage to Bengal. Ibid., p. 328.

80. Vasco Rebello was granted commercial privilege to send vessels to Bengal and Hormuz. Bibliotheca do Palacio da Ajuda, *Livro das Merces que fez D.João de Castro,* 51-8-46, fol. 241v.

81. Pedro de Liao was rewarded with a commercial voyaged to Bengal. Bibliotheca do Palacio da Ajuda, *Livro das Merces que fez D.João de Castro,* 51-8-46, fol. 164v.

82. Crown has acknowledged in his letter the help extended by these cities in lifting the siege on Diu. For details, see J.H. da Cunha Rivara, ed., *Archivo Portuguez-Oriental,* fasc. I, Nova Goa, 1857, p. 8.

83. For details, see Bibliotheca do Palacio da Ajuda, *Livro das Merces que fez D. João de Castro,* 51-8-46.

84. Ibid., p. 60.

85. Ibid., p. 64; J.F. Guilmartin, *Gun Powder and Galleys: Changing Technology and Mediterranean Warfare at Sea in the Sixteenth Century,* Cambridge, 1974, pp. 178-93.

86. Josef Wicki, *Documenta Indica,* vol. III, Rome, pp. 238-9, 252-3.

87. Diogo do Couto, *Da Asia dos feitos que os Portuguezes fizeram na Conquista e Descobrimento das Terras,* Decada X, Parte i, pp. 80-5; M.N. Pearson, *Merchants and Rulers in Gujarat: The Response to the Portuguese in the Sixteenth Century,* Los-Angeles, 1976, pp. 57-60.

88. Diogo do Couto, *Da Asia dos feitos que os Portuguezes fizeram na Conquista e Descobrimento das Terras e Mares do Oriente,* Decada X, pp. 82-4, 287-8; Decada IX, pp. 86-7; K.S. Mathew, 'Akbar and the Portuguese', in *Akbar and His India,* Irfan Habib, ed., New Delhi, 2005, pp. 260, 262.

89. John F. Richards, *The Mughal Empire,* New Delhi, 1993, p. 31; Shireen Moosvi, *People, Taxation and Trade in Mughal India,* p. 246.

90. Diogo do Couto, *Da Asia dos feitos que os Portuguezes fizeram na Conquista e Descobrimento das Terras e Mares do Oriente,* Decada X, pp. 300-4.

91. *The Akbarnama of Abu-l-Fazl,* tr. and ed. H. Beveridge, vol. III, Delhi, 2007, pp. 275-6.

92. William Foster, *Early Travels in India, 1583-1619,* Humprey Milford, 1921, pp. 191-2, 203; Rekha Misra, *Women in Mughal India (1526-1748),* Delhi, 1967, p. 68; Abul Fazl Allami, *Akbarnama,* tr. H. Beveridge, vol. II, Delhi, 1972, pp. 240-4.

93. This information is based primarily on the paper of Giancarlo Casale. For details, see Giancarlo Casale, 'Ottoman Imperial Ideology and the Politicization of Piracy in the Indian Ocean', paper presented to the panel on 'Piracy in the Indian Ocean', at the Second European Congress of World and Global History, 3-5 July 2008, Dresden, Germany.
94. Soren Mentz, 'The Armenian Merchants in the Indian Ocean', A paper presented at the international seminar on the Indian Ocean, held on 7 and 8 January 2008, at India International Centre, New Delhi.

CHAPTER SEVEN

From Merchant Capitalists to Corsairs: The Muslim Merchants of Malabar and their Responses to Portuguese Maritime Trade Expansion, 1498-1600

The Muslim merchants of Malabar formed an important commercial group that operated within the orbit of a World System encompassing the Indian Ocean and the Mediterranean. Their spheres of activity, though geographically originated in Malabar, were linked with the pan-Islamic commercial network, which ultimately terminated in the ports of the Red Sea and the Mediterranean. With the entry of the Portuguese into the Indian Ocean, and with their commercial expansion in the east, there was an attempt to incorporate this region into a new World System that had appeared in the Atlantic in an embryonic form. This move eventually led to a clash between the old World System and the emerging new World System, the effect of which was reflected eventually in differing degrees in the economy, society, religion and politics of Malabar.

This theme has generated a lot of academic interest and several scholars like Fernand Braudel, Niels Steensgaard, Genevieve Bouchon, Vitorino Magalhães Godinho, M.N. Pearson, Ashin Das Gupta, Sanjay Subrahmanyam, have already dealt with the nature of the response of Asian traders, who were operating in the old World System, to the commercial expansion of the Portuguese and the futile attempts of the latter for trade monopoly.[1] However, the scope for this study emerges from the fact that each spatial unit and each mercantile community reacted differently to the various challenges offered by the Lusitanians and that there were temporal variations in their responses. The Muslim merchants of Malabar—who on the basis of Portuguese

*This chapter was earlier published as an article in *Portuguese Studies Review* (Canada), vol. 12, I, Winter-Spring 2004-5, pp. 75-96.

description could be included into a wide variety of social groups like merchant capitalists, peddling traders, corsairs, etc.[2]—offer a challenging case of empirical study wherein these regional and temporal variations are evidently seen.

The central purpose of this study is to see how the different groups of the Muslim merchants of Malabar—who were the active feeders of the old World System—responded to the commercial expansion of the Portuguese and also unravelled the nature of transformation, which they underwent during this period, following the clashes between the old World System and the newly emerging World System. This point is made clear by focussing on two aspects: first, the Muslim merchant groups that collaborated with the Portuguese and second, those among them who developed alternative commercial arrangements to bypass Portuguese control systems for conducting trade with the ports of the Red Sea and the Mediterranean. In the historical evolution the attempts of the latter group to transfer their mercantile capital into the ventures for state building with a view to containing the Portuguese commercial operations gave an altogether new dimension to the very clash.

THE MUSLIM MERCHANTS OF THE
INDIAN OCEAN: A HISTORICAL SETTING

At the time of the arrival of the Portuguese, the Muslim traders were enjoying rather monopolistic hold over the maritime trade of India. However, the Muslim merchants engaged in the maritime trade of the Indian Ocean region were not a monolithic group; it had three main strands, which were cohesively held together by the commonality of religion and common Shafi'ite tradition linked with Arab origin.[3] On the one side there was the *paradesi* (foreign) Muslims, out of whom a good many were al-Karimi merchants engaged in the spice trade with Mamluk's Egypt.[4] They were controlling the long distance movement of the commodities, which had their termination in the Red Sea/Mediterranean world. These *paradesi* Muslims had wider networks and substantial capital for their ventures, which enabled them to operate almost as merchant capitalists. Two of these merchants trading in Cochin alone had as many as 50 ships for their commercial operations.[5] No other merchant groups in south India were said to have had so great a capital as these Muslims.[6]

While the transoceanic trade was increasingly appropriated by the *paradesi* Muslims, the Marakkar[7] Muslim merchants of Kayalpatnam, Kilakarai and Kunimedu controlled the coastal trade between Coromandel and Malabar. In fact, the Marakkar Muslims were natives of the coastal region between Kunimedu and Nagapattinam on the Coromandel coast.[8] They had established themselves along the coast of Malabar on the eve of the Portuguese' arrival and they used to carry (besides textiles) rice as well as provisions to the food-deficient zones of Kerala.[9] The wide family networks and partnerships deeply rooted in the rice belt of the Kavery region enabled the Marakkars to make a regular supply of food materials to their customers in Malabar in exchange for spices.[10] As the *paradesis* from the Red Sea ports and the Marakkars from Coromandel appropriated the major chunk of commerce, the local Mapilla Muslims of Malabar,[11] who seem to have engaged more in peddling trade, stood commercially at the lowest stratum. These native Mapillas[12] were increasingly looking for commercial partners who would enable them one day to compete with the merchants of Mecca and in that way to ensure upward mobility in the social and economic ladder.[13] It is against this background that one should see the support rendered by Koya Pakki (a Mapilla Muslim) to the Portuguese, who appeared to be potential partners for the Mapillas for realizing their dream of a carving out a commercial niche to their advantage.[14] The practice of temporary marriages (carried out through the institution of *mut'a*)[15] between the traders of Arab origin and local women was chiefly responsible for the change in the demographic profile of the Mapilla Muslims on the Malabar coast. The Mapillas of Malabar, the Marakkars of Coromandel, the Muslims of Sri Lanka and Indonesia, all following Sunni tradition, played vital roles in the emergence of an Islamic commercial world in South Asia, linked with Arabia and the Red Sea, whose ultimate door was opened to the Mediterranean. The Zamorin of Calicut who carried out his commercial and political expansionist career with the help of the money and personnel offered by the Muslim merchants, patronized the interests of the Muslim merchants in Malabar even by encouraging a male member from each family to be brought up according to the tenets of Islam.[16] As a result the pan-Islamic commercial venture had strong bases in the ports of Malabar, where the Zamorin succeeded in establishing his hegemony. The merchant guilds of the Jews and the St. Thomas Christians, which were earlier operating in the commercial zones of south India, lost their prominence and began to give way for the expanding commerce of the Muslims.[17]

Having established bases in the northern part of Malabar, the Muslim traders moved southwards along with the political expansion of the Zamorin in their attempt to control the commerce of central and south Kerala. When the Zamorin attacked the port of Cochin with the help of Arab merchants towards the end of the fifteenth century, the Nazaranis (St. Thomas Christians) who were trading there earlier, were denied the right to conduct trade in that port and the commercial privileges enjoyed by them were given over to the Muslims.[18] At the time of the arrival of the Portuguese, Quilon was the only port in Kerala, where the Muslim presence was relatively less and where the St. Thomas Christian traders still retained some commercial predominance. However, this state of affairs lasted only till the end of the second decade of the sixteenth century, when the Muslim attacks threatened the commerce of Quilon.[19] In fact, the discovery of the Cape route and the arrival of the Portuguese in India coincided with the flourishing phase of Islamic commerce in the maritime zone of south India. However, the wheels of commerce of Malabar moved in two opposite directions: the Red Sea oriented trade of the *paradesi* Muslims and the Coromandel oriented commerce of the Marakkar Muslims. Nevertheless the Mapilla Muslims, who were dwarfed by the two, were looking for an opportunity to create an economic identity of their own.

PORTUGUESE AND THE MUSLIM COLLABORATORS

The Portuguese response to the predominant presence of the Muslim merchants in south Indian ports was a mixed one. On the one hand, they found that the *paradesi* Muslims linked with Arabia and the Red Sea ports were their chief commercial enemy and that the latter were instigating the Zamorin against them (the inimical atmosphere commenced with the machinations of the Arab merchants in the court of the Zamorin against Vasco da Gama in 1498 when he visited Calicut for the first time).[20] On the other hand, the Lusitanians found that their Lisbon oriented long distance trade could be carried out successfully only with the help of the Marakkar and the Mapilla merchants, whose cooperation was indispensable to purchase spices. Moreover, the Marakkar merchants were the principal suppliers of food materials in the first two decades of the sixteenth century for the Lusitanian factories and colonies[21] established on the coast, cut off from the production centres. As a result, till the second decade of the sixteenth century, the 'crusading spirit' of the Portuguese was directed only against the *paradesi* Muslim traders, who formed the backbone of the Red Sea-Venice trade, whereas the Mapilla and the Marakkar Muslims were assimilated into the Portuguese commercial system as collaborators and partners. Nevertheless, while keeping the *paradesi* Muslims out, the Portuguese made attempts to ensure the commercial collaboration of the Marakkar and the Mapilla Muslim traders, for which efforts seem to have started in 1502 when Vasco da Gama contacted the leading merchants of Cochin and Cannanore for fixing the price of the spices.[22]

From 1503 onwards we find the Marakkar merchants actively cooperating with the Portuguese in procuring cargo for the *carreira* vessels. The initiative came from the great merchant called Charine Mecar (differently written as Cherina or Karine standing for Karim Marakkar), when he approached Francisco de Albuquerque on 7 October 1503 offering to supply pepper to the Portuguese vessels without the knowledge of the Zamorin.[23]

When Francisco de Albuquerque and Afonso de Albuquerque left Malabar, the Zamorin tried to create an artificial famine in Cochin as a war-tactic by blocking the supply of rice to the city. However, Duarte Pacheco overcame this hurdle by making friendship with Mame (Muhammad) Marakkar, who was the head of the Marakkar merchants in Cochin and who in turn saw to it that the regular supply of provisions was made to the city.[24] At a time when the Portuguese did not have a strong mercantile base in India, the Marakkar merchants helped them to procure spices from the various parts of Malabar for their Lisbon-bound vessels. In 1504, Cherina Marakkar and Mamale Marakkar supplied 3,000 *bhares* of pepper for 6,000 *cruzados* for the fleet of Lopo Soares.[25] In the initial days of the Portuguese establishment in India the Marakkar traders helped them in different ways: Nino Marakkar used to supply cinnamon from Ceylon to the Portuguese in Cochin[26] and he even supplied ships and fighting force consisting of 1,500 soldiers to confront the forces of the Zamorin;[27] Chilay Marakkar gave his own ship to the Portuguese to take commodities to Goa.[28] Meanwhile, the commercially dwarfed Mapilla Muslims, who were content with their role as peddling traders also began to come out as suppliers of spices to the Portuguese. Ali Apule, Coje Mapilla and Abraham Mapilla used to supply pepper to the Portuguese in Cochin regularly from the production centres of Edappilly.[29] This timely help was promptly reciprocated by the Lusitanians. The Muslim merchants of Cochin and Cannanore, who co-operated with the Portuguese commercial system, were given considerable freedom to send vessels and commodities to Red Sea ports, provided that they took *cartazes* or safe conduct from the Portuguese.[30]

The Portuguese commercial collaboration with the Marakkar and the Mapilla Muslims eventually led to the practice of forging matrimonial ties between the Lusitanians and native Muslim women. As Antonio Real writes from Cochin in 1512, many Portuguese preferred to have Muslim women as their partners.[31] These Muslim links, acquired through marriage, later helped some Portuguese citizens to develop a network of private trade and to penetrate into the ports of the Bay of Bengal and South-East Asia with the help of the Muslim relatives and partners.[32]

THE EXODUS OF THE *PARADESI* MUSLIMS AND THE
PRE-EMINENCE OF THE MARAKKAR MERCHANTS

The peace treaty, which Afonso de Albuquerque signed in 1513 with the new Zamorin, who ascended the throne after poisoning his uncle and predecessor, made the majority of the *paradesi* Muslims including the al-Karimis flee from Calicut to other safer ports of the Indian Ocean region like that of Gujarat, Vijayanagara, Hormuz and the Red Sea.[33] This peace treaty appeared more detrimental to their existence than the several battles which they had fought earlier along with the Zamorin against the Portuguese with a view to protecting their commercial links with Cairo and Venice. However, the mercantile group that took maximum advantage of the flight of the *paradesi* Muslims was the Marakkar merchants, who enjoyed greater freedom and a privileged position in the commerce of the Portuguese till the death of Afonso de Albuquerque. Even there was an attempt in 1513 from Afonso Albuquerque to bestow some special privilege on them in recognition of their commercial cooperation.[34] The favourable atmosphere that prevailed during the Albuquerquian period enabled the Marakkar traders to establish themselves as the principal mercantile community in south India and the exodus of the *paradesi* Muslims from Calicut accelerated this transformation process.

The period immediately after the death of Afonso Albuquerque (1515) witnessed the reversal of many of his policies related to administration and commerce. In fact the nomination of Lopo Soares de Albergia as the new governor in 1515 was a victory for the Portuguese private enterprisers of Cochin ('Cochin group'), who were demanding less state intervention and more an atmosphere of free trade. The new governor eventually demarcated for the *casado* entrepreneurs a space east of Cape Comorin, which was relatively free of state interference.[35] It seems that in the commercial expansion of the *casado* traders in the Bay of Bengal and South-East Asia, the Marakkar merchants, who were so far controlling the east to west coastal trade, played a very significant role. Matrimonial ties and commercial partnerships between the two, facilitated the Portuguese private traders to penetrate into the ports of the eastern space of the Indian Ocean, where Islamised traders were increasingly holding control. Some of the Portuguese *casados* started sending spices even to Red Sea ports with the help of these Marakkar merchants. In 1521 the governor Diogo Lopes and another Portuguese private trader joined hands with Kuti Ali, a Marakkar merchant, to send pepper to the Red Sea ports, though the attempt did not materialize, as the cargo was later confiscated by the governor himself.[36]

The commercial vacuum already created by the exodus of the *paradesi* Muslims was best utilized by the Marakkar merchants to penetrate deeper into the soil of Malabar. As early as 1507, with the accession of a new ruler in the kingdom of Kolathunad (who favoured the Muslims), Mamale Marakkar the leader of the Muslim merchants in Cannanore had emerged as a decisive political and commercial figure in the developments of Cannanore and

Maldives.[37] With a supporting king on the throne, Mamale began to look into the prospects of protecting the commercial interests of the native Muslims, which remained threatened with the entry of the Portuguese into the market of Kolathunad. He and his men were increasingly trying to explore new commercial avenues for their operation with a base in the Maldives, which very much strained their relationship with the Portuguese by the 1520s.[38]

The beginning of the third decade of the sixteenth century witnessed clashes of interests between the Portuguese and the Marakkar mercantile clan. It coincided with the expansion of private trade in the eastern space of the Indian Ocean by the Portuguese *casados*, which flourished with the tacit approval of the Portuguese officials. In fact these clashes originated as a reaction of the old World System to the eventual penetration of the new World System.

THE EMERGENCE OF KUNJALI MARAKKAR AND CORSAIR ACTIVITIES AS AN ALTERNATIVE ARRANGEMENT OF TRADE

By the 1520s, with the entry of the Portuguese *casados* into the intra-Asian trade, the Portuguese attitude towards the Muslim merchants changed.[39] The *Estado* officials frequently began to use *cartazes*, which authorized them to check and confiscate any vessel, as a convenient tool to weaken the commercial strength of the traditional Muslim traders, among whom the most affected were the Marakkar merchants. The frequent checking and confiscation of merchandise and vessels in the name of *cartaz* made many of the Muslim traders incapable of mobilizing capital for their further commercial ventures, and out of this situation the *casados* created a space for their expanding trade in the Indian Ocean region. Though *cartazes* were introduced from 1502 onwards, the Marakkar traders became the constant victims of being raided and undergoing torture, conducted in the name of this 'safe conduct', only after the death of Afonso de Albuquerque and with the assumption of offices by those who supported the private trade of the Portuguese *casados*.[40] This fact is suggestive of the involvement of the Portuguese 'private trade lobby' in these moves against the Muslims. Many of the Marakkar merchants became prey to the torture tactics, which the contemporary Arab writer Shaykh Zaynuddin refers to as Portuguese high-handedness.[41] The natural reaction to it was that some of the leading Marakkar merchants of Cochin eventually turned out to be corsairs. Kuti Ali, for instance, became a corsair, when the Portuguese governor Diogo Lopes de Sequeira (1518-21), who previously joined hands with him to send pepper to Red Sea ports, himself confiscated the cargo as contraband and appropriated the vessel.[42]

The most significant among these developments was the emergence of Kunjali Marakkar from the Marakkar clan of Cochin—estranged from the Portuguese—and the shifting of his residence and loyalty from Cochin to Calicut, where the Zamorin made him the admiral of his navy. It was because of the frequent confiscation of their vessels and cargo by the Portuguese that the leading merchants including Kunjali Marakkar, his brother Ahmad Marakkar, their uncle Muhammadali Marakkar and their dependents left Cochin by 1524 and settled down in Calicut, from where they decided to organize guerilla warfare and corsair activities against the Portuguese.[43] At the same time, Pate Marakkar, who had been a great friend and collaborator of the Portuguese in the early days of their establishment also turned out to be a corsair and went to Calicut to join his nephew, Kunjali Marakkar, when his two ships sent to Cambay were captured by the Portuguese.[44]

Meanwhile, the Zamorin's relationship with the Portuguese had already been strained by this time and he was eagerly looking for merchants and naval personalities to fill the gap created by the exodus of Arab Muslims in 1513. He found in the Marakkar merchants from Cochin what he looked for: capital for improving the commerce of his port, as well as for undertaking naval expeditions against the Portuguese. During the period of the peace treaty with the Portuguese (1513-25), the commerce of Calicut suffered very much not only because of the mass exodus of the *paradesi* merchant magnates but also because of the under-pricing of the commodities. With the extension of fixed prices to the spice market of Calicut during the period of peace with the Portuguese, the price of pepper and ginger in Calicut was reduced almost to half of the price that had prevailed there in 1500. Though this price fixation was done to bring the price of Calicut near to that of Cochin, it ultimately led to the under-pricing of the commodities, which adversely affected the commerce of the Zamorin's port.[45] The Marakkar clan under the leadership of Kunjali had the task of restructuring the commerce of Calicut, at a time when the Portuguese *casado* traders were fast penetrating into the principal trade centres of Asian waters. In this process it seems that even the native Mapilla Muslims accepted the naval and commercial hegemony of the Marakkars, in spite of the Coromandel origin of the latter, probably because of the commonality of religion.

With the estrangement of the Marakkar Muslim traders and their shifting of loyalty to the Zamorin, which came as a result of the process of coercion and violence, the Portuguese *casados* stepped into this commercial vacuum and emerged as the principal traders of the Indian Ocean region. While the second-rate Muslim Mappilla merchants, who continued to cooperate with the Portuguese, were reduced to the role of peddling traders or petty shopkeepers, the Marakkar merchants who moved over to Calicut began to develop corsair activities as an alternative arrangement of trade.[46]

In the initial phase Kunjali's men concentrated more on the Ceylon-Coromandel-Malabar trade, which was traditionally a Marakkar monopoly. Even after moving over to Calicut, the Marakkar merchants were enviously keeping the Gulf of Manar and the coast of Coromandel for their commercial operations, just as the Muslim merchants of Cannanore monopolistically held the Maldives. The possession of these bases in fact enabled both of them to join hands to evade the Portuguese control systems and to divert commodities to the traditional Red Sea-Venice route. However, the increasing Portuguese presence in this area alerted the Kunjali's men, who began to target at the Portuguese mercantile settlements of Nagapattinam, São Tome and Pulicat.[47] In 1527, Pate Marakkar captured near Pulicat a Portuguese ship coming from Malacca.[48] Nevertheless, the continued involvement of the Kunjali's men in the pearl trade of the fishery Coast and in the cinnamon trade of Kotte, invited direct confrontations with the Portuguese, who had already started trading there.

In the struggle for the control of the coasts of Coromandel and Ceylon, even some of the Portuguese *casados* who moved over to Coromandel from Cochin along with the Muslim merchants, came forward to join hands with Kunjali's men. These Portuguese *casados* were living almost five or six leagues away from Cochin in places like Culimute(?) making armaments for Kunjali's men and trading with them on contraband commodities. They built ships for the Muslim corsairs and helped the latter to enlarge their fleet.[49] These *casados* with the help of the corsairs even attacked the fleet of the *Estado*, an act which had come out of common economic interests. One Diogo Fernandes explained the reason for the association of the *casados* with the corsairs as being due to the Muslim origin of the wives of the *casados*. In 1537, he wrote to King John III that the Portuguese who were married to native Muslim women were giving protection and support to the corsairs.[50]

In the military encounter between the Portuguese and the Marakkars linked with Calicut (1537-9), the Muslim merchants were divided into two camps: one group stood with the Kunjali while the other supported the Portuguese. However, with the beheading of the first Kunjali and Pate Marakkar in 1539 in Ceylon,[51] the dream of the Marakkars to keep the ports of Coromandel and Ceylon as bases of operation for their Red Sea oriented trade shattered. Nevertheless, the Muslim merchants of Cannanore had by this time developed a parallel commercial network outside the Lusitanian control systems by keeping the Maldives as the base for diversion of merchandise to the Levant. The commodities of South-East Asia began to move to the Red Sea through the straits of Karaidu and Haddumati via the Maldives, a route which bypassed all the control mechanisms of the Portuguese.[52] By exercising control over this route, Mamale and later other *regedors* including Ali Raja could generate wealth from its commerce for their state-formation ventures at Cannanore.

By the 1540s the Muslim merchants of Kerala were engaged in two circuits of commercial operation: on the one side there were the channels of old World System, viz., the Cannanore/Calicut-Maldives-Red Sea route linked with Venice. With the increasing flow of commodities through these channels, trade was intensified in the Mediterranean after 1540.[53] On the other side there was the channel of the new World System, viz., Goa/Cochin/ Lisbon route of the Portuguese, in which some of Muslim merchants continued to collaborate as suppliers of cargo.[54] Some of these Muslim merchants also entered into contract with the Portuguese to supply annually about 150 *bhares* of coir from the Maldives to Cochin. As per this contract made in February 1560, Chaudela Marakkar, Ade Ramao, Ali Poera and Coje Ahmed, all belonging to both Marakkar and Mapilla segments of the Muslim community of Cochin and Palliport, took up the responsibility of supplying the stipulated quantity of coir to Cochin.[55] From there, the Lusitanians further took them to Lisbon for their shipbuilding purposes. A leading Muslim merchant who cooperated with the Lisbon oriented commercial operations of the Portuguese was Khwaja Shams-ud-din Giloni, a native of Persia, who conducted business in Cannanore. The Portuguese supported his business endeavours in Cannanore and even relaxed laws in order to buy land for him in Cochin in 1547 to extend his trading networks. However, he used to conduct trade through both the channels: while keeping the Portuguese in good humour, he frequently used to send commodities to Mecca, where his brother had commercial establishments.[56]

Meanwhile, by the 1540s the Kunjali's men, who were ousted from the Coromandel ports, began to increasingly resort to corsair activities, which had two types of operations: (a) to patrol the west coast of India with the tacit or explicit consent of the Zamorin, blockading and plundering the vessels of the Portuguese; (b) to integrate the native trade networks for sending spices regularly to Red Sea-Venice route. In this development, the agents of the old World System did rather circumvent the operations of the new World System: the first mode of operation provided them wealth for continued resistance and space for the movement of the vessels destined for the Red Sea ports. Most of the anti-Portuguese factors seem to have cooperated with these corsair endeavours, which appeared as both political and economic outlets for exercising freedom. The corsair activity developed by the Kunjali's men turned out to be an alternative arrangement of trade, where plundering and confiscation of enemy vessels went hand in hand with parallel shipment of commodities to the destination of their choice.[57]

THE STATE FORMATION VENTURES OF
THE MUSLIM MERCHANTS

On the basis of the experience of half a century, the Muslim merchants of Cannanore and Calicut, who were still clinging to the old World System, realized that the Portuguese trade expansion could be contained only by setting up a substantial state power of their own. As a result the Muslim merchant magnates made attempts to institute statehood in the territories under their influence and commercial sway. The Muslims of Kolathunad took the initial steps in this direction, where the Hindu ruler Kolathiri had already given great amount of administrative rights and political power to the Muslim *regedor*, Mamale and his successors Poca Amame and Pocaralle.[58] By keeping the Maldives as an integral part of the economic operations of Cannanore, these *regedors* could easily generate wealth from the Cannanore/ Maldives/Red Sea trade for setting up the infrastructure and the diverse apparatus of state in course of time.[59] However, the evolution of the Muslim *regedor* from a merchant to the head of a state became complete by 1545, when Ali Raja (on the assassination of his uncle Pocaralle by Belchior de Sousa) came to power and thereby laid the foundation of the Muslim dynasty of the Ali Rajas of Cannanore.[60] In the process of state formation and the expansion of instruments of power by Ali Raja, his mentor Kolathiri was reduced to the status of a puppet, who finally transferred his residence to Kasargod in the northern part of his country.[61]

The evolving Muslim state of Cannanore depended economically very much on the mercantile networks, which were increasingly utilizing the Maldives for diversion of contraband items to the Red Sea-Venice route. The Portuguese who apprehended the danger, reacted by building a fortress there and by intervening in the domestic affairs of the archipelago. In the ensuing troubles of 1552, the king of the Maldives fled to Cochin and embraced Christianity taking the name of D. Manuel. As Ali Raja could easily bring the Maldives back under his control and keep his nominee on the throne of the islands, D. Manuel, his sons (D. João and D. Paulo) and grandson (D. Filipe) had to live in Cochin in exile. In 1567, the Portuguese accepted Cannanore's nominee as the official ruler of the Maldives and thereby allowed it to be a political and economic appendage of the Muslim state of Cannanore.[62]

Meanwhile, with the acquisition of stately power, Ali Raja of Cannanore entered into alliance with the Kunjalis of Calicut to fight against the Portuguese[63] and probably also for joint commercial operations. In 1564, when the Portuguese were trying to confront Ali Raja and the Muslim force (who attacked the Portuguese fort of Cannanore), the Kunjali took up the spirit of the war to places where they had links. In the Bay of Bhatkal, the Kunjali and his men came upon the Portuguese force that was proceeding to Cannanore, which in turn delayed timely military assistance to the Portuguese engaged in war against Ali Raja.[64]

The Kunjali was very much taken up by the way the Muslim mercantile leader of Cannanore created a stately structure under himself, which the Kunjali wanted to emulate in his own territory. He realized that the expanding network of Portuguese commerce could be checked only by accumulating and institutionalizing power into the frame of a state. Eventually, the wealth accrued from the corsair activities began to be transplanted to Pudupattanam, where the Kunjali had already established a fortress of his own.[65] The Portuguese who had apprehensions about these developments sought the help of the ruler of Chaliyam in 1583 to get a site from his kingdom for the erection of a Portuguese fortress, from where the latter could easily control the developments in Pudupattanam and closely check the movements of the Kunjali's men.[66]

When Ali Raja built up a Muslim state in Cannanore with the Maldives as the principal feeding centre and trading posts along the rim of Indian Ocean as the satellite economic units, the Kunjali had less landed territory. Though Pudupattanam was enviously kept as the base of the Kunjali's evolving state, the limits of his authority were extended more along the coastal waters of western India making it rather a maritime state. He extended the diverse machineries of his evolving state (viz., administration of justice, law and order, regular coastal patrolling with a well equipped fleet) in the territory over which he claimed authority.[67] As a German document sent from India in 1588 testifies,[68] the entire western coast right from Diu up to Cape Comorin was under the control of these Malabar corsairs, which is suggestive of the boundaries for the exercise of their power. With the expansion of the Kunjali's spheres of influence, the Portuguese patrolling fleet of Malabar was given the double responsibility of curbing the corsair activities spearheaded by the Muslims of Malabar and of obstructing their links with the Red Sea ports of the Ottomans.[69] As an additional security measure the Portuguese merchant ships were also obliged to move in caravans or *cafilas*.[70]

In imitation of the title *regedor do mar* (meaning Regent of the Sea), which the leader of Cannanore Muslims used to bear in the transformation phase from mercantile stature to kingly stature, the Kunjali also began to assume the titles of 'Lord of the Arabian Seas', 'Prince of Navigation', and 'King of the Malabar Moors'.[71] This development naturally invited the suspicion of the Zamorin, who connecting these titles with the emerging state-building ventures of the Kunjali, feared that there would be a repetition of Cannanore situation in Calicut, where the emerging Muslim leader might dwarf the actual ruler. Now the mentor himself turned against the Kunjali. Though the Muslim maritime state structure that the Kunjali wanted to institute in Pudupattanam was mainly aimed at containing the commercial operations of the Portuguese, the venture as a double-edged sword did really hit at the sovereignty of the Zamorin, as well. As a result the Zamorin joined hands with the Portuguese to attack the Kunjali fort in Pudupattanam and to capture him.[72]

At this juncture, the state-building ventures of the Kunjali got the support of the king of Cochin, who promised to help him in his fight against the Zamorin and the Portuguese.[73] This intervention of the ruler of Cochin was probably to show his displeasure towards the peace treaty recently established between the Zamorin and the Portuguese, and to keep the Muslim mercantile community in his camp. This had its results. The Muslim merchants, both belonging to the Marakkar and Mapilla groups, joined hands with the king of Cochin to send about 4,000 quintals of pepper and timber to the Red Sea, under the cover of *cartazes*.[74] These Muslim merchants also began to collect pepper from the hinterland and to hide it for the ships of this native ruler, which even led to an increase in the price and created a shortage of the commodity for Portuguese commerce.[75] With the tightening of the siege of the Kunjali's fort, there was a pan-Islamic resistance to the Portuguese from the various Muslim groups of Malabar. Even the Ravuthar Muslims of Kanjirappally, who originally came from Madurai and settled down in the interior market places of central Kerala, staged their protest, but under a different pretext. The journey of D. Alexis Menezes, the Archbishop of Goa, to the settlements of the St. Thomas Christians in the spice producing centres to correct their so-called 'heresies' and his efforts to establish a church in such remote and interior market centre as in *Periate* (Vandiperiyar) were viewed by them as channels made by the Portuguese for their penetration into the hinterland of Kerala. As a result the Ravuthar Muslims of Kanjirappally instigated the Thekkenkur king to destroy this building, which they viewed as 'a fortress equipped with artillery'[76] and to obstruct the moves of the Portuguese and their allies in Malabar.

The state building ventures of the Kunjali enjoyed the support of the entire Muslim community of Malabar, who 'recognized him almost like their king'. He had in Pudupattanam 'the ambassadors of the most powerful Muslim kings of India, and even of the great Mughal, and of Mecca, all of them viewing him as the defender of the law of Mohammed.'[77] This still sent messages of caution and alarm to the Zamorin, who joining hands with the

Portuguese, tried to destroy the power structures of the Kunjali. Finally, as a result of the joint operation of the forces of the Zamorin and the Portuguese, the Kunjali was captured and later beheaded in Goa in 1600.[78] With this, the dream of the Kunjali and his men to establish a Muslim state in Pudupattanam died out.

Among the state formation ventures of the Muslims of Cannanore and Pudupattanam, which were aimed at countering the penetration of the new World System, only the endeavours of the former succeeded while those of the latter failed drastically. In both cases there was transfer of mercantile capital to empower their Muslim states. In Cannanore, the political atmosphere was rather favourable and with the accession of a pro-Muslim Kolathiri in 1507, the Muslim merchants wielded more power, which they easily succeeded in transplanting into the frame of an emerging state. The expansion of the Muslim state of Cannanore was realized at the cost of later Kolathiris, whose power was eventually undermined and who were in due course of time cornered to the northern limits of Kasargod. However, the state formation ventures of the Kunjali in Pudupattanam offer a different case. The Zamorin was not as weak as Kolathiri to be taken for a ride. Though the Zamorin knew very well that the empowerment of the Kunjali's base in Pudupattanam was meant for attacking the Portuguese vessels in a better way, he also realized that it was an alternative locus of power, which might turn out to be a threat to his suzerainty. With an apprehensive and assertive Zamorin as the immediate political superior, the Kunjali could not exercise power in the same degree as he transferred mercantile capital to institute the various machineries of the state. As a result, unlike the Muslim leader of Cannanore, the Kunjali had to fight against both the indigenous forces of the Zamorin and the European forces of the Portuguese to establish his stately and political identity. This is an evident case of fragmentation of the agents of old World System, which was caused by varying and mutually contradicting responses to the challenges of the new World System. With the extermination of the Kunjali, the state formation ventures of Pudupattanam were shattered and with it a major strand in the commercial activities of the old World System was also cut off.

THE VICISSITUDES OF MUSLIM TRADE

With the execution of the Kunjali Marakkar, neither the activities of the corsairs nor their involvement in the native trade networks for diversion of commodities to the Red Sea-Venice route came to an end. It took a new dimension with the establishment of the English and Dutch settlements along the coast of India. In 1615, a Malabar Muslim Mapilla merchant by name Mousa Attale entered into agreement with the English to make joint commercial operations ('to conduct mutual trade and traffique with one another').[79] The friendship between the corsairs of Malabar and the English must have been a part of the tactics to create a commercial partnership between the forces which opposed the Portuguese trade system. This arrangement helped the Malabar Muslims to send commodities to the Red Sea ports and other destinations even when the English and the Dutch blockaded Portuguese navigational lines. Thus, we find, for example, in 1621 vessels from India, including the one from Cochin—probably all operating from this network—reaching Mocha for trade.[80]

The joint operation of the Zamorin and the Portuguese against the Kunjali and his men reduced temporarily the gravity of corsair attacks and also the number of the Muslim competitors to the trade of the *casados*. The latter had by this time emerged as a 'bourgeoisie class' with the wealth they amassed from their earlier trading activities with the ports of the Bay of Bengal and South-East Asia. Some of the *casados* even began to lend substantial amount of money as loan to the bankrupt *Estado,* while some others began later to send *navetas* regularly to Portugal.[81] Eventually, with the accumulation of substantial capital in the hands of the Portuguese *casado* traders, the Muslim corsairs began to target at them as well, and this became frequent when their navigational lines collided with those of the former. The goods thus robbed from the Portuguese were sold by these corsairs in the market of Calicut, as observed by Pietro Della Valle in 1624.[82] However, with the increasing expansion of European powers in Indian waters, the number of the corsairs and their operations increased. Jean Baptiste Tavernier while mentioning the Muslim corsairs who operated under the patronage of the Zamorin says that they used to go in squadrons consisting of 10 to 15 vessels (sometimes 25 to 30 vessels, as when the English captain Mr. Clerc was attacked), with 200 to 250 men in each vessel.[83] By the middle of the seventeenth century, it evolved into an anti-European maritime campaign, in which all the Europeans including the Portuguese, the Dutch and the English became target of their frequent attacks.

While the Muslim merchants of Calicut continued to operate as corsairs for want of legally conferred commercial space and because of the economic subjection to which they were confined for more than a century, the merchants of Cannanore continued their trade with the wider world through their base in the Maldives. Though the Muslim merchants of Cannanore and the *casado* traders of Cochin competitively visited the archipelago, by 1627 the Portuguese accepted the Maldives as a dominion of the Ali Raja probably with a view to ensuring supply of cowries and coir from them for Lusitanian commerce.[84]

CONCLUSION

Thus, we find different strands in the relationship of the Muslim traders with the Portuguese. While the commercially powerful *paradesi* Muslims were predominantly hostile to the Portuguese, the Marakkar and Mapilla merchants were their collaborators in their economic operations. Eventually, the exodus of the *paradesi* Muslims from Calicut enabled the Marakkars to control the major part of the indigenous trade of Malabar, though the trade was later diversified into corsair-cum-trade activities under the Kunjali and a partnership trade under the Portuguese. However, it did not lead to the situation of the long-term accumulation of mercantile capital in Malabar, as it did in Europe. The main reason was that the *paradesi* merchant magnates with substantial capital kept themselves away from the commercial opportunities thrown open by the discovery of the Cape route and were still clinging on to the traditional trade links with the Red Sea ports. Before taking advantage of the impact of emerging global commercial revolution, they left Malabar to other promising trade centres of the Indian Ocean region, from where they continued to trade with the traditional caravan route.

With the beginning of a clash between the old World System and the new World System, the mode of response of the Muslim merchants of Malabar to the Portuguese commercial expansion changed. The Kunjali and his men in Calicut did amass a considerable amount of wealth from corsair-cum-trade activities as well as the partnership trade with the Portuguese; so did Mamale, as well as his successors, and his men in Cannanore. However, a major portion of this wealth, which should have been invested further for commerce and productive ventures, became frozen when diverted for the state building ventures of the Kunjali in Pudupattanam, and Ali Raja in Cannanore. In both the places a large amount was to be spent for setting up the diverse machineries of the state and for meeting the expenses of the recurring wars including the purchase of weapons. The Muslim ruler of Cannanore easily compensated it by empowering the state for expanded commerce. However, the Marakkar clan and the men of the Kunjali had to pay a heavy price for having used mercantile capital for state building instead of investing it for further productive commercial enterprises. With the destruction of Pudupattanam by the Luso-Zamorin force, it was in fact the surplus accumulated for nearly a century and transplanted into various state structures that got shattered. Though the formation of a Muslim state in Pudupattanam was one of the responses that the Kunjali gave to check and control the advance of the new World System, its bearing on Calicut's suzerainty created divisions in the two main closely-working agents of the old World system, viz., the Zamorin and the Kunjali. It was with the fragmentation in these agents by 1600 that the atmosphere was set ready for the full-fledged operation of the new World System. The tragic aspect of this transformation process was that a great many of the Muslims turned out to be economically poor by the beginning of the seventeenth century[85] and were incapable of undertaking any large-scale commercial activity that involved substantial capital.

NOTES

1. Fernand Braudel, *Civilization and Capitalism 15th–18th Century, vol. II: The Wheels of Commerce,* London, 1982, pp. 218-21; Niels Steensgaard, 'Asian Trade and the World Economy from the 15th to the 18th Centuries', in *Indo-Portuguese History: Old Issues, New Questions,* ed. Teotorio R. de Souza, New Delhi, 1990, pp. 213-26; Niels Steensgaard, *Carracks, Caravans and Companies: The Structural Crisis in the European-Asian Trade in the Early Seventeenth Century,* Copenhagen, 1973, pp. 80-95; Genevieve Bouchon, *Regent of the Sea: Cannanore's Response to Portuguese Expansion, 1507-1528,* tran. Louise Shackley, Delhi, 1988; Vitorino Magalhães Godinho, *Os Descobrimentos e a Economia Mundial,* 4 vols., Editorial Presença, Lisboa, 1981-4; M.N. Pearson, *Merchants and Rulers in Gujarat, the Response to the Portuguese in the Sixteenth Century,* London, 1976; Ashin Das Gupta, 'Indian Merchants and the Trade of the Indian Ocean', in *The Cambridge Economic History of India,* Tapan Raychaudhuri and Irfan Habib, eds., vol. I, Cambridge, 1982, pp. 427-30; Sanjay Subrahmanyam, *Improvising Empire: Portuguese Trade and Settlement in the Bay of Bengal, 1500-1700,* Delhi, 1990. The discussions within the frame of World Systems are based on the ideas from Fernand Braudel, 'The Expansion of Europe and the Long Duree', in *Expansion and Reaction,* ed. H.L. Wesseling, Leiden, 1978, pp. 20-3; Immanuel Wallerstein, ed., *Social Changes: The Colonial Situation,* New York, 1966; Immanuel Wallerstein, *The Modern World—System II: Mercantilism and the Consolidation of the European World Economy, 1600-1750,* New York, 1980; Janet L. Abu-Lughod, *Before European Hegemony: The World System AD 1250-1350,* New York, 1989.

2. Merchant capitalist here means a social agent who uses whole or a part of the accumulated capital for the generation not of 'use-values' but of 'exchange-values'. Here capital is invested for the exchange of commodities, that have use, based on the principle of exploiting price-differentials. In the organization of trade of this nature, which covers larger space and time, the invester needs greater resources, extensive networks and more personnel. Usually this is done on legitimate basis and confined within certain legal framework, even though illegitimate trade transactions may also at times betray fragments of merchant capitalism. For a detailed discussion on merchant capitalism, see Maurice Dobb, *Studies in the Development of Capitalism,* London, 1963, pp. 17, 83-129, 152-62.

The Portuguese used the word 'corsairs' in the sense of sea-pirates, into which category they included Kunjali Marakkar and his men. Some historians consider

Kunjali and his men as patriots and nationalists. See O.K. Nambiar, *The Kunjalis, Admirals of Calicut*, Delhi, 1963, pp. 14-16; M.N. Pearson pictures them as something between pirate and privateering. M.N. Pearson, *Coastal Western India*, New Delhi, 1981, pp. 25-6. Pirate is a sea robber acting on his own account, whereas a privateer is a private person who owns and mans an armed vessel with permission and authorization from the government to use it against a hostile nation, especially in merchant shipping. Here the concept of legality from the point of view of the plunderer does not necessarily coincide with how the plundered sees it. For more details, see Luis Filipe Thomaz, 'Portuguese Control on the Arabian Sea and the Bay of Bengal—A Comparative Study', *Commerce and Culture in the Bay of Bengal*, ed. Om Prakash and Denys Lombard, Delhi, 1999; Pius Malekandathil, *Portuguese Cochin and the Maritime Trade of India:1500-1663* (South Asian Study Series of Heidelberg University, Germany), Delhi, 2001, p. 131.

3. For details see A. Cherian, 'The Genesis of Islam in Malabar', *Indica*, no. 1, 1969, pp. 5-9; for a discussion on the Islamic commercial identity, see K.N. Chaudhuri, *Asia Before Europe: Economy and Civilization of the Indian Ocean from the Rise of Islam to 1750*, Cambridge, 1992, pp. 48-50.

4. For details about Al-Karimi merchants, see Walter J. Fischel, 'The Spice Trade in Mamluke Egypt', *Journal of the Economic and Social History of the Orient*, vol. I, Leiden, 1958, p. 165; Eliyahu Ashtor, 'The Venetian Supremacy in Levantine Trade: Monopoly of Pre-colonialism', *Journal of European Economic History*, vol. III, Rome, 1974, p. 27; Genevieve Bouchon, 'Calicut at the Turn of the Sixteenth Century', in *The Asian Seas 1550-1800: Local Societies, European Expansion and the Portuguese, Revista de Cultura*, vol. I, Ano V, 1987, p. 42.

5. 'Letter from King Manuel to Ferdinand and Isabella', in *The Voyage of Pedro Alvares Cabral to Brazil and India from Contemporary Documents and Narratives*, ed. William Brooks Greenlee, London, 1938, p. 49.

6. Raymundo A. de Bulhão Pato, ed., *Cartas de Affonso de Albuquerque seguidas de documentos que as elucidam*, tom. II, Lisboa, 1884, tom. I, p. 306.

7. Etymologically the word 'Marakkar' means captain or owner of a ship and is derived from the Tamil word 'Marakalam' meaning ship. For details, see O.K. Nambiar, *The Kunjalis*, p. 76.

8. Jayaseela Stephen, *The Coromandel Coast and Its Hinterland: Economy, Society and Political System (AD 1500-1600)*, Manohar, 1997, pp. 137-9.

9. As Kerala's topography does not favour rice cultivation except in scattered low-lying areas, a great part of it had to depend upon the rice imported from Coromandel, Orissa, Bengal and Canara. Tomé Pires says that the whole of the province was lacking in rice and the area from Tanur to Quilon had to depend on Kalinga for rice. For details, see Tomé Pires, *The Suma Oriental of Tomé Pires: An Account of the East, from the Red Sea to Japan written in Malacca and India in 1512-1515*, Nendeln, 1967, p. 77. During this period Cochin did not produce enough rice to support its population. Rice had to be imported from the Coromandel coast and distributed throughout the country by Muslim traders. The king of Cochin gave the monopoly in rice trade to Muhammed Marakkar. Cf. Gaspar

Correia, *Lendas da India*, tom. I, parte I, Coimbra, 1922, pp. 428ff; C. Achyuta Menon, *The Cochin State Manual,* Ernakulam, 1911, p.58.

10. Pius Malekandathil, *Portuguese Cochin and the Maritime Trade of India*, pp. 111-12; see also Jorge Manuel Flores, 'The Straits of Ceylon and the Maritime Trade in Early Sixteenth Century India: Commodities, Merchants and Trading Networks', in *Moyen Orient and Ocean Indien, XVIe –XIXe s.,* vol. VII, Paris, 1990, pp. 30-6.

11. For details about the Islamisation in Malabar, see Genevieve Bouchon, 'Quelques Aspects de l'Islamisation des Regions Maritimes de l'Inde à l'Époque Médiévale (XII-XVIe.s.)', *Puruṣārtha*, 9, 1986, pp. 29-30; see also Genevieve Bouchon, 'Les Musulmans du Kerala à l'Époque de la Découverte Portugaise', *Mare Luso-Indicum*, 2, 1973, pp.17-20.

12. The word 'Mapilla' is an abbreviation of the Malayalam word 'Mahapilla', meaning 'great son'. This appellation is given only to the indigenous Muslims having origin in Malabar as well as to the members of St. Thomas Christians of Malabar. The former are called Jona Mapillas or Muslim Mapillas while the latter are called Nazarani Mapillas or Christian Mapillas. While preparing the legal documents of the elder male members of the St. Thomas Christians, their proper name is invariably followed by the appellation 'Mapilla'. The use of common appellation 'Mapilla' for indigenous Muslims and the St. Thomas Christians, with differentiating prefixes 'Jona' or 'Nazarani', suggests that the term was in currency even before the Islamization of the region. Possibly it must have been a common word initially used to signify those people linked with the trading community and more probably with the Christian merchant guilds of *Manigramam* and *Anjuvannam*, as such people were viewed as 'great men' both by the rulers and the society. Even after Islamization also, such appellation of Mapilla continued; however the word 'Jona' is used as a prefix to make the social distinction that they are the Islamized segment in contrast to the Christian Mapillas. Though the Muslim Mapillas were indigenous traders of Malabar, their economic activity entered a phase of doldrums with the influx of larger numbers of foreign Muslim traders to Malabar ports with substantial amount of capital like the *paradesi* Muslims and the Marakkars.

13. Genevieve Bouchon, *Regent of the Sea: Cannanore's Response to Portuguese Expansion*, p. 53.

14. For the various help rendered by Koya Pakki to the Portuguese see, 'The Anonymous Narrative', in William Brooks Greenlee, ed., op. cit., pp. 83-6; Henry E.J. Stanley, ed., *The Three Voyages of Vasco da Gama and his Viceroyalty from the Lendas da India of Gaspar Correia*, New York, 1869, pp. 358-60; Fernão Lopes de Castanheda, *Historia do descobrimento e conquista da India pelos Portugueses*, tom. I, Coimbra, 1924, pp. 81-3; Joao de Barros, *Asia. Dos feitos que os Portugueses fizeram no descobrimento e conquista dos mares e terras do Oriente*, decada I, Lisboa, 1945, I-v-5,6 pp. 197-200.

15. V D'Souza, 'A unique custom regarding *Mahr* observed by certain Indian Muslims of South India', *Islamic Culture*, vol. 28-29, 1954-5, pp. 273-5. This

practice of temporary marriage was more common in the coastal society, where the traders used to stay only temporarily.

16. Pius Malekandathil, 'Merchants, Markets and Commodities: Some Aspects of Portuguese Commerce with Malabar', *The Portuguese, Indian Ocean and European Bridgehead: Festschrift in Honour of Prof. K.S. Mathew*, ed. Pius Malekandathil and Jamal Mohammed, Fundação Oriente, 2001, pp. 242-4.

17. Pius Malekandathil, 'St. Thomas Christians and the Indian Ocean: 52 AD to 1500 AD', *Ephrem's Theological Journal*, vol. V, no. 2, October 2001, pp. 197, 199; Andre Wink, *Al-Hind: The Making of the Indo-Islamic World*, vol. I, New Delhi, 1999, p. 71.

18. O.K. Nambiar, *The Kunjalis: Admirals of Calicut*, London, 1963, p. 40; Pius Malekandathil, 'St. Thomas Christians and the Indian Ocean', p.199.

19. In the Commentaries of Afonso Albuquerque we read that there was neither a single native Moor in Quilon in 1504 nor any foreigner there except the brother of Cherina Marakkar. See Walter de Gray Birch, ed., *The Commentaries of the Great Afonso Dalboqerque, Second Viceroy of India*, New York, 1875, p.11. At the same time we find that the St. Thomas Christian traders as emissaries of the queen of Quilon inviting Vasco da Gama in 1502 for trading with Quilon. Nationalbibliothek in Wien, Nr. 6948; Christine von Rohr, *Neue Quellen zur zweiten Indienfahrt Vasco da Gamas*, Leipzig, 1939, p. 51. For further details about the prominent St. Thomas Christian traders of the port of Quilon, see Raymundo Antonio de Bulhão Pato ed., *Cartas de Affonso de Albuquerque*, p. 268; tom. III, pp. 30, 258-9.

20. For details about the anti-Portuguese activities of the Arab merchants at the court of the Zamorin, see Gernot Giertz, *Vasco da Gama, die Endeckung des Seewegs nach Indien: ein Augenzeugenbericht 1497-99*, Tübingen 1980, pp. 92-8. The ignorance of the native language (Malayalam) was a great handicap for the Portuguese. The Arab traders who read and translated the Portuguese letters gave a wrong interpretation of the same making the decision taking machinery turn against the Portuguese. For more details about the Portuguese clash with the Arab merchants in the succeeding period, see 'Anonymous Narrative' in William Brooks Greenlee, ed., op. cit., pp. 83-5; Henry E.J. Stanley, op. cit., pp. 329-30; C. Achyuta Menon, *The Cochin State Manual*, Ernakulam, 1911, pp. 65-9.

21. By the 1520s, with the emergence of Portuguese *casado* traders, the monopoly of the Marakkar merchants in the rice trade was broken. At least from the 1540s onwards we have evidence of rice being imported to Malabar by the Portuguese *casado* traders. See Elaine Sanceau, *Colecção de São Lourenço*,vol.II, Lisboa, 1975, p. 275. A great bulk of it was return cargo for the spices taken to Bengal, Orissa and Coromandel. See for the details on the rice trade of the Portuguese *casado* traders, Pius Malekandathil, *Portuguese Cochin and the Maritime Trade of India*, pp. 199-201, 207-8, 213, 227-9; BNL, *Fundo Geral*, 1980, Livro das Despezas de hum Porcento, fols.12, 16, 25, 40.

22. For details about price fixation in Cochin (160 *panams* per *bhar*) and Cannanore (210 *panams* per *bhar*), see Thome Lopes, 'Navegação as Indias Orientales escrita em Portugues por Thome Lopes', in *Collecção de noticias para a historia e geografia das nações ultramarinas que vivem nos dominios Portugueses ou ilhes são vizinhas*, tom. II, nos. 1&2, Lisboa, 1812, p. 200; Genevieve Bouchon, *Regent of the Sea*, p. 72.

23. 'Reisebericht des Franciscus Dalberquerque vom 27 December 1503', in B. Greiff, ed., *Tagebuch des Lucas Rem aus den Jahren 1494-1541*, Augsburg 1861, p. 148.

24. Fernão Lopes Castanheda, op. cit., tom. I, p. 74; Gaspar Correia, *Lendas da India*, tom. I, Lisboa, 1921, pp. 430-1; Mamale Marakkar of Cochin was the 'richest man in the country'. See Ludovico di Varthema, *The Travels of Ludovico di Varthema in Egypt, Syria, Arabia Deserta and Arabia Felix, in Persia, India and Ethiopia:1503-1508*, London, 1863, p. 106.

25. *As Gavetas da Torre do Tombo*, tom. IV, Lisboa, 1964, p. 132; see also R.A. de Bulhão Pato, ed., *Cartas, de Affonso de Albuquerque seguidas de documentos que as elucidam*, tom. I, Lisboa, 1884, p. 320; tom. II, p. 361.

26. K.S. Mathew, 'Indian merchants and the Portuguese Trade on the Malabar Coast during the Sixteenth Century', in *Indo-Portuguese History: Old Issues— New Questions*, Teotonio de Souza, ed., New Delhi, 1985, pp. 6-7.

27. R.A. de Bulhão Pato, ed., *Cartas*, tom. II, pp. 377-8.

28. Ibid., tom. VI, p. 31.

29. Ibid., tom. V, pp. 503-4; K.S. Mathew, 'Indian merchants and the Portuguese Trade', pp. 6-7; K.S. Mathew, *Portuguese Trade with India in the Sixteenth Century*, New Delhi, 1983, p. 102. Even though the kingdom of Edappilly was an enemy of Cochin and the Portuguese, the latter succeeded in penetrating into its production centres with the help of the Mapilla merchants.

30. For details, see Pius Malekandathil, *Portuguese Cochin and the Maritime Trade of India*, pp. 125-6, 220-1; Luis Filipe Thomaz 'Portuguese Control on the Arabian Sea and the Bay of Bengal: A Comparative Study'.

31. Antonio da Silva Rego, ed., *Documentação para a Historia das Missões do Padroado Portugues do Oriente*, Lisboa, 1991, doc. 76, p. 171.

32. Cf. Infra nos. 43 and 44.

33. ANTT, *Chancelaria de Manuel I*, liv. II, fol. 83 'Capitulos de pazes entre Afonso de Albuquerque e o Samorin de Calicut', Lisboa, 26 de Fevreiro de 1515; Genevieve Bouchon, 'Calicut at the Turn of the Sixteenth Century', p. 46; R.A. de Bulhão Pato, ed., *Cartas*, tom. I, p. 126.

34. R.A. de Bulhão Pato, ed., *Cartas*, tom. III, p. 401.

35. For more details, see Vitor Luis Gaspar Rodrigues, 'O Grupo de Cochim e a Oposição a Afonso de Albuquerque', *Studia*, 51, Lisboa, 1992, pp. 119-44; Sanjay Subrahmanyam, *The Portuguese Empire in Asia 1500-1700: A Political and Economic History*, London, 1993, p. 97. Here the Portuguese *casado* traders clamoured for an atmosphere of free trade only for themselves and not for the non-Portuguese merchants of the region.

36. R.S. Whiteway, *The Rise of Portuguese Power in India: 1498-1550*, New Delhi, 1989, p. 196.

37. Pius Malekandathil, 'The Maritime Trade of Cannanore and the Global Commercial Revolution in the 16th and the 17th Centuries', in *'Cannanore in the Maritime History of India'*, ed. M.O. Koshy, Kannur, 2002, p. 47. Though Bouchon assigns Mamale a native origin, it seems that he was a Marakkar merchant from Coromandel settled down in Cannanore, as Tome Pires and Ludovico di Varthema call him Mamalle Mercar and Malmavicar respectively. Armando Cortesão, ed., *The Suma Oriental of Tome Pires*, vol. I, New Delhi, 1990, vol. II, p. 359. Ludovico di Varthema, *The Travels of Ludovico di Varthema in Egypt, Suria, Arabia Deserta and Arabia Felix, in Persia, India and Ethiopia, AD 1503-1508*, ed. George Percy Badger, New York, 1863, p. 282.

38. Genevieve Bouchon, *Regent of the Sea*, pp. 153-64.

39. Initially it was Afonso Albuquerque, the protagonist of the policy of mixed marriages, who encouraged the Portuguese *casados* (married citizens) to take up local trade and small business as a means of livelihood. The taste of profits generated by this trade induced in them a desire to participate in wider commercial activity, for which an opportunity came to them when the entire eastern space of the Indian Ocean was demarcated for their commerce by Lopo Soares de Albergia in 1515. By the 1520s they had already reached the main exchange centres of maritime Asia and started supplying commodities in the Portuguese settlements both for local consumption and for Lisbon-oriented trade. As the *casados* started supplying goods to the Portuguese, the Marakkar merchants ceased to be an indispensable element in Portuguese commerce. For details, see Pius Malekandathil, 'Portuguese *Casados* and the Intra-Asian Trade:1500-1663', *Proceedings of the Indian History Congress*, Millennium (61st) Session, Kolkata, 2001, pp. 385-7.

40. Ibid., pp. 387-8.

41. Shaykh Zaynudin, *Tuhfat-ul-Mujahidin*, tran. S. Muhammad Husain Nainar, Madras, 1942, pp. 89-91. Shaykh Zaynudin, an Arab, who was residing in Malabar gives elaborate details in his work *Tuhfat-ul-Mujahidin* about the raid and torture carried out by the Portuguese against the Muslims, principally the Marakkars. Though some scholars consider him to be a Malayali Muslim, it is highly probable that he was an Arab trader. This inference is made not only from the Arab language in which the work was composed but also from the title Shaykh, which is altogether absent among the Malayali Muslims. However it is very much in use among the West Asian Muslims.

42. R.S. Whiteway, op. cit., p. 196.

43. Faria y Souza, *Asia Portuguesa: The History of the Discovery and Conquest of India by the Portuguese*, tran. John Stevens, vol. I, London, 1695, p. 284; Shaykh Zaynudin, op. cit., p. 66; A.P. Ibrahim Kunju, *Studies in Medieval Kerala*, Trivandrum, 1975, p. 60.

44. *As Gavetas de Torre do Tombo*, vol. X, Lisboa, 1975, p. 577; Genevieve Bouchon, 'Les Musulmans du Kerala', pp. 52-3; Diogo Couto, *Da Asia dos feitos que os*

Portuguezes fizeram na Conquista e Descobrimento das Terras e Mares do Oriente, decada V, Lisboa, 1973, parte 2, p. 4.

45. In 1500 , the price of a *bhar* of pepper (166.3 kg) in Calicut was 360 *panams*, whereas in 1516 after the peace treaty, the price came down to 189.5 *panams* (10.17 *cruzados*). For details, see Pius Malekandathil, *Portuguese Cochin and the Maritime Trade of India*, p. 154; Duarte Barbosa, *The Book of Duarte Bnarbosa*, vol. II, Nendeln, 1967, pp. 226ff.

46. Pius Malekandathil, 'Portuguese *Casados* and the Intra-Asian Trade', pp. 387-8; For details about the Muslim merchants who put up small shops in Cochin, see K.S. Mathew and Afzal Ahmad, *Emergence of Cochin in the Pre-Industrial Era: A Study of Portuguese Cochin*, Pondicherry, 1990, doc.14, pp. 27-8. The trade organized by the Zamorin and his naval chieftain Kunjali was often referred to by the Portuguese as corsair activities as per the moral and legal perception they had.

47. João de Barros, *Asia. Dos feitos que os Portugueses fizeram no Descobrimento e Conquista dos Mares e Terras do Oriente,* Lisboa, 1973, decada IV, parte 4, p. 25.

48. Gaspar Correia, *Lendas da India*, tom. III, Lisboa, 1921, p. 235.

49. Gaspar Correia, *Lendas da India*, tom. II, p. 830; tom. III, p. 712. The exact geographical location of Culimute could not be identified. It could be Calmutão which Georg Schurhammer identified as Muttamtura in Travancore. See Georg Schurhammer, *Die Zeitgenössischen Quellen zur Geschichte Portugiesisch—Asiens und seiner Nachbarländer zur Zeit des hl. Franz Xaver, 1539-1552,* vol. I, Leipzig, 1962, nr. 6147, pp. 461, 540.

50. ANTT, *Corpo Chronologico*, II, Maço 211, doc. 65, fols. 5-6. The Letter of Diogo Fernandes to D. John III dated 1-6-1537; Jorge Manuel Costa da Silva Flores, *Os Portugueses e o Mar de Ceilão 1498-1543: Trato, Diplomacia, e Guerra,* Dissertação de Mestrado em Historia dos Descobrimentos e da Expansão Portuguesa presented to the Faculdade de Ciencias Sociais e Humanas da Universidade Nova de Lisboa, 1991, pp. 200-5.

51. Jorge Manuel Costa da Silva Flores, *Os Portugueses e o Mar de Ceilão*, pp. 214, 221:João de Barros, decada IV, livro 8, cap.12-14.

52. For the details about this route, see Genevieve Bouchon, *Regent of the Sea*, pp. 118, 161.

53. For the revival of Venetian trade, see Frederic C. Lane, 'The Mediterranean Spice Trade: Further Evidence of its Revival in the Sixteenth Century', in *Crisis and Change in the Venetian Economy in the 16th and 17th Centuries*, ed. Brian Pullan, London,1968, pp. 47-58.

54. By the beginning of the 1540s the supply of ginger to the Lisbon bound-vessels amounted to 2,000 to 3,000 quintals per year. ANTT, *São Lourenço*, III, doc. 130. Letter of the Kolathiri to Martim Afonso de Souza; in 1547 and 1548, the pepper export from Malabar to Portugal was 19,10,138 kg and 12,49,941 kg respectively. Pius Malekandathil, *Portuguese Cochin and the Maritime Trade of India*, p. 179. It is highly probable that this export trade was made possible with the continued collaboration of some Muslim traders.

55. J.H. da Cunha Rivara, *Archivo Portuguez Oriental*, fasc. 5, New Delhi, 1992, pp. 425-6.

56. ANTT, Corpo Cronologico, I, Maço 76, doc.103; Maço 78, doc.108; , Maço 79, doc.134. Initially he was in the service of Asad Khan of Belgaum (protector of the kingdom of Bijapur when Ismail Adil Shah died), who himself had a plan to buy a piece of land in Cannanore and to transfer there his enormous wealth. However, on his death Shams-ud-din Giloni inherited the entire wealth of Asad Khan, estimated to be about 10 million *cruzados*, which he used as capital for his commercial endeavours. In order to ensure the support of the Portuguese, he sent half of it to Lisbon in gold bars and the remaining half he invested in his commercial activities. Eventually, he bought land in Cannanore and made it the base of his trading empire extending up to Bassein and linked with Mecca. For more details, see Faria y Souza, *Asia Portuguesa: The History of the Discovery and Conquest of India by the Portuguese*, tran. John Stevens, vol. II, London, 1965, pp. 87-8; K.S.Mathew, 'Khwaja Shams-ud-din Giloni: A Sixteenth Century Entrepreneur in Portuguese India', in *Emporia, Commodities and Entrepreneurs in Asian Maritime Trade, c.1400-1750*, ed. Roderich Ptak and Dietmar Rothermund, Stuttgart, 1991, pp. 363-71.

57. Pius Malekandathil, *Portuguese Cochin and the Maritime Trade of India*, pp. 131-2.

58. Genevieve Bouchon,*Regent of the Sea*, pp. 151-75.

59. Pius Malekandathil, 'The Maritime Trade of Cannanore and the Global Commercial Revolution', p. 7.

60. Diogo do Couto, *Da Asia dos feitos que os Portugueses fizeram na Conquista e Descobrimento das Terras e Mares do Oriente*, Lisboa, 1973, decada V, parte II, pp. 431-7; Gaspar Correia, *Lendas da India*, tom. I, pp. 425ff; Genevieve Bouchon, *Regent of the Sea*, p. 172. This dynasty was to reign until the end of the nineteenth century.

61. For details, see Francois Pyrard Laval, *The Voyages of Francois Pyrard of Laval to the East Indies, the Maldives, the Moluccas and Brazil*, tran. Albert Gray, London, 1887, pp. 444-6; Diogo do Couto, decada VII-16-18; Genevieve Bouchon, *Regent of the Sea*, p. 173.

62. João Manuel de Almeida Teles e Cunha, *Economia de um imperio: Economia politica do Estado da India em torno do Mar Arabico e Golfo Persico Elementos Conjunturais:1595-1635*, Mestrado dissertation submitted to the University of Nova de Lisboa, 1995, pp. 397-400; Pius Malekandathil, 'The Maritime Trade of Cannanore and the Global Commercial Revolution', pp. 7-8.

63. K.K.N. Kurup, *The Ali Rajas of Cannanore*, Trivandrum, 1975; K.S.Mathew, 'Cannanore and the Portuguese: A Study of Trade and Urban Growth in the Sixteenth Century', paper presented at the National Seminar on 'Cannanore in the Maritime History of India', Kannur University, 8-9 March, 2001, p. 4.

64. F.C. Danvers, *The Portuguese in India*, vol. I, New Delhi, 1988, pp. 528-9.

65. See the picture of the fortress of the Kunjali given in Luis da Silveira, ed., *Livro das Plantas Fortalezas, Cidades e Povoações do Estado da India Oriental, com as Descrições do Maritimo dos Reinos e Provinciais onde estão situados e outros Portos*

Principais daqueles partes, Contribuição para a Historia das Fortalezas dos Portugueses no Ultramar, Lisboa, 1991, p. 86.

66. F.C. Danvers, op. cit., vol. II, p. 51.

67. Kunjali of course had his own version of justice and law. He used to execute it mercilessly. See F.C. Danvers, op. cit., vol. II, p. 51.

68. National Bibliothek Wien, Cod. 8961, fols. 891-892 letter dated 15-12-1588.

69. HAG, *Livro das Monções*, No. 3-a (1585-9), fols. 180-181. Royal letter sent to Duarte Meneses, dated 13-3-1587.

70. M.N. Pearson, *Merchants and Rulers in Gujarat*, p. 46.

71. F.C. Danvers, op. cit., vol. II, p. 112.

72. AHU, *Caixas da India*, Caixa 1, doc. 20, fol. 11; Faria y Sousa, op. cit., vol. III, pp. 99-100; F.C. Danvers, op. cit., vol. II, p. 112; A.P. Ibrahim Kunju, op. cit., pp. 81-2; Antonio de Gouveia, *Jornada do Arcebispo*, Coimbra, 1606, pp. 72-7.

73. BNL, *Fundo Geral*, Codice no.1976, fols.158-9, letter of Conde de Vidigueira to Philip, written in 1599.

74. HAG, *Livro das Monções, no. 7 (1600-3)*, fols. 192-5, royal letter sent to Aires de Saldanha, dated 15-2-1603; HAG, *Livro das Monções*, no. 6A (1604-5), fols. 71, 77, 79. All these three letters were dated 15-3-1605; ANTT, MSS, *S.Vicente*, 14, fol. 161, letter of Philip II (of Portugal) sent to D. Alexis de Menezes, dated 15-5-1605; ANTT, MSS, *S. Vicente*, 14, fols. 163-163v. Letter of Philip II (of Portugal) to the bishop of Cochin, dated 15-5-1605; Raymundo Antonio de Bulhão Pato, *Documentos Remettidos da India ou Livro das Monções*, vol. I, Lisboa, 1884, doc. 8, p. 36, Letter of Philip II to D. Martim Afonso de Castro, dated 6-3-1605.

75. HAG, *Livro das Monções*, no. 6A (1604-5), fol. 79, royal letter sent to the bishop of Cochin, dated 15-3-1605.

76. Antonio de Gouveia, *Jornada do Arcebispo*, pp. 208-9. The Ravuthar Muslims of Kanjirappally, an interior market place of central Kerala, trace back their origin to Moosavannan Ravuthar, Kulasekhara Khan and Mollamiya Labha who came to Kanjirappally from Madurai in AD 1373. From there these Ravuthar Muslims eventually spread to Erumely, Erattupetta and Thodupuzha. For details, see Jacob Aerthail, *Kanjiappally Noottandukaliloode* (Malayalam), 1985, pp. 88-97. Even now they use certain Tamil words in their Malayalam conversation.

77. Antonio de Gouveia, *Jornada do Arcebispo*, p. 94.

78. For details about the promise of the king of Cochin to help Kunjali to fight against the Zamorin and the Portuguese, see BNL, *Fundo Geral*, Codice no. 1976, fols. 158-159; Letter of Conde Vidigueira to king Philip written in 1599. For the details of the execution of the Kunjali, see C.R. Boxer and Frazão de Vasconcelos, *Andre Furtado de Mendonça (1558-1610)*, Lisboa, 1956, pp. 21-35.

79. William Foster ed., *The Voyage of Nicholas Downton to the East Indies:1614-1615*, London, 1939, p. 25.

80. M.A.P. Meilink-Roelofsz, *Asian Trade and European Influence in the Indonesian Archipelago between 1500-1630*, The Hague, 1962, p. 387.

81. The Portuguese *casado* traders of this period are viewed as a 'bourgeois class' by scholars like Dietmar Rothermund and Sanjay Subrahmanyam. Dietmar Rothermund, 'Introduction: The Fate of the Portuguese in Asia', *Portuguese Asia: Aspects in History and Economic History*, ed. Roderich Ptak, Stuttgart, 1987, p. vii; Sanjay Subrahmanyam, 'Cochin in Decline, 1600-1650: Myth and Manipulation in the *Estado da India*', in *Portuguese Asia: Aspects in History and Economic History*, ed. Roderich Ptak, pp. 63-79; For more details, see Pius Malekandathil, *Portuguese Cochin and the Maritime Trade of India*, pp. 207-18, 264-5.

82. James Talboys Wheller and Michael Macmillan, *European Travellers in India*, Calcutta, 1956, p. 34.

83. V. Ball, ed., *Travels in India by Jean Baptiste Tavernier*, vol. I, London, 1889, pp. 177-8.

84. A.R. de Bulhão Pato, ed., *Documentos Remetidos da India ou Livro das Monções*, vol. IV, Lisboa, 1935, doc. 954, pp. 295-6; João Manuel de Almeida Teles e Cunha, op. cit., pp. 400-4.

85. Authors like Jamal Mohammed say that the inland movement of Muslims from coastal areas and their involvement in agriculture started from this period onwards, with their impoverishment following the hundred years' wars with the Portuguese. Cf. Jamal Mohammed, 'Muslims on the Malabar Coast: A Study of the Nature and Activities of the Society (1600-1800)', in *The Portuguese and the Socio-cultural Changes in India, 1600-1800*, ed. K.S. Mathew, Teotonio R. de Souza and Pius Malekandathil, Fundação Oriente, 2001, pp. 269-75.

CHAPTER EIGHT

Information Networking between India and the Mediterranean in the Sixteenth and Seventeenth Centuries

The discovery of a sea route to India via the Cape of Good Hope by Vasco da Gama did not totally do away with the traditional linkages that the Indian Ocean had with the Mediterranean world. On the other hand, the Mediterranean connections were maintained through diverse mechanisms by different categories of Indian merchants, who were engaged in parallel movement of commodities to Europe. The basic aspect for the sustenance of trade that had by this time criss-crossed several continents was the ability to garner information about the market conditions of the places of procurement and distribution. Even when the Portuguese developed the Cape route for their commerce, information used to travel frequently between India and eastern Mediterranean through the medium of traders and hajj pilgrims going to Mecca. Eventually, the traders through the caravan route also acted as carriers of information between the two. Later, by the third quarter of the sixteenth century, the German traders developed a well-structured information networking system for the purpose of gathering information about the market conditions of the Mediterranean countries, which was also eventually used for collecting news about the nature and size of the Dutch vessels moving to the Indian Ocean from the Atlantic. This chapter dwells chiefly upon the nature of the information networking that different categories of traders resorted to for linking the commercial activities between India and the Mediterranean and shows how this parallel networking system became inevitable for the Portuguese in the seventeenth century for sustaining their commercial establishments, when threatened with frequent attacks from the Dutch and the English.

*An earlier version of this paper was delivered at Nirmala College, Murattupuzha, 28 September 2003.

THE CARRIERS OF INFORMATION
THROUGH THE RED SEA

The traditional merchant groups conducting trade with Mamluk Egypt and the hajj pilgrims were the early carriers of information to the Red Sea area about the arrival of the Portuguese in India. The traders of Alexandria and Venice received this news with great astonishment, which was evidently reflected in the reaction of the markets of these places. The price of pepper at Venice shot up from 56 ducats per quintal (in 1498) to 100 ducats in February 1500, when the pepper price was to be actually low because of the immense supply of cargo following the harvest in the months of December and January. In Cairo the price rose from 78 ducats in 1498 to 90-102 ducats in 1500.[1] The impact of the news of the Portuguese discovery of a sea route to India was such that the leading merchants of Europe, like the Fuggers and the Welsers who were conducting trade in Venice for a long period of time, closed their business establishments of Venice and moved to Lisbon in 1501.[2]

How did the information about the market conditions and other economic developments spread between India and the Mediterranean at a time when the Portuguese tried to control the movements of vessels and cargo to the Red Sea and Mediterranean oriented routes? The Portuguese used to exercise official control over the information and details about the sea voyages and expeditions made to new lands so that news about their navigational lines and market conditions of the discovered land might not reach other nations of Europe.[3] On 13 November 1504, King Manuel of Portugal decreed that complete secrecy, under pain of death, should be kept with regard to eastern and south-eastern and north-eastern voyages.[4]

One of the most important channels for dissemination of information between India and the Mediterranean was the hajj pilgrimage to Mecca from different zones of the Indian Ocean. Very often the pilgrims used to carry commodities along with them to sell them at the great fairs of Arabia and meet their travel costs, and the hajj was viewed by some as the largest bazaar of Islam.[5] Obviously the role of different categories of Indian traders, who managed to bypass the control systems of the Portuguese in exchanging information cannot be ignored. However, it was the pilgrims on hajj who turned out to be the greatest carriers of information in the Indian Ocean. By this time the hajj pilgrimage which the enterprising merchants managed to develop from the level of a religious ritual to a networking mechanism, had also become an effective device for the trading groups to exchange mercantile information and in this process Jidda as well as Mecca became the hubs of information networking between India and the Mediterranean.[6] The hajj pilgrims used to come back to India from the Arabian ports with the most updated information about the market conditions of the Mediterranean world.

Against this background of intense networking through the hajj pilgrimage, the fluctuations in the Mediterranean markets were immediately noticed by Indian merchants. As the Portuguese had fixed the price of pepper to be 2.5 ducats per quintal in the spice ports of Kerala in January 1503 on the initiative of Vasco da Gama and they did not change the price till 1624 despite the inflation factor and the radical changes that the European markets expressed during this long span of time,[7] Muslim traders who offered higher price got the best quality of pepper from the spice production centres of Kerala. In this process of quoting prices in the pepper ports of Kerala they banked upon the information from the markets of the Mediterranean world. The price of pepper in Cairo on the eve of the Ottoman occupation (in 1516) was 135 ducats per quintal, while its price at Venice was 80 ducats per quintal (1516).[8] It is interesting to note that this information about the pepper price immediately reached India, particularly the spice growing pockets of Malabar, where the Muslim traders were quoting far higher prices than the Portuguese. The king of Cochin said in 1516 that it was very difficult to arrange spices at the low rate paid by the Portuguese, as much of it was purchased by other traders at a very high price and in full cash payment.[9]

The words of Caesar Frederick (1560s) are more indicative of the advantages that the merchants conducting trade with Mecca had in the spice ports of Kerala, obviously because of their ability to garner market news from the Mediterranean world. They used to buy spices at a higher price, evidently on the basis of market indices of Europe and hence they could get clean and better conditioned pepper.[10]

The synagogue of Cairo acted as a hub of mercantile information for the Jewish merchants linked with the commerce of India and the Mediterranean. The trade documents obtained from the Cairo Genizza attest to the long-standing role that the synagogue of Cairo used to play in disseminating commercial information between India and the Mediterranean regions from the eighth to the thirteenth centuries.[11] In the sixteenth century, when the Portuguese tried to establish monopoly over the Indian Ocean trade, the Jews revived their connections with the Egyptian synagogue, which was eventually developed as a platform for passing on strategic commercial information from Indian markets to European markets. By the 1540s we find the Jews of Cochin and the Christian converts from Judaism (often called the new Christians) entering into an alliance to get linked with this information hub of Cairo. Consequently, big Jewish merchants from Cairo, like Isaac do Cairo, started settling down in the Jewish colony of

Mattancherry and conducted trade supplying cargo to the new Christian traders of Portuguese Cochin.[12]

The information networking through the Red Sea ports was later utilized advantageously for increasing movement of commodities to the Mediterranean and through this route about 40,000 hundredweight of pepper and other spices used to enter Alexandria, as Lourenço Pires de Tavora reported in the 1560s.[13]

THE PORTS OF THE PERSIAN GULF AND
THE CIRCULATION OF INFORMATION

The ports of the Persian Gulf formed another channel for the circulation of information between India and the Mediterranean. After the establishment of Portuguese hold over Hormuz in 1515, the Portuguese traders were frequenting this port for transporting horses principally to Goa, and at times to Cannanore as well as to Cochin.[14] They formed only one category of news-carriers, while the strongest strand was that of the illegal traders dispatching commodities via Damascus or Tripoly to the Mediterranean. These channels of information and trade passed through the markets of the Ottoman Turks and the Saffavid Persia either by the Basra-Arabian desert-Damascus route or by the Basra-Baghdad-Aleppo-Tripoly route.[15] Leonhard Rauwolfd, who visited the Persian Gulf region in 1574 attests to the intensified movement of Indian commodities through this channel.[16]

These were also the channels that many people, including Caesar Frederick (the Venetian traveller who reached India in 1563),[17] and Mar Abraham (the bishop of St. Thomas Christians who went to Rome and Venice to get legitimately consecrated as a bishop by the Patriarch of Venice in c.1564/5),[18] Ralph Fitch and Dom Matheus Castro (the first Brahmin Catholic from Goa to be appointed by Propaganda Fide as the bishop for the Apostolic Vicariate of Bijapur in 1637)[19] who used to travel between the Levant and the Indian Ocean. Ralph Fitch, whose travel was financed by the Levant company, made his journey accompanied by other Englishmen, viz., John Newbery, John Eldred, William Leedes and James Storey, to Basra through this route via Tripoli and Aleppo. From Aleppo they moved to Bir on the banks of Euphrates and sailed up to Fallujah on the river. Having crossed southern Mesopotamia, they entered Baghdad and then proceeded to Basra via the Tigris. From Basra, Ralph Fitch sailed down the Persian Gulf to Hormuz where he was captured by the Portuguese and taken to Goa.[20]

The route through the Persian Gulf, which was then used frequently for the movement of commodities and people, formed a significant channel of communication between the Levant and India. However, most of the information networking that was done till the 1570s was almost in an informal way and mainly through the media of caravan traders and travellers. A change was perceptible after the 1570s, when the nature of Indo-European trade necessitated an updated communication system and postal net-working.

FORMATION OF A POSTAL SYSTEM AND
COMMUNICATION NETWORKING

The establishment of a postal device between India and the Mediterranean became inevitable with the stepping down of the Portuguese King Sebastian from being a merchant monarch and the subsequent handing over of Indo-European trade into the hands of German, Italian and Portuguese private traders in the 1570s.[21] The private traders including Konrad Rott,[22] later the Fuggers as well as the Welsers[23] from Germany and Giovanni Rovallesca of Milan from Italy,[24] who took up an Asian contract (to fetch spices from India and supply them at *Casa da India* at Lisbon)[25] and the European contract (to collect spices from *Casa da India* and distribute them all over Europe)[26] from 1575 onwards could no longer depend upon the communication system of the Portuguese running through the Cape route as intrinsic component of their *carreira* system. These business houses sent their own trade agents to India, who were to operate under the instructions of their masters located at Augsburg or Milan.

The different trade agents of the German and Italian merchant magnates including Gabriel Holzschuher, the agent of Konrad Rott in India,[27] Ferdinand Cron the agent of the Fuggers and the Welsers in India[28] and Filippo Sassetti, the agent of Giovanni Rovallesca in India[29], had to correspond frequently with their masters in Europe. Very often they sent their correspondence in the ships which these trade agents resorted to for carrying cargo from India to Lisbon. Eventually a parallel postal device was developed by them to gather information overland from the Mediterranean.

In fact, the overland courier service was opened by the Fuggers in the early 1590s, when the English were increasingly concentrating in Lisbon and frequently blocking sea communication with India. This postal system, via the Levant and the Persian Gulf was devised so that the Fuggers could communicate regularly with their agent Ferdinand Cron in India, the firm Otto in Venice and the Welser factor in Lyons.[30] Usually the letters from the house of the Fuggers of Augsburg reached Goa (via Venice, Aleppo and Hormuz) within a period of 6 to 8 months. The distance from Augsburg to Venice (through the Alps) was 450 km, from Venice to Aleppo it was 2,750 km, from Aleppo to Hormuz 2,400 km, and finally from Hormuz to Goa

2,500 km. Thus, the overland courier service maintained with India by the Fuggers covered 8,100 km.[31] Later, when the Portuguese crown terminated contract trade and took up the Indo-Europe commerce again in 1598, many of the trade agents of the German and Italian business houses began individual business ventures for expanding operations, and they banked upon the overland communication network between India and the Mediterranean for burgeoning their enterprise.

Detailed information about this communication networking is obtained from the writings of Ferdinand Cron, who was the former trade agent of the Fuggers and the Welsers in India, and who started his own business at Goa when the latter terminated their Indian contract in 1591.[32] Cron took over this news-service and extended it to Malacca and Macao, which formed the eastern terminus of his commercial network.[33] Through the overland communication system via Venice-Aleppo-Baghdad-Ormuz, he used to get news about the political and economic developments of Europe, which he managed to make use of for his commercial advantage, or passed such news on to the Portuguese authorities to get acceptability before them and thus ensure mercantile privileges and legitimacy for his enterprises. Thus on 9 May 1598, Ferdinand Cron received letters from the *Fucares* (the Fuggers) and the *Belsares* (the Welsers) sent from Augsburg through the overland postal system in 1597, providing information about the Dutch fleet moving to the east from the Atlantic. Ferdinand Cron immediately passed on this information to the Portuguese viceroy Conde de Vidigueira (1597-1600), who soon sent a fleet to Malacca for its protection.[34]

The Dutch threat got intensified in the Indian Ocean after 1602, when the various Dutch companies were amalgamated to form *Vereenigde Oost Indische Compagnie* (VOC). Against this background of changed situation Ferdinand Cron began to capitalize on the overland courier service for collecting timely information from Europe about the timing of departure, nature and size of the Dutch fleet moving to India, and to pass it on to the Portuguese authorities. This in turn secured for Cron's courier service a larger acceptability before the Portuguese authorities, which he conveniently utilized for furthering his personal business activities. In 1605, Ferdinand Cron received a report through overland news service that the Dutch were preparing a great fleet for Malacca. He passed on this information to the Portuguese captain Andres Hurtado de Mendonça, who immediately took measures to fortify Malacca and to provide it with arms and supplies. Andres Hurtado later testified that had he not received the information well in advance from Cron, Malacca would have fallen into the hands of the Dutch.[35] In July 1605, about eleven Dutch vessels departed from the Atlantic to Malacca and the news reached Cron in 1606 through the overland information network. The information was passed on to the viceroy Martin Afonso de

Castro, who in turn convened a meeting with Archbishop Alexis de Menezes and Ferdinand Cron to decide on how to handle the situation. Cron suggested that two ships should be immediately built for the purpose of equipping the Viceroy's fleet, and Cron lent the Portuguese an amount of 6,000 *xerafins* for the same.[36] Later in 1607, Cron's overland courier service saved Malacca from being captured by the Dutch. On getting news about the departure of the vessels, Cron met viceroy Archbishop Alexis de Menezes and discussed the Dutch strategies with him. The Archbishop immediately sent a fleet to Malacca for its defence, for which Cron also contributed an amount of 5,000 *xerafins*. [37]

Meanwhile, seeing the importance of the overland news service in the defence and the commerce of Portuguese territories in the Indian Ocean in general, and in India in particular, against the increasing threat from the Dutch on the Cape route, Philip II of Portugal wanted to make use of Cron and his information network for the establishment of an official transcontinental courier service between Asia and Europe. Accordingly, a contract was signed with Sebastian Bader on 6 December 1608 in Lisbon in the house of Dom Francisco da Gama, Conde de Vidigueira. The agreement demanded that Cron and his information network had to take letters from Lisbon to Goa, where they would be personally handed over to the viceroy by Cron. In return, the letters from the viceroy or governor would be collected by Cron, who had to send them to Lisbon with a covering letter of his own. This overland postal service from Madrid to Goa was maintained by a network connecting Marseille, Genoa, Venice, Alexandria, Aleppo and Hormuz. In this network, there was a long line of agents including Ferdinand Cron and three associates in Goa, Jacome Artigo in Hormuz, Guilhes Quinto in Alexandria, and the Fugger factor Philip Litscher in Madrid.[38] In Venice the connecting man was Helman, who was originally from Antwerp and had good relations with the Dutch merchants of Amsterdam as well as Rotterdam. However, this courier service seems to have functioned only for a short period, as Bader soon went bankrupt.[39]

Meanwhile, Ferdinand Cron used this courier service to gather market information as well as for expanding his business. He extended his business to Bijapur and Golconda to obtain precious stones and the extent of his commercial enterprise stretched from Diu in the north-west, Mughal terrains in the north, Malabar in the south and Macao in the east. Cron used the overland route also to send diamonds and precious stones from the Deccan mines to Europe, where they were highly priced. His friends and former associates residing in different parts of Europe used to give him necessary information on the market conditions there and helped him in distributing the precious gems in European markets. Even some of the former Portuguese authorities, like Francisco da Gama, who returned to Lisbon after his tenure, continued to conduct negotiations with Ferdinand Cron for getting diamonds from India. In 1615, we find Cron sending diamonds from Goa to Lisbon for him.[40] However, this information networking eventually collapsed when Ferdinand Cron was arrested in 1619 and deported to Lisbon accusing him of having secret transactions with the Dutch.[41]

THE OVERLAND COURIER SYSTEM
OF THE PORTUGUESE

When the English and the Dutch obstructed the navigational lines of the Portuguese in the Indian Ocean, and particularly after the collapse of the overland courier system of Ferdinnad Cron, the Portuguese tried to develop an alternative news-service between India and Europe through Hormuz and the Mediterranean. This was done principally through the Augustinian monks, who established their houses at Muscat, Kung and Tebriz. It was Archbishop Alexis de Menezes who took up initiative to dispatch Augustinian monks from Goa to the court of Shah Abbas I, about which detailed information is given in *Jornada do Arcebispo*.[42] Eventually, their houses in different parts of Saffavid Persia were used as nodal points for the transmission of messages to Europe. In the 1640s, letters were first sent from Goa to the Portuguese factor at Kung, from where they were further sent to the Augustinian monastery in Isfahan. They were then taken to the Apostolic legate in Jerusalem and finally to Europe. Urgent messages were sent often through this route, even though it was expensive.[43]

The Carmelites also used to provide courier service through the overland route. Usually they used to take four to six months for delivering materials in Europe; however, they were reported to be much more reliable than the Augustinians as well as the Armenian and French private traders. In the 1670s the Carmelites used to give a written receipt of the letters that they received and employed their own runners through the Syrian desert to take them to the Mediterranean.[44] As the different religious orders like the Franciscans, the Jesuits, the Dominicans and the Augustinians operating in different parts of India had to send their periodical reports to their immediate superiors in Portugal and their highest authorities in Rome, they had to maintain a courier service of their own. Very often they used to resort to *carreira* vessels for sending letters to their authorities in Europe. However, with the increasing threat from the Dutch and the English blocking the Portuguese vessels in the Indian Ocean and with the establishment of their houses in Saffavid Persia and in terrains of the Ottomans, some of these religious orders preferred to send communication first to their houses in West Asia and from there to Europe through the overland route, employing their own runners wherever necessary.

The above discussion shows that though the information networking between India and the Mediterranean initially emerged as a parallel mechanism to the Cape route circuits, by the first decade of seventeenth century information coming through the Mediterranean channels became inevitable for sustenance of the Portuguese imperial edifice in the Indian Ocean. In the sixteenth century, the circulation of information between the two worlds was realized mainly through the hajj pilgrims or through the caravan traders. Very often the Portuguese failed to get the required amount of pepper and that too the best quality of spices, mainly due to the fact that the Arab and indigenous Muslim traders who had updated information about the market conditions of the Mediterranean world through the informants from Mecca/Jidda used to quote higher prices for the cargo. The Persian Gulf was a significant door for the movement of commodities, people and information from India to the Mediterranean and vice versa.

However, the postal system that the Fuggers developed during the time of contract trade between India and Europe linking the various markets of Europe and Asia proved to be one of the earliest attempts to organize a communication system between the two worlds. When the Fuggers terminated their Indian contract in 1591, individual private traders like Ferdinand Cron developed it still further for eliciting information about the political and economic developments of Europe to use it for their business advantages. Cron used to pass on to the Portuguese authorities the news that he got from the overland courier service about details of the Dutch vessels dispatched from Europe to Asia, which eventually prompted Philip II of Portugal to develop a highly organized overland courier system with Cron as the key figure in India. Eventually with the accusation of espionage on him, this overland postal system collapsed following which the various religious orders (through their houses scattered in Saffavid Persia and Ottoman terrains) maintained overland communication system, often employing their own runners. At a time when sea communication was increasingly becoming impossible because of Dutch and English threats, the overland courier service maintained by the various religious orders in the second half of the seventeenth century became the only source for linking communication between Portugal and India. In this entire development the Mediterranean once again became the major hub for information-sharing between Eurasian worlds.

NOTES

1. Vitorino Magalhães Godinho, *L'Economie de L'empire Portugais aux XVe et XVIe Siecles*, Paris, 1969, pp. 720-5. However, the price of pepper in Lisbon fell drastically from 80 ducats (in 1498) to 40 ducats in 1500-2. See Donald F. Lach,

Asia in the Making of Europe, vol. I, (The Century of Discovery), book I, Chicago, 1965, p. 143. Interestingly the price of pepper per quintal at Cochin was only 2.98 ducats in 1498 and 2.5 ducats in 1502. Pius Malekandathil, *Portuguese Cochin and the Maritime Trade of India, 1500-1663,* New Delhi 2001, pp. 154-5.

2. Franz Hümmerich, *Die erste Deutsche Handelsfahrt nach Indien 1505/06: Ein Unternehmender Welser, Fugger und anderer Augsburger sowie Nürnberger Häuser,* München, 1922, p. 9; Konrad Häbler, *Die Überseeischen Unternehmungen der Welser und Ihrer Gessellschafter,* Leipzig, 1903, p. 6; Pius Malekandathil, *The Germans, the Portuguese and India,* Münster, 1999, p. 43. The Fuggers were associated with Fondaco dei Tedeschi since the second half of the fifteenth century. See Götz Freiherr von Pölnitz, *Fugger und Medici: Deutsche Kaufleute und Handwerker in Italien,* Leipzig, 1942, p. 30.

3. Jaime Cortesão, 'Do sigilo nacional sobre os descobrimentos, Cronicas desaparecidas, mutiladas e falseadas. Alguns dos feitos que se calaram', in *Lusitania,* I, 1924, p. 50.

4. Ramos Coelho, ed., *Alguns documentos do Archivo Nacional da Torre do Tombo acerca das navegações e conquistas portuguesas,* Lisboa, 1892, p. 139.

5. R.J. Barendse, *The Arabian Seas: The Indian Ocean World of the Seventeenth Century,* New Delhi, 2002, pp. 38, 44; M.N. Pearson, 'Pious Passengers' Motivations for the Hajj from Early Modern India', in *Studies in Maritime History,* ed. K.S. Mathew, Pondicherry, 1990, pp. 112-26.

6. For details on the economic meanings of hajj pilgrimage, see M.N. Pearson, *Pilgrimage to Mecca: The Indian Experience,* Princeton, 1996.

7. For details about price fixation in Cochin (160 *panams* per bhar-166.3 kg) and Cannanore (210 *panams* per bhar), see Thome Lopes, 'Navegação as Indias Orientales escrita em Portugues por Thome Lopes', in *Collecção de noticias para a historia e geografia das nações ultramarinas que vivem nos dominios Portugueses ou ilhes são vizinhas,* tom. II, nos. 1&2, Lisboa, 1812, pp. 199-200; Luis da Costa, 'Tratado da Pimenta', in *Documentação Ultramarina Portuguesa,* ed. Antonio da Silva Rego, vol. III, Lisboa, 1963, p. 373.

8. Vitorino Magalhães Godinho, *L'Economie de L'empire Portugais aux XVe et XVIe Siecles,* pp. 720, 725. The price at Venice was much lower than that at Cairo, which happened because of pepper supply at Venice from Lisbon.

9. Pius Malekandathil, *Portuguese Cochin and the Maritime Trade of India, 1500-1663,* p. 115; See also ANTT, *Corpo Cronologico,* I, Maço 50, doc. 65.

10. Richard Hakluyt, *The Principal Navigations, Voyages, Traffiques and discoveries of the English Nation,* vol. V, Glasgow, 1905, p. 392.

11. For detailed discussion on Geniza papers, see S.D. Goitein, *Letters of Medieval Jewish Traders,* Princeton, 1973; idem, *A Mediterranean Society,* 4 vol, Los Angeles and Berkeley, 1967-84; idem, *Jews and Arabs: Their Contacts through the Ages,* New York, 1964.

12. For details on Isaac of Cairo, see Jose Alberto Rodrigues da Silva Tavim, 'Os Judeus e a Expansão Portuguesa na India durante o Seculo XVI. O Exemplo de Isaac do Cairo: Espião, Lingua, e Judeu de Cochim de Cima', in *Arquivos do Centro Cultural Calouste Gulbenkian,* vol. XXXIII, Lisboa, 1994, pp. 167-87.

13. Lourenço Pires de Tavora quoted in F.C. Lane, 'The Mediterranean Spice-Trade', in *American Historical Review*, vol. XLV, 1939-40, p. 585.

14. Karl H. Dannenfeldt, *Leonhard Rauwolf: Sixteenth Century Physician, Botanist and Traveller*, Massachussetts, 1968, pp. 121-2; Richard Hakluyt, *The Principal Navigations, Voyages, Traffiques and Discoveries of the English Nation*, vol. V, Glasgow, 1905, pp. 285, 333-4; J.H. da Cunha Rivara ed., *Archivo Portuguez Oriental*, fasciculo 3, New Delhi, 1992, p. 301; HAG, *Livro das Monções*, no. 4 (1595-8), fols. 672-8. The royal instruction given to the viceroy dated 2 January 1596.

15. Nycolão Gomçallves, *Livro que trata das cousas da India e do Japão*, p. 74.

16. Karl H. Dannenfeldt, *Leonhard Rauwolf: Sixteenth Century Physician, Botanist and Traveller*, Massachussetts, 1968, p. 121.

17. For details of his account see 'Caesar Frederick' in Richard Hakluyt, *The Principal Navigations, Voyages, Traffiques and discoveries of the English Nation*, vol. V, Glasgow, 1905.

18. For details on Mar Abraham, see Joseph Thekkedath, *History of Christianity in India*, vol. III, Bangalore, 1988, pp. 47-50; Josef Wicki, *Documenta Indica*, vol. XI, Rome, 1975, p. 64.

19. Matheus Castro left India in 1621 via Persia and Syria and reached Rome in 1625. He was ordained a bishop in 1629 and came back to Goa through the same route in 1633. Since he was not accepted by the Archbishop of Goa, he went back to Rome where the Propaganda authorities appointed him as the Vicar Apostolic (bishop) of Bijapur in 1637. Joseph Thekkedath, *History Christianity in India*, vol. II, pp. 417-20; D. Ferroli, *The Jesuits in Malabar*, vol. II, Bangalore, 1939, pp.173-85.

20. For more details, see J.C. Locke, *The First Englishmen in India: Letters and Narratives of Sundry Elizabethans*, London, 1930; Michael Edwardes, *Ralph Fitch: Elizabethan in the Indies*, London, 1972.

21. Francisco P. Mendes da Luz, *O Conselho da India*, Lisboa, 1952, pp. 73-4; Vicente Almeida d'Eça, *Normas Economicas na Colonização Portuguesa ate 1808*, Coimbra, 1921, chapt. II; Pius Malekandathil, *The Portuguese, the Germans and India*, Münster, 1999, pp. 75-78.

22. Konrad Häbler, 'Konrad Rott und die Thüringische Gesellschaft' in *Neues Archiv für Sächsische Geschichte und Altertumskunde*, ed. Hbert Ermisch, vol. 16, 1895, p. 179.

23. M.A. Hedwig Fitzler, 'Der Anteil der Deutschen an der Kolonialpolitik Philipps II. von Spanien in Asien', *VSWG*, vol. 28, 1935, p. 249; Reinhard Hildebrandt, Die '*Georg Fuggerischen Erben*': *Kaufmännische Tätigkeit und sozialer Status, 1555-1600*, Berlin, 1966.

24. Donald F. Lach, *Asia in the Making of Europe*, vol. I, book I, Chicago, 1965, p. 134.

25. Konrad Rott was obliged to buy 20,000 quintals of pepper from India and supply to the *casa da India* in Lisbon. Konrad Häbler, 'Konrad Rott und die Thüringische Gesellschaft', pp. 184-6.

26. Ibid., pp. 178-91.
27. See the letter sent by Gabriel Holzschuher on 10 January 1580 from Cochin, *Nationalbibliothek* Wien, cod. 8953.
28. *Fürstlich und Gräflich Fuggersches Familien und Stiftungs Archiv*, Dillingen Donau, Mss. Cod. 46.1. The letter of Fernand Cron, sent from Cochin , dated 26-12-1587; see also Charles R. Boxer, ed., 'Uma raridade bibliografica sobre Fernão Cron', *Boletim internacional de bibliografia luso-brasileira*, vol. XII, no. 3, 1971, pp. 323-64.
29. Ettore Marucci, ed., *Lettere edite e inedited di Filippo Sassetti*, Florence, 1855.
30. Hermann Kellenbenz, 'Ferdinand Cron', in Wolfganf Zorn, Hg., *Lebensbilderaus dem Bayerischen Schwaben* (Veröffentlichungen der Scwäbischen Forschungsgemeinschaft bei der Kommission für Bayerische Landesgeschichte), Reihe 3, Bd. 9, 1974, pp.195-6.
31. Hermann Kellenbenz, 'Le front hispano-portugais contre l'Inde et le rôle d'une agence de renseignements au service de marchands allemands et flamands', *Studia*, vol. XI, Lisboa, Janeiro 1963, p. 280.
32. Pius Malekandathil, *The Portuguese, the Germans and India*, pp. 98-9.
33. Hermann Kellenbenz, 'Ferdinand Cron', pp. 195-6.
34. Charles R.Boxer, ed., 'Uma raridade bibliografica sobre Fernão Cron', p. 327.
35. Ibid., pp. 327-8.
36. Ibid., p. 328.
37. Ibid., pp. 328-9.
38. Archivo Historico Nacional, Madrid, Estado, Libro 81-d, fols. 240-3; see Hermann Kellenbenz, 'Le front hispano-portugais contre l'Inde', pp. 269, 284-6.
39. Hermann Kellenbenz, 'Ferdinand Cron', pp. 208-9.
40. ANTT, *Convento da Graça*, II-E, Caixa 3, fols. 81-3, Letter of Cron sent to Conde de Vidigueira from Goa dated 22 December 1615; see also fols. 87-9, Letter of Cron sent to Conde de Vidigueira from Goa, dated 20 December 1616; Sanjay Subrahmanyam, 'An Augsburger in Asia Portuguesa: Further Light on the Commercial World of Ferdinand Cron, 1587-1624' in *Emporia, Commodities and Entrepreneurs in Asian Maritime Trade, c. 1490-1750*, ed. Roderich Ptak and Dietmar Rothermund, Stutgart, pp. 423-5; Pius Malekandathil, *The Portuguese, the Germans and India*, pp. 102-5.
41. Charles R. Boxer, ed., 'Uma raridade bibliografica sobre Fernão Cron', pp. 338-9, 343; Pius Malekandathil, *The Portuguese, the Germans and India*, pp. 105-11; Sanjay Subrahmanyam, 'An Augsburger in Asia Portuguesa', pp. 417-19.
42. See the original work Antonio de Gouvea, *Jornada do Arcebispo*, Coimbra, 1606. It is translated into English and edited by Pius Malekandathil, *Jornada of Dom Alexis de Meezes: A Portuguese Account of the Sixteenth Century Malabar*, Kochi 2003. For the details on the Augustinians being sent to the court of Shah Abbas I, see ibid., pp. 542-79.
43. R.J. Barendse, *The Arabian Seas: The Indian Ocean World of the Seventeenth Century*, p. 166.
44. Ibid., p. 167.

CHAPTER NINE

Bengal and the Commercial Expansion of the Portuguese *Casados*, 1511-1632

During the medieval period, the Bay of Bengal was an intermediate maritime zone in the larger exchange network linking the Indian Ocean world with the Mediterranean and Atlantic worlds. Covered by the pattern of the northeast monsoon winds, this region exhibited a remarkable degree of unity and commonality as far as the movements of commodities, people and ideas were concerned. Bengal, occupying the core position in the *micro-weltwirtschaft* that evolved in this maritime space, became a trade destination of great significance with the entry of the Portuguese into Indian waters. While the official Portuguese establishments were concentrated more on the west coast of India, making it the principal platform for their Indo-European commerce, the private Portuguese *casado* (the word *casados* literally means married Portuguese citizens; however, their wives were mostly Indian in origin) traders engaged in intra-Asian commerce were expanding more and more towards the eastern space of the Indian Ocean making Bengal a principal base for their operation. Keeping its one arm extended to South-East Asia, as well as China, and the other extended to the west coast of India as well as West Asia, Bengal tried to muster up commercial vitality through the enterprising skills of the *casados*.

Both commercially and politically the most strategic spot for the Portuguese in the Indian Ocean was coastal western India, because of being the source for highly priced spices and textiles and due to its geophysical closeness to the ports of the Red Sea, the Persian Gulf and the eastern Mediterranean, where the wares of the Indian Ocean used to flow before the Portuguese entry. The Portuguese tried to control the west coast of India by erecting a chain of fortresses at the junctional points of riverine and land

*This was earlier published in *Trade and Globalisation,* ed. S. Jeyaseela Stephen, New Delhi, 2003, pp. 161-90.

routes along the coast and a regular patrolling fleet along the vast coast was introduced for the purpose of preventing diversion of spices and other cargo, reserved to the Portuguese crown as per the norms of royal trade monopoly, to the ports of Red Sea and the eastern Mediterranean.[1] The chain of fortresses and patrolling fleet were meant to protect the monopoly claims of the Portuguese crown and the system of licences or *cartazes* (indicating port of origin and port of final destination) was introduced in the ports of the west coast to ensure that no monopoly item, including spices, moved to Europe through channels other than that of the Portuguese. While trade in the western space of the Indian Ocean was characterized by the several checking and controlling mechanisms of the Portuguese state, the eastern space of the Indian Ocean was earmarked as a space for the free trade of the *casados* of Goa and Cochin. In this process of movement of Portuguese *casado* traders to the eastern coast of India, there appeared several Portuguese enclaves in places like Nagapattinam, Mylapore, Satgaon, Chittagong, etc., where the Portuguese private traders thrived initially without fortifications and operated without the support of the official control devices like the patrolling fleet. Nor were there *cartazes* for checking the cargo destinations of their commercial competitors, either. The *casados* conducted their trade as any merchant group would do in the eastern space of the Indian Ocean, and very often their trade circuits through the different economic zones of eastern Indian Ocean revolved round their settlements in Bengal.

Bengal's encounter with the Europeans is a theme of great interest among the academicians and several scholars (like Armando Cortesão, J.J.A. Campos, George D. Winius, Sanjay Subrahmanyam, Genevieve Bouchon as well as Luis Filipe Thomas) had already dealt with the different aspects of Portuguese expansion in Bengal.[2] However, the discovery of several new source-materials related to Portuguese trading activities in Bengal and their interpretation against the background of recent researches give scope for undertaking this study, which proposes to throw light into the several of the neglected phases of Portuguese interlude in this micro-region. The central purpose of this chapter is to locate Bengal against the background of the commercial expansion of the Portuguese private traders in the eastern space of the Indian Ocean and to see how far it was made a base for furthering their private interests. It is analysed by focussing on two aspects: first, the nature of Portuguese trade with Bengal and second, the increasing utilization of the politico-economic developments of this region by the Portuguese *casado* traders to eclipse the commercial interests of the crown in Bengal for a considerable span of time. The resulting socio-economic order took a decisive turn in its course with the increasing inflow of Portuguese *casados* from the western seaboard of India and with their eventual settlement in Bengal's nodal points of exchange.

FROM PERIPHERY TO CORE

Bengal, which had been confined to the periphery level both in political and economic activities for a considerable span of the medieval period, moved more and more towards core position by the sixteenth century thanks to the combination of various developments. With the emergence of Malacca around 1400, Bengal lying on its peripheral orbit experienced resurgence of trade, which continued to gather further momentum in the following centuries.[3] It is interesting to note that Chatgaon or Chittagong, located on the frontiers of the regional economic unit of Malacca, played a vital role in this transformation process, which took a decisive turn after 1500. The closeness of Chittagong to Gaur, which as the headquarters of Sultanate power provided a large bulk of consumer class,[4] was an added reason that accelerated its evolution as the principal centre of Bengal's maritime trade in the early part of the sixteenth century.

In the first decade following the Portuguese entry into Indian waters, Bengal came to their attention and as early as 1508 the Portuguese crown asked Diogo Lopes de Sequeira to explore Gramjes (Ganges—evidently referring to the Bengal region located at the mouth of the river Ganges) and China to which pepper was flowing.[5] However, with the conquest of Malacca in 1511, the Portuguese started exploring the extent of commercial networks emanating from Malacca, a process which took them to a vast world of regional economies of the eastern space of the Indian Ocean.[6] In this explorative venture the Portuguese married citizens or the *casados* (to whom were granted by Afonso Albuquerque and the succeeding governors the privilege of conducting trade for their sustenance)[7] were the most enterprising and daring group. It seems that some of them must have reached Bengal during the course of their roaming voyages to sell their merchandise from Portugal. This is inferred from the letter of Afonso de Albuquerque of 1513, where he wrote: 'Bengal needs all our merchandise'.[8] These words are indicative of the fact that the nature of demand for Lusitanian wares in Bengal must have been ascertained by the Portuguese traders themselves.

The first private Lusitanian traders, who made daring voyages to Bengal, came from the Portuguese settlement of Cochin, where the lobbying group, known as the 'Cochin group', played a vital role in effecting a transition from state-controlled trade to free trade in Asian waters. These Portuguese *casado* entrepreneurs found a champion of their cause in Lopo Soares de

Albergaria who was appointed as the new governor of *Estado da India*, following the death of Afonso de Albuquerque in 1515. The policy of the former to decentralize trade by demarcating the maritime space east of Cape Comorin for the commerce of the Portuguese *casados* gave a radical twist to the very structure of the Portuguese trade in Asia.[9] It is against the general background of the Portuguese state's compromises with the evolving trading group of Portuguese *casados* and attempts for accommodating their private initiatives that one has to see their commercial expansion in Bengal.

From 1515 onwards, the crown also entered into the fray for exploring the Bay of Bengal and China along with the Portuguese private traders for expanding commerce, for the voyage of which Fernão Peres de Andrade was appointed the captain.[10] Though he explored the coast of China by 1517, he could not reach Bengal; but he sent his envoy João Coelho in a ship of a Muslim merchant to Chittagong. There João Coelho, who enjoyed the goodwill and support of the Muslim merchants, was well received by the local ruler, while D. João de Silveira, who came as an official envoy of Portuguese governor to Bengal in 1518, a little after Coelho's arrival, for securing from the local ruler trade facilities including the permission for erecting a factory, was looked upon with suspicion and animosity for his earlier capturing of two Bengali ships going to Cambay. Thanks to his anti-Muslim antecedents, João de Silveira achieved nothing of his mission; however, his voyage paved the way for the introduction of the *Carreira de Bengal*, sent annually by the Portuguese to the ports of Bengal.[11] This development in Chittagong is indicative of the fact that there was no such thing as a universal clash between the Portuguese and the Muslims, though personal conflicts and problems were not rare. However, with the introduction of the *Carreira de Bengal*, there was an attempt to extend to Bengal some of the maritime and commercial institutions linked with the central power of the Portuguese government in Goa. The commercial route of this *Carreira* was later strengthened by the Portuguese embassy sent to Gaur in 1521 under the leadership of Antonio de Brito and Diogo Pereira, a leading private trader of Cochin.[12]

From 1526 onwards, there is evidence of Bengali cloth being brought to Cochin for sale. In that year Manoel da Gama, the factor and captain of the coast of Coromandel brought textiles from Bengal to Cochin.[13] In fact, the enterprising *casados* of Cochin and Goa formed the major mercantile intermediaries who took the greatest advantage of the favourable atmosphere of Bengal markets, which was created by the diplomatic voyages of the annual *Carreira de Bengal*. As the share of the Portuguese state trade through *Carreira de Bengal* was meagre in the Bay of Bengal, the *casados* jumped into the expanding markets of Bengal, initially as distributors of cargo from Portugal and spices from Cochin, to which textiles, sugar and long pepper moved as return cargo. Seeing the huge profit amassed by the *casados* of Cochin from this trade, the native ruler of Cochin started putting claims, as early as 1529, of customs duties on all their ships coming from Bengal and also from Malacca, though it ultimately resulted in his internment in his own palace by the governor Lopo Vaz de Sampayo.[14]

For another two decades, or so, Bengal seems to have continued as a stable satellite economic unit for the commerce of the Portuguese crown, with which linkages were maintained through the *Carreira de Bengal*. However, by the mid-1530s, the politico-economic and geophysical changes in Bengal paved the way for a chain of developments, which necessitated greater involvement of the Lusitanians in its politico-commercial affairs. On the one hand, there was an active and direct Portuguese intervention in Chittagong with their attack of this port city in 1534, which ushered in an offensive phase in Luso-Bengal relations.[15] On the other hand, the new port of Satgaon which emerged following the change of the course of river system of the Hughli, began to increasingly attract traders as the nearest accessible gateway to Gaur. By the time Diogo Rebello reached Bengal in 1535 to liberate Martim Afonso de Mello and his men, the sultan had already extended his control over the port of Satgaon through his governor appointed there.[16]

Why were the Portuguese *casado* traders moving increasingly to Bengal, especially from 1540s onwards? It was mainly because of the fast expanding economic activities of the region, which provided a lot of opportunities of commerce for a wide variety of enterprising people. In fact, the affairs of Bengal had an altogether different but decisive turn with the entry of Sher Shah on the soil of Bengal, with which this land located away from the heartland of India turned out to be the focal centre of political action. In the battles of 1535-6, waged between the forces of Sher Shah and Mahmud Shah,[17] Martim Afonso de Mello and the available Portuguese forces fought for the latter. As a reward for this timely help in his battle against Sher Shah, Mahmud Shah permitted Martim Afonso de Mello to build Portuguese factories, besides conferring the right to collect customs duties at Chittagong upon Nuno Fernandez Freire, and that of Satgaon upon João Correa.[18] Though the Portuguese demand was for the construction of fortresses in both the places, with the help of which they wanted to extend to Bengal the militarized controlling power structure of the western coast of India, the sultan granted only commercial privileges of customs collection and site for setting up the trading establishment of factories at Chittagong and Satgaon in 1537. In fact, this decision of Mahmud Shah refusing the Lusitanian demand to erect fortresses was a turning point in the history of the commercial expansion of the *casados*, as it restricted the scope for the extension of militarized institutions of Portuguese central government to Bengal for a considerable period of time. This was most favourable to the emerging mercantile group of Portuguese *casados*, who started settling down in Satgaon from 1537 onwards and who entered into commercial operations of the region in an atmosphere of freedom without being controlled by the pulls of the central power at Goa.

The political transition of Bengal to the core position took a decisive turn with Sher Shah's occupation of Bengal in 1538 and with his eventual conquest of Delhi, whereby he kept the entire northern and eastern India, including Bengal, under Afghan domination, for the next sixteen years.[19] With this political integration and the subsequent construction of the Grand Trunk Road connecting Bengal with Delhi, the commercial importance of Bengal increased considerably, which fact is attested to by the intensification of trade in the ports of Bengal by the 1540s. In fact, the ports of Bengal turned out to be the principal gateways for the entry of overseas wares into the consumer markets of Sher Shah's empire, which extended from Bengal to Delhi.

PORTUGUESE SETTLERS AND THE DIFFERENT
STRANDS OF PRIVATE TRADE

What was the nature of the economic atmosphere of Bengal in which the commercial expansion of the Portuguese *casados* took place? It is obvious that they did not operate in an atmosphere of a complete economic vacuum. On the contrary, scholars like W.H. Moreland, Irfan Habib, Shireen Moosvi and Richard M. Eaton give a very promising picture of Bengal for the sixteenth and seventeenth centuries, when its economic space was fast expanding.[20] About 8 per cent (4,27,726,681 *dams*) of the total amount assessed as income for the Mughal empire in 1595/6 was from Bengal and it went on increasing all through the seventeenth century, as is evident from the *Jama* records for Bengal.[21] Richard M. Eaton estimates that there was 62 per cent increase in the revenue demand in Bengal during the period between 1595 and 1659.[22] These facts are suggestive of an expanding economy in this region, whose beginnings one has to trace back to a much earlier period.

It is against the background of a growing regional economy that the trading activities carried out individually in private vessels by the *casado* traders or in the crown vessels by the official agencies of the king, and the establishment of permanent Portuguese settlements in Bengal are to be viewed. Obviously, with the erection of trading establishments at Chittagong and Satgaon by 1537, and also with the eventual incorporation of Bengal into the wider market systems of the Delhi administration, realized through the wielding of power from the Mughals by Sher Shah, the commercial activities of the Portuguese *casados* got increasing momentum. The demand for luxury goods, particularly spices, from a wide variety of consumer classes[23] of the Delhi regime and its satellite units necessitated the involvement of a considerable number of Portuguese *casados*, as commercial intermediaries, to make available pepper and other spices in Bengal ports from the western seaboard of India.

As early as from 1540 onwards, we find evidence of the intensification of Portuguese commerce with the ports of Bengal, which fact is attested to by the presence of several treatises on navigation to Bengal, originating during this period.[24] The activation of Portuguese private trade with this region was followed by considerable increase in the size of the Portuguese settlements in coastal Bengal. Initially, the Portuguese were distributed on the coastal fringes of Bengal, where they stayed and carried out business initially on a temporary basis. In fact, there was a chain of Portuguese settlements in the Gulf of Bengal like Pipli on the Orissa coast (established in 1514),[25] Hijili located at the mouth of Rupanarayan (established in the second decade of the sixteenth century),[26] Chittagong, Satgaon, etc., of which the last two were the principal ones because of the Portuguese trading establishments attached to these two places.[27] The *casado* traders bringing pepper from Cochin in exchange for the sugar and textiles of Bengal, seem to have been the initial settlers of this region with commercial orientation, whose transition from temporary halt to a relatively permanent stay gave an added economic dimension to their settlements. Later, with the increasing commercial operations there was a corresponding increase in the number and size of settlements in Bengal. Even near Satgaon, the Portuguese had established a chain of huts and bamboo structures at Buttor (Betor–Howrah) along the river as temporary residences and commercial establishments, which they used to set fire on their departure, as is attested to by Caesar Frederick in 1565.[28] Many of these settlers spread into different parts of the Bengal littoral in the process of procuring wares for their commerce with China and South-East Asia and operating as distribution links in Bengal for the *casado* traders coming from Goa and Cochin, who eventually laid the nucleus for the diverse Lusitanian settlements in this region that emerged in the second half of the sixteenth century.

Taking advantage of these developments, several private Portuguese entrepreneurs from the west coast of India with substantial capital began to increasingly extend their commercial activities to Bengal. The New Christians (*Cristãos novos*—or the Jews newly converted to Christianity out of compulsion), who came to Cochin in 1533 from Portugal fearing persecution and the enforcement of anti-Semitic laws, also formed an important mercantile segment involved in the Cochin-Malacca-Bengal trade. Luis Rodrigues, a leading new Christian merchant used to take merchandise from Bengal, which he sold along with those of Ceylon and Malacca in Cochin at the beginning of the 1540s. In return he used to collect spices and other wares for these destinations with the help of the native Jews of Cochin.[29] Isaac of Cairo, a white Jew residing in the native city of Cochin (Mattancherry) was also said to have made rather frequent commercial trips to Bengal along with another white Jew during this period.[30]

By the 1540s, with the increasing commercial activities of the Portuguese *casados* in Bengal, the Portuguese officials followed a liberal policy of issuing frequent licences to carry pepper to its ports. After continuing it for a period up to 1545, opinions were sought from ex-officials to know whether this licensed trade should be allowed to continue further in Bengal. The experts opined that the flow of pepper to Bengal and other destinations in the eastern space of the Indian Ocean would make it difficult to get sufficient pepper in Cochin for the Lisbon-bound vessels[31] and that it would raise the pepper price of Cochin.[32] In fact Bengal offered a high price for the spices, perhaps because of its high demand in the consumer markets of the Delhi administration and of Ming China, which also must have been the highly probable reason for making Bengal the chief destination for the diversion of spices from Cochin in the 1540s. In 1545, the Portuguese governor made a secret enquiry to discover the price of pepper in Bengal, which revealed the fact that a quintal of pepper was sold there at 950 *reais*.[33] Seeing the prospects of Bengal trade, merchants engaged in commerce with other ports of Indian Ocean regions wanted to shift their activities to the markets of Bengal. Thus in 1546, as for example, Henrique de Sousa Chichorro asked permission to conduct trade with Bengal and to take sugar, rice and lac from Satgaon (Porto Pequeno of Bengal) to Cochin, since the horses taken to Cape Comorin from Ormuz via Cochin did not yield much profit.[34]

The Portuguese in Bengal also extended their trading networks to Malacca, South-East Asia and China.[35] With the rise of Aceh in the mid-sixteenth century, there began export of a considerable volume of textiles, rice and slaves to this Sumatran port in exchange for Indonesian copper, silver, gold and war animals.[36] Very often the ports of Bengal operated as intermediate zones for the *casados* and the private traders, who were taking wares from the ports on the western seaboard of India to China and South-East Asia, which also helped them in realizing commercial penetration into these regions.

During the 1540s several trade voyages were conceded to individuals as honour and reward in recognition of their meritorious service in Portuguese

India. Most of these commercial voyages had Bengal as the destination point.[37] Thus, for example, we have the case of Manuel Lourenço, the legal advocate of the Order of the Franciscans of Cochin, who was conferred a commercial voyage to Bengal on 21 February 1547, in recognition of his service to this monastery.[38] On 25 June 1547, he was again allowed to send one more ship to Porto Grande (Chittagong) of Bengal.[39] Many Portuguese, who fought in the war of 1546 to defend Diu from the Ottomans, were rewarded with the grant of commercial voyages by D.João de Castro, in most cases to Bengal. On 16 December 1546, Antonio Leme was given the permission to get a ship built in Malabar and to send commodities to any of the ports in Bengal.[40] On 19 February 1547, Antonio Correa, the factor of Cochin, was given a commercial privilege to send one ship to Bengal every year, in reward for his service for the defense of Diu.[41] On 21 February 1547, Manoel de Sousa de Sepulveda was permitted to send a ship to Bengal, for having served in Diu and for having spent a lot of money feeding the fighting forces.[42]

On 4 May 1547, Fernão Peres de Andrade was permitted to make or buy a ship and to send commodities to Bengal, as a reward for his participation in the defence of Diu with his own vessel and fighting personnel.[43] A certain Francisco Fernandes Moricalle was allowed to send a vessel to Bengal on 6 May 1547.[44] Later, on 22 November 1547, Alvares Teles had been granted the permission to send ships from Chittagong to Pegu and Malacca.[45] Another voyage was granted on 17 February 1548 to Sebastião Luis, *alcaide-mor* of Cochin, who was entitled to take commodities from Cochin to exchange with textiles and other goods in Bengal.[46] Another *casado* trader of Cochin, Francisco da Silva was given a grant of voyage on 23 November 1547, by which he could send every year one ship each to Bengal, Arakan and Moluccas.[47] In 1548, D. Pedro de Silva was given permission to bring yearly 20 *bhares* of mace and 80 *bhares* of nutmeg in the royal ship (obviously from South-East Asia) and also the privilege of sending a ship twice a year to Bengal, Pegu and Moluccas.[48] This long list of commercial voyages conceded to a wide variety of Portuguese settlers of Cochin and Goa suggests that Bengal had by this time turned out to be one of the most profitable commercial destinations in the Indian Ocean region.

When Bengal was the principal destination for the commercial voyages conferred upon the *fidalgos* and the upper strata of the *casados*, the ordinary *casado* entrepreneurs of lower strata resorted to smuggling activities to reap the harvest from high demands which pepper had in the ports of Bengal. Invariably, pepper formed the principal commodity that went to Bengal from Cochin during this period, and through this commodity stream the *casados* infiltrated into the markets of Bengal and its satellite exchange units. Through the gateways of Bengal pepper flowed to the extensive markets of the Delhi administration as well as to China. By 1545, pepper smuggling to Bengal, China and Pegu (besides its diversion to Mediterranean ports) became so frequent that the European trade began to dwindle considerably.[49] Interestingly, these regions were fed by the pepper not only of Cochin, but also of Malacca and other South-East Asian production centres.[50] However, the large volume of pepper that reached Bengal and China was not consumed in these places alone; they were further taken to inland markets. There was, thus, an overflow of this commodity in Bengal markets with the increased supply from Cochin and South-East Asia. On 26 November 1545, Benaldim de Souza wrote that Bengal needed much less pepper than what was sent there.[51] Though a lot of pepper was going to China every year, in 1543 pepper was even brought back from China because of the excesses and disproportionate supply, caused by private trade and smuggling.[52] The excess flow obviously reduced the profits, as well.[53] Consequently, very often pepper was also distributed and diverted to other places, once they reached the safe pockets of the eastern space of the Indian Ocean. Thus, in 1545, we come across at least some instances when many Ottoman Turks coming to Bengal, Pegu and Tenasserim to take pepper from there to their ports in the Red Sea.[54] This hazardous and time-consuming venture to buy pepper from the ports of Bengal, which seems to have been an exceptional attempt to trade in the pepper diverted to Bengal, was undertaken by the Ottoman Turks following the failure of the proposal of Turkish Sultan Sulaiman Pasha made on 28 May 1544 to buy 4,000 quintals of pepper from the Portuguese at Aden, as the French and the Venetians used to buy from them.[55] When this proposal was rejected by the Portuguese, the Turks tightened their control in the Persian Gulf and their vessels moved to Bengal to buy the smuggled pepper from there. As we have already seen earlier this was a time when the Luso-Ottoman conflicts were spread to different parts of the Indian Ocean, with its core being the Gujarat coast.

By the beginning of the 1540s the Cochin group of *casados* widened the network of their private interests in cooperation with the *Estado* officials. In fact, the top officials including Martim Afonso de Sousa (who was the governor of Portuguese India during 1542-5), Tome Lopes (who was the judge for the orphans, Pedro de Sequeira, the treasurer), and later the new captain of Cochin, Henrique de Sousa Chichorro, whom D. João de Castro sent in 1545 to check the private trading lobby of Cochin, were all themselves involved in the different processes of smuggling pepper to Bengal.[56] The governor Martim Afonso de Sousa tried to market the smuggled pepper in Bengal through his intermediaries, most of whom had already become the settlers of Chittagong, Satgaon and other pockets in the Gulf of Bengal. In fact a great part of the *Estado* structure turned out to be instruments at his disposal to carry out his commercial operations in Bengal. Tome Lopes, who was appointed as the judge of the orphans of Cochin by governor Martim Afonso de Sousa, used to lend orphanage funds to the enterprising *casado* traders to buy pepper from the native kingdoms of Malabar for Bengal-bound vessels.[57] Henrique de Sousa Chichorro the captain allowed free movement of these illegal traders for their participation in the Bengal trade. It was alleged that he permitted a considerable part of the Portuguese population of Cochin to go to Bengal and Malacca for trade, leaving the Malabar coast open for piracy.[58] This increased movement of commodities and people from Cochin to Bengal seems to have had significant impact on the developing mercantile settlements of the Portuguese in Bengal.

In fact, the entire commercial activities linked with Bengal were carried out within the frame of a particular kind of mixed economy, evolved by the beginning of 1540, in which there were three operational components: There were the Portuguese officials linked with the Portuguese governor Martim Afonso de Sousa who used to sponsor the entire project by issuing licences, or by diverting funds (earmarked for other heads) for buying pepper for Bengal or even by relaxing the controlling-cum-monitoring machineries with regard to the movement of vessels carrying contraband items to Bengal. These Portuguese officials transshipped commodities to Bengal with the help of commercial intermediaries drawn from the *casado* segment of Cochin. However, the different processes of the marketing of these wares in Bengal were taken care of by the Portuguese settlers of Chittagong, Satgaon and other enclaves, who also operated within the wider commercial network linked with the west coast of India, China and South-East Asia. In fact Martim Afonso de Sousa was the protagonist of this policy of mixed economy[59] that had eventually evolved in the west coast incorporating the commercial zones of Bengal. It was the knowledge that Bengal could no longer be brought under complete control of the Portuguese power localized at Goa, which made the governor evolve a commercial policy of mixed economy for Bengal by incorporating the enterprising skills of the *casado* traders with the private interests of the *Estado* officials. In order to make pepper available in Bengal in sufficient volume to meet the needs of the satellite markets of Bengal, licenses were issued in large numbers from the beginning of 1540 onwards. However, a considerable part of pepper also moved to Bengal without licenses and sometimes the vessels used to take double the amount of pepper than what was stipulated in the licence paper.[60]

A large number of middle-class and lower middle-class *casados* were employed in the process of marketing the commodities in Bengal and other ports of eastern space of the Indian Ocean by the leading merchants among the *casados*. Some of them residing in important port centres acted as collection agents for the bourgeoisie *casados*. An evident example of this was that of João Fernandes Correa who claimed that the entire eastern coast of India from Cape Comorin to Satgaon and the whole of Bengal belonged to him. He used to take a large number of *casados* with him for his commercial operations. In 1547 he took with him 70 *casados* and went to the fishery coast and Nagapattinam from where he and his mercantile team moved 300 leagues (1200 miles) along the coast up to Bengal. On 25 December 1547, Ruy Gonçalves de Caminha wrote to the governor that João Fernandes Correa was doing all this illegally and without permission.[61] This commercial operation with a group of traders under a principal merchant shows that the trade of Bengal linking the various exchange centres of the east coast of India was rather highly organized with significant capital investment. Most of these traders going for Bengal commerce used to procure cargo directly with the help of *casado* peddling traders who collected pepper from the kingdoms of Rapolim (Edappilly), Vadakkenkur, and Parur, sometimes in exchange for weaponry.[62] The mutual links and the intrinsic bonds of commonality enabled the *casado* group to operate jointly and collectively in the different stages of commerce, including the procurement of commodities, shipping, distribution and marketing, in which the Portuguese settlers of Cochin and Bengal had decisive roles to play.

CHANGING PATTERNS OF COMMERCE AND SETTLEMENT

The patterns of Portuguese commerce and settlement in Bengal underwent a significant change during the 1580s. The conquest of Bengal by Akbar in 1574[63] and the consequent granting of *farman* to Pedro Tavares (1579)[64] for settlement in Hughli ushered in an atmosphere of freedom for the Portuguese in matters of commerce and movement. This resulted in the concentration of Portuguese settlers in Hughli, to which place eventually there was an increasing shift of trade from Satgaon. Henceforth, Hughli came to be called the Porto Pequeno of Bengal. On the other hand, liberalization of Indo-European trade, which was later taken up by the Luso-Germanic and Italian syndicates during the period from 1575 to 1598 resulted in the relative relaxation of control measures on the west coast of India,[65] which also greatly favoured the private trade including the commerce of Bengal. Even before the liberalization of the Indo-European trade, the royal shipping to Bengal was stopped completely by the mid-1560s and commercial voyages were increasingly granted to *fidalgos*, of long service and merit, to the destinations of Chittagong, Satgaon and Pipli.[66] Caesar Frederick who had been travelling in the Indian Ocean regions during the period between 1563 and 1581 mentions that every year about 30-35 ships used to leave Satgaon laden with rice, cloth, sugar and other merchandise,[67] out of which sugar formed an important commodity stream flowing to Cochin.[68]

With the incorporation of Bengal as a part of Mughal administration in 1574, the ports of Bengal turned out to be the most profitable destinations of the Portuguese private traders. This is evidenced by the *Livro das Cidades e Fortalezas que a Coroa de Portugal tem nas Partes da India* written around 1580, which gives details of the selling price of voyages to the ports of Bengal.[69] The value of commercial voyages to Satgaon was 3,000 *cruzados*, while that of Chittagong was 2,000 *cruzados*,[70] a fact which evidently suggests that the Portuguese commerce of Porto Pequeno had taken precedence over that of Porto Grande by this time. This could also be seen as a development showing the shift from eastern Bengal to western Bengal in the trading activities of the Portuguese *casados* following the increasing economic pulls from the markets of Mughal administration.

However, this shift in the trading activities of the Portuguese *casados* towards the ports of western Bengal does not conclusively prove that the economic activities in the eastern part of Bengal had already entered a phase of slumber. Richard M. Eaton, on the other hand, says that south-east of Bengal experienced the highest rate of increase in the revenue demand in Bengal (i.e. 117 per cent increase) during the period 1595–1659,[71] which is suggestive of the fact that the economy of this region was well actuated. If the economy of Chittagong and south-east Bengal was strong, then why did the *casados* prefer south-western seaports of Bengal for their commerce? The answer is very simple. The latter ports were the principal maritime gateways for entry into a much larger market network under the Mughals and they provided easy linkages with a large cross-section of consumer classes under the Delhi regime,[72] from whom there was an increasing demand for luxury goods including spices. Against this backdrop of constantly growing demand for pepper from this consuming class, it was quite natural that the Portuguese *casados*, who were principally traders and suppliers of spices, preferred the south-western ports of Bengal particularly Hughli to Chittagong, which was still operating within the orbit of the Arakan-centered regional economy.

The principal single commodity taken from Cochin to Bengal for trade was pepper, whose value during this period (the peak period of intra-Asian trade) as Antonio Bocarro testifies in 1630, was about 400,000 *xerafins*.[73] In 1587, Ferdinand Cron, the trade agent of the German merchant syndicates the Fuggers and the Welsers, says that a great volume of pepper from the production centres of Malabar was diverted to the Coromandel coast through the 'ghat-route', which finally moved to Mogor (Mughal) territory and China, besides Pegu.[74] It is quite evident that pepper to the Mughal markets entered through the gateway of Bengal. In 1603, Francisco da Costa, the clerk of the factory of Cochin, writes that pepper was taken in large volume to Masulipattanam and Bengal from the production centres of Malabar across the ghat-route.[75] From Bengal the *casado* traders brought to Cochin large quantities of sugar, rice, laciron, textiles, long pepper, wheat and saltpetre, etc.[76] Though there were frequent orders, as in 1589, to prevent the illegal trade in pepper with Bengal and other parts of South-East Asia, they remained as dead letters for all practical purposes.[77]

Meanwhile, the rice ports of Bengal were also very active. During this period rice was in high demand all through Kerala, taking advantage of which the Portuguese private traders of Bengal started taking rice to Malabar frequently. It was a time when agrarian activities were fast expanding in Bengal following the intensification of forest clearing and the involvement of Muslim peasantry in paddy cultivation, as Richard Eaton argues.[78] During the period 1590–7 we find several references to rice being imported to Cochin from Bengal,[79] and, on certain occasions, the rice was transported on to the Maldives in return for cowries. For example, on 17 May 1590, the Portuguese *casados* carried about 900 *candis* of rice from Bengal to Cochin.[80] As rice was a return cargo for the vessels taking pepper to Bengal, the transportation cost was highly reduced, which enabled the *casados* to supply this commodity in Cochin at a reasonable price.[81] The total volume of rice imported to Cochin from the eastern coast during the period between 1587 and 1598 was 31,115,257 kg, which would mean an annual average of 386,830 kg.[82] Besides rice, textiles formed another major cargo of Bengal's trade. A part of it went to Cochin and Goa, from where they were taken by the vessels of *Carreira da India* to Portugal.[83] Textile items of Bengal, such as *khasas* and *malmals* used to figure frequently in the commodities taken from Cochin to Portugal, as we see, for example, in the case of goods carried by the ship *Nossa Senhora da Luz* in 1615.[84]

Meanwhile, the sacred spaces of Bengal also formed a considerable factor to cement the commercial linkages established by its traders. Against the background of frequent commercial contacts the rulers of south India used to go to Bengal to immerse the ashes of the deceased members of the royal family in the sacred waters of Ganges. Thus, for example, we find the king of Cochin Kesava Rama Varma going to Bengal to immerse the mortal remains of his mother in the Ganges. Sadly, he died about 80 leagues (320 km) away from the Ganges, while carrying the ashes of his mother.[85]

Meanwhile, with the increasing conflicts between the spice-producing St. Thomas Christians and the Portuguese on the question of changing the customs, practices and ritual traditions of the former into those of the Lusitanians (often known as Latinization or Lusitanization),[86] there evolved a new trend in the commercial operations linked with Bengal. As a part of the resistance to the Portuguese attempts to Latinize and Lusitanize their customs and ritual practices, the spice-producing Christians refused to supply spices to the Portuguese factory at Cochin; instead they started diverting pepper to the ports of Coromandel through the ghat-route, from where they where further taken to the ports of Bengal. In the new turn of events, the Tamil traders used to take a large bulk of spices from the hinterland of central Kerala across the ghats to Coromandel ports, viz., Nagapattinam, Mylapore, Masulipattanam and Pulicate, where the Portuguese *casados* came forward to carry them further to Bengal.[87] During this period, from Kanjirappally market alone about 3,220,000 kg (9,000 *bhars*) of pepper were taken through the ghat-route to Coromandel ports, while from Erattupetta 166,830 kg (1,000 *bhars*) of pepper moved over to Tamil country through ghat routes. About 500,490 kg (3,000 *bhars*) were taken from Erumely to Coromandel ports via the ghats. The diversion of pepper from Chalakudy to Tamil ports was 834,150 kg (5,000 *bhars*) of pepper and from Korattykara was 500,490 kg (3,000 *bhars*) of pepper. From Palghat another 500,490 kg (3,000 *bhars*) of pepper were diverted to the routes terminating in the Coromandel ports.[88] The *casado* traders operating in the Bay of Bengal, on their turn, took spices from the Coromandel ports of Nagapattinam, Mylapore, Masulipattanam and Pulicate for further distribution in Bengal.

The emergence of this new pattern in the commerce made many *casados* linked with the Bengal-Cochin-Goa trade to shift their spheres of activities from Cochin to the Coromandel ports, from where they could easily maintain their commercial links with Bengal, Pegu and Malacca. In this transition process, there was a mass migration of Portuguese *casados* from Cochin to the important ports of the eastern space of the Indian Ocean region by 1617, a development in which about two-thirds of the citizens of Cochin shifted their residence to the various ports located on the rim of Bay of Bengal including Nagapattinam and Mylapore, where they eventually settled down to take advantage of this new situation. Bengal seems to have been the major destination for the movement of people and commodities, while the ports of Nagapattinam and Mylapore were kept as principal bases for operations.[89] This commercial route began to acquire great significance from 1600 onwards not only because of the huge profits this trade brought to the entrepreneurs, but also because of the fact that it had less risk of being attacked by the Dutch while circumnavigating Cape Comorin. Following the increase in commercial transactions, and the following migration from Cochin, there was significant demographic growth in these places, as for example, the numerical strength of ordinary Portuguese citizens in Nagapattinam rose to 800 and *fidalgos* to 20 by 1644.[90] However, the Portuguese traders who used to take commodities from Nagapattinam to

Bengal, China and Malacca were required to pay to the Portuguese Exchequer, the entry tax at the same rate as paid by the settlers of Cochin.[91] In spite of the migration of Portuguese *casados* to Coromandel and Bengal following diversion of spices to Tamil coasts from the production centres of Malabar and the consequent commercial re-alignments, Cochin-Bengal trade continued to be active in a rather less degree. However, in the third decade of the seventeenth century, we hear that the smuggling to Bengal was on the increase, as the punishment given to the smugglers was not corporal, but merely pecuniary. In the then existing punitive frame mere payment of a part of the profit accrued from these transactions would entitle the smugglers to get out of legal tangles.[92]

Almost all the commercial settlements of Bengal were principally the result of private ventures; however, the vestiges of official elements were visible only at the time of the arrival every year of the crown vessels, whose captains took with them some elements of the central power of Goa. In fact, the captains of *Carreira de Bengal* carried with them a 'fluid state' with powers of a diplomat and ambassador of the central power of Goa, which was solidified in Bengal vaguely only towards the end of the sixteenth century. Later, with the increasing voyage concessions the Captains-Major turned out to be the links of continuity and distant successors of the captains of crown vessels, who carried with them some vestiges of the authority of Goa to Bengal.[93] However, the commercial expansion was carried out chiefly by the Portuguese private traders, who spread out to a wide range of geographical areas that were located on the waterfront and very much conducive for commerce. Corresponding to these developments we find the intensification of Portuguese settlements in several parts of Bengal like Dacca (particularly at *Feringhi Bazar*), Sripur (near Sonargaon), Chandecan (on the banks of a branch of Hughli), Bakla (identified with Chandradwip pargana), Catrabo (Katrabuh), Loricul (28 miles south of Dacca), Dianga (which got prominence when the Portuguese were expelled from Chittagong by the Arakan rulers towards the close of the sixteenth century), Bhulua, etc.[94] In fact, these settlements arose following the commercial penetration of Portuguese *casado* traders into the scattered market systems of Bengal, which were integrated by the frequent joint commercial operations of the *casados*. With the accumulation of mercantile surplus some of the most daring personalities among them like Sebastião Gonçalves Tibau, Manuel de Matos and Domingos Carvalho set up power structures in this region, as 'shadow-empire',[95] which was a matter of great concern for the local ruler because of their political repercussions in the region.

Thus, we find, maritime Bengal experienced a process of economic transition following the commercial expansion of the Portuguese *casados*. At one level the private Portuguese traders supplied the markets of Bengal with pepper from the ports of west coast of India, while on the other they took textiles to South-East Asia and rice to Malacca, Malabar and the Maldives. Coinciding with the commercial expansion, there was increasing distribution of the Portuguese in Bengal followed by the emergence of several Lusitanian settlements of various size in coastal Bengal, the nuclei of which could be linked with the economic activities of procurement or distribution of wares. The inflow of Lusitanian elements from Cochin and Goa, the greatest of which was the mass migration from Cochin that took place between 1600 and 1615, made the size of these settlements in Bengal swell. Since a great part of the Portuguese commerce in Bengal was carried out by Portuguese private traders outside the orbit of the official control systems of *Estado da India*, private entrepreneurs held key positions in the social order and regional economy of the areas dominated by the Lusitanians, and new power structures were created around the entrepreneurs and daring personalities like Sebastião Gonçalves Tibau, Manuel de Matos and Domingos Carvalho. Their transition from being merchants into rulers of territorial units is indicative of the considerable empowerment the Lusitanians gained in the process of surplus accumulation. Equally significant was the shift of the economic activities of the Portuguese from the ports of eastern Bengal to the ports of western Bengal like Satgaon, Hughli and Pipli following the economic pulls from the wider market systems of the Delhi administration, into which Bengal was incorporated from 1540 onwards. The commercial orientation of the Portuguese towards the Mughal-controlled part of Bengal continued further against the background of the favourable policies of Akbar and Jahangir; however the capture of Hughli from the Portuguese by Shah Jahan's general Qasim Khan in 1632 gave a restructuring to the Lusitanian trade in Bengal.

NOTES

1. For details on the nature of Portuguese expansion on coastal western India, see Luis Filipe F.R. Thomaz, *De Ceuta a Timor*, Lisbon, 1998.
2. Armando Cortesão, 'Os Portugueses em Bengala-Primeira Visitas', in *Boletim da Sociedade de Geografia de Lisboa*, 62, nos. 7 & 8, July-August 1944, pp. 433-47; J.J.A. Campos, *History of the Portuguese in Bengal*, Patna, 1979; George D. Winius, 'The Shadow-Empire of Goa in the Bay of Bengal', *Itinerario*, vol. VII, no. 2, 1983; Sanjay Subrahmanyam, *Improvising Empire: Portuguese Trade and Settlement in the Bay of Bengal, 1500-1700,* Delhi, 1990; Genevieve Bouchon and Luis Filipe Thomaz, ed., *Voyage dans Les Deltas du Gange et de l'Irraouaddy. Relation Portugaise Anonyme (1521)*, Paris, 1988.
3. For details, see M.R. Tarafdar, 'Trade and Society in Early Medieval Bengal', in *The Indian Historical Review,* vol. IV, no. 2, 1978, pp. 274-86; B. Schrieke, *Indonesian Sociological Studies*, pt I, The Hague, pp. 9-15; M.A.P. Meilink-

Roelofsz, *Asian Trade and European Influence in the Indonesian Archipelago Between 1500 and about 1630,* The Hague, 1962, pp. 15, 18-21. The sultans of the mercantile state of Malacca used to participate directly in commerce by sending their own ships frequently to the ports of the Bay of Bengal. For details, see Luis Filipe Thomaz, 'Malacca's Society on the Eve of Portuguese Conquest: A tentative interpretation based on the extant Portuguese documents', Paper presented at the *Persidangan Antarabangsa mengenai Tamadun Melayu,* Kuala Lumpur, 1986; Luis Filipe Thomaz, 'Malaka et ses commnautes marchandes au tournant du 16e siecle', in *Marchands et hommes d'affaires asiatiques dans l'Ocean Indien et la Mer de Chine, 13e-20e siecles,* ed. Denys Lombard et Jean Aubin, Paris, 1988, pp. 31-48. The maritime traditions of Bengal in the medieval period were recently highlighted by Rangan Kanti Jana by studying the Bengali *Mangalkavyas,* which were composed during the period between the fifteenth and eighteenth centuries. These *Kavyas* particularly *Manasamangal* and *Chandimangal* give a lot of information on boats, boat-building techniques, commodities, riverine routes and coastal trade, etc., a fact which is suggestive of the resurgence of Bengal trade after 1400. For details, see Rangan Kanti Jana, 'Medieval Bengali Texts on Boats-Boat Building Technique- Commodities and River Routes', *The Historical Review,* Calcutta, nos. 1&2, 1996, pp. 35-45.

4. Sanjay Subrahmanyam, *Improvising Empire,* p.118.

5. ANTT, *Corpo Cronologico,* I, Maço 6, doc. 82, letter dated 13-2-1508.

6. ANTT, *Corpo Cronologico,* III, Maço 5, doc. 87, letter of George de Albuquerque to the crown, dated 8-1-1515.

7. R.S. Whiteway, *The Rise of Portuguese Power in India, 1497-1550,* New Delhi, 1989, pp. 176-7; K.M. Panikkar, *Malabar and the Portuguese,* Bombay, 1929, p. 180; Pius Malekandathil, 'Merchants, Markets and Commodities: Some Aspects of Portuguese Commerce with Malabar', in *The Portuguese, Indian Ocean and European Bridgeheads: Festschrift in Honour of Prof. K.S. Mathew,* ed. Pius Malekandathil and Jamal Mohammed, Fundção Oriente, 2001, p. 251.

8. Jose Ramos Coelho, ed., *Alguns Documentos da Torre do Tombo acerca das navegações e conquista Portuguezas,* Lisboa, 1892, p. 300.

9. Vitor Luis Gaspar Rodrigues, 'O Grupo de Cochin e a Oposição a Afonso de Albuquerque', *Studia,* 51, Lisboa, 1992, pp. 119-44; Luis Filipe Thomaz, 'Diogo Pereira, O Malabar', *Mare Liberum,* 5, 1993, pp. 49-64; Genevieve Bouchon and Luis Filipe Thomaz, ed., *Voyage dans Les Deltas du Gange et de l'Irraouaddy. Relation Portugaise Anonyme (1521),* pp. 58-68; Sanjay Subrahmanyam, *The Portuguese Empire in Asia 1500-1700: A Political and Economic History,* London, 1993, p. 97; Maria Emilia Madeira Santos, 'Afonso de Albuquerque e os feitores', in *Actas do II Seminario Internacional de Historia Indo-Portuguesa,* ed. Luis de Albuquerque and Inacio Guerreiro, Lisboa, 1985, pp. 201-20; Pius Malekandathil, 'The Portuguese Casados and the Intra-Asian Trade: 1500-1663', *Proceedings of the Indian History Congress,* Millennium (61st) Session, Kolkata 2000-1, pp. 384-5.

10. Document dated 26-3-1515 summarized in Luciano Ribeiro, *Registo da Casa da India*, vol. I, Lisboa, 1954, p. 3. The first report on the arrival of the Portuguese in China was given by Giovanni da Empoli on 15-11-1515. See for details *Archivio storico italiano*, Appendix, 3, Firenze, 1846, p. 85.

11. João de Barros, *Asia. Dos feitos que os Portuguezes fizeram no Descobrimento e conquista dos Mares do Oriente*, Lisboa, 1973, decada III, parte I, chap. 3, pp. 135-6; J.J.A. Campos, *History of the Portuguese in Bengal*, Patna, 1979, pp. 26-30; Armando Cortesão, 'Os Portugueses em Bengala-Primeira Visitas', *Boletim da Sociedade de Geografia de Lisboa*, 62, nos. 7 & 8, July-August 1944, pp. 433-47; Sanjay Subrahmanyam, *Improvising Empire: Portuguese Trade and Settlement in the Bay of Bengal*, pp.103-5.

12. For details about Diogo Pereira, see Luis Filipe Thomaz, 'Diogo Pereira, O Malabar', *Mare Liberum*, 5, 1993, pp. 49-64.

13. ANTT, *Nucleo Antigo*, no. 808, fols. 5-6; see also Sanjay Subrahmanyam, *Improvising Empire*, p. 122.

14. ANTT, *Corpo Cronologico*, I, Maço 52, doc. 23; K.M. Panikkar, *Malabar and the Portuguese*, pp. 111-3.

15. In fact, the Portuguese under Antonio da Silva Menezes set fire to the port city of Chittagong in their attempt to liberate Martim Afonso de Mello and his men who were detained by Mahmud Shah in the midst of their expedition, for the alleged involvement of a certain Damião Bernaldes in corsair activities. For more details, see Diogo do Couto, *Da Asia dos feitos que os Portuguezes fizeram na Conquista e descobrimento das Terras e Mares do Oriente*, decada IV, Lisboa, 1777-8, parte I, livro, IV, capitulo X; João de Barros, *Da Asia dos feitos que os Portuguezes fizeram no Descobrimento e Conquista dos Mares e Terras do Oriente*, decada IV, Lisboa, 1777-88, parte II, livro IX, capitulo V.

16. Gaspar Correa, *Lendas da India*, vol. III, Lisboa (1858-64), p. 649; J.J.A. Campos, *History of the Portuguese in Bengal*, Patna, 1979, p. 37.

17. Iqtidar Husain Siddiqui, *Mughal Relations with the Indian Ruling Elite*, New Delhi, 1983, pp. 78-89.

18. Fernão Lopes de Castanheda, *Historia do Descobrimento e Conquista da India pelos Portugueses*, Lisboa, 1921-25, liv. VIII, cap. CXXVIII; João de Barros, *Da Asia*, decada IV, parte II, livro IX, cap. VII, p. 500; J.J.A. Campos, *History of the Portuguese in Bengal*, pp. 38-40.

19. Abul-Fazl 'Allami, *Akbar-nama*, ed. Abdur Rahim, vol. I, Calcutta, 1873, pp. 151-3; Richard M. Eaton, *The Rise of Islam and the Bengal Frontier*, New Delhi, 2000, pp.138-40.

20. Irfan Habib, *Agrarian System of Mughal India 1556-1707*, New Delhi, 1999, pp. 454-6; W.H.Moreland, *The Agrarian System of Moslem India: A Historical Essay with Appendix*, Delhi, 1968, pp. 189-200; W.H. Moreland, *India at the Death of Akbar: An Economic Study*, Delhi, 1962; Shireen Moosvi, *The Economy of the Mughal Empire, c.1595: A Statistical Study*, Delhi, 1987, pp. 26-7; Richard M. Eaton, *The Rise of Islam and the Bengal Frontier*, pp. 194-227.

21. For details on the *Jama* of Bengal for the period from 1595 to 1720, see Irfan Habib, *Agrarian System of Mughal India*, pp. 454-6.

22. Richard M. Eaton, *The Rise of Islam and the Bengal Frontier*, p. 199.

23. For details about this consuming class, see W. H. Moreland, *India at the Death of Akbar*, pp. 59-89.

24. During the 1540s we find a lot of treatises on the navigation to Bengal, attesting to the frequency with which the ships used to visit the ports of Bengal. For example, see, A. Fontoura da Costa, ed., *Livro de Marinharia de Bernardo Fernandes (cerca de 1548)*, Lisboa, 1940, pp. 89-91; Jacinto Ignacio de Brito Rebello, *Livro de Marinharia: Tratado da Agulha de Marear de João de Lisboa. Roteiros, Sondas e outros Conhecimentos realtivos a Navegação, Codice do seculo XVI*, Lisboa, 1903, pp. 231-3.

25. W.W. Hunter, *Orissa*, vol. I, 1872, p. 37; J.J.A. Campos, *History of the Portuguese in Bengal*, p. 98.

26. The Portuguese were said to have established this settlement immediately after their settlement in Pipli (1514). For further details, see J.J.A. Campos, *History of the Portuguese in Bengal*, pp. 94-95.

27. Chittagong and Satgaon had the principal trading establishments of the Portuguese; however, there were many other minor Portuguese enclaves in Bengal, which developed at different phases of history. For details about these minor Portuguese enclaves, see J.J.A. Campos, *History of the Portuguese in Bengal*, pp. 66-99.

28. Frederick Caesar in Richard Hakluyt, *The Principal Navigations, Voyages, Traffiques and Discoveries of the English Nation made by Sea or Overland to the Remote and Farthest Distant Quarters of the Earth at anytime within the Compasse of these 1600 Yeeres*, vol. V, New York, 1969, pp. 411, 439.

29. ANTT, *Inquisição de Lisboa*, Proc. 12292, fols. 17-22, 36-8, 42-3, 72, 77-9.

30. ANTT, *Inquisição de Lisboa*, Proc. 7296, fol. 77.

31. ANTT, *Corpo Cronologico*, I, Maço 76, doc. 8.

32. ANTT, *Corpo Cronologico*, I, Maço 77, doc. 26. The details are analysed in Sanjay Subrahmanyam, *The Portuguese Empire in Asia, 1500-1700: A Political and Economic History*, London, 1993, pp. 98-9.

33. ANTT, *Corpo Cronologico*, II, Maço 240, doc. 60.

34. Elaine Sanceau, *Colecção de São Lourenço*, vol. II, Lisboa, 1975, p. 275.

35. ANTT, *Corpo Cronologico*, I, Maço 68, doc. 86; ANTT, *Corpo Cronologico*, III, Maço 9, doc. 94; Luis Filipe Tomaz, *Os Portugueses em Malacca, 1511-1580*, Dissertação de Licenciatura (inedita), Faculdade de Letras, Universidade de Lisboa, vol. II, pp. 35, 122, 177; Sanjay Subrahmanyam, *Improvising Empire*, pp. 107, 116, 124-5; Ralph Fitch, 'The Voyage of Master Ralph Fitch Merchant of London to Ormus and so to Goa in the East India, to Cambaia, Ganges Bengala...', in *Hakluytus Posthumus* or *Purchas his Pilgrimes*, by Samuel Purchas (1625) vol. X, Glasgow, 1905, p. 185.

36. Sanjay Subrahmanyam, *Improvising Empire*, p. 124.

37. Pius Malekandathil, *Portuguese Cochin and the Maritime Trade of India, 1500-1663* (South Asian Study Series of Heidelberg University), Delhi, 2001, pp. 123-5.

38. Antonio Baião, *Historia Quinhentista (inedita) do Segundo cerco de Dio*, Coimbra, 1927, p. 321.
39. Bibliotheca do Palacio da Ajuda, *Livro das Merces que fez D.João de Castro*, 51-8-46, fol. 129.
40. Antonio Baião, *Historia Quinhentista (inedita) do Segundo cerco de Dio*, p. 298.
41. Ibid., pp. 306, 309-10.
42. Ibid., p. 312.
43. Ibid., p. 321.
44. Bibliotheca do Palacio da Ajuda, *Livro das Merces que fez D.João de Castro*, 51-8-46, fol. 121.
45. Bibliotheca do Palacio da Ajuda, *Livro das Merces que fez D.João de Castro*, 51-8-46, fol. 170.
46. ANTT, *Chancellaria de D.João III, Doações* 69, fol. 98v.
47. Bibliotheca do Palacio da Ajuda, *Livro das Merces que fez D.João de Castro*, 51-8-46, fol. 193 v.
48. Bibliotheca do Palacio da Ajuda, *Livro das Merces que fez D.João de Castro (1545-1548)*, 51-8-46, fol. 57.
49. R.O.W. Goertz, 'The Portuguese in Cochin in the Mid-Sixteenth Century', *Indica*, vol. 23, nos. 1&2, March-September 1986, pp. 63-78; Elaine Sanceau, *Colecção de São Lourenço*, vol. II, p. 283; Pius Malekandathil, *Portuguese Cochin and the Maritime Trade of India*, pp. 128, 170-81.
50. About 12 to 15 Chinese junks were sent annually to these places to collect pepper. ANTT, *Corpo Cronologico*, I, Maço 77, doc.18; ANTT, *Corpo Cronologico*, II, Maço 240, doc. 57.
51. ANTT, *Corpo Cronologico*, I, Maço 77, doc. 30.
52. On 15 May 1546, Henrique de Sousa Chichorro wrote to the governor that Alexis de Sousa permitted the Chinese junks to load pepper from Cochin. Bibliotheca do Palacio da Ajuda, *India Portuguesa*, 51-8-43. In 1543 and 1544 the pepper that reached China seem to have caused excess supply. So in these two years the traders had to bring pepper back to the port of Cochin. See the letter of Duarte de Miranda d' Azevedo, Goa, dated 27 November 1545. ANTT, *Corpo Cronologico*, I, Maço 77, doc. 31.
53. See the remarks of Domingos Rabelo about pepper diversion to China written in 1545 in ANTT, *Cartas dos Vice-Reis da India*, no. 75. He says that the pepper that reached China was in such a great quantity that the profit from it was very little.
54. See the remarks of João Fernandes Galego about the flow of pepper to various destinations in the Indian Ocean. See ANTT, *Cartas dos Vice-Reis da India*, no.75.
55. The letter of the Sultan to the Portuguese crown in ANTT, *Corpo Cronologico*, I, Maço 74, doc. 108.
56. R.O.W. Goertz, 'The Portuguese in Cochin', pp. 63-7.
57. Ibid., p. 66.
58. Ibid., pp. 66-7.

59. For details on this policy of mixed economy, see Pius Malekandathil, *Portuguese Cochin and the Maritime Trade of India,* p. 25.

60. For details, see Elaine Sanceau, *Colecção de São Lourenço,*Lisboa, vol. II, pp. 230, 300-1, 308; vol. III, pp. 80, 501, 505; Sanjay Subrahmanyam, 'Cochin in Decline, 1600-1650: Myth and Manipulation in the Estado da India', in *Portuguese Asia: Aspects in History and Economic History (Sixteenth and Seventeenth Centuries),* ed. Roderich Ptak, Stuttgart, 1987, pp. 66-7.

61. The Letter of Ruy Gonçalves de Caminha to the governor, Cochin dated 25-12-1547 in Elaine Sanceau, *Colecção de São Lourenço,* Lisboa, vol. III, p. 408.

62. Pius Malekandathil, *The Germans, the Portuguese and India,* Münster, 1999, p. 41; Elaine Sanceau, *Colecção de São Lourenço,* vol. II, p. 309.

63. Richard M. Eaton, *The Rise of Islam and the Bengal Frontier,* pp. 142-6.

64. J.J.A. Campos, *History of the Portuguese in Bengal,* pp. 49-60.

65. Pius Malekandathil, *The Germans, the Portuguese and India,* pp. 75-96; Pius Malekandathil, 'Merchants, Markets and Commodities: Some Aspects of Portuguese Commerce with Malabar', in *The Portuguese , Indian Ocean and European Bridgeheads: Festschrift in Honour of Prof. K.S. Mathew,* ed. Pius Malekandathil and Jamal Mohammed, Fundação Oriente, 2001, pp. 259-60.

66. Sanjay Subrahmanyam, *Improvising Empire,* pp. 109-10.

67. Caesar Frederick in Richard Hakluyt ed., *The Principal Navigations, Voyages, Traffiques and Discoveries of the English Nation,* pp. 410-40.

68. Ibid., p. 393.

69. *Livro das Cidades e Fortalezas que a Coroa de Portugal tem nas Partes da India,* ed. Francisco da Luz in *Boletim da Biblioteca da Universidade de Coimbra,* vol. XXI, Coimbra, 1953. It gives details about the selling price of the voyages to the ports of Bengal, South-East Asia, China as well as Japan. For detailed table of voyages, see Luis Filipe Thomaz, 'The Portuguese in the Seas of the Archipelago during the 16th Century', in *Archipel,* 18, 1984, p. 87.

70. Sanjay Subrahmanyam, *Improvising Empire,* p. 112; Luis Filipe Thomaz, 'The Portuguese in the Seas of the Archipelago during the 16th Century', p. 87.

71. Richard M. Eaton, *The Rise of Islam and the Bengal Frontier,* p. 199.

72. For details on the purchasing power of this consuming class, see W.H. Moreland, *India at the Death of Akbar,* pp. 59-66.

73. Antonio Bocarro, *Livro das Plantas de todas as povoações, cidades e fortalezas do Estado da India Oriental,* in A.B. de Bragança Pereira, ed., *.Arqivo Portugues Oriental,* tomo IV, vol. II, parte I, Goa, 1937, pp. 353-54.

74. *Fürstlich und Gräflich Fuggersches Familien und Stiftungs Archiv, Dillingen/Donau,* MSS Codex no. 46.1, fols. 50-51 v; Pius Malekandathil, *Portuguese Cochin and the Maritime Trade of India,* p. 202.

75. Francisco da Costa, 'Relatorio sobre o Trato da Pimenta', in *Documentação Ultramarina Portuguesa,* ed. Antonio da Silva Rego, vol. III, Lisboa, 1963, p. 315.

76. *Relação das Plantas & Dezcripções de todas as Fortalezas, Cidades e Povoações que os Portuguezes tem no Estado da India ,* Lisboa, pp. 38-9.

77. *Boletim da Filmoteca Ultramarina Portuguesa*, no. 2, Lisboa, 1955, p. 457.

78. Richard M. Eaton, *The Rise of Islam and the Bengal Frontier*, pp. 194-267.

79. BNL, *Fundo Geral*, Cod. No. 1980, *Livro das Despezas (Taboada)*, fols. 12, 40.

80. BNL, *Fundo Geral*, Cod. No. 1980, *Livro das Despezas (Taboada)*, fol. 25.

81. As a result of surplus production, the price of rice was very low in Bengal, which is testified by Caesar Frederick who writes in 1565 that a sack of rice in Bengal could be obtained 'for a thing of nothing'. Caesar Frederick as quoted by Richard M. Eaton, *The Rise of Islam and the Bengal Frontier*, p. 201.

82. BNL, *Fundo Geral*, Codice No. 1980, 'Livro das Despezas de hum porcento' *Taboada*, fols. 7-15.

83. See for details, the table of export given for the period between 1587 and 1609 by Niel Steensgaard, *Carracks, Caravans and Companies: The Structural Crisis in the European Trade in the Early Seventeenth Century*, Copenhagen, 1973, p. 166; Om Prakash, *The Dutch East India Company and the Economy of Bengal, 1630-1720*, Princeton, 1985, pp.183-6; Sanjay Subrahmanyam, 'Cochin in Decline', p. 65.

84. AHU, *Caixas da India*, Caixa 3, doc. 152.

85. Francisco da Costa, in Antonio da Silva Rego, *Documentação Ultramarina Portuguesa*, vol. III, pp. 355-6; see also Antonio de Gouveia, *Jornada do Arcebispo*, Coimbra, 1606, p. 213.

86. For details about Latinization, see Joseph C. Panjikaran, 'Christianity in Malabar with special Reference to the St. Thomas Christians of the syro-Malabar Rite', *Orientalia Christiana*, vol. VI, 1926, pp. 103-5. For a critical study of Diamper synod, see Jonas Thaliath, *The Synod of Diamper*, Rome, 1958. For details about the mercantilist motives behind the entire exercise, see Pius Malekandathil, ed., *Jornada of Dom Alexis de Menezes: A Portuguese Account of the Sixteenth Century Malabar*, Cochin, 2003.

87. AHU, *Caixas da India*, Caixa 2, doc. 107. The letter of the city council of Cochin sent to Philip II (Philip III of Spain) giving an account of the economic condition of Cochin dated 21-12-1613; Pius Malekandathil, 'The Portuguese and the Ghat-Route Trade: 1500-1663', *Pondicherry University Journal of Social Sciences and Humanities*, vol. I, nos. 1 & 2, 2000, pp. 145-6.

88. The report of Francisco da Costa, 'Relatorio sobre o Trato da Pimenta', in Antonio da Silva Rego, *Documentação Ultramarina Portuguesa*, vol. III, p. 315; Pius Malekandathil, 'The Portuguese and the Ghat-Route Trade: 1500-1663', pp. 137-48.

89. AHU, *Caixas da India*, Caixa 2, doc. 107; AHU, *Caixas da India*, Caixa 3, doc. 29 dated 25-1-1615; AHU, *Caixas da India*, Caixa 3, doc. 31 dated 25-1-1615. The Viceroy D. Jeronimo de Azevedo in his letter addressed to the Portuguese crown refers to the reduction of the population of Cochin to one-third following these developments. HAG, *Livro das Monções*, no.12 (1613-17), fols. 254-80, dated March 1617. These *casados*, with their new base in Coromandel, began to reap significant profit by trading on the pepper coming through the ghat-route, which they used to take primarily to Bengal, Pegu and China. Even the Dutch in

Masulipattanam and Pulicat also began to buy pepper coming directly through the ghat-route from the spice-producing hinterland of Kerala. BNL, *Fundo Geral* 1815, letter of Philip II sent to Conde de Vidigueira, dated 26 March 1625, fol. 78; AHU, *Caixas da India*, Caixa 8, doc. 38, dated 29-12-1624; Antonio Boccaro, *Livro das Plantas de todas as fortalezas, cidades, e povoações do Estado da India Oriental*, vol. II, Transcrição de Isabel, Lisboa, 1992, pp. 353-4, 360-2; Pius Malekandathil, 'The Portuguese and the Ghat-route Trade', p. 146. Sanjay Subrahmanyam, *Improvising Empire*, p. 113.

90. AHU, *Caixas da India*, Caixa 16, doc. 34, dated 12-2-1644; AHU, *Caixas da India*, Caixa 17, doc. 42, dated 3-12-1644.
91. Ibid.
92. BNL, *Fundo Geral*, Codice 1816, fol.151. Report on the illegal pepper trade of Cochin with Bengal, dated 25-1-1624.
93. Sanjay Subrahmanyam, *Improvising Empire*, p. 113.
94. J.J.A. Campos, *History of the Portuguese in Bengal*, pp. 66-80, 88-99.
95. George D. Winius, 'The Shadow-Empire of Goa in the Bay of Bengal', *Itinerario*, vol. VII, no. 2, 1983, pp. 94-6; for details about the exploits of these personalities, see J.J.A. Campos, *History of the Portuguese in Bengal*, pp. 67-8, 72, 78-87.

 CHAPTER TEN

Mercantile Wealth and the *Estado da India*: The Changing Pattern of Portuguese Trade with India, 1570-1663

The official renouncement of royal monopoly over the spice trade and the liberalization of Indo-European commerce in 1570 ushered in a new commercial situation in India, which favoured the accumulation of capital in private hands to an unprecedented degree. During the period 1570–98, when the business houses of Germany, Italy and Portugal controlled the Indo-European trade, the Portuguese *casado* traders of Goa and Cochin were increasingly engaging themselves, either independently or in association with the natives, in intra-Asian trade and in carving out larger commercial space in the Indian Ocean region for the expansion of their private initiatives. The immediate result emanating from this development was the accumulation of sizeable capital in individual hands and in the Portuguese settlements, making both the entrepreneurs and their city centres fabulously rich.

The trading activity emanating from the Portuguese settlements of India was never monolithic; it included several strands and streams out of which the official strand was evidently visible at the top, and the strand of the Portuguese *casado* entrepreneurs often ran closely parallel to it and at times strengthened it. The *casados* always maintained an Asian dimension to their commerce, a policy by which the wealth accumulated from trade was made to concentrate in their Indian settlements, without letting it flow to the mother country.[1] Eventually, the bourgeoisie class of *casado* traders, who by the last quarter of the sixteenth century had emerged as merchant capitalists,

*This is a revised version of the paper earlier published under the title 'Merchant Capitalists and the Estado da India: Changing Pattern of Portuguese Trade with India, 1570-1663' in *The Proceedings of the XI International Seminar on Indo-Portuguese History: Global Trends,* ed. Charles Borges, Fatima Gracias and Celsa Pinto, Panjim, 2005, pp. 345-60.

or as a leading entrepreneurial mercantile group with substantial capital and extensive networks in the Indian Ocean,[2] began to play a very significant role in the economic life of *Estado da India*, very often financing and contributing substantially for several of the royal enterprises, and pumping capital for the fast growing urban centres of Portuguese India.

This chapter tries to see the different phases of organizational and managerial innovations made during this period in the pattern of Portuguese trade incorporating the entrepreneurial skills of the Portuguese *casados*. It tries to answer the following questions: what were the circumstances that favoured the transition of *casados*, who were actively involved in the intra-Asian trade since 1520s, into merchant capitalists? How far did the temporary renouncement of Indo-European trade by the crown accelerate this transformation process? Did the distance factor from the centre of power in Goa contribute to the emergence of several traders with substantial capital in the semi-periphery and periphery zones of Portuguese India? To what extent did the crown succeed in incorporating the mercantile capital of the *casados* for continuing Indo-European trade in the later phase? These questions are answered by analysing the socio-economic developments of the sixteenth and the seventeenth centuries.

HISTORICAL SETTING

A lot has already been written on the Indo-European commerce of the crown and the intra-Asian trade of the *casados*. Several scholars have attempted to show how the *casados* initially found the very state as a competitive trader and on how they wanted to get out from its overwhelming intervention by resorting to the lobbying strategy under the banner of 'Cochin group', and later by getting champions of their cause like Lopo Soares de Albergaria as the governors of *Estado da India,* who could set aside the maritime space east of Cape Comorin for the commerce of the Portuguese private entrepreneurs.[3] A close examination of the socio-economic developments accompanying it would explain the process through which the *casados* emerged as principal trading group in the Indian Ocean.

When the *casado* traders started their commercial apprenticeship, the Muslim Marakkar merchants were the prominent traders involved in intra-Asian trade, who were also the chief collaborators of the Portuguese for their European trade in the first two decades of the sixteenth century.[4] By 1520s, their relationship with the Lusitanians strained and as a result of frequent clashes between the two, the Marakkar traders of Cochin migrated en bloc to Calicut in 1524 under the Kunjali Marakkar for carrying out their trading activities safely with the support of the Zamorin.[5] In the process of transferring their trading activities as well as their commercial networks into the Zamorin's territory, the Marakkar merchants left behind a relatively considerable commercial vacuum, particularly in Cochin, into which the commercially fast expanding *casados* stepped. The new and favourable atmosphere of trade in Cochin was promptly utilized by several Portuguese *casado* traders for commercial expansion to Chaul, Cambay and Homuz on the one hand, and to Bengal, Pegu, Malacca, South-East Asia, Ceylon as well as Maldives, on the other hand.[6] A few *casados* even made use of their matrimonial links with Muslim wives, whose relatives incorporated them happily as their trade partners, for widening their mercantile networks. The result was that *casados* started penetrating into a wider world of commerce mostly on their initiative and also at times with the help of their Muslim partners.[7]

With the support of ecclesiastical dignitaries, the *casados* (ordinary married Portuguese settler) opposed the hegemony of the *fidalgos* (Portuguese nobility) in political, as well as ecclesiastical realms, and eventually they even developed a system parallel to, and relatively independent of, the trading arrangements of the *Estado*, though at times it was also used for strengthening the *carreira* commerce.[8] Eventually, the *casados* accommodated the other prominent indigenous traders particularly the Gujarati traders by resorting to a strategy of 'ware-vessel exchanges'. In fact, they exchanged wares and vessels mainly to enable the banias to evade the high customs duty payable at Goa. The goods of the Gujarati merchants that were coming from South-East Asia and destined to Cochin or Goa were cleared under the name of Portuguese *casados* at Cochin, where they had to pay only 3.5 per cent as against 6 per cent at Goa. By claiming ownership over the wares of the Gujarati traders, the *casados* could easily clear the customs duty at a lower rate (i.e. 3.5 per cent, a concessionary rate applicable only to the *casados* alone) and enabled their Gujarati commercial partners to avoid the extra journey to Goa and also saved them from paying excessive customs duties, even though the revenue loss incurred thereby on the *Estado* was considerable. The king of Cochin to whom the customs money went encouraged this partnership, as it enriched his coffer and empowered his hands.[9]

Another side of this commercial partnership was the use of the vessels of the Gujarati and other indigenous merchants for transshipping the goods of the *casados*. This had two advantages for the partners: first, the native traders could evade the excessive customs duties for their commodities, by attributing ownership of the entire cargo to the *casados*. Then, the *casados* used native connections to dispatch commodities to non-Portuguese ports and destinations. The crown asked the *casados* not to send commodities that actually did not belong to them.[10] On 9 October 1596, the Portuguese king issued an order asking the *casados* of Cochin not to use the ships of the *chatins* (the native private traders) for carrying out trade with the northern ports, under the penalty of losing both the ship and the merchandise.[11] Even in the early seventeenth century, many *casados* used to send commodities in the vessels of the natives, especially banias, mainly as an arrangement to avoid the blockade imposed by the Dutch and the English.[12] In fact, the partnership with the indigenous traders helped the *casados* to expand their commercial networks to wider regions as well as to safeguard their vessels along with the commodities from the attacks of the enemy.

THE CHANGING PATTERN OF PORTUGUESE TRADE

The Portuguese trading activities experienced a significant change with the liberalization of the spice trade in 1570 by King Sebastian.[13] The Indo-European commerce including the spice trade, which the crown kept as a royal monopoly for almost seven decades, was taken over by the big business houses from south Germany and Italy as well as the New Christian trading groups from Lisbon on contract basis. There were two types of contracts: the Indian contract and the European contract. Those who took up the Indian contract had the obligation to collect and transport cargo from the various trade centres of south-west India and transship them to *casa da India* in Lisbon, while those who took up the European contract had the responsibility of taking spices from *Casa da India* and distributing them all over Europe. The Indian contractors were required to equip five vessels for spice trade, invest their own capital (about 170,000 *cruzados* per year) and send their own trade agents to the spice ports of India. The purchase price of the pepper was fixed at five and two-thirds *cruzado* per quintal. However, the pepper taken to the *Casa da India* in Lisbon was to be sold at 12 *cruzados* per quintal and they might receive an additional amount of 4 *cruzados* for freight and transshipping costs.[14] The contractors were to make their own arrangements including their own trade agents at their own cost to procure spices from India. Konrad Rott from Augsburg, who took up the Indian contract in 1579,[15] sent Gabriel Holzschuher as his trade agent to the principal spice port of Cochin.[16] Later, Giovanni Rovellasca from Milan whom Rott incorporated as his partner in 1580, sent the great Florentine humanist Filippo Sassetti to Malabar as his trade agent.[17] They together managed to send 1,127,675 kg of pepper from Cochin to Lisbon.[18]

The second contract was taken up by the German-Italian merchant syndicates consisting of the Fuggers, the Welsers and the Italian business house of Giovanni Rovellasca in 1586 and they together held the Indian contract for next five years.[19] The German business families sent Fernand Cron[20] as their main trade agent to Cochin and Goa, and he was further helped by sub-agents like Christian Schneeberger in Cochin, Gabriel Holzschuher in Quilon and Max Wolfmüller in Cannanore. Rovellasca's main agent in Cochin was Filippo Sassetti, who was also assisted by Oratio Nereti.[21] The Germans and the Italians had to set up their own networks all over Malabar to procure the required quantity of spices for Europe. In 1587, the German-Italian consortium distributed 629,715 kg of pepper. But in the succeeding years the volume of export was more than doubled: in 1588 the pepper export amounted to 1,204,409 kg, in 1589 to 1,575,703 kg and in 1590 to 1,242,121 kg. For want of vessels for transshipment, what was collected in 1591 was sent only in 1592 and the cargo then exported was about 1,870,000 kg of pepper.[22]

During the period between 1592 and 1597 the Europe-oriented trade of India was carried out by a Portuguese syndicate from Lisbon consisting of Pero Rodrigues, Fernão Ximenes, Andre Ximenes, Heitor Mendes de Brito, Jorge Rodrigues Solis, etc., all belonging to the New Christian mercantile community of Lisbon.[23] In spite of the wide network that they established in Malabar for the purpose of collecting spices for European trade, the volume of their export remained far lower than that of the Germans and the Italians. In 1593 they sent only 262,336 kg, which increased to 341,792 kg in 1594. Though in 1595 they sent 923,697 kg to Lisbon, the situation deteriorated in 1596 when the volume of export came down to 142,149 kg. However, they managed to procure 887,821 kg in 1597.[24] During this period, pepper that reached Lisbon from India was further taken up by the European contractors headed by the Fuggers and the Welsers for distribution in Middelburg, Amsterdam and the Hanseatic cities of Lübeck, Hamburg and Danzig. Hamburg, which was least affected by the Anglo-Dutch-Spanish war, turned out to be the safest distribution center for spices in northern Europe. Out of the pepper that was sent in 1591, Hamburg received the greatest share with 48.3 per cent, Amsterdam stood second with 28.3 per cent and Lübeck 23.4 per cent.[25]

When the Europe-oriented trade from south-west India went into the hands of contractors and private traders from Europe, the commercial developments in India were fast changing in favour of the private trade of the *casados*. The European contractors invested large amounts of money each year for procuring spices from the exchange centres of south-west India. But it was during the period of contract trade (1570-98), when there was liberal and favourable commercial atmosphere for the private enterprise, that a sizeable number of merchant capitalists from the Portuguese *casados* and the private traders began to emerge. Interestingly, this period also corresponds with the increasing attempts of the Portuguese private traders to convert Goa and Cochin into the biggest entrepots and richest trade settlements of Asia.[26]

THE VALUE OF PRIVATE TRADE AND THE INTENSITY
OF CAPITAL ACCUMULATION

The volume of private trade carried out during this period cannot be quantified commodity-wise, for want of continuous records. But the record of 1 per cent tax, which the city of Cochin levied on various wares brought by the *casados*, gives a rough picture of the private trade carried out in Cochin. During the period 1587–98, the total amount of wealth received as 1 per cent duty from the various commodities imported by the *casados* of Cochin was 88,195 *pardaos*, 4 *tangas* and 32 *reais*, which means that the total value of private trade in Cochin during this period was more than 8,819,500 *pardaos*.[27]

TABLE 1: THE VALUE OF PRIVATE TRADE IN COCHIN: 1587-98[28]

Year	Amount in Pardaos	Commodities Rice (kg)
1587	849,200	154,423
1588	529,300	1,235,876
1589	846,000	3,965,760
1590	948,100	2,776,532
1591	634,200	2,026,944
1592	632,500	2,777,232
1593	769,500	463,972
1594	699,100	3,657,712
1595	838,300	2,203,500
1596	866,600	4,670,804
1597	512,200	3,569,234
1598	694,700	3,613,268

Table 1 shows that the *casado* traders involved in intra-Asian trade used to import non-food commodities to the value of 8,819,700 *pardaos* per year in Cochin during the period 1587–98. The annual average import was about 734,900 *pardaos*.[29] It is quite reasonable to infer that the value of the export trade of the *casados* from Cochin during this period also must have been closer to this figure, if not more. On the other hand, the annual average of rice import during this period was about 386,830 kg.[30]

The graphic presentation (Fig. 1) gives a glimpse into the ups and down of the import trade. The rice import to Cochin seems to have increased considerably from 1588 onwards, probably because of the great increase in the demand for foodstuffs in Malabar, following the severe drought about which Ferdinand Cron made mention in 1587.[32]

As years passed by the volume of private trade of the *casados* went on increasing, as is evidenced by the fact that by 1605 the king of Cochin

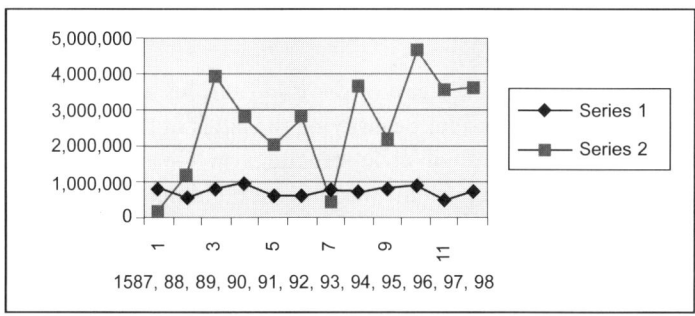

Series 1 = Trade in Food Materials
Series 2 = Trade in Non-Food Materials valued in *pardaos*

FIG. 1. VOLUME OF THE PRIVATE TRADE OF THE PORTUGUESE
CASADOS IN COCHIN 1587-98[31]

received about 60,000 *pardaos* annually by way of customs duty from the
wares of the *casados* and other private traders.[33] It later increased to 80,000
pardaos by 1612.[34]

There was a considerable increase in the private trade of Goa, as well,
which is attested to by the stark difference in the rate at which customs duty
was farmed out in Goa. Collection of customs duty on spices was farmed out
in 1540s for 1,350 *pardaos*, which in 1590s was farmed out for 7,755 *xerafins*,
evidently suggesting more than 500 per cent increase in the private trade in
spices in Goa during this period. Meanwhile the rate at which the food grains
were farmed out for the collection of customs duty rose from 2,500 *pardaos*
in 1540s to 11,630 *xerafins* in the 1590s evidently indicating more than 450
per cent increase in the rice trade of Goa.[35] Similarly, there was a corresponding
increase in the trade of pearls,[36] silk, horses,[37] textiles,[38] spices,[39] betel-leaf,[40]
food-stuffs,[41] etc., whose profit along with the surplus accruing from the
chain of commercial voyages emanating from Goa, made the *casados* of the
city rich and affluent. In 1570s about 58 per cent of the total income of the
Estado came from the customs house or the *alfandegas*,[42] which is suggestive
of the intensification experienced in the sector of private trade.

Some of the *casado* traders of Cochin were exceedingly rich as is
evidenced by the list of moneylenders who were being mentioned by Diogo
Couto as supporting the *Estado* in times of emergency. During the period
between 1610 and 1611 Francisco Barbosa gave an amount of 40,028 *xerafins*
to the state, out of which the latter could give back only 10,000 *xerafins*.
Manoel de Lacerda Pereira gave 20,000 *xerafins* and Manoel Fonseca 15,213
xerafins to the state to purchase spices for the European trade. Antonio
Guedez de Morais gave an amount of 14,182 *xerafins*. All these suggest that

the intensity and degree of capital accumulation in the hands of Portuguese *casado* traders was relatively high.[43]

Meanwhile, a sizeable share of the trade surplus accrued from intra-Asian trade was transferred for beautifying the cities of their habitation and also for building churches or civic structures in Goa and Cochin. It is interesting to note that many of the magnificent buildings of these two towns were carried out during this period. By the mid-1540s, there were about 14 churches and chapels in the city of Goa and surroundings with 1,600 citizens and 3,000 soldiers.[44] But by the end of 1580 Goa had reached its apex of prosperity, with manifold increase in the churches and posh living quarters, which earned for it the epithet Golden Goa.[45] The golden glitter of Goa and Cochin came from the wealth accumulated by the private traders.

The hilly slopes of Old Goa were crowned with elegant edifices and the ground below had magnificent palatial buildings, churches and private houses encircled by little gardens or orchards. It is estimated that by the beginning of the seventeenth century there were around 3,500 Portuguese houses in the city of Goa, out of which 800 were made of stone and lime. They had beautiful windows and balconies, and were covered with tiles, with alluring frontage and bordering the street in beautiful symmetry. The population at the beginning of the seventeenth century was about 225,000. The most beautiful street of the city of Goa was *Rua Direita* (Straight Road), which was occupied on both sides by lapidaries, goldsmiths, the rich, and well-to-do merchants and craftsmen, while each class of artisans and traders stayed together in their own localities.[46] Even in Cochin the wealthy segment of the city population lived on both sides of its main street also named *Rua Direita*, where the principal buildings of Cochin including the bishop's house, the municipal chamber, *Misericordia*, the Dominican monastery, etc., were also located.[47]

A considerable share of the trade surplus from the *casados* was diverted for the construction works of Old Goa and Cochin, out of which the main edifices so built were the monastic houses of the religious, the churches and the elegant civil structures. The most elegant and magnificent buildings of old Goa like the houses of the Dominicans, the Augustinians, the Bom Jesus Basilica, the Se Cathedral, the São Paulo College were either fully completed or partially built during this period of private trade.[48] Here one should remember that the royal subsidy was relatively meagre and was just sufficient to maintain and support the members of the religious houses and the liturgical services; but not for constructing such elegant buildings.[49] In 1550s only 10.5 per cent of the total expenditure of the *Estado* was used for the expenses incurred on church related affairs.[50] Then, where did the wealth for their building activity come from? The various contemporary tombstones of the St. Francis Assissi church, the Augustinian monastery and the Se Cathedral of Goa suggest the predominant role which the wealthy *casado* traders and the *fidalgos* played in the process of building or maintaining these church institutions.[51]

Similarly, the building process of the three-storeyed magnificent Madre Deus College of Cochin, the Dominican and Augustinian monasteries of Cochin were completed during this period,[52] when private trade of the *casados* was rampant.[53] It is suggestive of the fact the hectic building activities in Goa and Cochin, particularly the ecclesiastical ones, were sustained by the surplus accruing from the private trade of the *casados*. New epithets like 'Rome of the East' were given to Goa to boost this building process and to give legitimacy to the ventures to mobilize support for it. The *casado* capital along with the *fidalgo* wealth seems to have relieved much of the burden of the crown in erecting the ecclesiastical institutions in areas lying under the *Padroado* jurisdiction.[54]

DEPENDENCE OF *ESTADO DA INDIA* ON PRIVATE CAPITAL

In the seventeenth century, when the Portuguese navigational lines were increasingly blocked by the Dutch and the English, financial and personnel resources from Portugal did not reach India in time, and at times what reached the Portuguese trade centres was not sufficient enough to meet requirements. Hence, the *Estado* began to bank increasingly on the wealth of

TABLE 2: DETAILS OF MONEY BORROWED BY THE STATE
FROM THE PRIVATE TRADERS OF COCHIN BETWEEN
DECEMBER 1610 AND JULY 1611[56]

Manoel de Lacerda Pereira	20,000 *xerafins*
Joao Leitão	1,100 *xerafins*
Aires de Limos	2,000 *xerafins*
Antonio de Pinho da Costa	2,400 *xerafins*
Tristao Vaz de Carvalho	5,000 *xerafins*
Thome Rebello	5,000 *xerafins*
Antonio Guedez de Morais	14,182 *xerafins*
Pero Vaz de Figueirao	8,020 *xerafins*
Francisco da Fonseca Pinto	1,600 *xerafins*
Gabriel Mendez	2,000 *xerafins*
Francisco Pinto dazevedo	6,000 *xerafins*
Vasco da Gama	3,000 *xerafins*
Manoel de Fonseca	15,213 *xerafins*
Francisco Barbosa	40,028 *xerafins*
TOTAL	125,543 *xerafins*

the private traders, particularly the *casados* for mobilizing funds needed for its commercial and political ventures. For example, in 1610 the amount that came to India for the purchase of spices was 124,000 *xerafins*. Diogo Coutinho the *veador da fazenda* borrowed an amount of 140,345 *xerafins* from the *casados* of Cochin to conduct the crown's trade with Europe at an interest rate of 10 per cent.[55]

This shows that the degree of dependence of the *Estado* on the capital of Portuguese private traders in the early decades of the seventeenth century was relatively high. Eventually by 1613 the amount, which the state owed to the Portuguese *casados* of Cochin was 76,972 *xerafins* and by 1616, the loan given by the *casados* to the state amounted to 60,000 *cruzados*.[57] However, since the Portuguese state could not repay this huge amount because of the increasing financial burden consequent to the Dutch blockades, many enterprising *casados* had eventually been deprived of the necessary liquid capital for investing in further commercial operations, which adversely affected the further economic activities of a segment of *casados*.

This does not mean that the *casados* of Cochin were wiped away from the commercial scene. A sizeable segment of the enterprising *casado* traders of Cochin continued to be economically vibrant. Later the crown wanted to incorporate this segment for the conduct of European trade. By 1628, the *casados* of Cochin were invited to send *navetas* annually from Cochin to Lisbon with a cargo of 2,000 quintals of pepper.[58] Though the conditions of the contract stipulated that the pepper money be provided by the crown, in reality the price for the purchase of pepper was paid by the *casados* in advance and was later realized from Portugal, once the commodity reached Lisbon safely. That way the entire risk of this trade was on the shoulders of the *casados*; moreover the *navetas* of the *casados* did not put any financial burden on the mother country. The new arrangement of trade incorporating the capital and entrepreneurial skills of the *casados* worked, and against all odds, the *casados* continued to send their *navetas* regularly to Portugal till 1638.[59]

The *casados* were not the only mercantile group supporting the Portuguese in Goa and in Cochin. The *Estado da India* relied, in times of emergency, also on non-Portuguese traders like the Augsburg trader Fernand Cron, who married a Portuguese lady and settled down in Goa, with extensive commercial links stretching to Coromandel as well as Cochin on the one hand and to Venice, Augsburg and Madrid on the other hand. He contributed liberally to *Estado da India* when it was confronted by severe crises. He used his linkages with German cities to collect information about the departure of the Dutch fleet and passed it on to the Portuguese promptly.[60] Of course such help necessitated reciprocity and these traders obtained privileges in return.[61]

In the first half of the seventeenth century, we find several private traders of Goa, particularly the Hindu traders, playing vital roles in the Portuguese trade. Many of the Hindus entrepreneurs took advantage of the fast changing socio-economic conditions of Goa and the changing pattern of Portuguese trade to carve out a commercial niche.[62] One evident case is that of Rama Queny (Rama Keni). He managed to get himself appointed as the chief officer in charge of collecting pepper for the Portuguese India Company. He was permitted to collect in his warehouse, 60 *candis* of pepper every year. But under this pretext, he collected a large quantity of pepper coming from Cochin. By 1633, he was said to have become very rich and the principal merchant of Goa, mainly through his trade in pepper. Often the Portuguese India Company itself had to buy pepper from Rama Queny.[63] By mid-1634 Rama Queny emerged as the principal contractor of Goa for supplying saltpetre to the Portuguese.[64]

The tax-farmers from the Saraswat Brahmins and the banias began to emerge as significant supporters and bankers for the Portuguese system in Goa.[65] We find Mangoji Sinay[66] (Salcete), Vitula Naique[67] (*rendeiro* of the incomes from the customs of the passo de Santiago—the main ford between Goa and the mainland), Krishna Sinay and Nanna Chati (the *rendeiros* of the revenue of striking gold in the mint), as prominent tax-farmers of Goa in 1640s, who appear on the scene as bankers.[68] Some of these tax-farmers were only agents of big traders and capitalists operating elsewhere. Thus, for example, Nana Sinay, to whom was farmed out the *renda* for coral in Goa in 1655, though mentioned as a citizen of Nossa Senhora do monte, was merely a local representative in Goa of Gema Bhai Vena from Sanguiser (near Bombay).[69]

We also find that the *Estado da India* was responding on the basis of global trends: while the crown started depending on private capital of the German-Italian business houses and the Portuguese New Christian traders for carrying out Indo-European trade, the *Estado* was increasingly depending on the capital of the Portuguese *casados* and private traders for sustaining its commercial and politico-military activities. Liberalization of trade in 1570 was the turning point that made private trade rampant and hectic in Portuguese India. The tendency of the *casado* traders not to allow their accumulated wealth flow out of India took a decisive turn with the increasing borrowing of sizeable amounts by the state from the Portuguese *casados*. The individual traders of Cochin and Goa were eventually emerging as a money lending class for the state enterprises and pumped in liquid capital in times of emergency. Meanwhile the tax-farmers of Goa, who accumulated trade surplus by way of customs collection during this period, turned out to be the significant banking group in Goa. Thus, locally accumulated capital became a supportive and supplementary source for the Portuguese activities in the East including trade, at a time when the Dutch and the English were increasingly blocking the Portuguese navigational lines and preventing the Iberian capital from reaching India.

NOTES

1. For more details on this theme, see Pius Malekandathil, 'The Portuguese Casados and the Intra-Asian Trade: 1500-1663', *Proceedings of the Indian History Congress*, Millennium (61st) Session, Kolkata, 2000-1, pp. 385-406; for a detailed account of the *casado* trade, see Sanjay Subrahmanyam, 'Cochin in Decline, 1600-1650: Myth and Manipulation in the *Estado da India*', in *Portuguese Asia: Aspects in History and Economic History (Sixteenth and Seventeenth Centuries)*, ed. Roderich Ptak, Stuttgart, 1987, pp. 59-85.

2. Merchant capitalist here means a social agent who uses whole or a part of the accumulated capital for the generation not of 'use-values' but of 'exchange-values'. For a detailed discussion on merchant capitalism, see Maurice Dobb, *Studies in the Development of Capitalism*, London, 1963, pp. 17, 83-129, 152-62.

3. Vitor Luis Gaspar Rodrigues, 'O Grupo de Cochin e a Oposição a Afonso de Albuquerque', *Studia*, 51, Lisboa, 1992, pp. 119-44; Luis Filipe Thomaz, 'Diogo Pereira, O Malabar', *Mare Liberum*, 5, 1993, pp. 49-64; Genevieve Bouchon and Luis Filipe Thomaz, ed., *Voyage dans Les Deltas du Gange et de l'Irraouaddy. Relation Portugaise Anonyme (1521)*, pp. 58-68; Sanjay Subrahmanyam, *The Portuguese Empire in Asia 1500-1700: A Political and Economic History*, London, 1993, p. 97; Maria Emilia Madeira Santos, 'Afonso de Albuquerque e os feitores' in *Actas do II Seminario Internacional de Historia Indo-Portuguesa*, ed. Luis de Albuquerque and Inacio Guerreiro, Lisboa, 1985, pp. 201-20; Pius Malekandathil, 'The Portuguese Casados and the Intra-Asian Trade: 1500-1663', pp. 385-400.

4. The Muslim traders were not monolithic; they had different strands: while the foreign or *paradeshi* Muslim traders, including the al-Karimi, who had links with Mamluk Egypt and were feeding the Venice route opposed the Portuguese, the indigenous Muslim community of the Marakkars and the Mappilas of Malabar were the initial collaborators of the Portuguese for their commerce. Generally speaking, for almost two decades a large number of Marakkar Muslim merchants including Cherina Marakkar, Mamale Marakkar, Mitos Marakkar, etc., acted as principal suppliers of spices in Cochin for the Europe-oriented trade of the Portuguese. They also used to take copper from Cochin to Malacca to obtain spices coming from South-East Asia and to Gujarat to procure textiles, which finally found their way to Portugal. See Raymundo Antonio de Bulhão Pato, *Cartas de Affonso de Albuquerque*, tom. I, pp. 197, 265, 273; tom. III, pp. 52, 83, 269; tom. IV, pp. 41-2, 78; tom. VII, pp. 41-2. ANTT, *Nucleo Antigo*, No.804, fol.10 ff; Pius Malekandathil, 'The Mercantile Networks and the International Trade of Cochin, 1500-1663', in *Rivalry and Conflict, European Traders and Asian Trading Networks*, ed. Ernst van Veen and L. Blusse, Leiden, 2006, pp. 150-65.

5. Faria Y. Sousa, *Asia Portuguesa: The History of the Discovery and Conquest of India by the Portuguese,* tran. John Stevens, vol. I, London, 1695, p. 284; Shaykh Zaynuddin, *Tuhfat-ul-Mujahiddin,* trans. S. Muhammed Hussain Nainar, Madras, 1942, pp. 89-91; A.P. Ibrahim Kunju, *Studies in Medieval Kerala,* Trivandrum, 1975, p. 60; Pius Malekandathil, 'Portuguese Casados and the Intra-Asian Trade', pp. 387-8.

6. Raymundo Antonio de Bulhão Pato, *Cartas de Affonso de Albuquerque,* tom. I, p.197; Luis Filipe Thomaz, 'Diogo Pereira, O Malabar', *Mare Liberum,* 5, 1993, pp. 50-64; Pius Malekandathil, 'Bengal and the Commercial Expansion of the Portuguese Casados, 1511-1632', in *Trade and Globalisation* ed. S. Jeyaseela Stephen, New Delhi, 2003, pp. 163-6.

7. There were cases when some Portuguese private traders of Cochin developed trading networks in collaboration with the Muslim merchants. They viewed the very Portuguese state as the greatest stumbling block in the development of their entrepreneurial talents. On certain occasions these *casados,* particularly those living in Culimute in the vicinity of Cochin, even supplied armaments and vessels to Kunjali's men and joined hands with the Marakkars to attack the *Estado* vessels, as Diogo Fernandes reports in 1537. The *casado*-Muslim commercial linkage evolved out of marriage ties and it was pointed out that the marital relationship with Muslim ladies made these *casados* turn against the *Estado.* ANTT, *Corpo Cronologico,* II, Maço 211, doc. 65, fols. 5-6. The letter of Diogo Fernandes to King John III dated 1-6-1537; Gaspar Correia, *Lendas da India,* tom. II, Lisboa, 1921, p. 712.

8. The *casados* and the ecclesiastical dignitaries like Dom Jorge Temudo, the first bishop of Cochin strongly opposed the mass reservation given to the *fidalgos.* The bishop wrote that India needed only two dozens of good *fidalgos* to be appointed as governors and captains. The rest the *casados* could manage themselves. The move against the *fidalgo*-dominated *Estado* by the *casados,* who had acquired sufficient financial basis and had established trade networks all over Indian Ocean regions independent of *Estado* control, had alarmed the Lisbon administration. The crown felt it necessary to appease this group and made attempts to protect the *casado* trade from competition as well as to reserve some lines for their regional trade. Luis Filipe Thomaz, 'A Crise de 1565-1575 na Historia do Estado da India', in *Mare Liberum,* no. 9, July 1995, pp. 507-8; Josef Wicki, 'Duas Relações sobre a situação da India Portuguesa nos anos de 1568 e 1569', *Studia,* no. 8, 1961, pp. 200-1; Luis Augusto Rebello da Silva, *Corpo Diplomatico Portugues,* vol. IX, Lisboa, 1910, p. 303.

9. AHU, *Caixas da India,* Caixa 2, doc. 4, dated 12-1-1612; Caixa 2, doc. 73, dated 23-12-1612; K.S. Mathew and Afzal Ahmad, *Emergence of Cochin in the Pre-Industrial Era: A Study of Portuguese Cochin,* Pondicherry, 1990, doc. 53, pp. 77-83; Sanjay Subrahmanyam, 'Cochin in Decline, 1600-1650: Myth and Manipulation in the Estado da India', pp. 67-8.

10. HAG, *Livro das Monções,* no. 7 (1600-3), fols. 35-44, letter of the king to Viceroy, Aires de Saldanha, dated 6-1-1601.

11. J.H. da Cunha Rivara, *Archivo Portuguez Oriental*, fasciculo 3, New Delhi, 1992, pp. 660-1.

12. This was the usual way resorted to by the *casados* to escape the English blockade. The natives could either escape the enemy for being a native or would be made the scapegoat. Thomas Best gives a striking example, where the English captain Hermon capturing a vessel, tortured some bania merchants mistaking them to be Portuguese *casados*. Hermon did not believe that they were natives and he caused them hung upon a tree by 'their hands, fingers and heads' to make them confess that they were Portuguese. William Foster, *The Voyage of Thomas Best to the East Indies, 1612-1614*, London 1934, pp. 129-30. The transshipment of wares in the vessels of the banias usually provided some sort of immunity to the *casados* from the blockade of the enemies.

13. Francisco P. Mendes da Luz, *O Conselho da India*, Lisboa, 1952, pp. 73-4; Vicente Almeida d'Eça, *Normas Economicas na Colonização Portuguesa ate 1808*, Coimbra, 1921, chap. II.

14. For details see M.A. Hedwig Fitzler, 'Der Anteil der deutschen an der Kolonialpolitik Philipps II von Spanien in Asien', in *VSWG*, 28, 1935, pp. 243-81; Reinhard Hildebrandt, *Die 'Georg Fuggerischen Erben': Kaufmännische Tätigkeit und sozialer Status, 1555-1600*, Berlin, 1966, appendix, pp. 191-6; Pius Malekandathil, *The Germans, the Portuguese and India*, Münster, 1999, pp. 75-85.

15. For more details, see Konrad Haebler, 'Konrad Rott und die Thüringische Gesellschaft', in *Neues Archiv für Sächsische Geschichte und Altertumskunde*, ed. Hubert Ermisch, 16, 1895, pp. 177-218.

16. The letter sent by Gabriel Holzschuher on 10 January 1580, from Cochin to Sixtus Adelgaiss, Nationalbibliothek-Wien, Cod. 8953, fol. 25v; Konrad Haebler, 'Konrad Rott und die Thüringische Gesellschaft', p. 203.

17. Donald F. Lach, *Asia in the Making of Europe*, vol. I, book I, Chicago, 1970, pp. 134, 475-7; Ettore Marucci, ed., *Lettere edite e inedite di Filippo Sassetti*, Florence, 1855, pp. 204-10.

18. Victor von Klarwill, ed., *The Fugger News-Letters. Second Series: Being a Further Selection from the Fugger Papers specially Referring to Queen Elizabeth and Matters relating to England during the years 1568-1605*, trans. l.S.R. Byrne, London, 1926, p. 45.

19. M.A. Hedwig Fitzler, 'Der Anteil der Deutschen an der Kolonialpolitik Philipps II von Spanien in Asien', p. 249.

20. For details on Fernand Cron see Sanjay Subrahmanyam, 'An Augsburger in Asia Portuguesa; Further Light on the Commercial World of Ferdinand Cron, 1587-1624', in *Emporia, Commodities and Entrepreneurs in Asian Maritime Trade, c. 1400-1750*, ed. Roderich Ptak and Dietmar Rothermund, Stuttgart, 1991, pp. 401-25; Charles R. Boxer, 'Uma raridade bibliografica sobre Fernão Cron', in *Boletim internacional de bibliografia luso-brasileira*, XII, 3, Lisboa, 1971, pp. 323-64; Hermann Kellenbenz, 'Cron, Ferdinand 1559-1637', in *Lebensbilder aus dem Bayerischen Schwaben*, ed. Wolfgang Zorn, Reihe 3, Bd. 9, 1974, pp. 194-210.

21. Fürstlich und Gräflich Fuggersches Familien und Stiftungs Archiv, Dillingen Donau, Mss Cod. 46.1. The letter of Fernand Cron, sent from Cochin, dated 26-12-1587, fols. 54-66; Pius Malekandathil, *The Germans, the Portuguese and India*, pp. 83-8.

22. Pius Malekandathil, *The Germans, the Portuguese and India*, pp. 88-92; Reinhard Hildebrandt, *Die Georg Fuggerischen Erben*, pp. 158-63.

23. Antonio da Silva Rego, ed., *Documentação Ultramarina Portuguesa*, vol. III, pp. 314, 340; James C. Boyajian, *Portuguese Bankers at the Court of Spain 1626-1650*, New Jersey, pp. 6-8.

24. Luiz de Figueiredo Falcão, *Livro em que se contem toda a Fazenda e real Patrimonio dos Reinos de Portugal, India e Ilhas adjacentes e outras Particularidades*, Lisboa, 1859, pp. 59-69; Pius Malekandathil, *Portuguese Cochin and the Maritime Trade of India 1500-1663* (South Asian Study Series of Heidelberg University, Germany, no. 39), New Delhi, 2001, pp. 245-6.

25. Hermann Kellenbenz, 'Autor de 1600: Le Commerce du Poivre des Fugger et le marche international du Poivre', *Annales: Economies-Societies-Civilisations*, 11, 1956, pp. 9-11; Reinhard Hildebrandt, *Die Georg Fuggerischen Erben*, pp. 167-8.

26. The Account of Caesar Frederick in Richard Hakluyt, *The Principal navigations, Voyages, Traffiques and Discoveries of the English Nation*, vol. V, Glasgow, 1905, p. 392. For details on the private trade of the *casados* after the 1570s, see Pius Malekandathil, *Portuguese Cochin and the Maritime Trade of India*, pp. 207-18; Sanjay Subrahmanyam, 'Cochin in Decline, 1600-1650', pp. 65-78.

27. BNL, *Fundo Geral*, Codice no. 1980, 'Livro das Despezas de hum porcento' *Taboada section*, fols. 1-2.

28. Ibid., fols. 5-16.

29. BNL, *Fundo Geral*, Codice no. 1980, 'Livro das Despezas de hum porcento', *Taboada section*, fols. 5-16.

30. Ibid., fols. 7-15.

31. Ibid., fols. 6-16.

32. *Fürstlich und Gräflich Fuggersches Familien und Stiftungs Archiv, Dillingen Donau*, Mss Cod. 46.1. The letter of Fernand Cron, sent from Cochin, dated 26-12-1587, fol. 50; Pius Malekandathil, *The Germans, the Portuguese and India*, p. 89.

33. Antonio da Silva Rego, ed., *Documentação Ultramarina Portuguesa*, vol. III, p. 314; BNl, Cod., 11410, fol. 116 v.

34. BNL, Cod. 11410, fol. 116 v, *Orçamento de 1612* (*Cochin*).

35. Francisco Xavier Ernesto Fernandes, *Regimen do Sal, Abkary e Alfandegas da India*, Lisboa, 1905, pp. 23-7.

36. Corresponding to the intensification of trade in pearls there was a tax levied on the trade in pearls (*renda de aljofar*). The trade in pearls collection of this tribute was farmed out for a three-year period for a sum of 800 *xerafins* per year in 1592.

37. The taxes called *renda de sedas e chamalotes* (tax on silk and camel's hair cloth) and *renda de direitos de cavallos* (import duties on horses) are indicative of the

nature of trade carried out in these items. For details on these various types of taxes, see Francisco Xavier Ernesto Fernandes, *Regimen do Sal, Abkary e Alfandegas da India*, pp. 24-7.

38. There was a particular type of tax called *renda de boticas de panes d'algodao* (tax on retail trade in textiles) levied in Goa. Besides this there were other types of taxes levied on *sirgueiros* and *retrozeiros*, that is, silk weavers and haberdashers. The revenue on this was 1,140 *xerafins* in 1548 and it rose to 3,400 *xerafins* by the end of the sixteenth century.

39. The *renda de especiaria*, was farmed out, in 1541 and 1542, for a sum of 1,350 *pardaos*. But for the triennium ending in March 1595 this amount rose to 7,755 *xerafins*.

40. This impost was given as a monopoly to any *rendeiro* who quoted the highest rate. The total revenue collected in the years 1541 to 1542 was just 3,265 *xerafins*. But this amount shot up to about 7,050 *xerafins* in the year 1594.

41. The *renda de boticas de mantimentos* (medicines and foodstuffs) sold on retail was farmed out in 1541 and 1542, for a sum of 2,500 *xerafins*. This amount shot up to 11,630 *xerafins* per year, for the triennium ending in September 1595. For more details, see Francisco Xavier Ernesto Fernandes, *Regimen do Sal, Abkary e Alfandegas da India*, pp. 22-8.

42. Artur Teodoro de Matos, *O Orçamento do Estado da India, 1571*, CNCDP/Centro de Estudo, Damião de Gois, Lisboa, n.d., pp. 11-19; idem, *O Estado da India no Anos de 1581-1588, Estrutura Administrativa e Economica, Alguns Elementos para o seu Estudo*, Ponta Delegada, Universidade do Açores, 1982.

43. For a detailed list of the *casados* of Cochin with considerable capital, who used to lend money to the Portuguese state in times of emergency, see AHU, *Caixas da India*, Caixa 2, doc. 89, fols. 1-5; 11, dated 27 January 1613; Pius Malekandathil, *Portuguese Cochin and the Maritime Trade of India*, p. 217.

44. Georg Schurhammer, *Francis Xavier, His Life, His Times, vol.II: India, 1541-1545*, trans. M. Joseph Costelloe, Rome, 1977, pp. 187-91, 213; Antonio de Silva Rego, ed., *Documentação para a Historia das Missões do Padroado Portugues do Oriente, India*, vol. I, Lisboa, 1948, pp. 213-17; vol. II, p. 36; Gaspar Correa, *Lendas da India*, II, p.199, IV, pp. 140.

45. A wide variety of buildings including church buildings started appearing in Goa during this period, following the accumulation and channelization of commercial capital. The Franciscans started their house in Goa in 1517 with a Commissary to look after their affairs. Cf. A.A. Moreira, 'As Antigas Provincias Franciscanas Portuguesas da India', *Franciscanismo em Portugal*, vols. 3-4, Lisboa, 1996, p. 99. The Jesuits came to Goa in 1542 and erected São Paulo College, Bom Jesus Basilica, etc. Fortunato de Almeida, *Historia da Igreja em Portugal*, vol. II, Porto 1968, pp. 168-70. The Dominicans established themselves as a community in Goa in 1548 and eventually they built the Dominican monastery. Cf. Luis de Caçegas, *Terçeira Parte da Historia de. Domingos: Particular do Reino e Conquista de Portigal*, Lisboa, 1678. The Augustinians arrived in Goa in 1572 and eventually erected their monastery in this city. Arnulf Hartman, 'The

Augustinians in Golden Goa: A Manuscript by Felix of Jesus', *Anacleta Augustiniana*, vol. XXX, Rome, 1967, p. 21. The construction work of these monasteries and other church buildings as well as civic buildings was done primarily during this period, when private trade thrived. For details on the religious policy of the Portuguese during this period, see Teotonio R. de Souza, 'The Religious Policy of the Portuguese in Goa, 1510-1800', in *The Portuguese and the Socio-Cultural Changes in India, 1500-1800*, ed. K.S. Mathew, Teotonio R. de Souza and Pius Malekandathil, Fundação Oriente/ Tellicherry, 2001, pp. 437-48.

46. Joseph Velinkar, 'The Portuguese Conquest and Goa's Political and Adminis-trative History up to 1788', paper presented at the National Seminar on 'The History of Goa: Issues, Trends and Perspectives', organized by the Department of History, Goa University, 5-7 May 2003, pp. 5-7; The details of the city plan of Goa during this period are given by D. João de Castro and Linschoten. For a sketch of the city of Goa by D.João de Castro in 1539, see Georg Schurhammer, *Francis Xavier, His Life, His Times*, vol. II, p. 147. See also Jan Huyghen van Linschoten, *Histoire de la Navigation de Jan Hvgves de Linscot Hollandais et de son voyage es Indes Orientales*, Amsterdam, 1610.

47. Pius Malekandathil, *Portuguese Cochin and the Maritime Trade of India*, pp. 75; 110-11.

48. Cf. note 45.

49. For example, the Parish Church of Our Lady of Luz of the city of Goa received 147,680 *reis* in the mid-sixteenth century, out of which 27,300 *reis* went towards the expenses of wine, flour, host (small wheat-bread used for the celebration of Mass in the church), etc., while 110,000 *reis* went to the priest as salary and benefices. The remaining amount was spent for maintaining other office bearers of the church. P. S. S. Pissurlencar, ed., *Regimentos das Fortalezas da India*, Goa, 1951, p. 28. The amount of money set aside by the state for construction of the churches was very meagre (60,000 *reis* for six churches in Salcete, meaning ten thousand *reis* per church) when compared to the huge amount which the church dignitaries including the Chief Inquisitor drew as salary (the annual salary of the Chief Inquisitor was 400,000 *reis*). Ibid., pp. 28, 53.

50. This included the expenses for various rituals, church maintenance and salary for all priests. P.S.S. Pissurlencar, ed., *Regimentos das Fortalezas da India*, pp. 527-30.

51. A field-study conducted in these churches made it quite clear that most of the tombstones of these churches belonged to wealthy *fidalgos* and *casados*, who contributed liberally to their construction or maintenance. Interestingly, a good many tombstones belonged to the period of construction of these churches.

52. For detail, see Pius Malekandathil, *Portuguese Cochin and the Maritime Trade of India*, pp. 91-6; Gervasis Mulakara, *History of the Diocese of Cochin: European Missionaries in Cochin 1292-1558*, vol. I, Rome, 1986, pp. 35-70.

53. For detail on private trade, see Pius Malekandathil, 'Merchants, Markets and Commodities: Some Aspects of Portuguese Commerce with Malabar', in *The*

Portuguese, Indian Ocean and European Bridgeheads: Festchrift in Honour of Prof. K.S. Mathew, Fundação Oriente/Thalasserry, 2001, pp. 258-60.

54. Liberal contribution to the erection of church buildings played an important role in determining the social status of the donor besides ensuring legitimacy to his ventures. So the *fidalgos* and *casados* seem to have happily collaborated with this process.

55. For details on the wealthy *casados* of Cochin, who used to lend money to the state, see AHU, *Caixas da India,* Caixa 2, doc. 89; fols. 1-4, 11, 15, dated 27-1-1613. In order to understand the financial crisis which the Portuguese experienced during this period, see Pius Malekandathil ed., *Jornada of Dom Alexis de Menezes: A Portuguese Account of the Sixteenth Century Malabar,* Kochi, 2003, pp. 62-64.

56. AHU, *Caixas da India,* Caixa 2, doc. 89, fols. 1-5, 11, dated 27 January 1613; Pius Malekandathil, *Portuguese Cochin and the Maritime Trade of India,* p. 217.

57. AHU, *Caixas da India,* Caixa 2, doc. 89, fols. 14-15; Caixa 3, doc. 174, dated 2-1-1616; Caixa 4, doc. 133.

58. BNL, Cod. 11410, fols. 173-8, 'Contract to send *navetas* to Lisbon from Cochin'.

59. AHU, *Caixas da India,* Caixa 13-A, doc. 156; Caixa 13 –A, doc. 170.

60. Pius Malekandathil, *The Germans, the Portuguese and India,* pp. 97-111; C.R. Boxer 'Uma raridade bibliografica sobre Fernão Cron', *Boletim internacional de bibliografia luso-brasileira,* XII.3, Lisboa, 1971, pp. 323-64.

61. For details, see Sanjay Subrahmanyam, 'An Augsburger in Asia Portuguesa: Further Light on the Commercial World of Ferdinand Cron, 1587-1624', in *Emporia, Commodities and Entrepreneur in Asian Maritime Trade, c. 1400-1750,* ed. Roderich Ptak and Dietmar Rothermund, Stuttgart, 1991, pp. 407-11; Pius Malekandathil, *The Germans, the Portuguese and India,* pp. 98-104.

62. During the period between 1600-70, about 284 holders of the total known 355 holders of *rendas* were Hindus (about 80 per cent). About 178 holders of *rendas*, which is equivalent to 50 per cent, were Saraswat Brahmins. When the Christians held *rendas* worth only Rs.17,28,900, the Hindus held *rendas* to the value of Rs. 32,39,206 (69 per cent). M.N. Pearson, *Coastal Western India: Studies from the Portuguese Records,* New Delhi, 1981, pp. 98-9.

63. HAG, Livro das Monções, no.17 (1632-3) fol. 216; no.18 (1633) fol. 81.

64. HAG, *Conselho da Fazenda,* Mss. 1162, fol. 144. Rama Queny took up the contract for saltpetre from Vittula Naik. I express my gratitude to Dr Agnelo Fernandes, Goa for providing me with interesting information in this regard.

65. M.N. Pearson, *Coastal Western India,* pp. 97-111.

66. Mangoji Sinay was also a *rendeiro* of tobacco, silk and cotton during this period. HAG, *Conselho da Fazenda,* Mss.1163, fol. 19 v; Mss 1164, fol. 62 v; M.N. Pearson, *Coastal Western India,* p. 101.

67. To know more about the diverse types of commercial activities of Vitula Naique, see HAG, *Conselho da Fazenda,* Mss. 1161, fols. 88-89, Mss. 1162, fol. 144;

Sanjay Subrahmanyam, *Merchants, Markets and the State in Early Modern India*, Delhi, 1990, pp. 87-100.

68. ANTT, *Junta da Real Fazenda do Estado da India*, Lo. 6, Petição 12 November 1654; ibid., Provisão 15, ec.1654; ibid., Provisão 29 December 1657. M.N. Pearson gives a long list of Saraswat Brahmins who held different types of the *rendas*. For details, see M.N. Pearson, *Coastal Western India*, p.101.

69. HAG, 656, *Livro das arrematações das rendas*.

Index